Jon Connell

The New Maginot Line

ARBOR HOUSE / New York

Library of Congress Cataloging-in-Publication Data

Connell, Jon.
The new Maginot line.

Bibliography: p.
Includes index.
1. North Atlantic Treaty Organization. 2. Europe—
Defenses. I. Title.
UA646.3.C638   1986   355′.031′091821   86–14178
ISBN 0–87795–814–9

Manufactured in the United States of America

10 9 8 7 6 5 4 3 2 1

Contents

v

Introduction

Historians have not had many kind words for Charles VIII of France. He was, in most respects, utterly undistinguished: small, pale, and ugly, with an oversized head, blank, staring eyes, and a nervous twitch. "He was not better off for sense than for money," observed one of his followers. He died young—after bumping his head in a low doorway—and without issue.

Only one episode in his reign captures the imagination. In August 1494, in pursuit of a heroic dream, he set out to make good his family's claim to the kingdom of Naples, an objective he achieved with extraordinary speed, conquering a considerable part of the rest of Italy in the process. Unfortunately, he lost what he had gained with almost equal speed, when a hostile alliance of Venice, the pope, Milan, and Spain banded together to drive him out. In the end, his adventure did France the dubious favor of entangling it for generations in the byzantine politics of Italy.

But though his conquest was ephemeral, the manner in which

Charles achieved it earned him a small but important footnote in history.

Up until the late Middle Ages, the key to a successful defense had lain in fixed fortifications. Sturdy walls guarded towns, and castles with towering ramparts sat astride key invasion routes. True, gunpowder had been introduced to Europe more than a century earlier, but the standard artillery of the Middle Ages was cumbersome and crude, no match for a well-prepared defense.

It is not difficult, therefore, to imagine the discomfiture of the people of Italy when Charles rolled southward into Naples with what was then a modern miracle: a weapon as different from the traditional cannon of the Middle Ages as a tank loaded with armor-piercing shells is from horse-drawn artillery. Instead of firing laboriously sculpted balls of stone, and firing them while resting precariously on blocks of wood, the forty or so siege guns that Charles took with him fired balls of iron —much more lethal and accurate over an equivalent range—and even more to the point, were truly mobile. Instead of having to be hoisted onto ox carts to be moved, the guns had their own wheels.

Just how devastating these new weapons were emerges from an account by a contemporary historian. The cannons, he records, were "planted against the walls of a town with such speed, the space between the shots was so brief, and the balls flew so speedily, and were driven with such force, that as much execution was inflicted in a few hours as used to be done in Italy over the same number of days." The new mobile cannon, in short, changed the way people thought about warfare. The fortresses, which had been so central to defense in the Middle Ages, began to decline in importance. Charles VIII's Italian campaign was a rare instance in which technology—and technology alone— proved critical in enabling one side to defeat another in land warfare.

It is hard to find another example as clear-cut as this in the succeeding 500-odd years. One might cite the first use in Europe of the breech-loading rifle, in 1866, when the Prussians, who possessed it, defeated the Austrians, who did not, or the first use of breech-loading artillery, four years later, when the Prussians beat the French. But even here other factors came into play. In air and sea warfare, of course, examples of the triumph of technology are more plentiful since, unlike armies, air forces and navies are the creatures of technology and are thus inevitably more dependent on it. The British government's decision to develop chain radar in 1938, for instance, proved vital in the Battle of Britain; similarly, the atom bomb cut months of fighting off of World War II.[1]

But in general it is the human, not the technical, factor that has decided wars. The vast majority of battles, both ancient and modern, have turned not so much on differences in weaponry as on intangible qualities, such as training, morale, courage, leadership, and, of course, luck. When Napoleon destroyed the Hapsburg armies in 1805, his secret weapon was the confidence of his troops and their marshals in his invincibility. When the Japanese invaded Burma in 1942, their reputation as fearsome warriors preceded them, especially significant since the American public had been told the Japanese were too feeble and short-sighted to be effective. The exploits of American marines in the Pacific at the end of World War II owed more to their courage than to the quality of their equipment. The Germans defeated France in 1940, not because their hardware was better—it was not—but because they organized their troops, tanks, and aircraft in a devastating tactical formation. Similarly, the performance of the British army in the Falklands depended far more on professional skills than on sophisticated hardware.

This lesson now seems in danger of being forgotten. The greatest fallacy in modern military thinking is the notion that somehow high tech can do it all, that endless refinements in military hardware can be a substitute for the more traditional military arts. We may fondly imagine in a world of word processors and microwave ovens that scientists can take all the effort out of defense, and that microchips and pieces of metal, if only they can be configured in the right way, are all

---

[1]Two hypothetical examples from World War II illustrate the potential of key advances in weapons technology. Had the Germans brought their V-1 and V-2 rockets into service a few months earlier than they did, they might have been able to pound Britain's Channel ports before D-Day and prevent the landings in Normandy. Similarly, had their most sophisticated U-boat, the Type 21, gone into action in March 1944 as originally planned, instead of in March 1945, it might have made a dramatic difference to the Battle of the Atlantic.

we need. But history suggests this is a delusion. Defense is not a video game. You do not win wars simply by pushing buttons.

It is in America that push-button thinking has become most pronounced. There are various reasons for this. They involve the nature of the country, the ingenuity of American scientists, the lack of a military tradition, and perhaps most important of all, institutional pressures. There are enormous sums of money involved in modern defense. Everyone who is part of the procurement process has a vested interest in pushing technology to its limits, in "going to the next generation." The armed services—which are not, of course, spending their own money—are reluctant to settle for anything less than "the best." Industry knows that exploiting high technology is a means to stay in business and that, more often than not, the fancier the hardware, the larger the profits. Congressmen tend to worry more about bringing jobs to their constituencies than about preparing to fight the Russians. In his remarkable farewell address as president, Dwight Eisenhower drew attention to the dangers of a "military-industrial complex," which might take on a life of its own and work to its own distortion. His warning has come true.

Those who seek to justify the current obsession with high tech point across the Iron Curtain. We have no choice, they say. Hopelessly outnumbered by the Warsaw Pact in conventional forces, we must exploit our technological edge. But as Washington defense analyst Steven Canby has pointed out, "Trying to offset quantitative force inferiority solely by exploiting new technology is a policy marked by constantly diminishing returns." It simply doesn't make sense.

It makes no sense because there is not the dramatic gulf between NATO and the Warsaw Pact that existed, for example, between European nations and their opponents in nineteenth-century colonial wars, and because the West, unlike Charles VIII of France, is unable to spring startling new weapons on an unsuspecting enemy. Among a bunch of porous democracies in an age of mass communications, technological secrets do not remain secret for long. What the Russians cannot find in *Aviation Week* they can buy or steal. And what they know about they can react to, by imitating, by taking countermeasures, or simply by changing their tactics. Tightening up on "technology transfer" to the Eastern bloc is unlikely to have more than a marginal effect.

There are other reasons the current overreliance on high tech makes no sense.

First, instead of the careful, sensible application of technology, much of what goes on in modern military procurement consists of a mere fixation on gadgetry. The military want the best that scientists can dream up, but they also want to keep their traditional roles, and that means their traditional weapons platforms. Thus, unlike many weapons of the past—by today's standards comparatively cheap and easy to develop, and sometimes relying on very simple breakthroughs like the stirrup, which ushered in the age of cavalry—modern hardware tends to be extraordinarily complex and fragile, with a price tag out of all proportion to any conceivable benefit.

Second, new inventions are often swept into service prematurely. They tend not to work as well as anticipated, and they invariably cost more. *Imitating* technology, on the other hand, can prove easier and cheaper than making the breakthrough in the first place. Arguably, the Russians often *benefit* from being the slower horse in the technological race.

Third, creating modern weapons is, paradoxically, such a long drawn out process—it requires, on average, ten to fifteen years to take a new weapon from drawing board to battlefield—that any advantage a weapon might have given a country when conceived has frequently vanished by the time it comes into service. (The Russians have traditionally developed their weapons more quickly and enhanced them more incrementally than the West.)

Fourth, modern weapons cost so much that other vital elements of defense—ammunition stocks, fuel, training—are skimped on in order to pay for them. It has been argued, for instance, that only Israeli pilots get enough practice to be effective in America's supersophisticated front-line fighter, the F-15.

Thus, though they may enrich their manufacturers, many modern weapons do little to make us more secure. The constant sacrifice of *quantity* for *quality* leads to a vicious circle: fewer and fewer weapons are expected to do more and more, which in turn puts a premium on even greater sophistication. Some high-tech devotees advance the argument that the Russians are now developing supersophisticated hardware themselves, so we can do no less. There are many claims, and some evidence, that the Russians *are* beginning to fall into the same gold-plated trap as the West. But Western defense policy is not made in Moscow; its aim is not to ape what the Russians do.

The high-tech approach to defense has weakened America and threatens to weaken it further. Since the successful Inchon landing in South Korea in 1951, America's military record has been a catalogue of disasters: the army's uninspiring performance in Vietnam, where a cornucopia of sophisticated hardware failed to defeat an elusive, poorly armed guerrilla force; the *Mayaguez* incident, when Cambodians captured an American ship and the rescue effort was botched; the attempt to rescue the American hostages in Iran in 1980; and the storming of Grenada, which despite the Reagan administration's attempts to elevate it to a victory akin to Agincourt or Trafalgar, was in fact a badly bungled operation. Not all of these failures, it is true, can be traced directly to technological problems. They do, however, reflect the distorted priorities of the modern American military and a general lack of seriousness about warfare, a lack of seriousness manifest, perhaps above all, in its push-button mentality, its passion for hardware, and its neglect of strategy, tactics, and the intangibles of conflict.

Meanwhile, the West has suffered further from the inability of America's European allies to cooperate effectively with one another, and from Europe's long-standing reluctance to take on more of the burden of Western defense. "They could not agree among themselves about objectives, they trusted one another less than they did the United States, and they had no particular inclination to incur the costs and risks of greater independence," wrote William Kaufman, one of the wisest of America's postwar defense experts, in the 1960s. His charge still has a ring of truth.

What makes all this more disturbing is that conventional forces are crucially important, and, I will suggest, ought to become more so. It is only because of our pronounced conventional weakness that we are forced to rely on the inherently implausible threat to use nuclear weapons if we face defeat.

*   *   *

I have arranged this book in three sections. In the first I look at the West's conventional arsenal and illustrate, with examples, the fallacy of putting too much faith in technology. Inevitably, I concentrate mainly on American weapons, because America provides the best examples, and because America is by far the most important Western power, its research-and-development effort setting the pace for the rest.[2]

In the second section of the book I look at the West's nuclear arsenal. If gold plating conventional weapons is one way in which the West has become too hooked on technology, I argue that the overdependence on nuclear weapons is another. Some of the current plans for upgrading nuclear forces, and for developing new systems, are unnecessary, a diversion of energy and resources that would be better applied elsewhere. The fact that there has been no world war since 1945 may owe a great deal to the presence of nuclear weapons—on both sides—but theories of limited nuclear wars make little sense outside laboratories and think tanks, and attempts to make nuclear weapons more "controllable" (by constantly developing smaller, more accurate, "low-yield" warheads) are ultimately futile. We have long passed the point of diminishing returns. *Wars cannot be fought with nuclear weapons.* The notion that the West can save itself from conventional defeat by "going nuclear" is an illusion.

In the third section of this book, I concentrate on President Reagan's "strategic defense initiative," popularly known as Star Wars. This attempt to create a space-based defense against Russian nuclear missiles represents the search for the ultimate technological fix. In its purest form it is the product of millennial dreaming, like the peace

---

[2]In 1985, according to the *New York Times,* America spent $107 billion on research and development, "more than the combined research and development spending of Britain, France, West Germany and Japan. More than a third of this total [was] devoted to defense. . . . Defense claims only 4 percent of West Germany's research and development budget and less than 1 percent of Japan's."

movement; and it reflects, like unilateralism, a failure to think through the realities of the arms race. In its less utopian form—the form in which it is supposed to "boost deterrence"—I will seek to show that it is equally ill conceived, and furthermore that though it is unlikely to buy us more security, it is certain, if pursued, to drain away vast resources that would be better applied to badly needed "usable" and hence credible weapons.

The theme of this book, in essence, is that there is no technological solution to the problem of the Soviet Union, or to the problem of modern security. No amount of magical conventional weapons, or Stealth cruise missiles, or laser battle stations will remove the Soviet threat.

There is a school of thought, of course, that holds that if only we can keep the pressure up by constantly harnessing new developments in technology, we will force the Russians to keep reacting and spending ever larger sums of money simply to "stay in the game." In the end the hope is that their economy will be unable to take the strain, and that their political system will collapse, bankrupt, on the scrap heap of history.

This rationale is scarcely convincing. For one thing, in a world now spending around $700 billion a year on armaments, it is not only in Russia that high levels of defense spending are causing strain. America's recent military buildup has helped create huge federal deficits, which have caused distortions throughout the world economy. By 1990, according to Fred Hiatt and Rick Atkinson in the *Washington Post*, "nearly enough will have been spent on defense [by America] during the Cold War—$3.7 trillion in constant 1972 dollars—to buy everything in the United States except the land: every house, factory, train, plane and refrigerator." Besides, even if the existing Soviet system *were* to collapse, the world would not necessarily become a more stable, secure place. At the moment the USSR's thousands of nuclear weapons are at least under the centralized control of a regime that, however unpleasant, is notably cautious and wary of the risks of war. A breakup of the Soviet empire could make things decidedly worse for the West.

Technology, in short, is no substitute for diplomacy. International politics, as one scientist puts it, cannot be made "subject to an engineering solution."

Old habits die hard. The magic weapon mentality, I will show in these pages, is now deeply ingrained in Western defense. But we must hope the situation is not irreversible. With a more realistic approach to "the threat," with less emphasis on overcomplicated hardware, less worrying about nuclear weapons, and a realization that there are no Star Wars–type panaceas, we can make ourselves more secure. That, at least, is the belief on which this book is based.

PART ONE

THE ARSENAL OF DEMOCRACY

"Whatever happens, we have got
The Maxim Gun, and they have not."
—Hilaire Belloc

1

The Threat—and How NATO Proposes to Deal with It

The nightmare that the West lives with is of a massive Soviet assault across the border of the Federal Republic of Germany, sweeping with blitzkrieg speed through Germany's agricultural and industrial heartland into the Low Countries and on across the continent to the English Channel. That is what brought NATO into being, and that is what sustains it.

Many find the threat hard to take seriously. Why, after all, would the Soviet Union go to war? What could it possibly hope to gain by overrunning Western Europe? It already faces enormous difficulties coping with its existing satellites in Eastern Europe, so why would it want to add to them by taking on an even more turbulent empire full of troublesome Western Europeans?

The answer is that the USSR would stand to gain little. And at the moment the prospect of a Soviet tank assault on West Germany seems remote. Indeed, one of the thorniest problems facing those who devise NATO war games is in coming up with a plausible scenario for actually getting the war going. But though it is hard to imagine circumstances in which the Russians might choose to invade, it is not impossible. Wars happen. They do not always begin for rational reasons. They can arise out of crises—even, as in World War I, out of relatively trivial incidents. If a war arose out of a crisis between the superpowers, West Germany would almost certainly become the central battlefield. That is where, in one analyst's phrase, the troops are lined up like two football teams. And if war looked inevitable, the likelihood is that the Soviets would move first—since, for deep-seated historical reasons, they are determined not to fight on their own territory.

Besides, although the "steam may have gone out of the ideological balloon," in George Kennan's phrase, the Soviet Union remains committed to the Marxist doctrine and to the notion of the ultimate triumph of communism. Even at the height of détente, in 1976, the then Soviet premier, Leonid Brezhnev, told the Twenty-fifth Congress of the Soviet Communist Party: "Relaxation of tensions does not to the slightest extent abolish or alter the laws of the class struggle. No one should expect that because tensions have been reduced, Communists will reconcile themselves to the capitalist system or monopolists will become followers of the Revolution." The state of the Soviet empire, moreover, scarcely reassures many Western observers. With its huge defense establishment—seemingly larger than anything it could conceivably need for purely defensive purposes—its rickety economy, its starved consumer market, and its unhappy allies, the Soviet Union has become an ailing tyranny—and ailing tyrannies, like wild animals, can be dangerous. Just as the junta in Argentina attacked the Falkland Islands in 1982 largely to divert attention from an internal crisis, so it is possible to imagine that the Kremlin might be tempted to believe that the best hope of shoring up its empire might lie in becoming increasingly adventurous abroad.

Thus, however implausible the threat of war in Europe may seem, it nonetheless exists. And anyone who visits the "Inner German Border"—the dividing line between East and West—becomes instantly aware of it.

West Germany is divided from East Germany by two barbed-wire fences that are separated, for the most part, by about a hundred yards of dead ground. Stretches of this are mined, and most of it is patrolled by dogs. The fences themselves are made of razor-sharp wire, and parts of the inner fence are electric. At regular intervals are mounted SM-70 machine guns, which automatically open fire on people trying to cross the border from East to West. There are frequent watchtowers and the whole length is regularly patrolled by border guards. The fences are no respecters of history: they cut towns, sometimes even homes, in half.

Thousands of East Germans have attempted to cross this barrier since it was constructed in the 1950s and 1960s. Some have succeeded; others have been caught; yet others have died trying.

Seeing this monstrous barrier, as a CBS television reporter once put it, "your first thought is that a government that could do this could do anything, even go to war." Or as a veteran of NATO patrols of the Western side of the line put it to me: "You have to remember that it's built to keep people in . . . and you know that, whatever good there may be in communism, any system which built that must be rotten."

It is across this barrier that an attack on Western Europe, if it ever happened, would come. So supposing, in some dire crisis, the Russians did decide to breach their fence and invade West Germany. Could NATO stop them?

In the early 1980s, NATO's top soldier, General Bernard Rogers, toured a succession of gatherings of alliance politicians, officials, and defense analysts with a gloomy prognosis about the threat the West faced. The balance of forces was tilting dangerously in favor of the East, he said; if the Warsaw Pact ever invaded, the likelihood would be that he, as the supreme allied commander, Europe (SACEUR), would have no alternative but to request permission to defend Europe with nuclear weapons at a very early stage. NATO, he implied, now had a strategy scarcely distinguishable from the one developed in the early 1950s, under which its conventional forces, spread out along the central front of Europe like Kipling's "thin red line of heroes," were there simply as a "trip wire," which, if ever broken by the Red Army, would have triggered a massive nuclear retaliation from America. Nowadays, in Rogers's view, NATO simply had a "delayed trip wire," a frankly incredible position in an age when the two superpowers had rough parity in nuclear weapons and when massive retaliation might all too easily lead to a holocaust.

Rogers was never very specific about how long NATO would last —obviously it would depend on the circumstances of the attack, the margin of warning, and a host of other factors. But many seasoned analysts in the U.S. Army, both in Washington and serving under Rogers in his headquarters in Mons, Belgium, believe the alliance would be hard pressed to last more than two weeks. "The very best case for NATO I ever heard," one American officer, a veteran of countless war games, told me, "in which we assumed that NATO had plenty of ammunition and gas and spare parts, and that we were ready and the Warsaw Pact wasn't—that they were dragged reluctantly into this war, didn't want it, and showed up late!—had a catastrophic breakthrough [i.e., one requiring a nuclear response to save the war] occurring on *Day 16."* Another case, said this source, this time in a war game that began with a confused—and, for NATO, confusing—riot in East Germany (it turned out that the Soviets had deliberately staged the "riot" as a diversion), had the West going nuclear on *Day 13.* And the worst case, with the Warsaw Pact surprising NATO, and the West quite unprepared, had the West compelled to go nuclear as early as *Day 5.*

The conventional balance, of course, has always looked daunting. From the start, NATO failed to muster the political will to finance and construct a proper conventional defense of the West, and in this lies the source of all its problems. After getting off on the wrong foot, NATO never recovered, and though for a while in the 1960s things looked better, over the last twenty years they have been growing steadily worse. Let us briefly consider the history of NATO's struggle to match the Warsaw Pact.

In early 1949 a group of American and British army officers met secretly in London to discuss the requirements for a fully fledged conventional defense of Europe. The formal foundation of NATO was still eight months away, but it was already clear that Western Europe's security would depend, ultimately, on America and probably on the presence of U.S. troops in Europe. Ranged against an estimated 175 Soviet divisions in Eastern Europe were the forces of occupation left behind in Germany after the war—one American, three British, and three French divisions, two Belgian brigades, and some Dutch, Norwegian, and Austrian troops.

At the London meeting, the army officers discussed U.S. military aid to Europe—how much America might pay, and in what form. But in considering this they tried to work out how much the West might have to spend to provide itself with adequate troops and equipment to hold the Soviets if they ever attacked. The figure they eventually came up with, according to one man who attended the meeting, was $45 billion.

It was a staggering sum. In the late 1940s, Europe was still suffering acutely from the ravages of war. Rationing was widespread, raw materials in short supply. America, in an effort to breathe new life into Europe's faltering economic and political institutions, had just launched the Marshall Plan. The economic health of Western Europe was seen in Washington as vital to America's own and, moreover, vital if the seeds of communism were to be deprived of fertile soil. But the plan put together by the then secretary of state, George Marshall, envisaged spending a total of only $13 billion. The notion of spending more than three times that on the defense of Europe seemed out of the question. As Paul Nitze, a State Department official who attended some of the later sessions of the London talks, was keenly aware, it was beyond not just the Europeans, but America too. And so too, it seemed, was a robust conventional defense.

Yet by early 1949 many in Washington were convinced that the West should construct a conventional defense strong enough to contain a Soviet conventional attack. When the Russians exploded their first atomic bomb in June 1949, Harry Truman's secretary of state, Dean Acheson, talked in his office with Nitze, then deputy director of the State Department's policy planning staff and already an expert in European security. The two men agreed that the nuclear forces of both sides would eventually become "self-canceling"; that is, the incentive for a U.S. president to press the button on Europe's behalf would diminish rapidly as it became clear that the Soviet Union could retaliate in kind. A number of senior U.S. Army officers were making the same point, none more succinctly than General Omar Bradley. "When the Russians get a bomb to neutralize our bomb," he said in 1949, "we'd better get an army to neutralize their army."

The Truman administration began an energetic effort to persuade Europe to rearm—an effort kept up by successive U.S. administrations —but the results were scarcely dramatic. Even the outbreak of the Korean War, seen by many in Washington as a possible "blind" aimed at diverting attention before the Russians launched a second, major attack on Western Europe, did little to change things. It produced a brief flurry of activity and some grandiose promises from the allies, but as the danger of a European war receded and the pessimists were proved wrong, so the promises were forgotten. The last gasp of the Truman campaign came at a famous NATO meeting in Lisbon in 1952, when the foreign ministers approved an extraordinarily ambitious —and rather arbitrary—list of "force goals." Essentially, these anticipated NATO having 96 divisions and 9,000 aircraft by 1954, with 35 to 40 of the divisions ready for combat at all times and the rest capable of being mobilized within a month.

The force goals agreed on in Lisbon were clearly beyond NATO, and many have come to see the Lisbon conference as the last occasion the alliance seriously contemplated a full-scale conventional defense of the continent. Nevertheless, by the early 1960s the West seemed in a far stronger position than at one time had been thought possible.

In the first place, NATO by then had better intelligence. Although the Soviet Union might possess 175 divisions, theirs were much smaller divisions than NATO's, many were deployed in the East to guard against the threat from China, and the bulk of them were not at full strength. NATO meanwhile had gradually bolstered its own forces with more troops and equipment, and in the mid-1960s the odds looked more even than Western military planners in the early days of NATO would have dared hope. Against 56 to 57 small Soviet divisions were arrayed 25 to 26 larger Western ones; manpower figures were roughly equal. And in weaponry the Pact's advantage had shrunk from an estimated five to one in the late 1940s to one and a half to one.

The mid-1960s, however, were the high point for NATO. Since then, it has been downhill all the way. America became involved in a debilitating conflict in Southeast Asia, France left the military structure of the alliance, and the Soviets added extra manpower and huge amounts of extra equipment to their front-line forces. Five divisions and 70,000 men joined Soviet forces in East Germany, Czechoslovakia, and Poland as a result of the invasion of Czechoslovakia in 1968, bringing the total of forward divisions from 22 to 27 (though the overall figures of 56 to 57 in Eastern Europe and the western USSR has remained constant). More than 100,000 construction and support troops were added to these divisions. Much more significant than the manpower, however, was the equipment. According to Phillip Karber, a prominent American defense consultant who works for the BDM Corporation in Virginia, the Warsaw Pact, between 1960 and the early 1980s, added *four* new weapons for every one added by NATO. By mid-1985, the Pact had more than twice as many tanks as NATO (16,000 to 7,000), three times as much artillery (6,000 to 2,000 pieces), over six times as many multiple rocket launchers (1,000 to 150), and twice as many aircraft (3,000 to 1,500).

In addition, the Pact had—and has—other advantages over NATO. First, NATO, like the French in the 1930s, is committed to a strategy of forward defense, understandable enough since almost half West Germany's heavy industry and a third of its population reside within fifty miles of the border. Clearly, any strategy that envisages giving up a sizable chunk of West Germany is quite unacceptable to its people, who are committed to forward defense as an ironclad prerequisite for their continuing support for the alliance. But forward defense is a risky strategy; it denies the defender the ability to trade "space for time." In other words, he has to devote most of his forces to defending the front line and thus has difficulty creating large enough "operational reserves" to act as backup.

The second major problem the alliance has is geography. In a European war, the Russians would be able to bring the full weight of their forces to bear on NATO simply by moving them over land, a much easier prospect than the one facing the West, divided as it is by the Atlantic Ocean, with its major power 3,000 hazardous miles from the battlefield.

Finally, the Warsaw Pact would have the initiative in a European war. In 1977 the Pentagon began a study to measure the significance of this. For purposes of comparison, a team of military experts studied the battles between Germany and the Allies in 1940. By analyzing a number of factors—for example, equipment and manpower—they decided that Germany's "combat potential" was only four-fifths that of France and its allies. By most standards, then, the Germans looked, on paper, to be the weaker side; the secret of their success lay in their ability to concentrate their forces in key sectors, whereas the allied forces, for their part, were more spread out. In the actual places where the panzer divisions under General Guderian penetrated the line they usually enjoyed a superiority of two to one, and sometimes three to one. At one stage, the analysts examined fifty separate tank battles (mainly involving French and German forces); their overall conclusion is summed up by Phillip Karber, who took part in the Pentagon study: "A skillful opponent, even with only equal forces, will, if he seizes the initiative and orchestrates the action for decisive impact, have a sub-stantial edge over a side which is purely defensive." One of the lessons of 1940 was that even though the war itself had started nine months earlier, the attack on France still caught it, to some extent, by surprise. Similarly, even if NATO got two weeks warning of a Soviet thrust into Europe, the Red Army would almost certainly still catch the alliance less than fully prepared.

One of the most fraught questions, indeed, is whether, even if it got warning time, NATO would take the kind of action necessary. The signals would almost certainly be ambiguous; the pressures not to act would be strong. Say tension mounted in high summer; with the tourist season at its height, would European governments be prepared to close down airports, commandeer ferries and trucks, and in general take the kinds of action that some would argue might simply precipitate the very crisis everyone was trying to avoid?

So the odds against NATO are long. But they can be exaggerated. Military men tend to deal in worst-case scenarios; to wrest money out of democratic governments that have other priorities, they have to conjure up a vivid picture of the danger we face. They also worry, understandably, about being blamed in the event there is an attack and NATO forces fail to hold the line. The Warsaw Pact has a deeper front, and it can ultimately bring more force to bear than NATO. But as we will see, the Warsaw Pact has its problems too. The longer a war dragged on, for example, the more the Russians would have to worry about their supply lines and the reliability of their East European allies. And the immediate odds confronting NATO are far from impossible. In manpower, for example, NATO's 27 divisions comprise a total of 740,000 men; the 58 Soviet divisions assigned to the central front total 900,000 men. The advantage in equipment, though considerable, is not the five to one it was in the late 1940s (overall, it is now more like 2.2

to 1). It is not beyond NATO's power to mount a much more credible defense than it does now, and so buy precious time: time for negotiations and second thoughts, and time to let American reinforcements reach the battlefield.

But if NATO is to achieve this it will have to change the way it thinks about defense and, specifically, the way it buys its weapons.

That the West, and in particular America, should place great faith on technology is not altogether surprising. In the early days of the alliance, when the prospect of mobilizing a large enough ground force to match the Russians soldier for soldier and tank for tank seemed hopeless, Western inventiveness seemed the best, indeed the only, way to make up for Soviet numbers.

And there was no question that the West was more inventive. The democratic societies in the West provided conditions for science to flourish in a way that totalitarianism did not. The West led the way in most of the key developments in defense technology, from towed array sonar (the listening device used by surface ships and submarines) to the conversion of the torpedo into a guided weapon and the development of the vertical takeoff jet. A wide range of new inventions—from thermal imaging techniques to liquid crystals, satellites, and nuclear propulsion—were also pioneered in the West.

In America today, where military-related research and development provide the best opportunities for pushing technology to its limits, approximately 25 percent of the nation's scientists and engineers work for the defense industry and the Pentagon. The philosophy, therefore, was quite straightforward, and often repeated. The United States, said General George Brown, chief of staff for the U.S. Air Force and later chairman of the Joint Chiefs of Staff, "has never attempted to match the Soviet Union either on ground force personnel or matériel, relying instead on technology." In March 1975, Dr. Malcolm Currie, then the director of research and engineering at the Pentagon, testified to the Senate Armed Services Committee:

> In this increasingly competitive, often hostile and rapidly changing world Americans seem to have only one real choice. Clearly our national well-being cannot be based on unlimited raw materials or on unlimited manpower and cheap labor. Rather it must be

based on our ability to multiply and enhance the limited natural and human resources we do have. Technology thus appears to offer us our place in the sun—the means to insure our security and economic vitality.

Five years later, President Jimmy Carter's defense secretary, Harold Brown, echoed this. America's military strength, he said in autumn 1980, "rests on a scientific ability and a technology ability." "Technology," agreed Edmund Muskie, then secretary of state, "is another American advantage. 'Faster,' 'more accurate,' 'more advanced'—these generally are terms that apply to American weapons and American systems. Soviet technology has lagged behind."

America's technological prowess, therefore, was—and remains—beyond dispute.

At Hollaman Air Force Base in New Mexico is a "sled track"—a straight ten-mile-long railway that runs through the desert. Along this track, rocket-propelled sleds have traveled at phenomenal speeds. In December 1954 an air force pilot reached 632 miles per hour (the G force was so strong that his eyeballs almost popped out). Unmanned vehicles, however, have traveled considerably faster than that: one Pentagon official described to me how he watched a test in which an unmanned sled, propelled by nine rocket motors, shot down the track at 5,000 miles per hour. From a starting point three miles away, the sled took just two and a half seconds to whip past those watching. By the time observers had turned their heads it had vanished. Even that was a relatively modest exhibition; the unmanned land speed record, set at Hollaman Air Force Base in October 1983, is a staggering 8,900 feet per second—6,060 miles per hour.

The sled track at Hollaman has allowed defense engineers to enjoy the sheer technical challenge of making vehicles travel at enormous speeds. It has also, more practically, enabled the air force to test everything from the aerodynamic properties of a new wing design for a fighter to the stresses and strains that might bear on an aircraft ejection seat or a missile's reentry vehicle when released in space. Firing the relevant component along the sled track, say Pentagon researchers, is cheaper and simpler than testing it in space or in the air. The sled has also been used for testing human strain—by shooting dummies wired to computers down the track at extraordinary speeds.

The Pentagon is proud of its sled track in the desert.[1] It is an example, military men say, of a facility the Soviets could not match; for one thing, they have lagged behind America in the development of the computers and microelectronics that make the tests possible.

So why haven't technological advantages like the Hollaman sled track translated into better, cheaper, and more efficient military hardware? Why, despite Muskie's claim that American weapons are "faster," "more accurate," and "more advanced," haven't they given us a commensurate measure of extra security?

The short answer is that the West has got carried away. There is a story, apocryphal no doubt, about one of the passengers on the stricken liner *Titanic,* who happened to be in the bar as the ship began to sink. "I asked for ice," he is supposed to have quipped, "but this is ridiculous." In its effort to achieve technological supremacy over the Soviets, NATO has turned what should be an asset into a liability. It has tried, through sophisticated weaponry, to achieve "security without risk," and the consequences of this have been almost uniformly bad.

In the early 1930s, the French attempted something very similar. They constructed a line of fortifications along their southeastern border with Germany. The intention was to render France utterly secure against the threat that, even then, was looming from German rearmament. The French were determined never again to endure the huge losses they had sustained in World War I.

When it was completed in 1935, the Maginot line was hailed as a technological marvel, the most sophisticated set of fortifications ever constructed. It came to be dubbed "the shield of France," and almost until the eve of war the French government continued to express confidence in its impregnability. "Be reassured," said Édouard Daladier, the defense minister, in January 1937, "our fortified works are

---

[1]The United States has test facilities even more sophisticated than those at Hollaman. The air force, for example, has a series of state-of-the-art wind tunnels at Tullahoma, Tennessee, which it uses to test high-performance aircraft and rockets. NASA operates a similar facility near San Francisco.

sufficiently equipped to halt a sudden attack even on a Sunday. . . ."

The government's confidence, of course, was stunningly mis-placed. In the history of warfare, there have been few campaigns decided as swiftly and dramatically as the German conquest of Western Europe in May and June 1940. And though it was inevitable that Belgium and tiny Luxembourg should collapse rapidly under the supe-rior weight of the German forces, the fall of France—a country that had ended World War I with the strongest army in Europe—was a catastrophe that could and should have been averted. The evidence suggests that the Germans themselves were staggered by the speed of their victory.

What went wrong? Why did the supposedly invulnerable Magi-not line prove, in the end, so utterly useless?

What happened is that the Maginot line ended up not as *one* component of French strategy but as almost the *sole* component. This was not intentional; the government's plan had been to use the line merely to protect France's vulnerable southeastern border, thus freeing troops to block Germany from advancing through Belgium.

But projects as vast and ambitious as the Maginot line have a habit of consuming so much attention and energy that there is little left over for anything else. Whatever the military planners might have hoped, the Maginot line led France into a trap; it created, in itself, the illusion of security. It exhausted both the country's funds and its initiative. In the end, it cost close to 7,000 million francs—about $200 million—a staggering sum at that time, and more than twice as much as had originally been anticipated when the chamber of deputies gave the go-ahead in 1930. (This is a classic example of how big defense projects tend to generate huge cost overruns; even had France's planners voted to extend the line after the collapse of the Franco-Belgian accords in 1936, there simply would not have been the money with which to do it.)

As a result of the Maginot line, other military programs had been fatally squeezed: the French Air Force was neglected until it was too late; the army itself suffered all kinds of handicaps, with some units forced to fall back on horses for transport. There was interminable haggling over the replacement of the army's standard automatic rifle; a new model wasn't selected until 1936, and by 1939 only a few hundred thousand had been issued. In addition, on the eve of a war in which rapid communications between armored units was to prove vital, the French army continued to rely on the telephone—unlike the Germans, who had spotted the potential of radio and were experimenting with it intensively from the early 1930s onward.

The malaise went deeper. The army that had ended World War I as a fearsome fighting unit had, under the shadow of the old men who led it, declined; training had become inadequate, morale had sagged, and the fighting spirit that had seen France through to victory in 1918 had evaporated. As Alistair Horne wrote in his graphic book *To Lose a Battle:* "Rapidly, the Maginot Line came to be not just a component of strategy but a way of life. Feeling secure behind it, like the lotus-eating mandarins of Cathay behind their Great Wall, the French Army allowed itself to atrophy, to lapse into desuetude. A massive combination of factors—complacency, lassitude, deficiencies of manpower and finance—conspired to rust the superb weapon which the world had so admired. . . ."

As we consider modern weapons, and the mentality that creates them, the parallels with what happened in France in the 1930s will become clear. France lost its battle against Germany in 1940 because of a failure of imagination. The problem was not so much the decision to fortify part of a vital border—in itself, quite sensible—as the fact that, to be effective, French strategy required not just fortifications but substantial operational reserves to operate behind them. Because one great project absorbed so much money and energy, France got one but not the other. Modern defense planners have become similarly overdependent on microchips and data links and all the other attributes of space-age technology, while neglecting other crucial elements necessary for a coherent defense. (One could push the parallels further: just as France left itself open to General Guderian's daring thrust through the Ardennes and the rapid advance to Paris, so modern defense planners have made unrealistic assumptions about how the Russians would actually fight a war in Central Europe.) France misused technology; so has the West. France, through the Maginot line, tried to substitute equipment for men, minimize potential loss of life, and achieve an absolute security. In doing so, it ended up with far *less* security than it needed. The West has fallen into a similar trap.

2

Weapons

Geniuses, it has been said, think more simply than ordinary mortals. This clearly sets them apart from the Pentagon, which—collectively, at least—does not think simply about anything. The art of modern U.S. weapons procurement appears to be to find the most complicated and expensive way of performing even the slightest task.

On May 30, 1985, the Pentagon confessed that it had paid out $659 apiece for seven plastic ashtrays that were installed in the armrests of the navy's E-2C early warning planes. Saying there was "no excuse" for what he called a "silly transaction," Defense Secretary Caspar Weinberger questioned whether the navy might not explore the idea of using "old mayonnaise jars" in the future—or consider banning smoking on its planes. And responding to the clear need to take some form of punitive action, Weinberger decided to transfer the three senior naval officers responsible for the supply depot that had authorized the purchases.

But the three officers, one of them an admiral with thirty-three years service behind him, felt—with some justification—that they were being made scapegoats. For as the manufacturers, Grumman Corporation, pointed out, Pentagon-approved specifications, which included an extraordinarily elaborate drawing, called for ashtrays made up of eleven separate parts, which would take thirteen man-hours to assemble—the idea apparently being to ensure that they would withstand the jolt that occurs when an E-2C lands on an aircraft carrier. And though the company had clearly overcharged the navy—it agreed to a refund of $610 per ashtray—it was in part these absurdly detailed specifications that made the inflated price possible.

Thus, to single out three naval officers for punishment was ridiculous. In a Defense Department bulging with 36,000 officers and 359,-000 civilians (an estimated 54,000 of whom are directly involved in buying equipment), and in a defense industry with few incentives to keep down costs, overspecifying and overcharging are a way of life. In the billions of dollars spent by the Pentagon each year, $4,600 for seven ashtrays is a trivial sum, but it is an example that vividly brings home the way the American defense establishment does business. And the grotesquely overcomplicated, overexpensive ashtray at least has one virtue: it works. That is more than can be said for some of the equipment supplied to the U.S. arsenal.

The Divad Gun

General Sir Archibald Wavell, who commanded British forces in the Middle East in the early years of World War II, had an old-fashioned view of military equipment. He believed that, to survive on a battlefield, weapons ought to be sturdy. "Whenever in the old days a new design of mountain gun was submitted to the Artillery Committee," he wrote in his memoirs, "that august body had it taken to the top of a tower, some hundred feet high, and thence dropped onto the ground below. If it was still capable of functioning it was given further trial; if not, it was rejected as flimsy."

One wonders what General Wavell would have made of the U.S. Army's Divisional Air Defense Gun, or Divad for short. No one, so far as I know, ever dropped it from a 100-foot tower. Available information suggests they would have been ill advised to try. The Divad found it hard enough to cope with considerably lesser trials.

According to evidence that emerged at a Senate subcommittee hearing in early 1985, the Divad did not work in the cold. It was supposed to be an all-weather weapon, able to "acquire" its target automatically and line up on it by means of its elaborate, computer-driven fire control system. But when a Divad was tested in a cold chamber, with the temperature 25 degrees below zero, it registered readings 180 degrees off, meaning it aimed at targets in precisely the opposite direction to the ones its operator had in mind—"hardly reassuring to your reserve units," as Senator Mark Andrews of North Dakota pointed out to the assembled army brass. Only when the Divad had been heated for six hours with the field equivalent of a hair dryer did it seem ready to perform.

The news of the Divad's allergy to cold shocked Senator Andrews, who is a farmer (and incidentally a Republican who believes in a strong defense). On his farm, he said, his cattle would starve if machinery failed to work at 40 degrees below zero. "Unless the army plans to fight only in the balmy, 70-degree temperature of early summer," he pointed out, "this implement is far from satisfactory. . . ." In spite of constant attempts by the army to reassure its critics—the cold weather troubles, for example, were put down to a failure to use diesel fuel—the problems afflicting the Divad multiplied. It was a classic of its kind: a bafflingly complex and fragile weapon that showed little evidence of being able to withstand the rugged and unpredictable conditions of a battlefield (what the great Prussian strategist Karl von Clausewitz called "friction"). So bad did it prove to be that in August 1985, after eight years of development, and the expenditure of $1.8 billion, the Divad was canceled—a rare fate for a modern weapon, especially one so far into production. More clearly, perhaps, than any weapon before it, the Divad illustrated the excesses of the Pentagon procurement process: the tendency to exaggerate the threat, the incessant gold plating, the unrealistic tests, the lack of coherent thought about military missions and roles. And what was worse, it had actually been conceived to avoid these very pitfalls.

By the early 1970s, the U.S. Army was thoroughly convinced of the virtues of an air defense gun. The surface-to-air missiles (SAMs) on which it was becoming increasingly reliant were complicated and cumbersome, difficult to use against low-flying aircraft. They were expensive, too; and if a missile was fired, and missed, there was seldom time for a second shot. Fast-firing guns were different. They could pump a stream of shells or tracers into the sky, sometimes to devastating effect. Visually aimed guns shot down more than 4,000 jets in the Korean, Vietnam, and Arab-Israeli wars. The Falkland Islands conflict in 1982 certainly illustrated the value of the old-fashioned machine gun; on some of the British vessels that sailed to the South Atlantic, machine guns were hastily bolted to the deck to bolster what at times seemed patently inadequate missile systems.

In any war on the central front in Europe, air defense would be vital. America and its allies would be under fierce bombardment not just from fixed-wing aircraft delivering gunfire, napalm, or rockets, but from helicopters armed with precision antitank munitions. A helicopter is a tempting target: it lacks the speed and small radar profile of a low-flying jet. In Vietnam, the ill-equipped Viet Cong shot down some 4,643 American helicopters, almost 85 percent of them with simple rifles and machine guns.

In the early 1970s, the only air defense gun the army had at its disposal was a World War II–vintage model called the Vulcan. It was cheap and by all accounts quite effective, but it could fire only 20-millimeter ammunition, and by the 1970s it was clear that the new generation of Soviet aircraft and helicopters would have armor thick enough to withstand such a small round. The Vulcan was also of limited range and difficult to move around; it had to be replaced. The idea at first was simply to upgrade the Vulcan, but as the army's designers became embroiled in the project, and consultations with industry began, that changed. "Pretty soon," one of those involved told Gregg Easterbrook, a journalist who first exposed the shortcomings of the Divad gun in the *Atlantic Monthly* in October 1982, "we were adding every bell and whistle you could think of."

Three factors help explain the transformation of the new gun, which the army named the Sergeant York, after the World War I sharpshooter who single-handedly killed 25 Germans and captured 132 others in a battle in the trenches. First, the army couldn't make up its mind what it wanted. The procurement bureaucracy was divided about the merits of a new gun. Some, primarily civilian analysts, argued that ground-to-air missiles were more effective, and though these people lost, their arguments prompted the Sergeant York's advocates to promise the development of a very special gun. The second problem—closely related to this—was that, having settled on a gun, the army kept changing the requirements for it. And this, in turn, reflected a wider conceptual failure: a failure to think through with any precision the virtues and limitations of air defense guns as compared to surface-to-air missiles.

Perhaps the key catalyst in the development of the Divad, or Sergeant York, was a Soviet weapon called the Shilka. The American Army got its hands on one of these, officially designated ZSU-23-4 by the Russians, at the end of the 1973 Arab-Israeli War. It had been captured by the Israelis and was shipped back to the U.S. Army's testing range at Fort Bliss, Texas. There are differing accounts of its effectiveness. Some say it performed well in the 1973 war, shooting down a number of Israeli Skyhawks and Phantoms over the Golan Heights. But most experts I have talked to describe it as an unimpressive weapon; when tested at Fort Bliss, it apparently proved slow to pick up targets as well as inaccurate, and it rapidly exhausted its ammunition when fired. Agile aircraft, according to these skeptics, had little trouble eluding it. But whether or not the Shilka was evidence of wasted Soviet rubles, the U.S. Army was fascinated by it, especially by the radars that supposedly enabled it to pick up its targets and the computers that, in theory, permitted the gun to lock on to those targets automatically. As then available the Shilka might not be ideal, but what if the Russians perfected it?

The army set out to create a gun that, like the Shilka, would operate automatically, so that it could perform at night and in foul weather, too. To save time and money, it was decided to use components from existing weapons—the chassis from the old M-48 tank, the radar from the F-16 fighter, with two Swedish Bofors antiaircraft guns supplying the armament.[2] But for what the army had in mind, all this

---

[2]Some critics argue that a principal reason the Divad failed was that it consisted of a "cost-cutting hodgepodge" of existing technology. But this is hardly convincing.

had to be put together in an immensely complicated way. Initially, the Divad was conceived to knock down fixed-wing aircraft, but in 1978 that "requirement" was changed to include rotary wing aircraft (i.e., helicopters) as well—a *very* different target. Later still, another even more demanding requirement was added: in order to strike Soviet Hind helicopters before they could threaten forces the Divad was supposed to defend, the new weapon would have to be able to achieve "kills" at a range of 4 kilometers.

All of this, of course, necessitated a dazzling array of supersophisticated components, and aspiring contractors were soon putting them together: computers to track enemy aircraft, to "assess the threat levels" of these aircraft, to predict their movements, to monitor all the other computers and provide instant analysis of failure, to resist radar jamming, and to find out whether the aircraft flying overhead were friendly or not. In all, the Divad would require some 240 separate software programs. Then there was the laser range finder, the infrared night sight to back up the radars, and the air conditioner to keep all this apparatus cool. According to its eventual manufacturers, Ford Aerospace, Divad would require essentially no skill to operate. It would simply be a question of turning it on, waiting for a light on the control panel to flash "FIRE NOW," and pulling a trigger. Nothing would be simpler. Even the dumbest GI would be able to do it.

The first time the Sergeant York was tested was in early 1982, when some of the army's top brass assembled for a display at a Fort Hood firing range in Texas. It was a sunny day, and a small Huey helicopter hovered in the clear air above the range. This was the designated target. Given the weather, it didn't seem an exacting test. In this "optimized environment" the Divad might be expected to demolish the Huey the instant it was switched on.

The Divad was wheeled out—an ungainly-looking vehicle, closely resembling a tank, though with its radar and two Bofors guns mounted on top instead of the normal projecting barrel. A technician switched it on. Unhappily, instead of aiming at the Huey, its cannons swung round toward the reviewing stand and its audience of army brass. Officers dived for cover. Luckily, Ford technicians had thought to put a lock on the gun barrels to prevent them turning far enough to threaten any damage; but it was not an auspicious start. The technicians earnestly examined the Divad and it was tried again. This time it did point at the target, but only briefly. Then the cannons began blasting away at a patch of tumbleweed 300 yards away.

It is customary to dismiss the snags experienced in such tests as teething troubles. All the same, Ford's explanation for the debacle was hardly convincing: they said that the Divad gun used in the test had just been washed, and that its performance might have been degraded because of water affecting the electronics. But on the central front, or on any potential battlefield, military equipment is likely to have to survive all kinds of weather, not to mention dust and rough treatment. The evidence that Divad was no miracle weapon continued to accumulate: it could not hit an aircraft that "jinked" (dodged) in flight, or a helicopter that "popped up" (rose quickly from behind some trees or from the ground to fire antitank missiles before ducking down again swiftly). Indeed, it did not seem able to do any of the things it might be expected to do.

There was a ready explanation for this. The problem with guns that fire automatically is that the computers that make them work deal with the past rather than the future. Computers can track the "history" of an approaching aircraft and, based on that history, calculate where it will be. But they cannot allow (or allow *sufficiently*) for unpredictable movement. To shoot down a plane, you must aim ahead of it in the direction you anticipate it will follow, and since pilots flying over a modern battlefield weave and dodge for all they are worth, the Divad is relatively easy to foil. No pilot in his right mind, as one air force veteran put it, would fly straight and level over hostile terrain. There is only one truly effective device for tracking and aiming at an agile combat plane, and that is the human eye. A human gunner, aware of his surroundings, and of the kind of mission an enemy plane might be flying, is in an infinitely better position to predict its course than a computer. The human eye, for example, can see a plane banking before it turns; a computer can't.

The Divad, moreover, was expected to cope not just with aircraft but also with helicopters, which travel at very different speeds and which often have no momentum at all. Helicopters baffled the Divad;

a human gunner, by contrast, finds it relatively easy to adapt from one kind of target to another.

Even if the Divad had worked, its vaunted ability to shoot down aircraft at night and in fog seemed to some critics an overrated asset. Even modern jets have trouble flying successful missions in bad weather, and for night fighting a night sight called a FLIR (forward-looking infrared) would have been of more value than the computer wizardry of the Divad. Some U.S. fighter planes have FLIRs, which allow the pilot to see a narrow stretch of ground in front of him almost as clearly as if it were day. As Gregg Easterbrook notes, aircraft with FLIRs, however, might be countered by antiaircraft guns with FLIRs:

> In a flir-to-flir duel, ground gunners would have a distinct advantage. Aircraft flying against the cold, empty background of the sky provide an excellent thermal contrast, sharp and easy to see. Vehicles prowling amid the clutter and retained warmth of the ground, on the other hand, provide only a small thermal contrast; heat "camouflages" them against infrared detection the same way trees and colors camouflage them against visual detection.

Installing a FLIR on the Divad might have made sense. Installing an automatic fire control system demonstrably did not. It accounted for an estimated $2 billion of the program's $4.5 billion price tag, and it didn't work. Admittedly, trying to aim a gun *visually* at a target 4 kilometers away is a tall order—which is one reason the army was so keen on automatic fire control. But was the 4-kilometer-range requirement really sensible? In the first place, long-range shells have to be bigger than short-range ones; as a result, the ammunition chosen for the Divad was 40 millimeter, twice the size of the Vulcan's. It consisted of "proximity rounds," triggered to detonate several feet from a target and spray a cloud of shrapnel and tungsten pellets at it. These proximity rounds were very expensive—$200 apiece—and there was considerable doubt as to whether they would be able to penetrate heavily armored Soviet aircraft. In addition, the larger the shell the more difficult it is to create the "wall-of-lead" effect on which a gun depends; instead of being able to fire 3,000 rounds a minute, like the Vulcan, the Divad could manage only 600. The special nature of the shells, moreover, meant that in a war the guns would require a special logistical support system, although, as *Newsweek* noted, the guns "jammed so frequently" in testing that this might not have been a serious problem.

So was the emphasis on extralong range, and therefore extraspecial shells, a necessary one? Probably not. As the *New York Times* pointed out: "Knocking out a tank requires precision, and an attacking plane, armed with homing missiles, must first get close enough for the pilot to see the target and identify it as the enemy." Yet the obsession with range grew, rather than diminished, as the Divad was developed. In the early 1980s alarming reports began to reach U.S. intelligence from Afghanistan that the Russian Hind helicopters had become theoretically capable of firing guided missiles at a target up to 6 kilometers away, 2 kilometers beyond the Divad's maximum range. This sent a tremor through the Pentagon. Some officials began to argue that the Divad's range was too *short*. The army, to be fair, tried to point out that the Hind threat was being exaggerated. After all, as the *New York Times* noted, "Soviet pilots would not be able to hit targets from six kilometers in an actual battle, especially in the frequent overcast and rolling hills of Europe." The argument appeared to have little effect, even though the *real* trouble with the Divad was not that it could not shoot far enough but that it could shoot too far.

Meanwhile, the program struggled on, with the Pentagon preferring to attack the messenger rather than heed the message. With stout backing from Ford, it labeled the media and congressional criticism of the Divad inaccurate, unfair, and incomplete. "The program," says Major General James P. Maloney, who was in charge of the Divad, "is problem-plagued in the press only."

To be sure, the press sometimes overdid it. On one occasion the Divad's acquisition radar ignored the intended target on the test site and picked up instead a bathroom fan in a building 100 yards away. Though the gun never actually opened fire, subsequent jocular headlines in the newspapers (e.g., "BATTLE OF THE LATRINE FAN") gave, in the army's view, the false impression that it had. It was something for the army to seize upon as it tried to stem the tide of criticism.

Essentially, though, Maloney's claim was rather unconvincing.

The basic charge against Divad—that it could not "acquire," let alone hit, the right targets—was never properly answered, save by continual claims that the gun's problems were only minor ones. "I would say," declared General Maloney to a television reporter in mid-1984, "that practically all of the problems that we have found with this system have been corrected. If the totality of problems were 100 percent, I would say at this point, 97 percent of those problems have been corrected."

"Divad experienced normal start-up problems," echoed Ford spokesperson Susan Frutkin. "None of them are show-stoppers. Most of them have been fixed." By this stage, however, some powerful critics were joining the fray. In the summer of 1984, the Divad was put through its paces again. At the army's test site at White Sands, it mistook about half of 180 decoys sent against it for real targets, and hit only about one-third of its aerial attackers when they employed electronic countermeasures to fool the gun's radars.

The gun's inability to hit "pop-up" helicopters was still plainly evident. In one particular round of testing, when it seemed unable to hit a stationary helicopter placed on an elevated platform some distance away (an electric motor was used to turn the rotor blades), the army added "radar reflectors" to the target to provide a clearer signal for the Divad's radar. This was described in the *Washington Monthly* as "like testing a bloodhound's ability to track a man covered with beefsteak standing alone and upright in the middle of a parking lot." In this instance, the army argued it had been necessary to shorten the helicopter's rotor blades—so that it didn't take off—and that the reflectors had been added simply to compensate for the reduction in radar signature this caused. Still, the Divad seemed to need a lot of this kind of help —what was called "target enhancement" or "success-oriented testing." At one point, cans of gasoline were even loaded into the helicopters to increase their chances of exploding when hit.

The poor results of the 1984 tests proved, if not the last straw, at least sufficient to provoke an unusual step. With concern about the Divad widespread in official circles, the army's Operational Test and Evaluation Agency acknowledged in private meetings that the Divad's record of failure raised serious questions about its performance and reliability. And it wasn't just the "ultra" components that were giving trouble; even the relatively simple ammunition feeder on the Divad didn't work properly.

As the recriminations mounted, the army deflected some of the criticism to Divad's manufacturer, Ford Aerospace. In March 1984, it produced a report charging the company with a "totally unacceptable" performance. In fact, the army had created considerable controversy by giving the contract to Ford in the first place.

In the initial competition for the lucrative $4.5 billion contract, two firms had emerged as front runners, General Dynamics and Ford. The two, each of which had built a prototype Divad, held a shoot-off, which was won hands-down by General Dynamics. According to a Pentagon report, Ford's gun hit half as many targets as the General Dynamics prototype, and the longest range of a Ford hit was only just over half the longest range of a General Dynamics hit (in all, General Dynamics shot down fifteen helicopters, Ford only eight). Nonetheless, the army decided to opt for Ford. Ostensibly, this was for two reasons: first, said the army, Ford had technically superior ammunition; and second, Ford had more "near misses" than General Dynamics, and if near misses were counted as hits, Ford emerged the victor.

Needless to say, General Dynamics was outraged by the decision. There were suggestions that Ford had gotten the contract because it was in financial trouble, and that the Reagan White House, philosophically opposed to bailing out companies, yet anxious to help, had suggested the Pentagon look favorably on Ford's attempts to win defense contracts. Whatever the case, General Dynamics, already hugely dependent on Pentagon business, and in some difficulties with its submarine program, was not anxious to cause a public row. Still, the controversy only added more fuel to a roaring fire.

In the wake of the 1984 tests, Pentagon Inspector General Joseph Sherick produced a report that proved depressing reading for those involved in the Divad project. The inspector general is an important man in the Defense Department (he acts as an in-house watchdog), and now he charged Ford with unacceptable behavior. No sooner had the company won the contract, he told a congressional committee in late September 1984, than it proceeded to negotiate price reductions with its subcontractors. According to Sherick, this clearly indicated that Ford had overcharged the army in the first place. Not only that:

he complained that the prices for spare parts for the Divads were far too high. For example, after originally charging $7,900 for a power control assembly, Ford was now ready to charge $151,500—an increase of 1,840 percent.

But Sherick was not content simply to blast Ford for the way it had handled the contract, and for its seeming overeagerness for huge profits. He also told Congress that army charts supposedly illustrating test data from 1982, when Divad production was first authorized, and which attested to a high level of effectiveness in field trials, "were oversimplified, and therefore misleading and based on a selective analysis of the results." The Pentagon, in other words, had been so keen on the Divad that it had rigged the tests to make the gun look better than it really was.

Finally, in October 1984, after a series of hearings in Congress, and after the army had finally admitted that its Sergeant York had missed the target 75 percent of the time at a recent firing, Defense Secretary Caspar Weinberger decided he had had enough. It is unusual for a weapons system to be suspended once in production: there are too many vested interests tied up in it by then, and too many jobs at stake. But Weinberger suspended production of Divad anyway, ordering the army to stop purchasing it: the $4 billion program would await the results of new tests scheduled for 1985.

Already, however, 15 Divads had been delivered to the army and funds for a further 130 had been approved by Congress (each gun then cost $6.3 million). Over $1.5 billion had been spent, and this despite the appalling record of the Divad since it was first conceived. "What is so awful," one Pentagon skeptic told me at the time, "is that there is nothing we know now that we didn't know two years ago." Yet in the meantime a fortune had been wasted.

The army continued to insist that the Divad's problems were only temporary and would be solved. But even if this were true, the original concept of an air defense gun had long since been lost. "We've finally found a way of making a gun more expensive than a missile," commented one army skeptic.

In mid-December 1984, shortly after the Divad program was suspended, viewers of the ABC News current affairs program "20/20" were treated to a remarkable piece of film. Reporter Geraldo Rivera had

spent the best part of a year investigating the Divad gun: he had heard
the horror stories about it; he had also listened to the army's protesta-
tions about its effectiveness, and decided to hold back his report until
after the summer 1984 tests. These, of course, proved no more successful than any previous tests, but Rivera was anxious to see for himself,
and finally the army agreed to invite him to Fort Bliss to attend a
demonstration. Flanked by a group of high-ranking military officers
from around the world, Rivera and his camera crew watched as a Divad
was prepared for firing. "To demonstrate that the tracking and computer system of this gun is so sophisticated that absolutely anyone can
fire it, General Maloney made a bold decision," Rivera told his viewers.
"He allowed the gun to be operated by a civilian aide to the secretary
of the army. The aide had never done it before. Perhaps the general
should have selected someone more experienced."

What viewers of "20/20" saw next was the Divad gun opening
fire on a ground target 100 yards away. Given that, in a war, the Divad
would probably have to fire at ground targets as well as at aircraft and
helicopters—indeed it had been designed with this in mind—it was not
unreasonable that it should be tested in this manner. But judging from
the results, enemy ground forces would have little to fear. The Divad
fired a burst, and missed, the tracer shells exploding in the clear sunlit
air a safe distance away. It fired again a few seconds later and missed.
A third time . . . and a fourth. The target remained unscathed. Apparently, the world's most sophisticated gun, which had been designed to
be able to strike aircraft flying above it at great speed, was not even able
to hit a stationary target a mere 100 yards away. After this display,
however, the civilian aide at the Divad's controls turned his attention
to the "main event" of the day—a QH-50 helicopter drone hovering
gently 300 feet above. This is not the kind of height helicopters usually
fly in combat; they either hug the ground very tightly (Vietnam helicopter pilots often returned from missions with grass on their skids),
or they climb as high as possible to escape antiaircraft fire. As one
former Vietnam pilot put it, 50 to 1,200 feet "is dead man's height;
no helicopter in war would be performing as the QH-50 was during the
test." Still, the fact that the airborne target was a sitting duck did not
appear to help the Divad much. One round in the first burst appeared
to wing the helicopter, though it continued to hover peacefully 300 feet

up. Another burst missed entirely. Finally the QH-50 had descended
to closer range, by which time it scored a hit.

Following this display, reporter Rivera turned to General Maloney. "How do you characterize the demonstration we've just seen?"
he asked.

Maloney was unruffled. "Well," he said, "it was absolutely a total
success."

Eight months later, in July 1985, Caspar Weinberger finally canceled the Divad outright. To the end, the army continued to maintain
that the gun's problems could be solved. So did Ford Aerospace. Even
as late as March 1985, the ever-optimistic General Maloney was telling
Congress he believed that "testing in the future will prove that the
Sergeant York is the finest self-propelled antiaircraft gun in the world."
Maloney also impugned the motives of the gun's leading congressional
critic, Representative Denny Smith, a Republican from Oregon.
Smith, he said, was "not doing this [attacking Divad] for the good of
the country." And Weinberger, once described as a man "who never
saw a weapons system he didn't like," knew that the army had nothing
else in its stocks to close the air defense gap.

But the Divad's final test, in June 1985, proved as ludicrous as any
that had gone before. At first it seemed otherwise. Ford put out a paper
saying that, in a "live-fire" exercise, the Divad had managed to destroy
"six out of seven high-performance aircraft and three of three helicopters presented." But this, it turned out, was highly misleading. First,
as Denny Smith quickly learned, the army had presented its targets
many more than ten times; second, the targets appear to have flown
in straight lines with little or no maneuvering, except for a roll in front
of the guns to provide a *larger* target. And third, four of the six planes
that were brought down were not hit by the Divad at all but destroyed
by the range safety officer on the ground. The army was worried that
they might veer off course and cause damage, a spokesman said, even
though the test took place in the middle of the New Mexico desert.
So the target aircraft, which were filled with explosives, were "command destructed." For its part, the army claimed that the Divad's
proximity shells would eventually have brought the planes down. The
evidence suggested otherwise.

In the end, as Bill Keller of the *New York Times* put it, the Divad could be said to have "died of embarrassment." It had managed to combine *all* the drawbacks of a surface-to-air missile system—namely, elaborate fire control, complexity, and cost—with *none* of the advantages of an air defense gun. Guns make sense if they are cheap and simple enough to be produced in large numbers so that on the battlefield they can throw up a "wall of lead" in front of enemy aircraft and helicopters. Unlike missiles, lead can neither be decoyed nor spoofed because it does not depend on "locking on" to the heat or radar signature of a target. It depends, or should depend, on the eye of the gunner. (Not least of the Divad's drawbacks was the likelihood that, in a war, its powerful active radar would act as a homing device for the Soviets' radar-seeking missiles.) Had the Divad been properly designed —had the army, in other words, pushed for less elaborate requirements, settled for a shorter range, and thought more about tactics and less about technology—a formidable weapon could have emerged, inexpensive enough to be produced in large numbers. As it was, the army wasted a lot of time and money. For even if all the proposed 618 Divads had been purchased, and had worked, they would still not have been available in anything like the necessary numbers.

The Bradley Fighting Vehicle

The job of an army is the most fundamental in warfare: it is to take or regain land, and traditionally the PBI—"the poor bloody infantry" —has been less susceptible to gadgetry than its sister services. In World War II the U.S. Army relied on abundant quantities of simple, rugged, easy-to-maintain equipment. Indeed, U.S. procurement became synonymous with basic and mass-produced weapons such as the Tommy guy and the Sherman tank. The idea was to overwhelm through sheer numbers, and there was logic to it. In war, numbers count.

Now, however, the philosophy in the Pentagon is that a few "ultra" weapons are better than a lot of less sophisticated ones, and the army has become a true believer in that philosophy.

But ultra weapons, like the Divad, built "at the leading edge of technology," are extraordinarily expensive. And because they are so expensive, and you can thus build so few of them, they have to be very good indeed because (1) you are presenting fewer targets for the other side to destroy, and (2) you are leaving the other side with more "weapons platforms" to fire from and more targets to lose. It is commonly assumed, in fact, that if you wish to equal the strength of an enemy who outnumbers you by two to one, then your weapons have to be between two and four times as good as his. The Divad gun hardly lived up to this equation. And nor does another example of the shiny new hardware that, in the early 1980s, began to arrive on the battlefield as part of the army's ambitious, across-the-board, "weapons modernization" program.

The Bradley Fighting Vehicle, or M-2, is built by the FMC Corporation, a company that until the early years of World War II specialized almost entirely in building fruit-processing and canning equipment. When America entered the war, FMC adapted its expertise in metal bending, welding, and mechanical engineering to the military, securing a contract to produce tracked amphibious vehicles for the army. The model FMC built was simple and sturdy. The company christened it the Water Buffalo, and churned out 11,000 of them by the time the war ended. FMC followed this up in the 1950s with another armored personnel carrier, the M-113. It was poorly protected and built of aluminum, but it served its purpose—depositing soldiers on the edge of a combat zone—and it was cheap ($183,000 each when the army bought the last batch in 1984). In all, FMC has sold a total of more than 70,000 M-113s throughout the world, and it proved one of the few notable successes of the Vietnam War. Christopher Foss, editor of the authoritative *Jane's Armoured Fighting Vehicles*, describes it as "one of the most successful vehicles ever in the U.S. Army service."

To understand why the Bradley will never win such praise one has to go back to 1964, when the U.S. Army, after consultation with the West German army, changed its doctrine. There was now a need, it decided, for a vehicle that would not simply deposit mechanized infantry at the edge of a battlefield, but be able to carry troops into the thick of any fighting—indeed, allow them to fight while they were still aboard. Even at the time, some army experts doubted the wisdom of this. They pointed out that it is very difficult for infantry to shoot at enemy forces while rolling across what would undoubtedly be rough countryside. They also noted that mechanized infantry tend to be used in terrain where tanks are highly vulnerable; and if tanks are highly vulnerable in such terrain, so-called "mechanized infantry combat vehicles" would be, too.

Nonetheless, the new requirement stood, and the army, which was already considering a replacement for the M-113, began to investigate ways of meeting it. Though it dismissed as too large, too heavy, and too underpowered three 52,000-pound prototypes built for it by a company called Pacific Car & Foundry (now Paccar, Inc.), its conception of what it *did* want grew steadily more ambitious—and as with the Divad gun, more and more confusing.

In 1972, FMC sent the Pentagon a detailed and comprehensive package, which included a foot-high stack of documents and a wooden model of the envisaged end product. FMC knew that the army was worried about a new Soviet infantry fighting vehicle, first fielded in the late 1960s, which was armed with a cannon, able to carry eleven men into combat, and supposedly capable of crossing rivers and being dropped by parachute. Nevertheless, given that the army was already demanding something vastly more complicated than the M-113, the company put forward a relatively simple design, emphasizing ruggedness, reliability, and prompt delivery. The army was impressed. FMC got the contract.

It was at this point that the trouble started. By all accounts, FMC found itself bombarded with specifications from different army departments—the Infantry Center in Georgia wanted to be able to move men around; the U.S. Army Armor Center wanted to kill tanks; the army's light cavalry disliked the whole project because it was keen on a new scout vehicle—and the new carrier began to sink in a morass of bureaucratic indecision, design changes, and gold plating. FMC executives were bewildered by their dealings with the Pentagon: the days when the army issued simple specifications and let contractors get on with the job appeared to be over. Washington had changed. "What we're dealing with now is a multiheaded monster," said one executive. "The Bradley project is rather like a tree," commented another. "The army keeps pulling it up by the roots to see if it's still growing."

The project stumbled on and the problems multiplied. The new vehicle must be able to go as fast as modern tanks, said the army, in order to keep up with them on the battlefield—a requirement that meant that the vehicle kept "throwing its tracks" in testing (centrifugal force around the drive gear, which built up when the vehicle was traveling fast, caused the tracks to slip off). In addition, the transmission system installed by GEC broke down frequently, and the price began to rise. The anticipated 1976 production date came and went and then a high-level army study group rewrote the specifications yet again, insisting that the vehicle should have two TOW missiles, a night-vision system, and a stabilized Swiss cannon. The TOW—a tube-launched, optically tracked, wire-guided missile—is a useful enough weapon for infantry when operated on the ground. But it had a drastic effect on the design of the new vehicle. It required a large turret to accommodate it, and this in turn meant that the number of soldiers who could be squeezed aboard would have to drop from twelve to nine. And instead of one man, three of the nine—the driver, the gunner, and the commanding officer—would have to remain aboard at all times. In effect, the vehicle would be able to carry *half* as many men as had originally been anticipated.

Meanwhile, as FMC slowly drowned in a sea of specifications, the army decided to rechristen its new creation in order to reflect its increased importance. Choosing the name of a distinguished general, Omar Bradley, they called it the Bradley Fighting Vehicle.

The Bradley Fighting Vehicle, when it finally emerged, after much prodding from Congress, was a kind of hybrid between a traditional battlefield taxi and a full-blown tank. Ten feet tall, and weighing 50,000 pounds, it was, however, less well armed than a tank (it had only a 25-millimeter gun) and, of course, more vulnerable because it was taller and less heavily armored. "If it gets blown up there where everybody can see it, it does not make any difference how sophisticated the gun is or anything else," said Senator Sam Nunn, one of Capitol Hill's most respected defense experts, in June 1983. He might have added that if the Bradley is hit, it will burn—very fast: it is largely made of aluminum. Senator Gary Hart has described it as a "powder keg." Moreover, it is so cumbersome that the C-141 aircraft intended to carry it can only hold one at a time. And getting one Bradley into a C-141 is hard enough. In one test, it took no less than 153 minutes in all— 72 of them spent unbolting the side armor and squashing the vehicle down on its springs to make it shorter, and then another 81 winching it onboard because, having been squashed, it could no longer move itself.

Despite its bulk, however, the Bradley is so cramped inside that is has been aptly described by one analyst, Paul Hoven of the Washington-based Project on Military Procurement, as "an infantry fighting vehicle with almost no room for the infantry." It is also extremely heavy. An early effort to demonstrate its supposed amphibious capability ended when a Bradley, complete with a rubberized collar around its frame, plunged into the Ohio River at Fort Knox, Kentucky—and sank like a stone.

By the time the Bradley began rolling off the production lines in the early 1980s, the army was saying that its troubles were over and that all the problems had been solved. "An infantryman's dream," said the Pentagon. But in the course of its tortuous route to the battlefield, the costs of the infantryman's dream had soared. Set in 1968 to cost $108,000 ($363,000 in 1985 dollars), by 1985 its price tag had risen to $1,459,000; allowing for inflation, it was four times more expensive than originally anticipated. Not only that: you could have bought at least eight improved versions of the M-113 for the price of one Bradley, and each of those eight would have been able to transport eleven, instead of six, soldiers to the battlefield.

What did this huge increase in the price buy the army? More weapons, to be sure, and thicker armor, thanks to new materials and new techniques (mainly the application of lightweight fibers). But did this really make up for all the additional money and lack of space in the Bradley? The fact is that the M-113 was (sensibly) designed not to enter the thick of battle but to deposit soldiers on the edge of a combat zone. And the chances are that for all the army's plans, this is precisely what the Bradley Fighting Vehicle will have to do. Like the Divad, it has been trapped by its own technology. As the distinguished military expert Edward Luttwak has observed:

> Unfortunately, while the Bradley was slowly being developed, becoming more and more elaborate in the process, the antitank revolution was under way. The modern rockets, more modern guns and recoilless weapons, and the many kinds of antitank

missiles that now saturate the battlefield are not really very effective against the latest 50–60 ton battle tanks. But they are devastating against all tank-sized targets that do not have tanklike levels
of protection. With its thin armor, the 20-ton Bradley cannot
survive on the battlefield—i.e., within the inner zone of close
combat—any better than the one-tenth-the-price M-113 could.
But if the Bradley is employed as a mere troop carrier, to be left
behind by the infantry before it enters a fight, then its million-plus
dollars' worth of weapons will be wasted.

The M-1 Tank

The keystone of the U.S. Army's modernization program is its new
tank, the M-1 Abrams. The M-1 is very sophisticated; its fans, and
there are many, describe it as "the Cadillac of tanks." Like the Bradley
Fighting Vehicle, the M-1 was a long time in the making. The U.S.
Army started shopping around for a new tank in the early 1960s. First,
Robert McNamara, U.S. defense secretary at the time, forced the army
to consider jointly developing and building one with the West Germans. The advantages that would accrue from shared ammunition,
spare parts, maintenance, and operational procedures seemed attractive
and desirable. But no one could agree on the design, and by 1969 the
MBT-70 (MBT for main battle tank) had foundered, as so many
NATO projects have, on the rocks of diverging national interests. The
army then redesigned the MBT-70 into another tank, the XM-803, but
Congress considered this too complicated and costly, and gave it the
thumbs down. Not until 1972 did the army finally come up with a plan
that Congress found acceptable: this was for the M-1.

    The initial estimates of the M-1's cost was about $500,000 each;
in the early 1980s, it was rolling off the production line at a price of
just over $2.7 million, though to be fair, much of the added cost was
the result of inflation and the sheer length of time it took to develop
the M-1. Still, $2.7 million is a lot for a tank.

    Is it worth the price? The M-1's main armament is a 105-millime-
ter gun capable of striking targets very accurately at great distances.
Thanks to its fire control computers, its laser range finder, and its

night-vision devices, it is theoretically capable of destroying enemy tanks when they are almost 2 miles away. But is this capacity worth the money it costs and the reliability problems it creates? Some army experts doubt it. They believe that long-range tank encounters would be the exception rather than the rule. History suggests, they say, that most tank engagements take place over quite a short range—1,000 meters or less. Certainly analysis of the tank battles of World War II, and subsequently in Korea and the Middle East, suggest that most took place when the gunners of both sides were able to see what they were firing at. There is a natural enough reason for this: tank battles rarely take place on completely flat land. Trees, hills, and often buildings get in the way, making it hard for tank gunners to get a definite fix on their targets. Even in the Arab-Israeli wars of 1967 and 1973, which were fought on relatively flat terrain, the average engagement range for tanks was between 300 and 800 meters. In West Germany, where much of the terrain is hilly and wooded, and where even when it is flat (as on the north German plain) it is heavily built up, with villages and towns very close together, tanks would be greatly hampered in long-range firing. Once a war had begun, and the two sides had become closely entangled, the problems, say the skeptics, would intensify.

The defenders of the M-1 argue that its computerized gear could make all the difference to NATO by giving its tanks perhaps three times as long to engage the enemy, and allowing them to knock out perhaps three times as many enemy tanks in each engagement. Even if true, the fact remains that the cost of extending the range of the gun means there will be fewer tanks than there otherwise might be, and the unreliability of the hardware—which would undoubtedly become more pronounced amidst the smoke and harsh conditions of the battlefield —would reduce numbers still further. According to George Kuhn, a Vietnam veteran and consultant to the Heritage Foundation, a conservative think tank, "The overwhelming evidence is that, as in air combat, ground conflict will be won or lost in close encounters. Yet it appears that over 90 percent of our anti-armor force development funds go to achieving kills at extraordinary ranges."

The emphasis on long-range kills is not the only questionable feature of America's new tank. The M-1 can travel at 45 miles per hour on roads (30 miles per hour over flat ground), and accelerate from zero to 30 in twelve seconds. Some argue that this is an unnecessary luxury: no advance, or retreat, they say, is likely to require speeds as high as 45 miles per hour. Certainly, nothing on the battlefield is likely to be able to keep up with the M-1. Others argue that the capacity to "sprint" across short distances would bolster the tank's chances of survival. But whatever the truth, the powerful Lycoming AGT 1500-horsepower gas turbine engine, which gives the tank its power, is scarcely ideal for the battlefield. Though quiet (tank crews in Europe call it "whispering death"), it gives off tremendous heat, making it especially vulnerable to heat-seeking missiles, and making it hard for infantry to shelter behind it. The M-1 is also a gas guzzler, consuming much more fuel than diesel-powered tanks. The British toyed with the idea of installing a jet engine in their own 1980s tank, the Challenger, but rejected the idea, as did the West Germans who, when offered a chance to buy the American engine—in exchange for the opportunity to sell the United States their 120-millimeter tank gun—balked at the prospect.

The gas turbine has added hugely to the M-1s reliability and service problems: it needs no less than seven different types of oil, each of which has to be applied in the correct place, and its fuel consumption (the M-1 gets just one-third of a mile to the gallon) means that it has to travel into battle with a wagon train of fuel trucks, technicians, and spare-parts vans. This "rolling traffic jam," as one army commander called it, would, of course, be highly vulnerable in a shooting war.

Meanwhile, doubts persist about some of the M-1's gadgetry. At a "tank Olympics" in West Germany in June 1981, for example, the Americans and the British entered tanks with laser range finders. (The M-1 was not yet in production, but the M60A3, which the Americans used, was fitted with most of its successor's accouterments.) Yet the Germans, whose Leopard 1A4s and 1A3s had no thermal imagers and no laser range finders, won the contest, and the Belgians, similarly handicapped, came second. "The competition is a test of marksmanship," reported *Defense Week*, "yet the laser range finder in the U.S. and British tanks seemed to help them little." "The optical range finder is better," a German tank commander told the magazine.

The M-1 has fewer detractors than the Divad or the Bradley Fighting Vehicle. It works, and its "stabilization system," which enables it to fire while on the move, has been highly praised. So has its Chobham armor, a secret mixture of superalloy reinforced with fiberglass invented by the British. But many wonder whether America would not be better off with greater numbers of simpler, cheaper, and lighter tanks. Because of its armor and its weaponry, the M-1 weighs a massive 67 tons, and there is only one aircraft in the world—the C-5A Galaxy—that can carry it. And just as the C-141 can only squeeze in one Bradley at a time, so the C-5A can only carry two M-1 tanks. Even fans of the M-1 admit this is a major problem.

There are also serious questions about the M-1's reliability. How much trouble it will give on the battlefield is hard to predict, but early test results were not reassuring. A study by Dina Rasor of the Project on Military Procurement, a Washington-based pressure group, found that the M-1 experienced a serious breakdown on average once every 34 miles. Rasor did her analysis, which was based on an internal army report, in 1980, when the M-1 was still a relatively new program. Two years later, things had not improved much. The General Accounting Office, a congressional watchdog, issued a study suggesting that of thirty-nine tanks that covered 178 miles in a test at Fort Hood, Texas, only twenty-one were able to complete the course without breaking down.

These results may not be an accurate guide to the future, but the experience of the air force in the 1960s suggests that maintaining and repairing the army's new generation of equipment on the battlefield is going to prove excruciatingly difficult. In the late 1960s, when the U.S. Air Force was in the throes of developing a new range of fighter aircraft, technical experts predicted that a new avionics system then being built —the Mark II—would make the F-111D a far more reliable aircraft. The Mark II was so good, it was said, that it would *increase* the mean time between system failures (MTBF) to more than 60 hours, and *reduce* the maintenance man-hours per sortie (MMHS) to only 1.4. In fact, the Mark II ended up experiencing a MTBF not of 60 hours but of less than 3; and an MMHS not of 1.4 hours but of 33.6.

This example was offered to the Senate Armed Services Committee in 1980 by a Pentagon analyst named Franklin "Chuck" Spinney. Spinney, a slim, fair-haired man who is not greatly liked by his superiors because of his tendency to deal in uncomfortable truths, also told the senators that the air force's star fighter, the F-15 (which we will examine shortly), required over 27 maintenance man-hours per flight hour compared with the 11.3 predicted, and was experiencing a major systems failure once every 1.25 hours in the air—not, as promised, one every 5.6. This sort of record scarcely augured well for the army in the 1980s and 1990s. Besides, the business of identifying faults and repairing them on the battlefield promises to be nothing short of a nightmare.

Amidst the extraordinarily delicate, computer-driven gadgetry of such weapons as the M-1 are buried small black boxes called BITEs (for "built-in test equipment"). When weaponry breaks down, BITEs are supposed to identify the fault promptly, thereby saving hours of painstaking labor by mechanics. But the air force's experience of the 1970s suggests that BITEs frequently *create* work by suggesting that a specific part has broken down when in fact it is working perfectly, and occasionally fail to identify the right part when there is a snag. As the Defense Science Board, a panel of scientists under the aegis of the Pentagon, noted in a 1981 report:

> In the early 1970s, the proliferation of complexity within avionics equipment, coupled with the advancing state of digital technology, led to the birth of the "Built-in Test (BIT)" cult. Concerns relative to the maintenance of equipment with a multiplicity of removable assemblies were quieted with the promise of automatic fault detection and isolation capabilities that stretched into the high ninety percentile range. While these promises looked good on paper and were incorporated into almost all specifications, the actual field performance has been nothing short of a disaster.

The same is likely to prove true for the bigger test sets that army maintenance engineers use to identify faults *not* identified by BITEs. Air force experience suggests that army logistics personnel may take up to eight times longer than planned to test the individual electronic components in major new weapons. "The Army's new test sets may accurately isolate faults only half as often as projections allow," notes George Kuhn. "The sets themselves may require major repairs and not be available for testing three times more often than planned." To take one small example, army maintenance engineers looking after the Hawk missile systems in the early 1980s spent almost a quarter of their time dealing with false alarms generated by the test equipment. Thus the army will not only face problems with its equipment; the sets supposed to identify the problems will break down a lot, too, especially on the battlefield. And even when they are working, they will identify problems that do not exist. The logistics problem this is likely to create on the battlefield—where the army will be using hundreds, if not thousands, of different electronic components for repairs—can be readily imagined.

The F-15 Fighter

The abiding preoccupation of the Pentagon, says George Kuhn, is with "fighting wars at a distance." Like the creators of the Maginot line, modern defense planners are anxious, above all, to insure that, if war comes, loss of life is kept to a minimum. In this respect, they are pursuing a noble goal. But as the Maginot line illustrated, elaborate attempts to reduce the risks, and "dehumanize" war, can backfire.

The emphasis in the exotic M-1 tank is on high speed, computerized fire control, long-range kill, and all the other wonders that science has made theoretically possible. With modern aircraft, such as the air force's F-15, and its navy equivalent, the F-14, the pattern, as I have indicated, is much the same. The story, once again, is one of soaring costs, "marginal" improvements, and declining numbers.

The F-15 is America's top-of-the-line fighter. It is astonishingly fast, with a top speed of almost three times the speed of sound, and its sophisticated avionics, data display indicators, cathode ray tubes, head-up visual display for the pilot, and forty-five computers are geared toward giving it the ability to shoot down other aircraft when they are still up to 80 miles away. (The missile supposed to enable it to achieve this, the AMRAAM, which we will examine in a moment, is still not in production.) It is this capacity to strike the enemy before he is even in sight that accounts most for the F-15's bulky size and high cost (almost $40 million in 1985 prices). The F-15 needs a large, powerful, active radar to search the sky in front of it; it is built to carry missiles that can be guided to their targets "beyond visual range" by that radar. Not for nothing is the F-15 known as the Eagle.

In 1977 and 1978 the F-15 Eagle was tested in an unusual and ambitious series of exercises at Nellis Air Force Base in Nevada. For almost two years, some of America's best pilots dueled with one another high above the desert, pushing both themselves and their planes to the limit. The lessons that were learned at Nellis in the course of these mock engagements taught the air force some surprising things.

On one side was the F-15 and its naval equivalent, the F-14; on the other were the comparatively small and cheap F-5 Tiger Shark, which the air force does not consider good enough to be a front-line fighter (though it sells some to its allies), and the Phantom F-4—both of which cost a fraction of the price of the F-15 and F-14.

It wasn't combat, but it was intended to be the next best thing. During the exercises, every possible kind of combination was tried out: one fighter meeting another in solitary encounter; two fighters taking on two others; one fighter ambushed by two, three, or four enemy ones; four taking on four; and so on. The controllers of the exercises, who monitored everything from the ground, assessing probable kills, were determined to find out exactly how America's best fighting aircraft measured up. And though you might have expected the F-15s to triumph every time, it did not work out that way.

To be sure, in the one-on-one dogfights, the F-15 invariably came off best, its superior technology allowing it to vanquish the less sophisticated F-5s and F-4s. But when the combat became more confused, the F-15's advantages faded. When it met two or three F-4s and F-5s it was not nearly so successful; it might get one of the smaller planes, but invariably it would be shot down by another. When four F-15s met four F-5s the results were usually fairly even; in the confusion of the battle, both sides would sustain losses and the F-15's technology simply did not appear to help it.

The results of the exercises at Nellis Air Force Base have been fiercely debated ever since, but they amount to a sobering reminder of the limits of high-tech defense. The organizers afterward confessed to some shock at the outcome. Writing in the air force's *Tactical Analysis Bulletin,* Lieutenant Colonel George Dvorchak commented that one finding of the tests was that "there isn't any way to out-technology the other guy. If he has some good basic capabilities, numbers are a basic driver. The reason that incremental weapons improvements wash out in the long run is that people learn to adjust to them."

It must be acknowledged that the F-15 pilots were denied one crucial luxury—the ability to shoot at their opposition before they could see them with the naked eye. As we have observed, much of the technology that goes into the F-15 is designed to provide it with just such a "beyond visual range" capability.

But the men who staged the exercises argued that in this respect they were a fair representation of what a war would actually be like on the central front. Just as tank experts argue that most tank battles in history have taken place at ranges of 1,000 meters or less, so history suggests that aircraft kills are achieved when pilots can see their enemy. And in a war in Central Europe this would almost certainly be the case. For—and this is a crucial point—NATO does not have a common IFF (Identification Friend or Foe) system, which means that American fighter pilots would have no foolproof way of establishing whether aircraft heading toward them were friendly or not; they would be able to exchange signals with fellow American pilots, but not with British, Dutch, Belgian, or German ones. The dangers therefore of shooting at enemy aircraft before they become visible are readily imaginable.

There is a further problem. The long-range missiles—like the Sparrow—introduced into the inventories of the U.S. Air Force and Navy in the 1960s and 1970s, have proved less than satisfactory in combat. Unlike shorter-range, heat-seeking missiles such as the Side-winder (essentially a very simple invention), they are full of complex, delicate mechanisms and are inherently less reliable. They are also easier to foil through countermeasures or evasive action, since enemy pilots can see long-range missiles approaching and have more time to try and avoid them. By flying in pairs, it would seem, enemy aircraft also have a good chance of outfoxing the Sparrow. Tests showed that the Sparrow, if faced with two targets, would sometimes split the difference—confused, according to air force sources, by the contradictory messages emanating from the two targets, it would be unable to work out which it ought to hit and end up flying harmlessly in between. In Vietnam, the air force had to fire one hundred Sparrows for every eight planes they actually brought down, whereas heat-seeking missiles brought down sixteen per one hundred firings, twice as good a strike rate.

Besides, to fire the Sparrow, or other radar-guided missiles, pilots have to switch on their own "active radar," which searches the sky for enemy aircraft but also risks giving away their position. Switching on active radar, in the view of one air force expert, is like switching on a torch in a darkened room when you know there's a killer inside: you may well get shot at before you can fire a round. Pilots, therefore, will be wary of using active radar in battles over the central front. Modern radar-guided missiles are also wildly expensive; the Phoenix, for example, which has a range of 80 miles and is carried by the F-14, cost $1.85 million apiece in 1985, making it a difficult missile to practice with.

An even more sophisticated missile in the works for both air force and navy is the AMRAAM, or advanced medium-range air-to-air missile. The AMRAAM is what the F-15 was developed to carry. It is intended to have a "fire and forget capability," meaning that pilots will not have to keep their active radar locked on to a target until the missile has actually struck, as they are forced to do with both Sparrow and Phoenix. In theory, AMRAAM will also enable pilots to fire several missiles simultaneously at different enemy targets. But the AMRAAM has had a troubled history: there have been disputes about testing, about whether pilots will be able to manage the complicated multishot launching sequence, about whether the new missile will be able to perform in the face of enemy electronic jamming—and, of course, about whether it is necessary at all. Meanwhile, the price has steadily climbed. Once intended to be a cheaper alternative to Sparrow, it now looks likely to be far more expensive. In 1979, Russell Murray II, then the assistant defense secretary for program analysis and evaluation, pointed out that it was set to cost 50 percent more than Sparrow— which, he said, "is already so expensive that we are not able to afford more than two missile loads per F-15." The AMRAAM, Murray predicted in 1982, will turn out to be "an expensive bird with limited utility." Nothing has happened since then to invalidate that judgment.

As a result of the 1977 and 1978 exercises in the Nevada desert, other attributes of the F-15 also began to look more questionable: its enormous speed, for example. The F-15 can travel at almost three times the speed of sound, but how often would that kind of speed be required? As far as I can tell, there is simply no need for fighters to be able to fly faster than Mach 1.5. The faster you go, the more fuel you burn up. Pilots have a saying: you only reach top speed in order to run out of fuel. Many, indeed, believe that agility counts for more than a high top speed in aerial combat—a successful plane, they say, should be agile and small.

Small the F-15 is not. Geared for speed, it has a large profile. It carries bulky engines and a substantial radar—in order to be able to pick up an aircraft 40 miles away, it has to have a 36-inch radar disk up front —which means that the aircraft's nose is considerably broader than it otherwise might be. As Bob Fay, an air force officer who monitored the Nevada exercises, put it: "When you're up in the sky searching for something in that gray mass or blue mass, your eyes tend to gravitate to the first object you see. And you can see large planes quicker than you can see small airplanes. Well, that's not too bad if you're a small-airplane driver, because the large airplanes are the enemy. But if you're a large-airplane driver, and all you're seeing is large airplanes, who are your wingmen or your colleagues, then you're in trouble."

In the melee of a war over the European battlefield, small, agile planes, with the surprise their size would help them achieve, would enjoy a number of advantages. In a war against the Russians, long-range, one-on-one dogfights would almost certainly be the exception rather than the rule. As Lieutenant Colonel Dvorchak noted in an article in *Tactical Analysis Bulletin:* "In massed fighting, similar to the swarm warfare everyone says would be likely in European battle, confusion plays a much larger role and exotic weaponry a much smaller one —most of the kills [in the Nevada exercise] came from visual sightings, as they had in the dogfights in World War II (and Vietnam), rather than from the elegant, computerized systems. High-performance capabilities, so impressive on paper, are blunted by the disorderly circumstances of war."

Critics make another point. Even if the F-15's high-performance capabilities might, in certain circumstances, make a difference, these very capabilities require considerable practice to use properly. Unlike the previous generation F-4 Phantom, the F-15 carries a crew of just one—meaning there is one less pair of eyes to see the sky, and correspondingly more dependence on complex cockpit controls. It has been said that only Israeli pilots train intensively enough to get the maximum benefit out of the F-15; American pilots find it hard to get enough time in the air to do so. When the budget is squeezed, it is usually training—hours spent in the air, or at sea, or in the field—that suffers. During the 1970s, when the price of oil (and, hence, jet fuel) shot up, the number of flying hours allotted to each pilot in the U.S. Air Force was cut dramatically, from twenty or twenty-five per month to sixteen or seventeen per month. And though flying hours rose sharply in the early 1980s, when the Reagan buildup began, they look certain, at the time of writing, to plunge again as the defense budget comes under increasing strain in the second half of the decade.

The real sacrifice forced on the air force by the emphasis on high tech is numbers: fewer and fewer aircraft are available each year to take on the Russians. The F-15 needs twice as much time in the hangar as the Phantom F-4; it needs almost fifty hours of servicing for every hour in the air.[1] The F-15 is an unusually complex aircraft, and its complexity is evident in almost every aspect, from its avionics, which cost a thousand times as much as World War II avionics, to its engines, which cost fifty times as much. Its fuel control alone consists of 4,500 parts, four and a half times more than the fuel control of the 1950s-vintage F-4 Phantom, which did so well against it in the Nellis tests. The radios and radars used by commercial airliners average about eight hundred hours between breakdowns, according to a report by systems analyst Pierre Sprey; their military counterparts, which cost between ten and a hundred times as much, average just five to ten hours. So the total number of F-15s possessed by the air force should not be mistaken for the total number that, on any given day, will be available to fight in a war.

That total number, however, is not very high to start with—only about 750 in 1985. The navy has the same problem with its equally

---

[1]When a squadron of twenty-four F-15s moves to a new base, a total of twenty-nine C-141 transport planes must follow behind, carrying support equipment and mechanics.

expensive F-14. Given the staggering costs of the aircraft, this is not surprising. In World War II the navy's main fighter was the Hellcat. At a price of $65,000 each, the country could afford to buy 12,000 of them. The modern navy, by contrast, can afford to buy just 900 F-14s. To put it another way, $7 billion in 1952 bought 6,300 jet fighters; today the Pentagon is paying $8 billion for just 270. In 1983, the navy and air force together were able to buy a total of just 399 planes—less than the number they lost that year through accidents and old age.

Norman Augustine, chairman of Martin Marietta, a major defense contractor, has a famous "law" for the direction in which complex technology is taking the U.S. Air Force. If the costs of military hardware continue to rise at the rate at which they have been rising for the last fifty years or so, he says, "in the year 2054 the entire defense budget will purchase just one tactical aircraft. This aircraft will have to be shared by the air force and the navy three and a half days per week, except for leap years, when it will be made available to the marines for the extra day."

By the mid-1970s, the rocketing costs and complexity, coupled with what they viewed as declining performance, led a small band of air force insiders to write a proposal for an alternative fighter. These dissidents, among them a former fighter pilot named John Boyd, believed that since the early 1960s fighter development had been going in precisely the wrong direction. What they proposed was a lightweight fighter in which the emphasis would be purely on agility. Doubtful that all the beyond-visual-range technology of the F-15 would be of much use in a real war, and aware that a plane carrying fewer "black boxes" and long-range missiles would be much more agile, they envisaged a fighter with a top speed of only Mach 1.6 but capable of outaccelerating and outturning any existing aircraft at all speeds below that.

The lightweight fighter ended up as the F-16, now undoubtedly the best fighter in the U.S. inventory. At $16 million, the F-16 costs just over half the price of the F-15. It might have been even cheaper than that had the air force not crammed back into it many of the gadgets the so-called "fighter mafia" had scrupulously removed, such as active radar and long-range missiles. In any case, the United States is now buying a "mix" of F-15s and F-16s. If it weren't, the financial picture would look even worse than it does.

The Tornado

America is not the only country to pin its faith on supersophisticated fighter aircraft. Europe has followed its example.

In the late 1960s, three European countries—Britain, West Germany, and Italy—developed plans for a fighter bomber that came to be called Tornado. Once described by former German chancellor Helmut Schmidt as "the greatest technological project since the birth of Christ," the idea behind Tornado was that by working together all three countries would save money: production lines could be longer and thus the unit costs of each plane would be lower. In an alliance plagued by unnecessary duplication in weapons procurement, the Tornado, it was hoped, would demonstrate the benefits of collaboration.

Like so many American weapons systems, however, the Tornado was plagued by spiraling costs and inefficiency. The problems once again arose from competing and complicated specifications: each country wanted a plane with different attributes. The British RAF wanted Tornado for two roles: long-range strike and defense of the homeland; the Italians wanted an "air superiority" fighter like the F-15 or F-16; the Germans wanted a plane for close air support on the battlefield. So the Tornado had to be light and agile enough to achieve air superiority in combat, while at the same time able to carry enough fuel and payload for long-range strike, and in order to operate on the battlefield, be capable of short takeoff and landing. Thus, Tornado became a truly multirole aircraft (though the British developed a separate "interceptor" version for strategic air defense).

Meanwhile, the costs have shot up. In 1970, for example, the German Luftwaffe estimated that Tornados would cost them 15 million deutschmarks ($8.4 million) each. Ten years later that "fly away" price (extras not included) had risen to at least 35.2 million deutschmarks each ($18.9 million), while the overall system price (including spares, cost of pilot training, etc.) jumped to 67.36 million deutschmarks ($36.3 million). In Britain it was the same story, and in all three countries the plane produced enormous pressures on defense budgets.

During the 1980s the price continued to rise. The cost of Tornado is now roughly equivalent to the cost of the F-15.

Of all the roles for which it was intended, Tornado is clearly best suited for "deep strike." Expensive and full of modern technology, it is ill designed for the role the Germans initially had in mind: close air support. Its technology is primarily intended, as one British air marshal pointed out, to enable it to reach and hit "critical military targets behind the front line, such as concentrations of armor, headquarters, and airfields in all weathers, day or night."

Thus, like the F-15, Tornado reflects the trend in NATO's attitude toward air power. The emphasis is on long-range striking power —hitting the enemy before he can even reach the battlefield. In the air force view of a third world war, according to defense analyst William Kaufman, the idea is to create such havoc for the enemy behind his lines that his front-line forces "will simply wither on the vine," and the various NATO armies will be, if not quite reduced to passive spectators, left with a relatively small role to play. Indeed, Kaufman estimates that a mere 640 aircraft on the central front would have as their primary role close air support of ground forces; the remaining 2,400 that would be initially available for war would be dedicated to long-range missions.

This arrangement strikes many defense analysts as absurd. They argue, with good reason, that NATO ground forces would benefit from more aircraft dedicated to their support—and to killing enemy tanks. Yet not only is the air force disinclined to take on the task, but the army is forbidden to purchase the aircraft that would enable it to do the job itself. This self-defeating division of labor is the result of Congress's decision, in the aftermath of World War II, to establish the air force as a separate entity (previously, it had been part of the army) with complete control over all land-based aircraft, except for training planes and helicopters.

The army has therefore been forced to rely heavily on helicopters for close air support (and now has some 9,000 of them). Though many experts argue that helicopters are much less effective in this role than fixed wing aircraft, the air force has the planes—and it has consistently shown itself to be unenthusiastic about helping the army.

The A-10

The air force does have one tank-busting aircraft: the A-10. Regarded by many defense experts as one of the most effective weapons in the U.S. arsenal—and a weapon that illustrates of the sensible, economical use of new technology—it was built in the early 1970s, in part, it seems, in response to the rapid growth of the army's helicopter fleet. Evidently concerned that the army's demands for increasingly exotic helicopters might affect their own budget, air force planners believed they could design a plane that would perform the close-air-support role more cheaply and more effectively. They were right.

The plane they came up with is indubitably ugly: barrel-shaped, with short, stubby wings protruding from which are two cannons and eight missiles, the A-10 is a single-seater with a cockpit surprisingly free of any kind of gadgetry. Set against sleek, elegant monsters like the F-15, it looks like a relic of World War II. It cannot fly very fast—less than the speed of sound (pilots joke that when flying it they are in danger of being hit in the rear by birds), but it can stay in the air a long time and fly very low. It is agile, and is heavily armored. It is also, in the view of some experts, the most lethal tank-killing aircraft in the world. The reason is that its primary weapon is not a missile but a simple cannon.

This cannon—called the GAU8/A—has seven barrels and the 30-millimeter armor-piercing shells it uses—made of "depleted" uranium of low radioactivity—are an example of high technology that works. The shells are heavy, twice as heavy as lead, and move at enormous speeds—3,240 feet per second—enabling them to cut through the side and rear armor of tanks with relative ease. They can be fired at a rate of 4,200 rounds per minute. And because they are extraordinarily cheap, they are affordable in large quantities. Each shell costs $20, which means that a thirty-round burst—judged adequate, in most circumstances, to cripple a tank—costs only $600, less than the cost of one of the navy's ashtrays, and the same as just three of the Divad's proximity rounds.

In a series of tests at Nellis Air Force Base in 1975 and 1976, A-10s destroyed six out of ten Soviet T-62 battle tanks, by striking them in the rear or in the sides, and put the other four out of action. As Morton Minz noted in the *Washington Post:* "The 60 percent kill rate was four times higher than had been predicted by computer studies during development of the gun. . . ."

The only problem with the A-10, which itself costs only just over $3 million (about a fifteenth the cost of the F-15), is that its gun cannot be used for long-range kills. The attraction of missiles is that a pilot can fire them long before he reaches his target, thus theoretically giving him a better chance of escaping antiaircraft fire. This argument might make more sense if pilots were confident that air-delivered antitank missiles would work properly. But as we will see, they have little reason to be confident. "If the question is, which would you rather take in against the target of interest, I would unhesitatingly say guns," says Colonel John Verdi, a retired Marine Corps weapons expert who led one of the first marine fighter squadrons in the Vietnam War and now holds the Legion of Merit, along with thirty other medals. "You have to have a gun on a plane that's going to fight somebody. Anything else is absurd." And though, as Verdi acknowledges, guns force a pilot to risk going in very close, the problem with "standoff" missiles is that, if they miss you wind up having to get in close anyway for a second shot. So the argument is strong for having cheap, simple, reliable, effective aircraft that can do the job and are cheap enough to be affordable in huge numbers.

This kind of logic, however, counts for little in the modern American military, or in Congress. The A-10 was never regarded with much enthusiasm by air force leaders, who had kept the project simple and cheap—in large part, critics charged, because they did not want to waste money on the unglamorous mission of protecting the "grunts" on the battlefield. In 1981, for example, the air force tried to drop sixty A-10s it was due to purchase. To his credit, Defense Secretary Weinberger promptly reinstated them. And in 1982, by which time the air force had acquired some eight hundred A-10s—seventy-two of which it had managed to give away to the Air National Guard, the air force reserve—the program finally died.

Just as the A-10 never excited Pentagon imaginations, neither did its gun. Air force leaders "don't like the gun," says Thomas Hahn, a one-time staff member of the House Armed Services committee. "Missilery is what people are all enthused about." For politicians fascinated by glamorous high-tech weaponry, guns, as another analyst put it, "are far too simple." Much more stirring was the A-10s alternative armament, the Maverick.

The Maverick

The Maverick is everything the GAU8/A is not. It is expensive, complicated, and it doesn't work—precisely the characteristics likely to insure it a long and successful life in the Pentagon procurement system. It costs a hundred times as much as the thirty-round burst from the GAU8/A required to fulfill a similar mission. Its testing record is a joke. It has attacked telephone poles, fence posts, and rocks. And the second, more sophisticated, version promises to be even worse than the first.

The Maverick has its origins in the mid-1960s. As the West sought to place greater reliance on conventional weapons, so the air force decided it needed a standoff air-to-ground weapon that would enable its planes to attack ground targets while staying away from the thickest air defenses. The army had the 20-millimeter Vulcan, the predecessor to the Divad gun, but though this worked quite respectably against aircraft, it "pelted a tank," in the words of one commentator, "as ineffectually as raindrops pelt a window." Clearly what was needed was a lethal missile that could pelt tanks more effectively from a safe distance.

The missile that came to be called the Maverick was designed to be slung under the wings of tactical aircraft. It was to be "television guided"; that is to say, it was to have a tiny video camera in its nose that would enable it to spot and then home in on an enemy tank. It was a beguiling idea, very much in tune with Congress's love affair with high tech, and the air force got the go-ahead. Eventually the air force spent $500 million on some 20,000 of the eight-foot-long, first-generation Mavericks, sending them to Europe and—most important—to Southeast Asia.

There was, of course, a war going on in Southeast Asia. This gave the Maverick early and ample opportunity to demonstrate its capacity to kill tanks. Instead of doing that, according to General John W. Vogt, who commanded U.S. air operations in Vietnam, it proved almost totally useless. "Clearly it didn't do the job out there," he said in early 1982. In bad weather (fog or heavy rain), he added, "this kind of weapon craps out completely." One problem with the Maverick was its tiny field of view: the sensor in its nose can see only about a 3-degree-wide segment in front of it. "It's like looking at the world through the end of a drinking straw," according to one weapons analyst. Thus, unless the missile was lined up very accurately in the first place it would almost certainly miss its target.

A second problem was described by General Vogt, who tried to use the Maverick to stop the enemy on the Ho Chi Minh Trail. To use a Maverick, a pilot had to climb to a higher altitude in order to have a straight, clear view of his target. The TV sensor in the Maverick's nose needed a clear contrast between target and background if it was to find its target. But according to Vogt, the "pop-up" maneuver used by Maverick-carrying aircraft was usually sufficient to alert the Viet Cong to move exposed tanks in amid foliage or into the shade, thus degrading the visual contrast between target and background and making it hard for the Maverick to strike home. Indeed, according to a later set of tests, the Maverick's sensor locked on to a tank that was camouflaged or parked close to a tree line less than 5 percent of the time. Against moving tanks, its record was even worse: the Maverick never locked on to any moving target long enough to hit it.

Yet the fact that it did not work in tests—or, according to a top general, in combat—was not enough to deter the air force. By the early 1970s, it was developing a new version of the Maverick, this one a heat-seeking infrared model that would be able to work in the darkness and have a much longer range—up to 8 miles. Congressional testimony and other analyses on the new missile already run to thousands of pages, and by all accounts it has been one long history of trouble, delay, and failure. To fire the new Maverick, the pilot has to study a small 5-inch video screen in his cockpit. On this he is supposed to be able to detect his target, enemy tanks. But what tests showed was that the images appearing on the pilot's tiny scope made it very difficult to distinguish between all kinds of "hot objects" (sun-warmed rocks, bonfires, burning armor hulks, even flare grenades) and actual tanks. According to Thomas Hahn, the former staff member of the House Armed Services

Committee who also happens to be a physicist: "What you get on your display is a bunch of bright spots. . . . You don't know what you're looking at. . . . If you can't determine there's a gun barrel, all you can determine is that there's a blob and it's hot."

Even on a test range at Fort Polk, Louisiana, in February 1977, when the pilots knew exactly where the tanks would be, and where there were no competing "hot targets" to confuse the Maverick, the missile's success rate was hardly encouraging. Of 123 passes made by pilots, less than 60 percent produced "lock-ons" (i.e., occasions when the missile recognized and homed in on its target without losing sight of it). A year later, at a series of tests in West Germany, the Maverick fared even worse. Again, pilots knew exactly where the "enemy" tanks would be. The record shows that 317 practice runs simply weren't counted by the air force. Of the 215 that were, only 113 (or 53 percent) achieved lock-ons. Despite urgings from the General Accounting Office to stage a test in "a realistic battlefield environment," and despite unease among many congressional staffs, the air force pressed on with the development of the Maverick. Eventually, between October 1981 and January 1982, it scheduled five operational live firings. One aborted, two failed, and the other two had to be postponed. After this, the air force apparently decided to rethink the matter; the decision to produce the 61,000 new Mavericks the air force wanted was put off indefinitely. In 1984, however, it was decided that the Maverick Mark II would overcome its problems, and Congress gave it the go-ahead once again.

The Viper

The preoccupation with complex tank-killing weapons extends far beyond the Maverick. I will end this dismal catalogue by glancing at three other examples, all of which have been developed by the U.S. Army. The first, the Viper, is a weapon that was intended to be a lightweight, shoulder-fired, bazooka-type rocket for use by the infantry. It was priced at $76 each when first proposed in 1976, though over the next six years its price rose tenfold, partly because of persnickety Pentagon specifications relating to maximum weight and noise, and partly because its manufacturer, General Dynamics, tinkered endlessly (with the army's blessing) with what had been an ingenious original design.

And while the Viper's cost had soared, by 1982, to $787 a round, its chances of knocking out Soviet tanks dropped equally rapidly. It had become clear that the rocket's small charge had no hope of penetrating the frontal armor of the T-64s, T-72s, and T-80s that were rapidly coming to constitute the sharp end of the Red Army tank force. The army's response to this discovery, in 1980, was not to scrap the project but to "clarify" the Viper's mission. That meant reduce it. From now on the Viper would only have to perform against the older T-55 and T-62 tanks, or strike modern tanks in more vulnerable places than the front. Many former army men believe its newly clarified mission scarcely justified the investment, especially since the Viper's effective range was only about 250 yards. Their view was summed up by Hyman Baras, the director of Land Warfare Audits at the General Accounting Office, who wrote a critical report on the Viper in 1981:

> I'd have grave doubts about hanging around with my Viper until the enemy tank is only 250 yards away. For one thing, if I miss, they're going to blast away with machine guns, and I've had it. And if I have to attack the tank from the side or rear, what they're saying is that I have to ambush a tank. Now that strikes me as a very risky thing, particularly if I have a low probability of killing it. I think I'd want to be out of there. I'd want to be as far away as I could be.

Another critic went further, calling the Viper a "Medal of Honor" weapon—meaning you would only use it if you were prepared to die. When White House budget director David Stockman talked of the "swamp of $10-, $20-, $30 billion of waste" in the Pentagon budget in a 1981 magazine interview, it seems likely that the Viper was one of the projects he was referring to. Unlike the army, which committed itself to buying nearly 650,000 Vipers, the Marine Corps turned the missile down. "You want something that hurts the enemy," said Senator Warren Rudman, "not just pisses him off." It was only after Senate and congressional critics of the weapon forced the army to test it against cheaper, European-made antitank weapons that the project was canceled. (Among other things, Congress had become concerned about the tendency of its launch tube to explode during testing.) That was in 1983, by which time the original $76 price tag on the "fire and discard" Viper had risen to a staggering $1,200.

The Copperhead

A weapon the army has stolidly refused to cancel, however, is the Copperhead, a "smart" artillery projectile of dubious merit. An army brochure about Copperhead boasts that "its accuracy is so good that it can literally drop down the open hatch of a moving tank"—though there was little evidence of this in its testing program, and the concept behind Copperhead has given critics a field day.

Firing a Copperhead involves a complicated and exacting sequence. A soldier crouching on the forward edge of the battlefield selects his target, an enemy tank, and aims a so-called "laser designator" at it. He then focuses a laser beam on the tank. The beam is reflected skyward, enabling the Copperhead missile, fired from several miles away, to "ride" it down to the tank. That, at least, is the theory. The critics are troubled by three things.

First, the whole operation depends on a lonely soldier who will be perilously exposed on an open battlefield. Unlike the target spotter of old who called in artillery, and who was equipped simply with a pair of field glasses and a radio, his successor in today's army would have to keep a laser beam on his target until the Copperhead struck home —a dangerous exercise, since the laser would quickly give his position away. Besides, the actual "designator" has been criticized in an official army report as being "too bulky and heavy" and presenting "too high a silhouette," requiring "the operator to assume a sitting or kneeling position."

The second problem, also identified in the internal report, is that Copperhead will only function in perfect weather: laser beams do not work well in mist, rain, or even smoke. Critics point out that mist and rain are not unknown in Europe, and smoke not unusual on a battlefield. Third, even the army has admitted that the coordination necessary between the artillery battery in the rear and the soldier up front would have to be "excessive," especially for "a fast-moving battlefield or in high-stress situations."

Finally, some critics—notably the Project on Military Procurement—complain that the Copperhead has a minimum range of 1 kilometer, and cannot be used if a tank is closer. "Thus," says the project, "it will be unusable for approximately 85 percent of real tank engagements."

While on the subject of Copperhead it is worth noting another U.S. Army device that may be used in conjunction with it. This is a new "remotely piloted vehicle" (RPV), currently being developed and now, after years of gold plating and soaring costs, expected to enter service in 1989.

Like many of the army's weapons, the new RPV is based on a simple—and sensible—idea. RPVs, essentially radio-controlled model aircraft, can be extraordinarily effective on a modern battlefield. They can play a variety of roles—eavesdropping on enemy radio traffic, jamming enemy radio transmissions, delivering missiles, and most important of all, taking pictures of enemy emplacements. RPVs survive by being small enough to escape being tracked by radar or hit by missiles, and by operating beyond the range of antiaircraft guns. Their virtue is (or should be) that they are cheap, available in large numbers, and expendable.

The United States made limited use of fairly basic RPVs in Vietnam, but it is the Israelis who have best understood—and exploited—their value. The Israeli Air Force bought a cheap and simple RPV in the 1970s. It was armed with a zoom lens video camera that could relay back live pictures, it cost about $40,000 per plane, and it proved highly effective. In 1982, the Israelis used their RPVs both to achieve detailed reconnaissance of the Syrian antiaircraft batteries in the Bekaa Valley and to jam Syrian radar. Largely as a result, they were able to destroy no less than eighteen batteries within an hour. When the United States attempted to destroy new Syrian batteries the following year, it did so without the help of RPVs—and lost two planes in the process. As a result, according to an investigation by the ABC Television program "20/20," the U.S. military borrowed several Israeli RPVs and used them to good effect in Lebanon. The RPVs tracked the salvos of the battleship *New Jersey,* enabling the ship's gunners to correct their aim.

So why didn't the U.S. Army simply buy its RPVs from the Israelis, or at the very least imitate their design? The answer is that the army was already developing its own model: an RPV with a difference, called Aquila, after the Latin for eagle. Initially, when the army began serious work on the Aquila in the mid-1970s, it hoped that the RPV might cost only $100,000—which, though expensive compared with the Israeli RPV, was not excessive by U.S. Army standards. Since the mid-1970s, however, the Aquila has been transformed.

First, it has become extraordinarily complex. Instead of following the trail blazed by Israel, creating a basic RPV and developing different models for different specialized roles, the U.S. Army created an "all purpose" RPV, to perform all kinds of roles, one of which is to designate targets by laser for attack by Copperhead or other artillery shells. According to *International Defence Review,* the Aquila is crammed full of electronics and carries a sophisticated data link "including two steerable EHF antennae in dorsal and ventral thimble radomes. It has its own strapdown inertial-navigation system and it is nuclear hardened." And that is not all.

> The airframe for Aquila is highly blended and has an ultralow radar cross-section, which imposes restrictions on payload weight and volume, so that any payload has to be specially designed and developed. Aquila has also been designed for fully automatic recovery, requiring the development of a special electro-optical precision guidance system to steer the vehicle into the landing net.
>
> Finally, Aquila was designed from the outset to meet all U.S. Army specifications for compatibility with other systems, operability in all climates, and quality of construction.

Despite, or more probably because of, all this gear, the Aquila has had a sorry track record. Ever since the mid-1970s, test models have kept crashing. A champion flyer of model airplanes, Garry Korpi, who was a test "pilot" for the Aquila program in 1975–76, described some of the early crashes to "20/20," suggesting that several could have been avoided had the army taken more precautions, and that the army might have wasted less money if it hadn't insisted on installing expensive video cameras in the test models.

But the crashes did not end in the mid-1970s. Using the Freedom of Information Act, "20/20" obtained footage of much more recent test flights showing that though some went well—with the Aquila taking off, completing its mission, and then landing safely in a net—others did not. For example, in 1984, according to the film, at least three went badly wrong, two ending in crashes.

This might not have mattered much had the army stuck to its original budget. But by 1984, the Aquila no longer cost $100,000 apiece. Rather, the price had now risen to $1 million—a staggering increase, even allowing for inflation. Moreover, the army had by now spent some $700 million on the program, and after eleven years of development was still not ready to deliver. Indeed, according to a special army investigation, so many Aquilas had crashed in tests by the end of 1985 that there was some doubt as to whether there were enough left to complete the testing program. Whether the U.S. Army will get the funds to make that possible is, at the time of this writing, unclear. But even if it does, the point of the device has long since been lost. RPVs make sense if they are cheap and simple, and Aquila now represents a valueless investment. Indeed, the combination of Aquila and Copperhead—one a simple device wrecked by gold plating, the other a complicated missile dependent on an overelaborate firing sequence—seem destined to do more damage to the army's budget than to any enemy.

Hellfire and the Apache

Working on the same principles as the Copperhead, but on a much grander scale, is the army's new missile-firing helicopter program.

Since the late 1970s, both superpowers have been putting tank-killing missiles on helicopters. But the project the U.S. Army plans to have operational by the late 1980s threatens to become the most exotic —and expensive—in its entire modernization program.

The missile-firing helicopter has been code-named the AH-64

Apache, and as helicopters go it is bulky, heavily armored, and bristling with weapons. The original idea was that it should fire TOW missiles, but in 1976 this changed: the TOW concept was replaced by a much more glamorous system called Hellfire. Under Hellfire, a designator in the helicopter would have to fasten a laser beam on an enemy tank; then a missile would be fired down the beam. But Hellfire required a helicopter with a special turret filled with exotic gadgetry, and since, by the early 1980s, the Apache was set to cost $11 million a piece, the army felt the time had come to think again. The result was yet another change. Instead of there being one helicopter, there now would be two: the Apache, which would actually fire the missile; and a smaller, cheaper "scout" helicopter, which would fulfill a similar function to the Copperhead's laser designator.

More precisely, the system would work like this: the scout helicopter would hide behind trees and use a novel electronic periscope perched just above its rotors to spot tanks and to fasten a laser beam on one of them. The Apache would pop up from behind a tree or hill, fire a missile locked on to the scout's beam, then drop down again out of danger.

Whether this system will prove successful is anyone's guess. But it would appear to suffer from many of the same defects as the Copperhead. By 1983, the small, "cheap" scout helicopter—originally designed to cost $700,000—was set to cost $4.3 million, partly because of the complex engineering involved in its pop-up periscope, with its TV sight, infrared sight for night operations, laser designator, and laser range finder. That means the whole package—Apache, scout, plus Hellfire—will come to about $16 million.

Helicopters, bravely piloted, provide a vital means of transporting soldiers to the front lines of a battlefield, and armed with sensible weapons, especially in a hilly or tree-covered landscape, they can be effective tank killers. But at $16 million for the system, the Apache AH-64 will cost more than eight times as much as the M-1—and the M-1, of course, is the world's most expensive tank. At that price, how many Apaches will the army end up being able to buy?

The weapons I have described in this chapter are, for the most part, egregious examples of gold plating, unnecessary complexity, and dubious effectiveness. Some, as we have seen, scarcely work at all, let alone yield advantages commensurate with their cost. I do not mean to suggest that every American weapon—or every European one—is as overtechnologized as those we have examined. If that were the case, we would be in dire straits. But these weapons are indicative of a trend, and it is not a healthy trend.

A prominent military analyst once observed that too much faith in high-tech wizardry might one day mean that we in the West would be reduced to depending on an army of men clad in skins and wielding clubs. "Indeed," he added, "those who come to rely too much on technology may find one morning that just such an army has captured them, lock, stock, and laser."

3

People

"We can spend billions on the most modern and sophisticated weaponry," commented Republican Senator Roger Jepsen in 1981, "but in the final analysis it is the infantryman, sailor, pilot, and medic that will determine our nation's strength."

History suggests that the senator is right. Yet the prevailing philosophy seems quite different. The U.S. defense establishment appears vastly more concerned about weapons than about the human aspects of war. Indeed, its obsession with high-tech gadgetry suggests a belief that somehow war can be dehumanized, and that an array of "smart" hardware can enhance the chances of victory and minimize the risks to human life.

Consequently, a gulf has opened up between the sophistication of modern equipment and the skills of the modern servicemen who are called upon to operate and maintain it. And while the aim in creating much modern equipment has been to install gadgets that require little or no skill to operate, the gadgets have scarcely compensated for the many and varied problems that have beset the American military during the 1960s, 1970s, and early 1980s: low morale, inadequate training, low pay, poor leadership. These problems intensified when the draft was ended after Vietnam, and the American middle class virtually opted out of the military. At the beginning of the 1980s, the service chiefs were unanimous in telling Congress that they faced grave problems with personnel: the army was declared "hollow," the navy was said to be suffering a "hemorrhage of talent," and the air force was in "critical" condition.

Under President Reagan, things began to improve. Indeed, some believe that boosting the sense of purpose and morale in America's armed services has been one of his most significant achievements. But the improvements were inevitably limited. The prevailing philosophy did not change. And the problems run very deep.

The classic case, of course, is the U.S. Army. After the Vietnam War, the army's morale and confidence plummeted, and the drive for sophisticated hardware hardly made up for it. As a former Pentagon official, Thomas Etzold, noted in 1981: "America's much-vaunted computer edge loses some of its keenness in the face of . . . reports that 77 percent of the people who operate computer and automated systems in the field failed their skill qualification test in 1978." In other words, almost four-fifths of the soldiers who had to operate and maintain sophisticated equipment were unable to do so properly. And as Etzold added, the 1978 test occurred a year before the American army took in one of the worst batches of recruits—in terms of intellectual caliber —in its history. Another survey in the late 1970s found that 40 percent of new army recruits were unable to read above seventh-grade level (that is, very inadequately). Not for nothing was the U.S. Army dubbed the world's largest remedial reading program. Worse, units stationed in Europe were plagued by alcoholism and drug abuse. In NATO exercises, they rarely distinguished themselves. Often they finished last.

The top brass has struggled to put things right. In 1982, for example, the army unveiled a new doctrine: after a history of fighting wars of "attrition"—heavy firepower allied to mass production back home—the plan from now on would be to rely on more subtle tactics. In a ninety-page booklet, the army outlined its thinking: highly mobile units would operate independently and be prepared to yield ground temporarily if need be before mounting swift counterattacks. "Airland

Battle," as the new doctrine was called, represented the outcome of the army's post-Vietnam soul searching. It had much to recommend it. But there was one fundamental snag, as critics were quick to point out. Maneuver warfare entails high risks. It envisages fighting battles without flanks, and risking being cut off from supply lines in the rear. As defense consultant Steven Canby has observed, this requires high standards of training and equipment very different from the kind the army is currently buying.

The army has tried to improve its training. At Fort Irwin in California, for example, it has established what is intended to be the most realistic training area in the world. Amid a thousand square miles of desert, U.S. Army units come to practice against a division that imitates Soviet tactics and whose armored vehicles, though American, are "visually modified" to look like Soviet ones. The men who make up the division even wear red stars on the front of their black berets. While video cameras and radio relay stations monitor all the activity, the visiting units get a chance to try to defend themselves against the "Opfor" (opposing force), as well as attack it. To make the effect even more realistic, the tanks and guns at Fort Irwin are equipped with what is called "Miles," the Multiple Integrated Laser Engagement System, which means that when fired they project a laser beam toward their targets. The targets—all infantrymen and vehicles on the battlefield— are in turn equipped with laser receivers that register direct hits and even near misses. If a tank is "hit"—that is, struck by a laser beam— a strobe light on its casing begins to flash, indicating that it has been "killed." Similarly, if a soldier is "hit," the laser activates a continuous high-pitched alarm in his helmet.

Yet though Fort Irwin is clearly a step in the right direction, many army experts insist that overall training is not nearly rigorous enough. The U.S. Army's priorities, they say, become evident if you compare its basic infantry training manual with the Israeli Army equivalent. In the course of a twelve-week training course, American recruits are obliged to spend a mere twenty-eight hours on forced marches and camping out ("marching and bivouacking"). The Israeli program, by contrast, subjects its recruits to a nineteen-week basic training course, in which the stress is almost entirely on forced marches and bivouacking (first week, 10-kilometer forced march; second week, 15-kilometer march and 3-kilometer jog with one loaded stretcher for each four men; third week, 15-kilometer forced march and then 10 kilometers with stretchers; and so on, steadily increasing, until the nineteenth week, when the recruits undergo an 85-kilometer forced march). Through bitter experience, the Israelis have learned that you cannot depend on high-tech alone; to win wars, you need highly trained soldiers.

But if a doctrine of maneuver calls for highly trained soldiers, it also calls for equipment that is flexible, reliable, and easy to maintain. If you are engaged in a counterattack, perhaps behind enemy lines, cut off from your main force, the last thing you want are tanks—or antiaircraft guns—that are liable to break down. Yet instead of acquiring these, the army, by 1982, was busy buying some of the most elaborate, fragile, and hard-to-maintain equipment ever conceived.

One exception to this was the army's Ninth Infantry Division (motorized), based at Fort Lewis in the state of Washington. The Ninth Infantry—the army's experimental high-tech division—*is* seeking to turn itself into a leaner, more effective fighting force. To this end, it has created a "fast attack vehicle" (FAV), a small, agile "dune buggy for the Pepsi generation," as the *Wall Street Journal* called it, armed with an antitank missile. Unfortunately, few army experts believe that the FAV would be very useful against Soviet tanks on the central front or anywhere else. And although the Ninth has undoubted virtues (". . . its tactics—in-and-out attacks, surprise, night-fighting— put it squarely in the mainstream of the Army's new doctrine of mobility and surprise," the *Wall Street Journal* observed), it appears to suffer from the standard disease: a predilection for technological rather than operational solutions to problems.[1]

---

[1]The "division of the future," as the Ninth calls itself, has certainly come up with its share of zany ideas. One that didn't last long was a helicopter that could be "folded" to fit into a suitcase. Unfortunately, its fuel tank was so small it would have been able to stay aloft for only thirty minutes. Another project that fizzled was what the *Wall Street Journal* dubbed "the flying trash can"—a machine straight out of James Bond that enabled individual soldiers to levitate. Too noisy and too expensive.

So though the army got itself a new strategy in 1982, it was (and is) still a long way from being able to implement it.

In some respects, all four American services have pulled themselves up from the nadir of 1980. President Reagan's attitude toward the military helped; so did the 11.4 percent across-the-board pay raise that he instituted in 1981. As a result of better pay, growing unemployment from the recession of 1981–82, and intensive recruiting campaigns, the services managed to stem the "hemorrhage of talent" and attract more high school graduates into their ranks. But even if recruiting standards continue to rise, the problems of the U.S. military are too deeply entrenched to be solved without some fundamental rethinking.

A few months before Reagan took office, the Pentagon made its ill-fated attempt to rescue the American hostages being held in Iran. It was a disaster, a classic failure. As Jeffrey Record, a defense consultant at Georgetown University and critic of the high-tech mentality, describes it, the episode was "one of the few military miscarriages the responsibility for which—the entire responsibility for which—can be laid at the doorsteps of the military." The problems extended well beyond any single shortcoming; they stemmed from interservice rivalries, lack of leadership, ridiculously bureaucratic procedures, and an apparent inability among Pentagon military planners to think things through. Because all the services wanted in on the act, no one was really in charge: while an army captain ran the assault force, the helicopters (which were not checked properly, and broke down) were run by the marines, the C-130 aircraft by the air force, and the overall operation was directed by a navy admiral 2,000 miles away in the Persian Gulf. The actual plan was never properly rehearsed and never checked for possible shortcomings. The communications gear did not work properly, and the different services involved could not communicate with each other. And when the operation began to fail, the assault force was unable to withdraw without a humiliating and fatal accident in which eight men died. Reading the report on that disaster, one journalist noted: "You are left to wonder if our military leaders are capable of successfully staging even a small joint operation."

Any notion that the Reagan administration affected the underlying problem was rudely dispelled three years after the Iranian hostage rescue attempt by another uninspiring military performance. This was the storming of the small Caribbean island of Grenada.

Grenada, of course, was not a disaster. Quite the opposite. After all, America won. The Pentagon managed to lay on an operation to defeat a mighty force of 679 Cubans, 43 of whom were professional soldiers (the rest were construction workers). And this was a matter for celebration.

In fact, many of the problems that had surfaced in Iran surfaced once again in Grenada. All four services wanted to be involved (the army was especially eager because it wanted to justify its request to Congress for a new Ranger battalion), and the navy's original plan was overruled by the Joint Chiefs. Instead, an enormous armada sailed off into the Caribbean—the aircraft carrier *Independence* with its associated battle group, complete with naval fighter bombers; helicopter gunships; a 1,250-man, heavily armed marine amphibious unit; and eventually (after the reinforcements arrived) a total of eight army battalions, six of infantry and two of elite Rangers.

Yet in spite of this breathtaking display of force, it took the U.S. forces no less than three days to conquer Grenada, in the course of which they lost nine of the eighty-five helicopters they deployed in combat (more than the British lost during the Falklands War), as well as the lives of eighteen servicemen. Less than half of these men were killed by the enemy; the rest died in accidents. Twenty-one Grenadans also died, due to a misaimed American bomb.

Though the marines and the army Rangers performed adequately, the regular army units (attached to the famous Eighty-second Airborne Division) advanced across the island with such caution that General John Vessey, the chairman of the Joint Chiefs, is said to have complained at one point: "We have two companies of marines running all over the island and thousands of army troops doing nothing. What the hell is going on?"

Altogether, Operation Urgent Fury, as it was called, gave plenty of cause for concern. As in Iran, the root of the trouble was the inability of the four services to work together. There were difficulties in coordinating naval fire support. There was no unified land commander (as Britain had in the Falklands), with both marine units in the north of the island and army units in the south reporting direct to Admiral Joseph Metcalf aboard the U.S.S. *Guam*. There were a host of logistics problems, despite the fact that a new Joint Deployment Agency (JDA) had been set up in the Pentagon in 1979 specifically to coordinate the rapid deployment of forces. The new agency was excluded from the planning of Urgent Fury because, as a congressional staff report noted, "it did not have adequate communications gear to process highly classified messages." As retired General Volney Warner, a former chief of the army's Readiness Command, put it afterward: "The JDA's major purpose in life is planning that kind of situation. To rule them out is unconscionable."

But according to the congressional report, the biggest single problem was the inability of certain units to communicate with each other. The reason for this was that each of the services "continues to purchase its own communications equipment, which all too frequently isn't compatible with the equipment of the other services." Sometimes this resulted in situations that were quite farcical. As the report noted:

> . . . the Army elements initially on the ground were unable to speak to the Navy ships offshore to request and coordinate naval gunfire. It has been reported that one Army officer was so frustrated in his efforts to communicate with the Navy ships that he used his AT&T calling card to place a call on an ordinary civilian pay telephone to his officer at Ft. Bragg in an attempt to coordinate fire support. It has also been reported that some of the early communications were conducted via a ham radio operator.

At the end of Urgent Fury, Admiral Metcalf, the man in overall command, declared proudly: "We blew them away." Clearly the army agreed. Unlike the marines, who downplayed their role in securing victory, the army enthusiastically congratulated itself, handing out a total of 8,612 decorations, including 170 medals for valor.

The fundamental problem with the U.S. military is that, consciously or unconsciously, it sees its prime task in peacetime as *buying* hardware, rather than using it: the main aim of each service is to wrest money out of Congress for the weapons platforms it wants—tanks, armored personnel carriers, ships, aircraft—and the main enemy in this process is not the Russians or the Iranians or the Cubans, but the other services. "The main game in town," says one Washington veteran, "is not the U.S. versus Russia, but the navy versus the air force versus the army."

Thus, as Edward Luttwak points out in his caustic study *The Pentagon and the Art of War*, all three services are now grotesquely top-heavy with officers, most of whom spend most of their careers thinking and acting like bureaucrats. The United States has eight times as many admirals per ship as it did in World War II, seven times as many air force generals per aircraft, and two to three times as many army generals per soldier. Or to put it another way, the American military now has nearly as many officers at or above the rank of army colonel and navy captain as it did at the end of World War II. On June 30, 1945, when the United States had more than 12 million men in uniform, the number of senior officers stood at 17,057—one officer for every 703 enlisted men. On May 31, 1983, with just over 2 million men on active duty, there were 15,455 senior officers—one for every 129 enlisted men.

As Luttwak observes: "Very few of these officers can find normal command or staff duties in the small peacetime forces. So the vast majority are placed in layers of higher headquarters and a multitude of administrative, logistic and equipment-acquisition commands, all of which have been expanded over the years to keep officers busy in peacetime, in readiness for the day when all might be fully employed in the war-mobilized forces."

Thus the emphasis in the peacetime American military has shifted away from fighting skills toward procurement and technological management: the overelaborate bureaucracy in the Pentagon, as Luttwak notes, reproduces itself on the battlefield (in overelaborate weapons), and this, in a kind of synergistic effect, has a corrupting effect on attitudes throughout the military. The best way to promotion these days is through running a successful procurement program in the Pentagon; leading troops in the field is a secondary occupation. The emphasis on procurement and management has even permeated officer selection boards, which tend to be dominated by what Luttwak calls "maintenance and support types."

But if the Pentagon is chock-full of ribbons and rank, and thousands of officers are engaged in overspecifying equipment and supervising its progress from laboratory to battlefield, the services are still chronically short of skilled leadership at vital levels. Good noncommissioned officers, or NCOs, are crucial to any army; they form the link between the elite, specially trained senior officers and the men; on them hinges the discipline, training, attitude, and morale of an individual unit. (The regimental sergeant-major has long been the key to the success of the British Army, to take the best example.) But the all-volunteer army has consistently found it hard to attract recruits capable of rising through the ranks to become NCOs. At the time of writing, the U.S. Army was short by almost 25,000 skilled NCOs.

There are deep-seated reasons for the state of the armed services in America—reasons that make it unlikely the situation will dramatically change. In Europe, where war has been a central part of life for centuries, military men are still highly regarded; belonging to the armed services is a matter of pride. There is a tradition of martial exploits, of heroism, and of sacrifice that is largely absent in America. To some extent, the technological bias—the desire to create weapons that can kill at a distance and save lives, and the failure to create well-motivated, well-trained military forces—reflects a national revulsion against war, a failure to come to grips with the realities of it. It has been said, brutally but with an element of truth, that as a nation the United States is essentially frivolous about defense. No one, for example, is ever punished for failure.

In 1757 the British executed Admiral Byng for gross incompetence after he had lost a battle with French men-o'-war. The British did it, observed Voltaire, *"pour encourager les autres."* Byng behaved no worse than many who have led American military operations over the last twenty years. I am not suggesting that Congress begin executing senior officers, but the nearest the Reagan administration has come to punishment was removing three senior naval officers from their posts for allowing too much money to be spent on ashtrays. And these officers were, I suspect, doing no more than countless senior officers do every day of the week. They were part of a cumbersome and inefficient procurement system. Their removal had nothing to do with their fighting skills.

Defense, then, has become a matter of buying weapons. There has been no overall guiding sense of strategy, no real attempt to decide priorities. The links between hardware and strategy have grown more and more tenuous. Each service has simply pursued its own chosen weapons systems, designed more to satisfy internal needs and long-standing traditions than to meet a plausible threat.

Nothing makes this clearer than a glance at the present state—and plans—of the U.S. Navy.

4

The Navy:
A Special Case

When President Reagan took office in January 1981 he launched the biggest peacetime military buildup in American history. He proposed to spend $1.5 trillion in four years— a sum whose vast proportions he had difficulty conveying. "I've been trying to think of the best way of illustrating how big a trillion is," said the president in his first major economic address after arriving in the White House. (He was talking about the evils of large federal deficits!) "If you had a stack of $100 bills 4 inches high, you would be a millionaire. A trillion dollars would be a stack of $100 bills 67 miles high."

The administration had a long list of things it wanted to spend the money on: the modernizing of America's nuclear forces, better command and control facilities, more pay for soldiers and sailors, and a variety of modern weapons (including most of those examined in Chapter 2 of this book). But it soon became clear that the most distinctive feature of the Reagan buildup was to be its emphasis on the navy. The president didn't mince words; what he was after, he repeatedly made clear, was naval superiority. If America was to be secure in the world, nothing less would do.

The man chosen as architect of the navy buildup was a one-time naval aviator named John Lehman. At the age of thirty-eight, Lehman was brought into the Pentagon as navy secretary. His plan was to expand a navy that stood at 480 surface vessels at the start of 1981 into a navy of 600 ships by the late 1980s, and within a year or two, his tough, single-minded approach and bureaucratic skills were drawing gasps of admiration from Washington. As Robert Komer, an undersecretary of defense under Jimmy Carter, put it, Lehman was "without doubt the most energetic service secretary we've had for twenty years."

Komer's praise, however, stopped short of the programs Lehman was so successfully promoting. Lehman's plan, Komer said, "would lead to strategic disaster in the event of a major conflict with the Soviet Union." It was a verdict shared by many strategists in the American defense community. They could see no sound military rationale for a 600-ship navy. It was "wildly wasteful," said one. "A classic example of spending without regard to strategy," said another.

It was certainly ambitious. The 600-ship navy, in the view of its proponents, held the key to being able to wage a global conventional war with the Russians. There were, of course, other more traditional rationales for surface ships: "showing the flag" or "projecting force" in the Middle East, the Third World, and elsewhere when the occasion demanded it (such as Lebanon in 1982 or Grenada in 1983), and in the event of a major war, controlling vital sea lanes so that weapons, soldiers, and supplies could be brought across the Atlantic to reinforce the defense of Western Europe. But none of these purposes demanded a 600-ship navy. Indeed, they scarcely required a navy of 480 ships. The only possible justification for such a huge surface fleet was to enable the United States to take on the Russians—worldwide—and the question was: was this either *possible* (in the way Lehman imagined it) or *necessary?*

At the heart of the Lehman plan was a new and daring concept of naval strategy. Lehman wanted to increase by three the number of America's aircraft carriers, from twelve to fifteen. That, in turn, would require a radical expansion of the number of surface escorts (frigates and destroyers), since each carrier operates as part of a large battle group. Lehman's plan was to deal much more aggressively with the Soviet Union's northern fleet, the one that, in the event of war, would pose the greatest threat to NATO. The traditional idea was (and is) to deploy naval forces along a defensive line connecting Greenland, Iceland, and Britain—the so-called GI-UK gap. That way, the Soviet fleet would be intercepted as it tried to head out into the Atlantic. Lehman wanted instead to attack the enemy in its home waters, and the strategy he envisioned would probably include a direct assault on the nothern fleet's home port of Murmansk. "I take an oath to defend Norway as if it was an attack on Long Island," he told me in 1983. "It makes no sense to turn the Norwegian Sea and the Baltic over to the Soviets in time of conflict if we can win in the northern flank with aggressive policies and aggressive defense."

Common sense alone would suggest that this is a tall order. Lehman may have taken an oath to defend Norway, but the American battle groups would be operating within easy range of Russian land-based aircraft, and history suggests that the dangers would be enormous.

In 1940, the British made an ill-fated attempt to recapture Norway from the Germans. But the expeditionary force they sent, lacking air support and fatally exposed to the Luftwaffe, was cut to pieces, losing four ships sunk and eighteen badly damaged, including a carrier and a battleship. Later in the war, Japanese kamikaze pilots—forerunners of guided missiles—again showed how devastating aircraft can be to surface ships. And though many of today's guided missiles, as we have already seen, are not nearly as effective as the glossy defense manuals suggest, technology has undoubtedly rendered surface ships even more vulnerable than they were during World War II. Even against a decidedly second-rate, though bravely and skillfully manned air force, the British Navy had a harrowing time during the Falkland War: it lost six ships, mainly due to aircraft of 1950s vintage operating at the extreme edge of their range and armed with old-fashioned iron bombs.[1] A U.S. naval force attempting to take Murmansk would have

---

[1]The total of British ships lost might have climbed as high as fourteen if a number of Argentinian bombs that scored hits hadn't failed to explode.

to brave the full might of the Soviet Air Force operating within easy striking range of their bases and including modern Backfire bombers armed with long-range cruise missiles.

The American aircraft carriers, of course, would provide their own air support. The huge *Nimitz*-class, nuclear-powered vessels, for example, carry some ninety planes each, ranging from the supersophisticated F-14s to radar aircraft, anti-submarine planes like the S-3, and helicopters. The snag is that most of these aircraft are there to defend the carrier herself and her accompanying flotilla of destroyers and frigates. Only a small number—thirty-four at most—would be free to attack land targets. Thus, the combined offensive punch of a formidable carrier group operating in hostile waters is relatively puny. "The mighty whale," as Edward Luttwak observes, "gives birth to a sprat."

So the chances of America being able to mount a successful assault on Murmansk look wildly small. Even John Lehman's own chief of naval operations, Admiral James Watkins, no slouch when it comes to extolling the capabilities of the U.S. Navy, privately confessed to doubts about it, though he later maintained that he and Lehman were "very much in harmony on strategy." And retired Admiral Stansfield Turner, director of the CIA under Jimmy Carter, declared: "I have yet to find an admiral who will attempt it." Many strategists believe that Murmansk is so well defended that it would be impossible to destroy without nuclear weapons.

But if the idea of taking Murmansk by sea lacks credibility, so do the assumptions underlying Lehman's strategy. The first is that if war breaks out in Central Europe, a badly outnumbered NATO could quickly be faced with the unacceptable choice of losing or going nuclear, and that the best hope of prolonging the conflict would lie in the U.S. Navy's ability to move quickly to assert control of the seas. The second assumption is a broader one. It is that a "big war" in Central Europe is not very likely—not nearly so likely, at least, as a brushfire war somewhere else (say, in the Third World)—and that America is therefore best served by a strategy that places considerable emphasis on a large, flexible, and powerful navy.

These propositions are less logical than they may seem. The problem with naval superiority is that it doesn't get you anywhere. As Robert Komer points out: "Even if Lehman knocked out all the Soviet naval bases and swept the Soviet navy from the seven seas, he could not prevent them from taking over Western Europe and the Persian Gulf and cowing Japan. The exercise would be like sticking pins in the hide of an elephant."

Nothing makes this clearer than the fallacy of "horizontal escalation." Horizontal escalation was a notion that surfaced in the Pentagon in 1981, its exponents maintaining that if America was attacked in a place where it faced heavy odds, it should counterattack the Soviet Union somewhere else—somewhere the Russians were vulnerable—in a kind of global tit for tat. But suppose the Russians attacked Western Europe or the Middle East, a favorite scenario when horizontal escalation was conceived. Should the United States then attack, say, Cuba or Nicaragua? It would scarcely be a fair exchange. "The problem with horizontal escalation," as one former Pentagon official put it, "is who the hell do you horizontally escalate against?"

As for the argument that America should plan not so much for the most dire contingency imaginable as for the likeliest—what Robert Komer calls "the likelihood fallacy"—this might make sense if America, and the West in general, had unlimited resources. But since it does not, it must surely concentrate on protecting its most vital interests, even if this means not being able to protect everything. Indeed, the danger foreseen by Komer and others is that the more America shifts its emphasis toward the navy and away from ground forces, the harder those vital interests will become to defend. "What is really happening," says Komer, "is that *the United States is drifting by default toward a primarily maritime strategy*" (italics in original).

Neither Komer nor other critics of the Lehman plan, of course, advocated abandoning the surface navy. But in a full-scale war against the Russians it would play a limited role, and the kind of ships being built—bristling with advanced radar and missile systems, and hugely expensive—made some critics even more uneasy.

At $3.4 billion each, 90,000-ton nuclear-powered aircraft carriers are the most expensive single items in the U.S. defense budget. Including the price of the escorts and the aircraft, the total for a carrier battle group comes to about $17 billion—a staggering sum to pay for a unit that has to devote most of its efforts to defending *itself*. Carriers are

easily tracked by modern surveillance systems and provide a tempting
target for attack by submarines and land-based aircraft. The admirals
are reluctant to acknowledge their vulnerability; according to former
defense official Thomas Etzold, who now works for the Arms Control
and Disarmament Agency, carriers are never "sunk" in war games, even
though a missile or a well-aimed bomb can put them out of commission. Even so, the admirals were reluctant to send a carrier into the
Persian Gulf during the Iranian hostage crisis; like the professional
armies in Europe in the seventeenth and eighteenth centuries, the
aircraft carriers of today sometimes seem to constitute too valuable an
instrument of force to risk using.

Yet the whole U.S. Navy is built around these carriers, and the
navy is currently investing in some extraordinary new technology designed to defend them. In particular, it is busy deploying an ultrasophisticated system called Aegis.

The Aegis was the magical shield used by Zeus and Athena for
protection against their enemies. Just looking at it was enough to make
them tremble. Critics, however, doubt whether the modern version will
be as effective. "The modern Aegis, alas," commented the *New York
Times* in April 1984, "has a way to go before it makes anyone tremble,
except maybe the taxpayer."

The U.S. Navy plans to spend $80 billion on all ships equipped
with Aegis—26 cruisers and 60 destroyers—by the early 1990s. It is a
computerized battle management system, an elaborate network of
computers intended to enable an array of radars to track up to 200
targets at a time and shoot down 18 missiles or planes in one salvo.
Lehman has called it "the key to the survival of the battle group," and
Defense Secretary Weinberger labeled it "the centerpiece" of the
navy's effort to defend the fleet against air attacks.

At the time of writing there was only one Aegis-equipped ship
afloat, the $1 billion cruiser U.S.S. *Ticonderoga*. The *Ticonderoga* has
a very high superstructure, protruding from which are antennae containing thousands of small radars, each of which seeks out potential
targets. Once the targets—attacking planes or missiles—have been
picked up, the system sends out signals to determine whether they are
"friend or foe." Then another radar bounces signals off the targets

identified as hostile so the cruiser's missiles can home in on the reflected radar energy.

There are signs that Aegis may not prove the magic shield of the fleet it is intended to be. In two sets of tests in April 1983, the *Ticonderoga* managed to hit only four out of sixteen missiles aimed at the ship. In another test five months later, it hit only two out of six targets. Moreover, four of the missiles fired at the ship in the earlier test were low-flying; the *Ticonderoga* hit none of them. In September, three of the targets flew in low: the ship hit only one. And the low-flying missiles "were not as low-flying or as fast as the kind the Argentinians used against the British in the Falklands war," according to one man who saw the test results.

Yet the Soviets would be bound to attack Aegis-equipped ships with low-flying and other antiship missiles. To be sure, in a fresh set of tests in May 1984, the *Ticonderoga* fared better. According to the navy, it hit ten out of eleven drone missiles in a simulated attack on a carrier battle group. But critics of this test maintain that it was unrealistic: a navy aircraft, they say, flew above the *Ticonderoga* during the test on a course parallel to that followed by the missiles, thus enabling the Aegis to get a fix on the plane before it had to follow the missiles.

John Lehman has maintained that the Aegis is the most carefully tested combat system ever built, and that "operational requirements have been met or exceeded" in the *Ticonderoga*. Critics dispute this, saying that there is no evidence that the system will be able to cope properly with the swarm of targets it might be expected to face—especially in hostile waters against low-flying, long-distance missiles. In 1984 Representative Denny Smith, an Oregon Republican and a leading critic of Aegis, charged that there was "a serious mismatch between the navy's publicly stated performance of the U.S.S. *Ticonderoga* and the navy's own test results."

But the Aegis has another drawback, one it shares with the navy's other principal air defense system, the F-14 interceptor aircraft. Both rely on active radar to find and destroy their targets. But as we have seen, active radar acts like a powerful beacon, making it much easier for the enemy to find its target—a problem that would be especially apparent at sea. Thus the Aegis and the F-14, called upon to defend huge, vulnerable battle groups, possibly close to the Soviet mainland, would have to cope with very intense, concentrated attacks.

Besides, as defense analysts have shown, the need for extra escorts to back up the new carriers is going to place a huge, and probably impossible, strain on the navy budget. According to one study by the Congressional Budget Office (CBO), the navy will need sixty new escorts in the water by 1992 to protect its new carriers. Yet even under Lehman's plan, there will only be twenty-five at sea by 1991. "The consequent imbalance between ships needing protection and the number of escorts will put tremendous pressure on the available escorts," George Kuhn has observed. Another CBO study suggested that navy budgets would have to keep rising 5 percent faster than inflation just to pay for the fleet Lehman has planned. The navy secretary dismisses this as an exaggeration, and it cannot be denied that he has had some success in improving the navy's contracting procedures, keeping prices down and reducing waste and fraud. But a principal reason the navy is expanding is not so much that new ships are being built as that old ones are being retired more slowly. This means that the navy's bill for maintenance and repairs is going to get bigger and bigger, and that in turn means that the overall pressure on the navy budget will grow, especially as it becomes clear that the new ships Lehman wants are going to cost more—far more—than had been anticipated.

The strain is already apparent. In October 1985, in one effort to save money, the navy ordered a cutback in the amount of time its ships were to spend at sea. There is already a drastic shortage of skilled seamen, with many ships lacking a full complement of men. On a visit to the aircraft carrier *Coral Sea* in 1985, Bill Keller, Pentagon correspondent for the *New York Times,* found that the engineering crew tending the ship's twelve boilers had "dwindled from 820 to 650 as the Navy stretches to man its expanding fleet."

No one questions that America needs a navy. In operating the ballistic missile submarines that form the most invulnerable part of the U.S. nuclear deterrent, the navy fulfills one of the most critical missions of Western defense. Clearly, too, there is a need to protect sea lanes in the Atlantic and Pacific. But Lehman's plans, which envision spending vast sums of money on huge and vulnerable carriers, might actually make "sea control" more difficult. The fact is, submarines and long-range aircraft operating from land bases increasingly seem the best means of performing many of the functions that once fell to surface ships. The navy, naturally, balks at this kind of thinking, fearful that it might lose one of its primary missions to the air force. Robert Komer's solution: "Give the navy responsibility . . . and let it have its own AWACS and F-15s." That would certainly make more sense than the baffling decision to build such a vast, carrier-heavy surface fleet.

However, the admirals wield considerable influence among the politicians on Capitol Hill, partly because a lot of jobs hinge on the nation's shipyards, and partly because support for the navy is deep-rooted, based as much on sentimental attachment as on practical realities. Unlike the Soviet Union, America is a sea power; it has long depended on the oceans for trade and access, and a mystique has clung to the navy since the days when U.S. admirals were received in foreign ports like government plenipotentiaries. Until 1947, the navy had its own representative in the Cabinet: there was no secretary of defense, but a secretary of war, responsible for the army, and a secretary of the navy.

There is a further reason for the navy's continuing success. The procurement system in the Pentagon works to promote narrow service interests rather than a broader strategic interest. In the committee of the Joint Chiefs of Staff, each chief tenaciously fights for his share of the budget and his own cherished programs; the chairman, under the present arrangement, is able to exert little influence. He can express his own views, but his job is merely to achieve a consensus within the committee. Most retiring chairmen have complained about the impotence of the post, but the navy—more than any other service—has a vested interest in its continuance: it knows that a reform of the system could lead to its share of the procurement budget, which has stayed more or less constant at about 40 percent since World War II, being substantially reduced.

Nothing illustrates the navy's skewed sense of priorities more clearly than the fact that while the surface fleet expanded rapidly under Reagan, the submarine force did not. Submarines are much less vulnerable than surface ships and, as was evident in World War II, can pose a potent threat to shipping during a war. They are also hard to detect:

technology has been used to much greater advantage in submarines than in surface ships, making them much quieter than their predecessors and able to travel much farther under water. Yet the navy has never been as keen on attack submarines as it has been on surface ships, and those it does have reflect the familiar bias for sophistication. The current generation of attack subs are large, fast, nuclear-powered craft, undoubtedly effective but also expensive. The navy has 90 to 100 of them and admits that it needs at least 130. Yet it will neither sacrifice surface ships to build them nor purchase any *smaller*—hence, cheaper —nuclear-powered submarines. Nor is it much interested in conventional diesel-powered submarines, which would cost a fourth as much. As George Kuhn points out:

> In rejecting the smaller nuclear boat the Navy balks at the loss of five knots top speed. Though such a speed difference can be useful in ocean transit and in escaping immediate attacks, it also makes the sub much noisier and more easily detected. The navy rejects the conventional sub, arguing that it is more vulnerable to airborne detection (since it must snorkel occasionally) and that it cannot perform the same range of missions as a nuclear boat.

Though they may be valid, these objections miss the point. If costs didn't matter, the navy could have as many large nuclear submarines as it wanted, just as the army could have an unlimited supply of M-1 tanks. But since money does count, and the navy prefers to spend most of what it has on gadget-ridden surface ships, the need for a larger submarine fleet suggests that it would make sense to build smaller boats.[2] Moreover, the critical areas in which American submarines would operate—choke points such as the GI-UK gap—would probably be *dominated* by friendly aircraft. This means the risks faced by conventional subs, which must occasionally surface for air, would be relatively small—far smaller, certainly, than the risks faced

---

[2]The same argument applies to Britain, where the Royal Navy, though obsessed with gold-plated cruisers, Type 22 frigates, and nuclear submarines, has shown itself decidedly reluctant to buy *conventional* attack submarines.

by surface vessels. What's more, as Kuhn observes, "because conventional boats are much quieter and smaller and could carry the same sensors and weapons load, they might actually better perform many stealth missions and the hunter-killer mission in barriers and shallow areas against Soviet attack submarines. Moreover, they can operate on long-range missions—they could be based abroad more readily than nuclear vessels." The navy, however, pays no heed to this kind of logic.

5

"Shooting Fish in a Barrel"

No one who believes defense should be taken seriously can fail to be appalled by America's system of military procurement. It comprises an obsession with high tech and an endless chase after superexpensive, supersophisticated weapons, many of which do not work—or, if they do, are irrelevant to any real "threat." This may satisfy the institutional and traditional needs of the individual services, but it can satisfy no one who believes that the task is to prepare for a possible war with the Russians or with anyone else.

It would, of course, be foolish to suggest that most of those involved in military procurement are anything other than decent, patriotic, well-intentioned people. There is no overarching conspiracy to defraud the taxpayer. (As the Pentagon joke has it: "Nothing so inefficient could ever be a conspiracy.") Nevertheless, the taxpayers do get defrauded: they pour money into a system wide open to abuse in which most of the checks and balances do not work properly.

What makes the situation all the more depressing is that there is little incentive for change. Too many vested interests are involved; too much money is at stake; too much of what happens has become accepted as common practice. In his farewell address as president, Dwight D. Eisenhower warned of the danger: "We have been compelled to create a permanent arms industry of vast proportions. . . . The potential for the disastrous rise of misplaced power exists and will persist." Gradually, the forces of what Eisenhower called "the military-industrial complex" have come to dominate procurement: a system has grown up that works to its own distortion, and is hard to escape.

Just how bad things are emerged with unusual clarity in a case that hit the headlines in 1984 and 1985. It involved General Dynamics, one of the Pentagon's top contractors and the supplier of an array of crucial military hardware, ranging from F-16 fighters to M-1 tanks to the Trident submarines that form the vital, sea-based leg of America's nuclear deterrent. The "defection" of one of General Dynamics' top executives, C. Takis Veliotis, a Greek businessman who absconded to Greece after retiring from the company, allowed investigators to gain a unique glimpse into the relationship between the government and one of its major defense contractors. Seeking to defend himself against charges that he defrauded the company, Veliotis made a series of charges against top General Dynamics executives, including the chairman, David Lewis. The picture he painted was one of scandalous behavior by the company.

By May 1985, it had been clearly established, among other things, that General Dynamics had given gifts worth $67,628 to retired Admiral Hyman Rickover, "the father of the nuclear navy," and that it had "ripped off" the U.S. taxpayer by charging the Defense Department millions of dollars for questionable expenses, ranging from $491,840 for Lewis's personal flights on corporate jets to a $155 kennel fee for an executive's dog. For its sins, General Dynamics—which at the time was doing $23 million of defense business *a day*—was fined $676,283. In addition, two of its major divisions were temporarily suspended from doing business with the Pentagon, and two existing contracts were canceled. Navy Secretary Lehman stopped short of accepting a recommendation from the Pentagon inspector general that Lewis and two fellow executives be barred from ever doing business with the military again. But even then General Dynamics was not out of the wood. A federal grand jury was investigating charges that the company had defrauded the government by putting in a bid for a submarine contract, knowing it to be too low, and then blamed the Pentagon for the consequent additional huge costs; that it attempted to blackmail the government into paying costs that resulted from its own shoddy workmanship; and that it tried to stop its stock price from sliding by lying about delivery timetables.

At the time of writing, it is true, none of these charges has been proved. But the allegations alone were enough to send shock waves through Congress. And it was becoming clear that the General Dynamics case was not unique. "I think the company's excuse is exactly correct," says A. Ernest Fitzgerald, the Pentagon whistle blower who exposed huge cost overruns in the 1970s. "Everyone's doing it." Indeed, by the beginning of 1986 nine out of America's top ten defense contractors were under criminal investigation for some abuse or other. Allegations swirled around General Electric of improper billing for nuclear warhead contracts, around McDonnell Douglas of "accounting irregularities," around Sperry of falsifying bills for the MX missile, around National Semiconductor of cutting corners in the testing of electronic chips, around Boeing of billing the Pentagon for contributions to political campaigns.

A spate of "small" spare-parts horror stories in the press—the $659 ashtray, the $640 toilet seat, the $7,600 coffeepot—added to the impression that the defense industry was not yielding value for money. It was perhaps these relatively trivial items that did the most to focus public attention on the procurement mess. "People have no idea what a fighter or a spare part for a fighter should cost," said one defense official, "but everyone knows that coffeepots shouldn't cost $7,600."

Indeed, according to Ernest Fitzgerald, the $7,600 coffeepot reflected a general trend. "What you're seeing when a military aircraft flies overhead," he said, "is an overpriced collection of spare parts."

The way the Pentagon procurement system operates, of course, provides the perfect climate for "rip-off." There is the enormous and unwieldly bureaucracy—compared by Thomas V. Jones, the president of the Northrop Corporation, to "a log floating down a river with 10,000 ants aboard, each one thinking he's steering." Within this structure, where control from the center is lax, and where the services compete fiercely for their share of the budget, officers win their spurs by running big weapons programs, and in their efforts to obtain the "best" possible weapons, constantly bombard manufacturers with elaborate and ever-changing specifications.

Thus, when drawing up specifications for the B-1 nuclear bomber, the air force included a demand that the pilot be able to eject while the plane was flying at 200 feet—upside down. Having the capacity to eject at 200 feet right side up just might make sense, but adding the technology necessary to permit upside-down ejection would have added $1 billion to the cost of the program. In this instance, the air force was eventually persuaded to drop the requirement, though not until money had been spent on research and development. The point is, defense contractors can argue legitimately that the services are continually making similarly absurd demands.

Norman Augustine, the shrewd and witty former Pentagon official who in the early 1960s became chairman of the Martin Marietta Corporation, likes to point out that the contract the Wright brothers signed with the army in 1908 to build the first military airplane was only two pages long. By contrast, the proposal for the building of the C-5A transport—a hugely complex piece of equipment—ran to 1.5 million pages and weighed 25,000 pounds. The most critical aerospace material nowadays, says Augustine, is not cobalt or titanium but the wood pulp that goes into a contractor's proposal. Hence, his "law": "If all the contract proposals were piled one on top of the other at the bottom of the Grand Canyon, it would probably be a good idea."

Hugely complicated specifications are not just the rule for large weapons systems. Even ashtrays, as we have seen, have to be made to a precise and elaborate plan. The specifications for the plastic whistle used by army drill instructors run to sixteen pages of single-spaced detail, dictating everything from the size of the tiny cork ball inside the whistle to the type of tissue wrapping paper it should be packed in.

Faced with such ridiculous demands, industry can justifiably protest that it is hardly being encouraged to save money. But the truth is that elaborate specifications, by and large, suit the defense industry as much as they suit the services, precisely because they afford an opportunity to push up costs. What makes the cooperation between services and industry especially close is the phenomenon known as "the revolving door." Every year hundreds of top military men leave the Pentagon to take lucrative jobs in industry, often with the very firms whose business they have been handling. A study by the New York–based Council on Economic Priorities found that 1,672 former military and civilian employees of the Pentagon and NASA were recruited by eight major contractors between 1970 and 1979. Over the same period, 270 executives from these firms joined the Pentagon and NASA.

Thus, it is often difficult to tell who is responsible for changes in specifications—though it is, of course, the Pentagon's responsibility to approve them. In any case, the Pentagon's fixation on high technology, and its determination to make tiny adjustments in the light of new information about the "threat," provide constant excuses for change.

For example, the "high-speed anti-radiation missile" known as HARM, designed to be fired from aircraft and then home in on enemy radar systems, was expected to cost $48,000 apiece in 1976. But in an effort to keep up with what was thought to be increasingly sophisticated Soviet radar technology, HARM steadily acquired extra "capabilities," and its price raced up to $600,000 by 1978. By 1981, when the first eighty HARMs were ordered by the navy, the missile was being built from 10,000 design drawings—and the price was $1.3 million.

Whether or not the HARM missile now being fitted to military aircraft will work properly is unclear. At the time of writing, its test record is undistinguished. But what is evident is that an air-to-ground missile initially designed to be used in large quantities against Soviet radar defenses had become instead a missile that would have to be used very sparingly for "the surgical removal of high-priority, extremely sophisticated enemy air defense systems," as an air force general put it. Once again, the Pentagon had put all its eggs in the high-tech basket; it had purchased a missile so expensive that it was quite un-suited to the role for which it had been originally planned.

Clearly, the Pentagon deserved much of the blame for this: as the customer, it encouraged the kind of tinkering that transformed HARM. But the manufacturer—in this case Texas Instruments—has much to gain and little to lose from increasingly elaborate specifica-tions. Talking of the defense industry generally, Navy Secretary Leh-man told the *Washington Post:* "They've got their order book out. 'The latest study shows you ought to have 20 miles more range? Sure,

we can give you that, piece of cake. We'll hire more engineers.'
. . . When you get paid for overrunning, and get profits on top of that
for overrunning, you're disserving your stockholders if you don't overrun."

As Lehman suggests, the defense industry often seems to work in
precisely the opposite way from the rest of the private sector. In
standard business practice, you make money by keeping overheads
down and prices low: that way you undercut your rivals and maximize
your profits. In what Reagan likes to call "the arsenal of democracy,"
however, the secret is to jack up your overheads as much as you can
and sell your product at the steepest price you can get: you don't, on
the whole, have to worry about competition. According to an estimate
by Republican Senator Charles Grassley, a leading Pentagon critic,
only a tiny fraction of Pentagon contracts are awarded on the basis of
genuine competition between two or more firms. Many firms are monopoly suppliers of particular pieces of equipment and get paid whatever they happen to charge. And what passes for competition often
turns out to be meaningless: firms routinely submit unrealistically low
bids, knowing that once they have secured a contract, the Pentagon will
probably proceed to dream up, or agree to, a whole series of new bells
and whistles that will provide them with ample excuse to inflate the
original contract price. The fancier the technological frills, the more
difficult it becomes for the Pentagon to estimate what a realistic price
should be.

But there is an even more fundamental problem. In many instances, the trouble starts before a final "fixed price" contract has been
agreed on between Pentagon and contractors, and before cost overruns
and the adding of new bells and whistles have entered the picture. For
until the Pentagon has "frozen" the specifications for a particular
weapon—and decided precisely what it is it wants to buy—the contractor is being paid for research, technology demonstration, initial development, development and initial production, and the building of a
prototype—all this usually on a "cost plus" basis. The Pentagon, in
other words, pays the company's costs, plus an agreed profit formula.
It is, therefore, clearly in the contractor's interest to stretch out this
process, encouraging gold-plating ideas, and delaying as long as possible

the fixing of a unit price. Defense contractors, after all, exist to make profits, not equipment.

Thus, the initial bidding for contracts is often a charade, one that is played out by both the contractors and the services procurement people. Anxious to win approval from Congress for their pet schemes, they indulge in what has been aptly called "a conspiracy of optimism." In an unusually frank moment, one Pentagon official put it like this: "If we told the truth we would never get our programs approved. So we have to understate the cost and overstate the performance. Our military bias is to get as much as we can—after all, we don't know who the future enemy is or what he will have in the way of weapons. We are the ones who have to fight the war, not the people in Congress or the average taxpayer."

So the services justify their yearning for high-tech equipment with the argument that only the best will do (even though it is often not the best at all), while the defense industry exploits their unwillingness to think economically by grossly overcharging them. There is little, if any, incentive to worry about offering value for money. "Everyone's missed the point of what we're buying," says Ernest Fitzgerald. "We're not buying products, we're buying costs."

In the rare instances when competition occurs, results can be dramatic. When the price of the HARM missile soared over $1 million, for example, the navy suggested to Texas Instruments that it might seek another bidder. Once before, while developing an earlier antiradiation missile, the navy had threatened the same thing—whereupon Texas Instruments found itself able to drop its price by 77 percent. This time the firm tried to block the navy's attempt to introduce competition, arguing that it was the only qualified antiradiation missile builder in the country and that it would cost the Pentagon millions to familiarize another contractor with the technology. Texas Instruments won its case, but the threat of competition did have an effect: in the following three months, according to the *Washington Post*, Texas Instruments dropped its price three times, reducing it from $1.3 million to $400,000 per missile. The company maintains it would have dropped its price anyway, as production techniques improved. Even if true, however, there is little doubt that the specter of competition was a potent catalyst.

Similarly, in June 1980 General Dynamics suddenly cut the unit price of its F-16 fighter by $6.2 million, or 30 percent. It did so because the Northrop Corporation had spent $800 million of its own money developing an alternative fighter, the F-20, and, frustrated by the air force's reluctance to hold a flyoff between the planes, had made the Pentagon an attractive offer. Threatened with this competition, General Dynamics felt compelled to make a new bid of its own: a stripped-down version of the F-16—minus some of the more exotic gadgetry—for $13 million apiece, with spare parts guaranteed at $554 per flying hour. As the *New York Times* put it: "The lesson is clear. Even if one plane should prove to have the overall edge in quality, the Air Force needs to buy at least some of each so as to keep both contractors competing."

More often than not, however, instead of fostering competition, the armed services hand contractors a license to spend. In Chapter 2 we examined the less than distinguished record of the Viper antitank missile. In 1979, however, the army was so desperate for an antitank missile that it ordered Viper's manufacturer "to get something that worked in the field, regardless of cost." Not surprisingly, the cost quadrupled, eventually getting so out of control that the army ended up paying $77 each for the simple cloth slings—worth 52 cents—used to carry the weapon. When Hughes ran into trouble producing another dubious missile, the Maverick, in 1982, it persuaded the Pentagon to renegotiate its contract: instead of paying $111 million for 490 missiles, the air force would pay $100 million for only 200 missiles. In addition, Hughes charged the Pentagon over $20 million for contract changes.

"What you're seeing," says one British defense expert, "is socialism in action. Anyone who has studied a nationalized industry will recognize exactly what is going on. The difference is that in the case of the defense contractors things are much worse. They have shareholders who are anxious to see big profits."

Or as another long-time observer of the U.S. defense industry put it: "If I were in the KGB, I would make enormous efforts to encourage this system. You could scarcely make it more inefficient if you tried."

In the first four years after Reagan took office, America's military procurement budget doubled. In all, the Pentagon spent over $1 trillion

—the equivalent of $28 million an hour, night and day, seven days a week. As a result, the defense industry enjoyed its greatest spending spree ever. Contractors reported record profits, and thanks to loopholes in the tax laws, many of them managed to pay little or no tax. Indeed, seven top defense contractors paid no taxes at all between 1981 and 1983. Some even claimed money *back* from the Treasury. General Electric, for example, reported profits of $6.5 billion between 1981 and 1983. Yet not only did it pay no income taxes in this period, it actually received a tax refund of $283 million. Thus, as Robert McIntyre, a tax lawyer who runs a pressure grouped called Citizens for Tax Justice, pointed out, these defense contractors managed to exempt themselves from paying so much as a dime toward the huge buildup from which they profited so handsomely.

The defense industry, then, boomed under Reagan. Lee Iacocca, chairman of the Chrysler Corporation, likes to ask fellow industrialists who sell to the Pentagon whether they think there's easy money in defense contracting. According to Iacocca, they usually start chuckling, look around to make sure no one else is listening, and then reply: "It's like shooting fish in a barrel."

To be fair, Defense Secretary Weinberger and his deputies, especially John Lehman, have tried to crack down on the pervasive waste and fraud. They themselves exposed a litany of horror stories, and attempted to encourage competition. But many believe they did little more than scratch the surface. Even a CIA report, completed well into the Reagan buildup, concluded: "Anything that succeeds in U.S. weapons acquisition seems to do so in spite of the system, rather than because of it." The evidence is that the huge Pentagon budgets of the Reagan years did vastly more for the contractors, their shareholders, and their employees than for American defense. Much of the huge influx of cash went into high costs and overheads rather than weapons, and the evidence of inefficiency mounted. F-18 aircraft came rolling off the McDonnell Douglas production lines with dangerous cracks in their tails. (The company tried to get the navy to pay to fix them. To his credit, Secretary Lehman refused.) Semiconductor chips produced by Texas Instruments turned out to be endangering the reliability and performance of a whole range of sophisticated weapons. According to documents supplied to Congress, one major defense company was paid for 5,050 hours of labor on the MX missile—even though its own "factory efficiency" data suggested the work should have taken only 370 hours. And the Hughes Corporation was found to be taking up to seventeen times as long as its own estimates said it should to produce each Maverick missile.

These were not unusual cases; in some instances, of course, the problems stretched back to the 1970s, but everywhere investigators looked, they found that the defense industry was far more inefficient than most firms in the private sector. Meanwhile, however, defense contractors were paying their executives proportionately much larger salaries—not insignificant, since 70 percent of contract dollars underwrite wages—and reaping proportionately much larger profits. One navy study cited by the *Washington Post* found that defense work in the early 1980s was in some cases proving ten times as lucrative as other business. To take one example: in 1983 Boeing earned three times as much profit on its military work as it did on its civilian work. The huge Reagan buildup, therefore, scarcely translated into a dramatic increase in security. Thanks to an inefficient defense industry, a top-heavy bureaucracy, and a technology-obsessed Pentagon, the United States got precious little bang for its bucks. Indeed, in the four years between 1981 and 1985, the Pentagon bought:

- only 6.4 percent more missiles despite a 91.2 percent increase in the missile budget;
- only 8.8 percent more aircraft despite a 75 percent increase in the aircraft budget;
- only 30 percent more tanks and combat vehicles despite a 147.4 percent increase in the budget for tanks and combat vehicles.

The buildup also promised trouble for the future. From early on, a number of seasoned defense analysts, such as former defense secretary James Schlesinger and MIT professor William Kaufman, had warned of this. They saw a clear pattern, based on experience in the past. The services, assured of large amounts of money, would order large quantities of new equipment. This would, therefore, pave the way for a bigger defense establishment—more ships, planes, and tanks to maintain. When the bills fell due, however, the services would find that they had wildly underestimated how much they owed. So they would have to "squeeze." How do services squeeze? By cutting back on vital things like flying and sailing hours, training, spare parts, and ammunition, all essential to military preparedness. So, although short-term readiness may have improved under Reagan (thanks to the size of the budget), the long-term effect of the Reagan buildup promised to be a defense establishment less ready for war than ever.

Some critics, such as Senator Grassley, argued that pumping ever-increasing sums into the Pentagon simply encouraged abuses. A conservative from Iowa, Grassley was appalled by the behavior of defense contractors. Isolated from competition—and from the consequences of their mistakes—with a government always prepared to bail them out if necessary, they appeared to him an anathema in a country based on competitive private enterprise. The envy of their "civilian" opposite numbers, they had become what Grassley called "the new welfare queens," sponging on the taxpayers and squandering public trust as speedily as they enriched their shareholders.

Grassley was not alone in his disillusionment with the Pentagon. As congressmen and senators grew sick of having to answer questions from constituents about $7,600 coffeepots and $658 ashtrays, the consensus for a steeply rising defense budget began to evaporate. In 1980, a Harris poll found that 71 percent of those who replied supported increased defense spending; in a similar poll taken in 1985 that figure had shrunk to a mere 9 percent. Just as Congress had discovered that the war on poverty would not be won simply by throwing money at social programs, so a similar feeling now set in about defense. For the first time, many politicians in Washington came to appreciate the significance of Eisenhower's dark warnings about the military-industrial complex.

But Congress, though grown collectively weary of the defense industry, is in fact part of the problem. Too many individual congressmen are prepared to acknowledge abuses in the abstract, but reluctant to punish firms that operate in their districts. And though it is ready enough to "micromanage" the Pentagon through a swarm of different committees, Congress rarely shows itself capable of seeing the broad strategic perspective.

It is not just that defense contractors make handsome contributions to campaign funds (though they do: the amount of money poured into political action committees by defense contractors doubled during the Reagan buildup). Nor is it just that the "conspiracy of optimism" —that is, the constant lying about costs and performance—makes it hard for congressmen to judge individual programs (though it does: both the baffling complexity of modern hardware and the ten to fifteen years it takes a new weapons system to progress from drawing board to battlefield militate against Congress's ability to make rational judgments). The real problem is that Congress has a stake in the system as it currently operates. For one thing, the economic recovery that began in late 1982 owed a huge amount to the upsurge in defense spending (financed, of course, in classic Keynesian fashion, by growing federal deficits). And the defense industry in the United States employs millions of people. Indeed, the jobs of one in ten Americans depend directly or indirectly on defense spending. There are twice as many defense workers as farmers; in some states, notably California, defense-related employment is the largest single source of personal income. So defense, as Senator William Proxmire once put it, has become "a public works program." Politicians may be genuinely outraged by the behavior of the defense industry and the Pentagon, but they are reluctant to take steps that will increase unemployment in their districts. The Soviet threat may seem shadowy at best, but the prospect of a major defense plant closing, or of a whole spate of new jobs for a struggling district, is a matter of more immediate concern in a country where the breathing space between elections is short.

Thus the late Representative Joseph Addabbo, who led the campaign to kill the B-1 nuclear bomber, realized the immensity of his task when he visited the headquarters of its manufacturer, Rockwell International Corporation. He saw on the wall a map of America with strings radiating from Rockwell's main plant in Los Angeles to dozens of subcontractors involved in building individual parts of the plane. The strings spread over the whole map. Addabbo knew that many of his fellow congressmen were unhappy about the B-1, a nuclear bomber designed to penetrate Soviet air defenses in the 1980s and 1990s, which had been canceled by Jimmy Carter but revived by Ronald Reagan (estimated cost: $20.5 billion for 100 planes). In the end, however, parochial considerations won out. Potential allies told Addabbo: "Joe, they've built a plant in my district. I need the jobs."

In fact, though the B-1 is an extraordinarily complicated aircraft —it is so full of tubes and wires that it is described as resembling a heart transplant patient—it may actually represent a sounder investment than many other Pentagon projects. It is, for example, a more sensible addition to America's arsenal than the MX missile because it can perform a dual nuclear/conventional role and is not as vulnerable to a preemptive strike. Nonetheless, support for the B-1 seemed to depend more on its job-creating capacity than its military value. Among its backers, for example, was Senator Alan Cranston of California. He made the establishment of a "freeze" on the nuclear arsenals of both superpowers the prime plank of his challenge for the Democratic presidential nomination in 1984. Despite this, and despite arguing that "one of the worst ways to provide jobs is through defense spending," Cranston has continued to be a fan of the B-1. And no one except perhaps his closest aides doubts for a moment that a principal reason he supports it is because Rockwell's main plant is in his state.

No congressman or senator is free of the kind of pressures that were operating on Cranston. Even as long-standing and vehement a critic of the Pentagon as Addabbo tenaciously looked after the interests of the Grumman Corporation, manufacturer of the navy's F-14 fighter. Grumman has a large plant on Long Island, and many of its employees live in what was Addabbo's Queens district. In 1983, when senators began to talk about cutting defense spending, John Tower, chairman of the Senate Armed Services Committee, wrote a letter to all ninety-nine of his colleagues asking them to list which defense projects they would be willing to give up in their home states. He got just six replies.

Consider the F-18, the navy's answer to the air force's relatively cheap and lightweight fighter, the F-16. Conceived in the early 1970s as an alternative to the horrendously expensive F-14 (which the navy could not afford in adequate numbers), the F-18 grew rapidly into an all-purpose, all-capable plane as the navy and its manufacturer, McDonnell Douglas, crammed into it the familiar technological wizardry: new engines, new radar, fancy computers. Originally designed to cost a relatively modest $5 million apiece, it was set by 1982 to cost $30 million—almost as much as the F-14.

By then, of course, cancellation was virtually out of the question. Weapons programs acquire a momentum of their own, and by the late 1970s thousands of jobs all over the country were tied up in the F-18. Some 20,000 companies in 44 states were building parts for the plane. Among the F-18's backers were two stalwart liberals, Speaker of the House Tip O'Neill and Senator Edward Kennedy—both of whom hailed from Massachusetts, where, as it happened, General Electric was making the plane's engines.

The F-18 has many backers. It also has many critics, among them hawkish defense analysts like Jeffrey Record, a former Capitol Hill staffer who charges that the F-18 is an aircraft without a role, and will not help the navy at all—but simply preserve its requirement for large carriers. But whatever its merits, the point is that the F-18 is not now what it was conceived to be, that Congress, having once given it the go-ahead, was powerless to insist that costs be kept down. Though strong on principle, its members are too bound up in the system they have helped create to exercise any real powers of supervision. And the services and industry, needless to say, do all they possibly can to insure that their pet projects survive unscathed. In addition to contributing heavily to political campaigns, defense contractors also spend large sums on sophisticated lobbying operations. The mere prospect of Reagan's five-year defense buildup, according to the *Los Angeles Times,* was enough to persuade several top defense contractors to double the size of their "government affairs offices" in Washington.

Just how thorough lobbying efforts can be emerged in June 1982, with the leaking of a computer printout from the Lockheed Corporation, manufacturers of the C-5 transport plane. First built in the early 1970s, the C-5A Galaxy is the world's largest aircraft. But its development was consistently plagued by engineering and design problems. First, the undercarriage proved unsatisfactory. Then the wings began to crack. And though Lockheed insisted the faults weren't serious ("We know that a new wing is not necessary," a company executive told a congressional committee in 1979. "We know that a report will not come out that a new wing is necessary"), new wings did have to be built, and the tab, of course (an extra $1.6 billion), was picked up by the taxpayer. The process dismayed many congressmen—among them, Democrat Allard Lowenstein, who felt the project was so scandalous it should have been terminated. "I speak with some sadness," he said in a speech on the floor of the House. "I love this place. To be elected to it is easily the greatest honor I shall expect to attain. Yet much that happens here leaves me feeling that we are not conducting ourselves as we should. . . . We have greater obligations to the country than we have shown in our behavior today."

When the air force decided to buy a new, modified version of the C-5A—to be called the C-5B—it anticipated a good deal of opposition. So did Lockheed. This fear deepened when Boeing came up with a competing proposal: it suggested adapting 747s for military purposes, which would have been cheaper and, in the view of some powerful legislators, more suitable. But the computer printouts that were leaked in June 1982 suggested what the Boeing forces had to contend with. Technically, the services are forbidden by law to lobby, though the law is largely ignored. The printout made it clear that a specially convened C-5 group, comprising air force officers and Lockheed executives, prepared a careful campaign to win congressional support for their project.

The group's activities provide an object lesson in American political tactics. It drafted a letter for Caspar Weinberger to send to the heads of key committees on Capitol Hill, for example; developed a "target list" of members who should be approached directly; prepared a soft-sell "Dear Colleague" letter for backers of the project to send to other potential supporters; persuaded U.N. ambassador Andrew Young to "work" the black caucus in Congress (knowing that he might have the clout to influence a group that is traditionally antidefense); compiled a list of members who were "PAC-wired" (i.e., were supported by political action committees through which financial contributions could be pumped), and persuaded congressmen from states where Lockheed was a major employer to play an active role in the campaign. The massive effort paid off: in the end, the requisite funds for the $5.35 billion C-5B project were safely appropriated, and Boeing's rival bid fell by the wayside.

Afterward, when the leaked printouts revealed the extent of the lobbying, Lieutenant General Kelly Burke of the air force, the senior officer responsible for the C-5 program, justified the approach as common practice: "You're just wrong if you think this is a highly unusual happening. Anytime you get competing views, it's customary for government to work with those contractors whose views are congruent with the president's. . . . I do not want to sound platitudinous, but all you're seeing is democracy in action. This is the way the system is supposed to work."

Among America's NATO allies, procurement problems do not loom as large as they do in the United States. This is largely a function of size: the Europeans have much smaller defense establishments; they are not nearly as rich. (It is also, in part, a function of secrecy; the procurement debate is much more open in America than it is anywhere in Europe.) To be sure, on a smaller scale, the fascination with high technology is apparent. The latest generation of British and German tanks, the Challenger and the Leopard II, contain much of the computerized gadgetry that adorns the M-1, though the Leopard took only five years to produce, a quarter of the time it took to build the M-1, and many consider it a better tank. The British armored personnel carrier, the MCV-80, has some disturbing similarities to the ill-fated Bradley fighting vehicle; it, too, is a hybrid of the traditional battlefield taxi and a tank, and many critics say it is both overpriced and overburdened with bells and whistles.

The British Army's new telephone switching system, called Ptarmigan, is also unnecessarily complicated. The handset alone costs nearly $5,000, and though it is capable of performing all kinds of marvels—from encrypting human speech into code so that the enemy cannot listen in, to transmitting pictures—the army was offered a handset only marginally less capable at a much cheaper price. However, Plessey, the manufacturer, was obliged to build a telephone "hardened to withstand nuclear weapons effects"—meaning it had to have an extremely expensive steel cover rather than the plastic one originally suggested. This and other elaborate finishing touches sent Ptarmigan's price through the roof (and also, incidentally, helped dash Britain's chances of selling the system to the U.S. Army, which opted for a cheaper, French-made alternative).

On the whole, however, European defense establishments are less obsessed with state-of-the-art technology than the Pentagon. With less money to spend, they tend to be willing to settle for less. Thus, Britain's Harrier jump-jet, which performed well in the Falklands, stems from a breakthrough in vertical-takeoff technology back in the 1950s. Since then the plane has steadily been improved. But the improvements have been incremental. There has been no attempt to add on a whole range of untried new gadgets.

Nevertheless, the history of European defense since the war has, like America's, been one of exploding costs and declining value for money. European inventories of tanks, planes, and ships are shrinking too. Europe, like America, is on what has been called the "road to absurdity": if costs keep rising at current rates, no one, in the end, will be able to afford any equipment at all.

A major problem is the lack of any real cooperation between the allies. There have, of course, been certain collaborative projects, most notably the joint effort by West Germany, Italy, and Britain to build the Tornado. But such undertakings do not always save money: with all the difficulties of competing specifications and liaison between different countries, Tornado, as we have seen, turned out to be formidably expensive, probably more so than it would have been had it been produced by any of the partners acting alone. And the fate of the European Fighter Aircraft, a new multilateral venture, may be precisely the same.

What militates against effective cooperation—against what NATO bureaucrats call "rat, spec, and stan" (rationalization, specialization, and standardization)—is each country's commitment to preserving balanced forces and its own "defense industrial base." At heart, the issue is one of national sovereignty. Effective cooperation would require each of the allies to surrender a significant amount of this, and the prospect of them agreeing to do so is slight. As a result, Western Europe, as a whole, is duplicating the inefficiencies of the Pentagon. Just as congressmen want their districts to have a fair share of defense work, so European governments, especially at a time of rising unemployment, are reluctant to close down domestic defense plants and buy from abroad.

Thus, according to one survey, NATO nations are now busy developing some twenty-one ground-to-air, air-to-ground, and antitank missiles, fourteen combat aircraft, four tanks, and six new tactical communications systems—none of which is compatible with each other. There is duplication in all kinds of other weapons, too, from recoilless rifles to fire-control radars to naval guns.

Instead of buying the U.S. Apache attack helicopter, the West Germans decided to build their own, expecting to be able to do it for half the cost. By 1985 the new West German helicopter looked as if it would cost twice as much as its American equivalent. Similarly, the British decided to build the Nimrod early-warning aircraft instead of buying "airborne warning and control system" (AWACS) planes from Boeing.

This was an especially silly decision. By 1985, Nimrod was millions of pounds over budget and still not airborne. The role it is intended to play is a vital one: to fly out over the North Sea during a war and, using its radars and highly sophisticated computers, track up to 1,000 Soviet Mig fighters and cruise missiles coming in from the northeast. But by 1985, two years after it was due to be in service, the Nimrod's radar still didn't work properly (performing, according to one account, at 40 percent of its required efficiency). In addition, the Nimrod's airframe, based on an ancient 1948 Comet aircraft, couldn't accommodate all the necessary gadgetry, including cooling equipment designed to prevent the whole system from overheating. "Without Nimrod, there is a bloody great hole in the U.K.'s air defenses," one source told the *Sunday Times* of London. "The Tornado is toothless and the Shackletons [Britain's 1950s-vintage early warning aircraft] are being held together with bits of glue."

To be fair, cases like this arise in part because of U.S. procurement policy. The Europeans complain that pressure from Congress means that America rarely buys equipment from Europe, leaving them with little incentive to buy hardware from America.

The lack of cooperation between the allies would cause all kinds of problems in a war. As defense expert Robert Kleiman has observed, NATO forces would often be unable "to refuel each other's planes, repair each others' tanks and shoot each other's ammunition." Worse, pilots would have great difficulty avoiding shooting down their allies. In an exercise in 1974, the lack of a common "identification friend or foe" (IFF) communications systems resulted in NATO forces "shooting down" thirty of their own aircraft. Ground forces would have a similar problem.

NATO pilots returning from bombing runs over enemy territory would be all right if they returned to their own sector, but in the confusion of battle this would not always be easy or possible. One Pentagon veteran of Vietnam and an expert on NATO's problems offers this assessment of the pilots' predicament:

> They all know there are privates on our side of the ground, armed with Stinger [antiaircraft] missiles, capable of taking them out. If you're coming back from a mission you're supposed to fly low, with your flaps down. The idea is, if you do that—which is like walking around with your drawers down—the private down on the ground will know you're not a Russian because no one expects a Russian to come in slow. So if someone comes in slow with his flaps down he has to be a NATO pilot. But the pilots know if they're in the position of having to trust a private on the ground with a Stinger, Murphy's Law will apply. So these pilots are telling me: "Screw these goddam procedures. I'm coming back at full bore 50 feet off the ground. I'll be past that goddamn guy before he knows I'm there." Another reason you don't want to fly low and slow is that you have to start being low and slow over Soviet air defenses. And that's the box we're in simply because the Germans, the British, and the U.S. cannot decide which goddam black box to buy and they're all buying different black boxes that are not interoperable. You're okay if you fly back in your own sector. But if you get knocked off course or for whatever reason get out of sector, all bets are off.

Like the Pentagon, the Europeans have also tended to concentrate on "big ticket" items (planes, ships, tanks) rather than on readiness. As a result, there are drastic shortages all over the central front. Among them are:

> *Ammunition.* In some sectors, stocks of the 155-millimeter ammunition used by most NATO artillery pieces would run out within a week to ten days after the start of a war. So, in about the same amount of time, would antitank missiles and even much

mortar and rifle ammunition. Air-to-air missiles are also in short supply.

Transport. NATO is very short of transport, especially of 5-ton trucks to take ammunition and supplies to the front line during a war.

Communications equipment. "If the C³I [for command, control communications, and intelligence] doesn't work, it doesn't matter what we have," says one Pentagon expert. "It's every man for himself, and that's no way to fight a war." Yet much of the equipment designed to facilitate this crucial role is very fragile. For example, there are a handful of microwave towers on the central front that would be critical in enabling commanders to communicate with each other in a time of war. They are currently protected by barbed wire and lightly manned guard posts. In a war, say U.S. Army experts, a skilled saboteur ("or even a good marksman with a rifle," said one specialist) would have little trouble taking them out. Inadequate communications—and differences in systems used by the allies—have led to farcical moments. In one exercise, an American general requested permission from his HQ to "go nuclear." There was no reply. An inquiry later revealed that his message had been routed to the Italian public telephone system, where it vanished.

Protected air bases. In the mid-1970s America's European allies agreed to provide a series of so-called "co-located operating bases" (COBs) for the U.S. Air Force. Consisting of maintenance facilities and hardened shelters on exposed runways near the front line, the bases were designed to give American aircraft flying across the Atlantic in time of war—and some 1,500 fighter planes would be expected in the first ten days—adequate protection when they arrived. So far none of these COBs has been built. (They were supposed to be paid for out of NATO's common, or "infrastructure," budget, but this has been kept short of the requisite funds. As a result, the U.S. Air Force is understandably worried that its highly prized modern fighters will arrive in Europe only to be-

come sitting ducks for the enemy—as likely to get destroyed on
the runway as in the air.

The American high-tech bias, combined with a lack of cooperation among NATO allies, has done much to weaken Western defense.
Fortunately for the West, however, the Soviet fighting machine is not
as formidable as it is often assumed to be. The Russians have their
problems, too, and though their attitude toward conventional weapons
remains, by and large, more sensible than the West's, they have fallen
into some similar traps.

The basis of Russian strength is numbers. They have consistently
managed to outproduce the West in everything from tanks and aircraft
to antiaircraft guns and personnel carriers. They have done this by
making simpler, cruder, cheaper weapons. In the early 1960s, General
Creighton Abrams (who was once described by his World War II
superior, General George Patton, as "my champion tank commander")
inspected a Soviet tank captured during the Korean War. Abrams, who
posthumously lent his name to the most complex tank ever built, the
M-1 Abrams, said afterward: "I got in the goddam tank, and it didn't
do all the fancy things the colonels want in our tanks. You couldn't
push the joystick and make the thing turn around, but it could do every
damn thing you want a tank to do."

In the late 1970s, a team of American engineers compiled a report
for the Pentagon on the different approaches taken by the superpowers
to weapons design. The engineers concluded that the difference lay not
so much in the amount of money spent as in the Russians' ability to
churn out greater quantities of equipment because they "think poor":
on the whole, Russian weapons systems have been less the victims of
technological complexity and cripplingly high costs than American
ones.

Among the examples the engineers used to illustrate their case
were tank tracks. The tracks of a tank, which enable it to move
smoothly over rough ground, clearly need to be solid and durable.
Those of the T-55 and T-62 (the mainstays of the Red Army throughout the 1950s and 1960s) were just that—simply a "rough casting
which did not even need machining," according to the design report.

This meant there were fewer parts to assemble and less danger of the tracks "slipping off" in combat—a problem of many modern tanks that has been compared to a boxer losing his shorts in the middle of a round.

Similarly, the standard Soviet jet engine, designed by the Tumansky Design Bureau near Moscow, was much simpler than its U.S. counterpart. "The total number of parts," said the U.S. engineers, "including fasteners, washers, and so forth, of Tumansky engines is estimated to be only 30 or 40 percent of the number found in American engines with comparable performance characteristics. One Tumansky engine, which was used in a Mig fighter, had less than one-sixth as many parts as the comparable J-79 engine used in American aircraft." The Soviet engine, according to the U.S. report, proved altogether more reliable than its American counterpart—and cost one-third as much. Indeed, it has been estimated that even if it was built in the United States with American materials and by a labor force earning American wages, the Tumansky engine would still be less than half the cost of the U.S. one.

The watchword in the Soviet design bureaus, then, was caution, and the U.S. study team suggested that the makeup of the Russian design bureaus themselves helped promote this. In contrast to the Pentagon, where program managers tended to change disconcertingly often, Soviet design bureaus tended to work together for long periods, sometimes twenty-five years or more. One key difference between the two sides was that whereas the average "lead time" for a weapon in the West (i.e., the amount of time it takes to progress from drawing board to battlefield) was ten to fourteen years, much of this made up of endless wrangling over specifications and constant design changes, the average lead time in the Soviet Union was much less—between eight and ten years. The advantages, as the engineers pointed out, were obvious. The West was always making quantum leaps from one generation of equipment to the next, with many more untried bells and whistles. The Soviet Union, on the other hand, could proceed more incrementally: there was less of a gap between one generation of equipment and the next, and less gambling on half-understood gadgetry. As former Pentagon official Leo Sullivan once put it, the Soviets appeared to have "made a conscious decision to stay below the leading edge of technology." To put it another way, they clearly took note of the precept of Soviet helicopter designer Mikhail Mil: "Comrades, make it simple, make it rugged, make it reliable, make it work."

Not that it did always work. But Soviet shortcomings tended to be more the result of sloppy engineering and poor construction than overambitious design. The gear change in the old T-55 tank, for example, was so stiff that drivers had to keep a sledgehammer by their side to hit the gear lever with when they wanted to change gear. And the T-55s were scarcely reliable: various accounts suggest they broke down frequently. Still, the Soviet approach emphasized numbers and has continued to do so. Because the Russians modernized more often but less dramatically, they managed to keep their numbers up more easily than the West. The Russians have also tended to build more different types of systems than the Americans: they have a whole range of antiaircraft guns, for example, rather than relatively few "all-capable" systems.

There are signs that this approach is changing, that the Russians are now "catching up" with the West's high-tech obsessions. Instead of being relieved by this, however, Caspar Weinberger believes that it justifies the current Pentagon shopping list. As he said in an interview on CBS television:

> There's a sort of myth around that what we should do is buy a great deal more of very much less sophisticated kinds of weapons and planes very much less expensively, and that this quantitative advantage is all we need. This myth is based on the assumption that the Soviets don't have very good equipment, and that is a myth. They have very good equipment, and they have an ability to produce very large numbers of very sophisticated, complicated, expensive and high-quality equipment. So we cannot do less.

Weinberger's argument begs a number of questions. For one thing, Weinberger makes the clearly false assumption that "sophisticated" is interchangeable with "good." For another, he disparages his critics by suggesting that they believe "quantitative advantage is all we need," which is not true at all. They simply believe that quantity should not be sacrificed lightly.

The fact is, the Soviet Union, in its attempt to close the "technology gap," is falling into many of the same traps as the West. The concern that has driven them to do this has been well expressed by Michael Binyon, a former Moscow correspondent of the *Times* of London. "The worry that what they have, not only in the military sector but in almost every aspect of life," he says, "is not as good as the West, and whatever they do it's not going to be as good; and that, therefore, they don't actually believe that they're superior, even when objective analysis of what they've got on the ground would say they are. They don't believe that they're better off, that they're stronger, until they hear the West saying it."

Even then they worry. Somehow, the West, they fear, with devilish cunning, is going to pull a technological rabbit out of its hat that will defeat all their efforts. So, as Andrew Cockburn charted in *The Threat*, his study of the Soviet military, the tendency has been to try and catch up with the West. "The Soviet Air Force," Cockburn says, "is now busily imitating [Western] 'advanced technology' systems, including 'all-weather' radar, and complex 'look-down-shoot down' systems—the same features that have made American fighters so expensive and unreliable."

Not only the air force: the Soviet T-64 and T-72 tanks have had plenty of problems too. Though ostensibly in the class of the American M-60, they are in fact much slower and break down twice as often. They are also highly flammable and are cursed rather than blessed with an "autoloader" that is intended to spare the tank gunner the task of ramming shells and charges into the breech. It is said that the autoloader has a tendency to try and load not simply shells but the gunner himself into the breech. Says one U.S. Army officer: "We believe this is how the Red Army chorus gets its soprano section."

The Russians have other problems, too. The Red Army may be large, but it is uneven in quality; it is plagued by problems ranging from nationalism (only 50 percent of conscripts are Russian) to alcoholism to lack of initiative. Until recently, at least, no one under the rank of company commander in the Soviet Army was taught map reading, so in the event of a Soviet invasion of Western Europe some Soviet units may simply get lost. Too much can be made of this ("even the Black Watch get drunk," points out a British official), just as too much can be made of the potential unreliability of the Soviet Union's allies. Were the Soviets to invade Europe, the Warsaw Pact would undoubtedly fight—"better a NATO bullet in the chest than a KGB one in the back," as Soviet defector Viktor Suvorov has observed. But the longer a war lasted, the more concern Moscow would have to feel about Eastern Europe, and about its long, vulnerable lines of supply.

The Soviet threat therefore is often exaggerated. The Red Army is not ten feet tall, and its equipment is not as wonderful as Caspar Weinberger suggests. Yet the tendency of Pentagon analysts to overestimate Soviet weapons has long been used to justify the American high-tech bias. The Shilka air defense weapon, which provided the inspiration for the Divad gun, turned out to be far less magical than had been suspected: it was inaccurate and unreliable. Similarly, the Soviet Foxbat Mig-25 fighter—supposedly capable of traveling at three times the speed of sound and made of titanium—turned out to be far less awesome once American experts got a chance to take one apart and evaluate its technology. (A defecting Russian pilot, Viktor Belenko, landed one on a Japanese airstrip in 1976. It was not built of titanium but of steel; and it was quickly clear that whereas it might just be capable of reaching Mach 3, it would only do so in time to run out of fuel.)

By overestimating the Soviet threat, and overtechnologizing its own weapons, American defense procurement is caught in a vicious circle. Outnumbered by the enemy, the Pentagon tries to even the odds through technology; the result is spiraling costs and fewer systems. So the Pentagon is even more outnumbered, and tries even harder to compensate, and so on. As Pentagon analyst Franklin Spinney puts it:

> By ignoring the real world, we have evolved a self-reinforcing yet scientifically unsupportable faith in the military usefulness of ever-increasing technological complexity. The costs . . . can be generalized into low readiness, slower modernization, and declining forces . . . our strategy of pursuing ever-increasing technological complexity and sophistication has made high-technology solutions and combat readiness mutually exclusive.

A Belgian general once suggested in a meeting with allied and American top brass that the alliance might be able to mount a more effective defense against Russia if it replaced all its existing equipment with men on bicycles armed with bazookas. It was a joke, of course, but maybe not that much worse an approach than the existing one.

The obsession with technology is threatening to bust budgets and sap the West's ability to fight. As Jeffrey Record puts it: "Technology proved indecisive in Korea, ultimately irrelevant in Vietnam, and unreliable in Iran. But this seems not to have shaken that faith [in] technical advance as the solution to most problems on the battlefield. . . ."

Every so often, a good and effective weapon *does* make it through the Pentagon's procurement system, though as a CIA report noted during the Reagan buildup, this is usually in spite of the system rather than because of it. One example is the A-10 antitank aircraft we looked at in Chapter 2. Another is a navy bomb called Skipper. Skipper was born after the Soviet invasion of Afghanistan in 1979, when the U.S. Navy worried that it might have to go into action in the Persian Gulf carrying nothing except 1960s-vintage bombs to attack Soviet surface ships. So the remote Naval Weapons Center in China Lake, California, produced a very simple design. Working against the clock, designers had a bomb ready to be dropped in just ten months. And they did it, as the *Washington Post* noted, by sticking to "off-the-shelf" technology—a 1,000-pound bomb, an existing rocket motor, a "seeker" in the nose capable of homing in on a target illuminated by a laser beam. "They used hacksaws and a sand blaster to shave superfluous parts from the motor. The ignition system was salvaged from the pilot ejection system in an F-104 warplane. Finally, the engineers tacked on a couple of matchbook-size pieces of metal worth 50 cents apiece to make the bomb spin during flight for stability."

After an early failure or two, the Skipper began to work well. It could be dropped 6 miles from its target and guided to it by a laser beam (easier to do from a naval aircraft than on the battlefield). But thought the naval officers and engineers were impressed by Skipper, they had to fight hard to enable the unsexy, indubitably ugly $20,000 bomb to survive. Competing against it, under a contract the air force awarded to Texas Instruments, was another bomb, called Triple L (low-level laser-guided), an altogether more sophisticated and more expensive weapon. Triple L, however, had some powerful backers in Congress and the Pentagon, and though Skipper fared well in tests, it almost fell by the wayside for lack of a patron. Only when Navy Secretary Lehman heard about it and personally intervened—and the Triple L was canceled because of cost overruns—did the Skipper finally earn itself a secure place in the U.S. procurement system. But the Skipper, as the *Washington Post* pointed out, started life as an "orphan." With no strong backing from industry or from a bureaucracy in love with "the expensive, complex, and sleek," it seemed to survive more by good luck than good management.

6

ET

It is known, like Steven Spielberg's famous character from outer space, as ET. To its advocates, and there are many, it could be NATO's salvation, a breakthrough that could finally enable the West to even up the balance of forces. To its detractors, it is a delusion, another example of NATO clutching at technological straws, as unreal as the eponymous hero of the Spielberg film.

In the Pentagon script, ET stands for "emerging technology." Many of the weapons involved, in other words, are still a gleam in developers' eyes. But the theory behind them is already complete. It goes like this.

NATO, though badly outgunned by the Warsaw Pact, might just be able to hold the line in the first phase of a war on the central front. The greatest danger would come later, for the Soviet attack would unfold in waves, or echelons. The first echelon would be followed, within forty-eight hours, by a second. Then, moving up from deeper in Eastern Europe and, ultimately, from the USSR itself, would come a third and possibly a fourth echelon. "It would be like a bloody battering ram coming at you," as one NATO general once put it to me.

In 1973, at the end of the Vietnam War, as the U.S. Army began to turn its attention back to Europe, a team of defense analysts began a secret and detailed assessment of Soviet operational plans. The analysts worked for the BDM Corporation, a major U.S. Army think tank situated in a large office building on the south bank of the Potomac. They concluded that the Russians had worked out very carefully how they might overrun Europe, with the armies in East Germany (the first echelon) taking West Germany up to the Rhine, the armies in Poland and the Slovak part of Czechoslovakia (the second echelon) moving up to take the Low Countries, and the armies in the western Soviet Union (the third echelon) completing the conquest.

Out of BDM's work in 1973 grew the concept of "deep strike" or "follow-on forces attack"—and ET. The idea was that if NATO could mount accurate strikes deep behind enemy lines at the outset of war, it might prevent the second and third echelons from ever reaching the battlefield. That way, NATO ground forces would have to deal only with the first echelon, and perhaps not even with all of that, since the rear elements of the first echelon would be vulnerable to deep strikes too. Thus, NATO would be able to exploit the principal weakness in the Soviet attack, disrupting its timetable and crushing its reinforcements before they could be brought to bear.

That was what BDM thought the Pentagon should seek to do. The question was, how? When the initial analytic work was done there seemed only one possible way—by using nuclear weapons. Only they could provide the combination of accuracy and blast needed to destroy the kind of targets BDM had in mind. The notion of going nuclear at the outset of a war, however, was unthinkable. Bernard Rogers, when he became Supreme Allied Commander, Europe, knew that he would never be given the political authority to do it. Neither a U.S. president nor any NATO head of government would consider going nuclear so early.

A second option might be to use aircraft, and indeed some of the ET bombs and rockets being developed have been designed for aircraft. But for all their computerized gadgetry, modern aircraft are still vulnerable to antiaircraft fire and scarcely constitute a foolproof way to implement the kind of precisely coordinated strike against small, well-defended targets that BDM envisaged. The best bet, it seemed to the most dedicated advocates of ET, would be to use long-range, conventionally armed cruise and ballistic missiles.

As it happened, the use of such missiles, by the late 1970s, was becoming feasible. Thanks to new propulsion fuels and better guidance systems, missiles were (in theory at least) becoming much more accurate. Similarly, it was becoming easier to spot and identify targets quickly, thanks to the development of the new high-resolution "doppler" radar, which could track not only stationary targets but moving vehicles as well. (This new radar was being incorporated in the huge AWACS early-warning aircraft that would fly high over the battlefield, and also in crucial surveillance satellites.) Most striking of all were the advances in computer technology that made it theoretically possible to carry out the mammoth tasks of "acquiring targets" (relaying the information from the satellites or radar systems back to a central point for assessment) and "battle management" (coordinating a series of precision strikes against a huge number of small targets).

According to Dr. Malcolm Currie, one-time director of research and development at the Pentagon, these developments, by 1975, had "brought us to the threshold of what will become a true revolution in conventional warfare." Many scientists agreed. So did the U.S. Army, which saw ET as the perfect complement to its new stress on more flexible "maneuver" warfare. But would ET really transform the military balance and give NATO the edge? Were the hopes of its backers justified?

There were two kinds of targets that the advocates of ET had in mind. The first of these were critical fixed targets and "choke points." They ranged from communications facilities and major airfields (80 percent of the Warsaw Pact air force are based at only twenty-four airfields) to railway lines (specifically the power stations that feed them and the rail yards where troops brought from the Soviet Union would disembark), and most important, the sixty or so bridges that span the main rivers in Eastern Europe (the Oder, the Elbe, and the Vistula). But to hit these targets and sever the Soviet advance would be a tall order. Putting airfields out of action, for example, is notoriously difficult. Despite successive British attempts to put the airfield at Port

Stanley out of action during the Falklands war, for example, the Argentinians managed to keep it operational until the very end. No sooner had it been bombed by Vulcans or Harriers in a night raid than it was swiftly repaired. Similarly, though the bridges spanning the Elbe, the Vistula, and the Oder seem attractive targets, bridges can be rapidly replaced. Whatever the Red Army's shortcomings, it is clearly well aware of the hazards it might have to face in crossing the three rivers; its inventory contains a formidable array of mobile bridges and bridge-building gear, including huge rafts that would carry tanks in an emergency. Some experts believe that the Warsaw Pact would be able to replace most of the bridges within two hours.

There is a further complication. Like so much of modern technology, ET assumes that the Russians will behave in a set piece, predictable fashion. Before we examine this, however, we must glance at the second set of targets that NATO was contemplating.

These were not fixed but, rather, moving targets—enemy tanks, to be precise, surging forward toward the battle area. Given that the only sure way to stop an enemy is to hit his actual forces, the ability to destroy Soviet tanks while they are on the move would clearly give the alliance a significant advantage. But developing that ability is enormously difficult—much harder than destroying fixed targets. According to one man who spent a year studying radar screens in Southeast Asia, all you see on the screen are white blips; you can't tell whether they represent tanks or trucks or cars or even houses.

By the early 1980s, a number of different systems were under study in the Pentagon, all of them involving extraordinarily complex technology. Typical of these was Assault Breaker. Assault Breaker is not a weapon. It is really a series of different technologies that have been harnessed together to form a weapon. In an interview in 1981, James Tegnelia, the Pentagon official in charge of the Assault Breaker project, explained how it would work. "I have an an airborne radar (mounted on a TR-1 plane, say, or a Boeing 707) that surveys a geographical area of 200 square kilometers," he said. "The airborne radar is at 30,000 feet and is normally 50 kilometers behind the battle line" to stay out of range of enemy surface-to-air missiles. This radar would find and track targets, and the targeting data it gathered would be transmitted to a special "tactical fusion" processing station. The station, 30 kilometers or more behind the battle line, would also receive intelligence from satellites, sensors, and other intelligence sources. Once information had been assessed, and a target identified (an enemy tank formation), an army or air force commander on the spot would make the decision to attack it. Then, according to Tegnelia, a missile would be fired and the radar plane would track both missile and targets, whether stationary or moving. The plane would issue midcourse guidance commands to the missile, which would have a range of 100 kilometers or more. Then, once the missile was in the vicinity of its targets, it would dispense a payload of as many as twenty-four "smart" submunitions, or bomblets, each of which would have its own infrared guidance system theoretically capable of homing in with devastating accuracy on an individual tank.

Will these missiles, with their tiny submunitions, actually work? The history of "smart" antitank missiles (such as Maverick) suggests that it is wise to be skeptical. The technology for success is exotic, to say the least.

One proposal, for example, involves a system called Skeet, the brainchild of the Avco Corporation. A total of 228 heat-seeking bomblets would be encased in special delivery vehicles. These vehicles would be released by the Assault Breaker missile and descend by parachute. At a predetermined height, the vehicle would release its Skeets in pairs, and each Skeet, with its infrared guidance system, would then seek out an individual tank (drawn by the heat from the tank's engine) and fire a molten lump of metal into the tank's relatively unprotected top. A similarly exotic system, called WASP, is being developed for the air force. In this instance, the submunitions would depend on millimeter wave guidance systems rather than infrared.

No one has any idea whether Skeet, WASP, or any of the other potential components of Assault Breaker can be made to work effectively. The only successful tests as of the time of this writing have been those conducted in the most benign environment. In 1982, for example, an Assault Breaker missile did manage to drop infrared submunitions onto five tanks in the White Sands desert in New Mexico. But according to the *National Journal*, the target tanks were old and stationary, and their engines more exposed than those of modern tanks, making it much easier for heat-seeking missiles to home in. These were not the only steps taken to make the test work. The land around the target tanks had been bulldozed and graded, and the vegetation removed so that the tanks stood out clearly amid the "ground clutter." And since the test occurred early in the morning, the "thermal contrast" between the desert surroundings and the tanks was strong.

With such carefully organized, success-oriented testing the Pentagon may yet convince itself that even in the Skeet project, an unmitigated failure in early tests, it has a winner on its hands. The snag is that the Russians have more or less been left out of the picture. This is unfortunate, since even if Assault Breaker worked perfectly in peaceful New Mexico, there would still be no guarantee that it will work on a battlefield in Central Europe.

Assault Breaker is what is known as a sequential system, and the best analogy for such a system is the "accumulator" bet, which inveterate gamblers sometimes make at racetracks. To win an accumulator, you have to pick not just one winner but a series. If all your selections win, you stand to make a considerable return on your investment; if just one fails, you lose your stake. The odds against success, therefore, are long. Prudent gamblers do not bet on accumulators.

Assault Breaker is the military equivalent of an accumulator. To work successfully, it requires a long string of extraordinarily complicated operations to work perfectly. To make it fail, the enemy would simply have to disrupt one link in the chain. The likelihood that they would be able to do this would seem to be strong. First, the airborne radar used to track the enemy's tanks could be jammed or shot down. It would clearly be a high-value target, according to one official who has worked closely on the research for ET, which the Soviets "will try to suppress just as we will try to suppress any Soviet equivalent." The process of relaying the information from the radar back to the ground-based "fusion" center would be equally vulnerable to disruption; so would the next link in the sequence, communicating with the relevant ground commander. The next step that would have to work perfectly would be the launch of the expensive munitions-carrying missile or missiles; then would come the separation of the delivery vehicle from the main rocket and the release of the individual heads. The tanks would still have to be roughly in the same area they were when the intelligence was first gathered, and the submunitions would have to home in on their separate targets and, since they would be very small, strike them with pinpoint accuracy in order to destroy them. As one analyst put it: "If you attach a 90 percent probability to each of the links in the chain, which is high, you still may end up with only a fifty-fifty proposition." Not for nothing has the Assault Breaker been called "a thirteen-miracle weapon."

The Soviets, to disrupt any of these miracles, could easily devise appropriate countermeasures, and probably at a fraction of the cost. If, for example, their tanks maintained an irregular speed on the way to the battlefield, it would become much harder—given the time between spotting them and delivering the warheads—to be sure of success.

In a detailed paper on Assault Breaker and its brethren, defense analyst Steven Canby has given some examples of what could be done first to stop the submunitions from achieving their end. They could deploy a World War II invention called chaff, thin metal or plastic rods that, when dispersed into the air, appear on radar screens as false targets. They could force civilian vehicles to mingle with their tanks in order to "draw the fire" of the submunitions as they descended. The high-resolution radar that NATO plans to use would supposedly be able to distinguish between tanks and other vehicles, but as yet there is no real evidence that it will be able to do so. The Soviets could even cover the trees along their attack route with "emitters" that give off heat or radar messages (strung parallel to roads like Christmas tree lights). And finally, since the new weapons would be unable to pack much of a punch because of their small size, the Soviets would probably find it cheaper to harden the tops of their tanks than the West would to increase the explosive power of their submunitions. (Canby even suggests that the judicious placing of bags of children's marbles along the top of tanks might be sufficient to defeat the bomblets.)

There is another, more basic, step the Russians could take to avoid the worst effects of ET, however. They could change their strategy.

In October 1981, the Soviet Union staged a major military exercise on the Baltic Coast. It was called Zapad 81, and Western intelligence, which took a close interest, noted that for the first time the Red Army was experimenting with a different concept of operations—one that depended not on applying force right across the front, but on making fast, concentrated attacks through the weakest sections of enemy lines.

NATO strategists were not taken unawares by what they saw. For several years, in the arcane pages of Warsaw Pact military journals, a debate had raged on the value of what have been called "operational maneuver groups" (OMGs). October 1981, however, provided the first glimpse of theory being turned into practice.

OMGs work by exploiting the weakness of the defense. Instead of trying to force breakthroughs all along the front line, the Red Army would instead launch a series of probing thrusts to try and find the most vulnerable points—like a pitchfork probing the soil, or water trying to find gaps in a gutter. As soon as the crack had been found, a fast, heavily armed, heavily mechanized force that had been kept in reserve would close in and follow up the initial probe, attempting to force rapid passage deep behind enemy lines. It was a tactic the Russians used with some success against Germany in World War II but abandoned in the late 1940s because the danger of a war on the central front going nuclear argued against too much concentration of force (offering a more attractive target for nuclear attack). Besides, as military strategists point out, OMGs are difficult to coordinate, especially in an army as bureaucratic as the Red Army, and pose considerable command and control problems. It is a risky strategy, too. "Nobody to get you out of trouble when you're deep in enemy territory," as one analyst of the Soviet military put it.

But the Russians are clearly working on it. They may be less worried now than they used to be about the likelihood that NATO would use nuclear weapons early in a conflict. (We will see why in the next chapter.) And they could reap considerable advantages in terms of surprise and catching NATO off balance by deploying OMGs. Some analysts believe that the Soviets might be able to take West Germany, if not the whole of continental Europe, without ever having to draw on the divisions stationed back behind the critical rivers in Eastern Europe and the USSR.

Thus, like the Maginot line, ET could turn out to be irrelevant, and in attempting to achieve it, NATO, like the French, might come to neglect more immediate concerns; before dealing with the second, third, and fourth echelons of the Warsaw Pact forces, after all, it would have to deal with the first.

If Zapad 81 is anything to go by, the Russians, as John Erickson, one of Britain's leading Soviet experts, puts it, "are not going to line up so that they can be bombed by NATO one sunny Friday afternoon."

There is no doubt that ET would also be very expensive: the missiles envisaged are veritable "silver bullets." Once the technology is properly developed, "smart" missiles may play a larger and more useful role in Western defense than they do now. And some of the systems contemplated may actually make it easier for aircraft to find and strike fixed targets, and even moving ones. Pilots, at least, can see what they are shooting at, and can also call in reinforcements.

But the Pentagon's hopes that ET will radically transform the military equation have little basis in reality. First, as in so many previous cases, they depend on inflated expectations of how well the new technology will work. Second, much of this technology is not even available yet. "It's pure Buck Rogers just now," says one army skeptic. "This stuff doesn't exist, much as we might wish it did. It's just a gleam in some developer's eye." Third, there are a whole range of countermeasures the Russians could deploy to defeat it, which seem likely to work out cheaper than the technology. Fourth, the Russians could attack in such a way as to render ET irrelevant. And fifth, history suggests that if the Americans deploy ET, the Russians will soon follow suit. ET fans suggest that this wouldn't matter. The virtue of ET, they say, is that it would benefit the defense more than the offense. But would it?

In 1977, Richard Burt, a young American analyst working in London (he subsequently became assistant secretary for European affairs in the State Department under Reagan, and later U.S. ambassador to West Germany), wrote an incisive paper pointing out that although ET might make land harder for an enemy to take, it might also make land—once taken—harder to regain. (He was assuming, of course, that the systems could be made to work effectively.) Burt also noted that if we move into an age of "one shot, one kill," in which conventional rockets unerringly find their targets, would not be good for NATO, since it has fewer weapons platforms to lose than does the Warsaw Pact.

ET, therefore, is as unlikely as the Divad gun or any of the Pentagon's other magical creations to transform the conventional balance in Europe or anywhere else. It would also create political problems for the Europeans, who are uncomfortable with the notion of beginning a war by launching a deep strike into enemy territory. The implications are stark. Attempts to solve the problem of conventional weakness through technology alone seem doomed to failure. What is more, they condemn the NATO alliance in Europe to what is becoming a more and more implausible strategy—the threat to use nuclear weapons first in order to stave off conventional defeat.

PART TWO

THE DILEMMA OF NATO'S NUCLEAR DOCTRINE

"Everything about the atomic bomb is overshadowed by the twin facts that it exists and that its destructive power is fantastically great."

—*Bernard Brodie,*
in The Absolute Weapon

7

Battlefield
Nuclear Weapons

If there is one episode that should have been seminal in the history of the U.S. nuclear policy, it came in the autumn of 1961. That, to borrow a phrase used at the time by the then national security adviser McGeorge Bundy, was America's "moment of thermonuclear truth."

Throughout 1961 a crisis had been building over West Berlin, the tiny allied enclave in East Germany that had long been a source of contention between the superpowers. On January 6, 1961, Soviet Premier Nikita Khrushchev raised the stakes. In a saber-rattling speech, he declared that "wars of liberation" would be supported by the Communists "wholeheartedly and without reservation," and warned that the occupation of West Berlin by America, Britain, and France could not continue. "These powers," he said, "cannot fail to realize that sooner or later the occupation regime in that city must be ended. . . . And should they balk, then we will take resolute measures. . . ."

Six months later, Khrushchev repeated his determination to end the division of Berlin at a summit meeting with President Kennedy in

Vienna, effectively threatening war if America resisted. Throughout the summer, tension mounted. Kennedy gave a dramatic televised speech about the dangers menacing Western freedom in Berlin; Khrushchev, who had apparently concluded from the Vienna summit that Kennedy was weak and lacked the will to resist, continued to increase the pressure. In the early hours of August 14, Soviet troops occupied the border between East and West Berlin and, with brick and barbed wire, began building what was to become known as the Berlin Wall.

In Washington, the Kennedy administration prepared for war. Everyone knew that if the Russians decided to occupy West Berlin and cut it off from the West, it would be immensely hard to prevent the seizure solely through the use of conventional weapons. West Berlin, after all, was in Soviet territory. So though Kennedy made plans to increase dramatically the size of the U.S. Army, Navy, and Air Force, the chances were that a war over Berlin would go nuclear.

In the light of this, Kennedy's defense secretary, Robert McNamara, reviewed existing plans for nuclear use. The official contingency plan for dealing with Berlin, the Joint Chiefs of Staff told him, called for sending a few brigades down the autobahn from West Germany to Berlin, and then, if Warsaw Pact troops resisted them, launching a huge, all-out nuclear strike. But as Fred Kaplan has documented in his book *The Wizards of Armageddon,* the crude thinking enshrined in this plan was refined during the summer of 1961 into something much more precise by one of McNamara's aides, Carl Kaysen. Working from the latest information about the Soviet nuclear arsenal (which revealed that the Russians at the time had only four operational intercontinental missiles, far fewer than anyone thought, only a few bombers capable of reaching the United States, and a small number of nuclear-armed submarines), Kaysen and a small task force did a detailed study on the possibility of a disarming "counterforce" strike. They decided that such a strike could be pulled off "with high confidence."

At the time, America was still vastly superior to the Soviet Union in nuclear strength. And according to Kaysen, if it came to war, the United States would be able to knock out most of the Soviet nuclear forces before they could be used. There was, however, one problem. Even under the Kaysen plan, some Russian nuclear weapons would survive. Indeed, it was calculated that Soviet retaliation could kill at least 2 to 3 million Americans (in the best case), and as many as 10 to 15 million (in the worst case). What's more, Europe would be left desperately vulnerable to a strike from Soviet short-range missiles. The Soviets had hundreds of these, and knocking out most, let alone all of them, would be impossible. As a result, the number of European fatalities was likely to be in "the low tens of millions."

In the abstract, the Kaysen plan might have made sense: the Soviet Union would lose (in the sense that it would end up much worse off than America). Certainly, its nuclear arsenal would be wiped out once and for all; and Western losses, as worked out in the cold statistical world of nuclear planners, might be considered "acceptable." But to leaders faced with a real crisis in the real world of political decision making, the plan seemed horrifying. Kennedy and his Cabinet balked. To students of Western nuclear strategy, it was a revealing moment. As Fred Kaplan observed: "If ever in the history of the nuclear arms race, before or since, one side had unquestionable superiority over the other, one side truly had the ability to devastate the other's strategic forces . . . the autumn of 1961 was that time. Yet approaching the height of the gravest crisis that had faced the West since the onset of the Cold War, everyone said: 'No.' "

Among those aghast at the notion of a nuclear strike was Defense Secretary McNamara. He remembers a meeting, as the crisis reached its climax, with the British chief of staff, Admiral of the Fleet Lord Louis Mountbatten. Mountbatten, during a trip to Washington, was invited by McNamara to visit him in his third-floor office in the Pentagon. Asked for his advice on Berlin, Mountbatten ran through a number of possible military options. When he had finished, McNamara said: "But you haven't mentioned nuclear weapons."

Mountbatten looked at him in disbelief. "Are you insane?" he asked.

The conversation left a deep impression on McNamara. As it turned out, the Berlin scare proved mercifully short-lived. The administration stood its ground (as it was to do in the Cuban missile crisis the following year), and Khrushchev backed down. But the question McNamara and other top Kennedy advisers had been forced to confront seemed to have profound implications for Western policy. If you

couldn't use nuclear weapons to defend Berlin—and their use, as
Mountbatten suggested, seemed to defy sanity—then when could you
use them? And if you couldn't use them *at all* (except in response to
a nuclear attack), then where did that leave Western military strategy,
which was then, and still is, predicated on the first use of nuclear
weapons?

McNamara now says that after this experience he became convinced that the first use of nuclear weapons could never be an option
for the West, no matter how grave the situation. He goes further. "In
long conversations with successive presidents—Kennedy and John-
son," he has written, "I recommended, without qualification, that they
never initiate, under any circumstances, the use of nuclear weapons. I
believe they accepted my recommendation."

Some of McNamara's former colleagues dispute this. They maintain that even if he gave such advice, which they doubt, it was not
accepted. But whether or not McNamara's recollection is accurate in
this respect, there is no doubt that he became rapidly concerned about
the implications of nuclear "first use." There is no doubt, too, that if
there was reason for concern then, there is much greater reason now.
Nuclear use looked far more plausible in the early 1960s than it does
in the mid-1980s.

Yet NATO still clings to a strategy that assumes that the West
is prepared, in certain circumstances, to be the first to press the nuclear
button. Because of their conventional weakness on the central front,
the argument goes, the Western powers have no alternative but to
threaten to unleash the unimaginable carnage of nuclear warfare to
stave off defeat on the battlefield. NATO has continued to stick with
this strategy despite the evidence that if war broke out no one, not the
Americans and not the Europeans, would want to see the threat imple-
mented.

In 1961, when Kennedy's Cabinet faced its "moment of thermonuclear truth," NATO's official nuclear doctrine was one of "massive retaliation." In theory, any Soviet conventional attack (in Europe
or elsewhere) would be met by automatic and massive retaliation by the
United States. Indeed, NATO's conventional forces on the central

front were seen only as a "trip wire" that, once broken, would unleash a tremendous nuclear assault on Soviet territory.

By 1961, however, massive retaliation was beginning to seem highly implausible. Indeed, it had begun to seem implausible even before the Berlin and Cuban crises concentrated official minds. The doctrine might have made sense in the very earliest days of the arms race, when the Soviet Union had no and then very few weapons of its own. But during the late 1950s and early 1960s that changed. If we could massively retaliate against the Soviets, it became clear, they could massively retaliate back. What had become a plan to "blow up Russia" was rapidly assuming the outlines of a plan to blow up the world.

So throughout the early and mid-1960s, pushed hard by McNamara, NATO struggled to find a replacement for "massive retaliation." Eventually, in 1967, after a bitter row within the alliance and the departure of France from the military structure, NATO settled for its current doctrine of "flexible response."[1]

Flexible response took it as given that the West could no longer hope to eliminate the Warsaw Pact's capacity to retaliate with one massive nuclear blow. Basically, it was a doctrine of minimal force: the alliance would use conventional weapons to resist an invasion, resorting to nuclear weapons only if the alternative was defeat. But though a less obviously suicidal doctrine than massive retaliation, flexible response failed to solve the essential dilemma: it anticipated using nuclear weapons in some *limited* way, but it continued to assume that the West would use them *first.* How could this be done? How did you use nuclear weapons in such a way as to prevent a war from escalating into an all-out nuclear exchange?

Even the three men who drafted the official document setting out the new doctrine—assistant defense secretary for NATO force planning Tim Stanley, General Gert Schmuckler of West Germany, and Sir Arthur Hockaday of the British Ministry of Defense—did not see

---

[1] In fact, NATO's formal adoption of doctrine, enshrined in a document called MC 14/3, lagged behind U.S. adoption of the same strategy by some six years.

it as more than a stopgap, a political compromise that everyone could accept until something more coherent was devised. They certainly felt that flexible response provided a less than perfect blueprint for fighting a war, and after completing the document, they repaired to a Brussels restaurant for dinner wondering if they would be fired for their plans. They weren't. Almost twenty years later, flexible response remains official NATO doctrine.

The best way to understand the dilemma of flexible response is to look first at the short-range, or "battlefield," nuclear weapons stockpiled on the central front in Europe. Because of their size and their proximity to the front line, these would almost certainly be the first to be used if a conventional conflict in Europe went nuclear.

With names like Long Tom (a 280-millimeter cannon), Honest John (artillery), and Matador and Regulus (early short-range cruise missiles), the first battlefield weapons began arriving on the Continent in the mid-1950s. They were made possible by developments in the accuracy of delivery systems and the creation, at nuclear weapons labs like Los Alamos in New Mexico, of small, low-yield warheads. According to John Foster Dulles, secretary of state under President Eisenhower:

> [The] resourcefulness of those who serve our nation in the field of science and weapon engineering now shows that it is possible to alter the character of nuclear weapons. It seems now that their use need not involve vast destruction and widespread harm to humanity. Recent tests point to the possibility of possessing nuclear weapons the destructiveness and radiation effects of which can be confined substantially to predetermined targets.

The hope was that battlefield nuclear weapons could be used to make up for NATO's conventional weakness. "If seventy divisions, for example, are needed to establish a conventional line of defense between the Alps and the Baltic," said General Alfred Gruenther, NATO's supreme allied commander, in a speech in Paris in January 1954, "then seventy minus X divisions equipped with atomic weapons are needed." The assumption, of course, was that X was a substantial number:

battlefield weapons were seen, quite simply, as bigger and better artillery.

Among those who believed strongly in battlefield weapons was physicist J. Robert Oppenheimer. Tormented by conscience after his work during World War II on the Manhattan Project, Oppenheimer had been struck by the crudeness of America's early plans for delivering nuclear weapons to the Soviet Union. The notion of dropping multimegaton weapons on cities, obliterating millions of civilians, appalled him, and tactical weapons at least appeared to offer a way of returning war to where it belonged: the battlefield. To many since, Oppenheimer's faith in battlefield weapons has come to seem a classic example of how the road to hell is paved with good intentions.

The central front in Europe is the most built-up area in the world. There are 4,000 towns and villages in West Germany alone, and much of the country has become a continuous urban sprawl—hence, the old NATO saying that the towns and villages of West Germany are less than 2 kilotons apart. Yet this is the area in which NATO, if it ever pushed the nuclear trigger, was contemplating fighting its nuclear battle.

The implications of using nuclear weapons in this environment were clear even in the 1950s. In 1955, NATO staged a war game in West Germany, the Low Countries, and northeastern France. For reasons of space, the game, code named Carte Blanche, was played on a north-south rather than on an east-west axis, but the casualty figures gave some indication of the fate that might be in store for Europe in the event of a real war. The weapons employed were bombs, dropped by aircraft. In all, the aircraft of the blue (NATO) and orange (Warsaw Pact) forces dropped 335 bombs on more than 100 military targets. German civilian casualties were estimated at 1.7 million killed and 3.5 million wounded, and that did not include the victims of radioactivity. Incredibly, the NATO hierarchy decided to publish the results of Carte Blanche in order to "reassure" people of NATO's determination to defend Europe. The reaction was widespread horror. In Britain and elsewhere the peace movement latched on to Carte Blanche as evidence of what they saw as the suicidal nature of NATO strategy; in Germany, politicians and public alike wondered whether NATO did not intend to blow up their country to save it. No one, in short, was reassured. And a year later, in an article that the State Department considered too sensitive for publication, General Maxwell Taylor noted: "In Europe, we have some 250,000 soldiers accompanied by thousands of dependents living in close proximity to superior communist forces deployed in the satellite countries. If the latter suddenly advanced west without warning, they would soon be locked in close combat with the NATO armies in such a way as to restrict the employment of atomic weapons against them."

Another American general, James Gavin, concluded after a series of war games carried out with his Seventh Army Corps that because nuclear war fighting would be so destructive, "more rather than less manpower would be required to fight a nuclear war successfully"— battlefield weapons, in other words, were no compensation for conventional weakness.

Under the old doctrine of "massive retaliation," however, this kind of logic scarcely seemed to matter. Little serious thought was given to the precise way in which battlefield weapons might be used. They would simply be fired, along with everything else, as part of the all-out strike that NATO contemplated in the event of war in Europe.[2]

It was only after the introduction of flexible response, in 1967, that battlefield weapons suddenly fell under the spotlight. Now NATO had to contemplate precise, flexible nuclear strikes in the event of conventional defeat. What was envisaged was a "ladder of escalation" under which NATO, if it faced an overwhelming breakthrough on the battlefield, would first mount a relatively small nuclear strike; if that failed to halt the enemy, it would then raise the stakes by authorizing a larger strike; finally, if all else failed, the awesome power of America's strategic arsenal—the intercontinental rockets and bombers based on the American mainland and the nuclear-firing submarines hidden beneath the seas—would be invoked.

The crucial rung of the ladder, however, was the first one, the one

---

[2]Purists might point out that in 1957 the United States *did* introduce a small degree of flexibility into its strike plan by dividing massive retaliation into two phases: in the first, NATO would fire its battlefield weapons; if that didn't work, there would be an all-out strategic attack on the Soviet Union.

comprised of battlefield weapons, of which NATO had almost 7,000 in place when flexible response was unveiled in 1967. These weapons —artillery shells, rockets, and bombs—were actually stationed on the central front. They would be used first because they were relatively small and low-yield, because they would offer the best hope of keeping a war "limited," and because, being near the front line, they might have to be used before the troops possessing them were overrun.

When NATO began to look in detail at the potential uses of battlefield weapons in the late 1960s and early 1970s, the concerns of such generals as Maxwell Taylor and James Gavin came to seem very prescient. However NATO contemplated going nuclear, at whatever stage in the battle, it was hard to see how it would benefit—and how it could avoid risking the destruction of the very prize it sought to save, namely, Western Europe.

In a series of secret studies carried out between 1968 and 1974, the alliance grappled with the difficulties of using nuclear weapons. The studies were conducted by the Nuclear Planning Group, a special committee set up by McNamara in response to European demands for a greater say in nuclear policy making. An early attempt by Washington to achieve this end by creating a so-called "multilateral nuclear force" (MLF) had failed dismally, and the Nuclear Planning Group emerged, essentially, out of the ashes of the MLF.[3] To an extent the Nuclear Planning Group was, and is, a public relations exercise—a means of keeping the nonnuclear allies, especially the West Germans, happy. Nevertheless, the NATO studies represent an exhaustive attempt to think through precisely how nuclear weapons might be used. The

---

[3]The multilateral force was an elaborate scheme dreamed up by the State Department. The idea was to give NATO a force of 25 surface ships equipped with 200 Polaris missiles and manned by crews from several member countries (each of whose governments would have to agree before any missiles could be fired). It sounded grand, but there were too many snags: the cost, the vulnerability of the ships, the exact composition of the fleet. Above all, there was the question of command and control. How would the release procedure work? Who would give the orders? How could it be done quickly enough? The idea was shelved in December 1964.

intention was to provide a clear set of political guidelines for Western leaders should they ever be faced with the awesome decision to cross the nuclear threshold.

Not surprisingly, such guidelines proved difficult to write. European ministers and officials, led by British Defense Secretary Denis Healey, were from the outset firm in their belief that it was pointless to plan to *win* a "theater" nuclear war in Europe. And what worried them was that the Pentagon and the strike planners at SHAPE—the Supreme Headquarters, Allied Powers, Europe, now based at Mons, Belgium—appeared to be planning exactly that.

The Nuclear Planning Group undertook two sets of studies—one on "initial use," and another, even more detailed, on "follow-on use" (i.e., what NATO might do if the Warsaw Pact kept coming after one side or the other had "gone nuclear"). Both studies made it abundantly clear that the idea of NATO benefiting from massive use—and of "winning" nuclear wars in Europe—was a fantasy. In almost no circumstances, the studies suggested, would the alliance reap *military* gains from using nuclear weapons.

The reasons for this were simple enough. No nuclear strike, however massive, would be able to remove the Soviet capacity for an equally massive counterstrike. And even a small, selective strike aimed at a handful of military targets raised all kinds of problems. There was, in the first place, no guarantee that the Soviets would play by the same rules. What if they simply responded, even then, with a massive counterstrike—precisely what Western intelligence anticipated they *would* do (at least during the 1960s and 1970s)? But that did not illustrate the full extent of the problem, for suppose the Soviets merely responded in kind—the minimum assumption NATO could make. In other words, say NATO exploded two or three warheads over a Soviet armored division, and the Soviets did the same over a Western division. Would NATO then be better off?

The answer, it soon became clear, was that it would not. Even after an *equal* exchange of nuclear fire, NATO would end up worse off than the Warsaw Pact. NATO, after all, is conventionally the weaker side. In a war it would start with fewer soldiers and fewer tanks. If, in a nuclear exchange, both sides lost the same amount of men and equipment, then the odds against NATO would have worsened. (If you start with ten men, and your opponent with twenty, and each of you loses five, then the odds against you have lengthened from two to one to three to one.) There were other difficulties. NATO would probably be firing at well-dispersed Soviet troops, while the Soviets would be firing at Western troops retreating into an ever more crowded area. The Soviets would have an easier task getting reinforcements to the battlefield than NATO—theirs are able to approach by land, while the bulk of NATO's, those from America, have to cross 3,000 miles of ocean. Finally, NATO's key assets—ports, airfields, military storage and communications facilities, and the like—are much closer together and more vulnerable than the Warsaw Pact's. Thus, in military terms, going nuclear would not help the alliance; it would hinder it. The use of nuclear weapons would actually accelerate defeat. By crossing the nuclear threshold, NATO would *lose faster* than if it stuck to conventional weapons. That is the dilemma of flexible response.

There were, it must be acknowledged, a few isolated scenarios in which nuclear use looked more feasible. If the Warsaw Pact, for example, attempted to take, say, Norway or Denmark by sea, then NATO might be able to detonate a nuclear weapon or two over the beachhead. In such an instance, the theory went, the act of aggression would be so distinct—and the use (perhaps of only one weapon) so clear in its purpose—that the risk of escalation might be worth running. Unless NATO was staging an amphibious landing elsewhere—an unlikely eventuality—then the Soviets would be hard pressed to respond in kind.

Attacking a beachhead was a rare exception, however. In almost every other scenario, the Nuclear Planning Group found that the military gains to be derived from going nuclear first—assuming an equivalent Soviet response—would be temporary and illusory, that the dangers of the strike leading to rapid and possibly uncontrolled escalation would be severe.

The conclusion that NATO drew from its studies was that the only purpose of going nuclear first would be to send a "political signal" to the Soviets. By going nuclear, NATO would not be trying to *win* in a military sense, it would merely be trying to show that it was determined not to *lose*. It would, thus, deliberately, and in the face of terrible dangers of escalation, raise the stakes to demonstrate to the

Kremlin that its actions had become unacceptable and to signal that NATO was not prepared to surrender.

In this context, one of the options the officials examined was the "demonstration shot," the nuclear age equivalent of firing a shot across the enemy's bow. This would be accomplished by exploding one or more warheads over an uninhabited area (the Black Sea, the Baltic, the Polar icecap—a strong contender—or some deserted area in the Ukraine). That way, some argued, you could demonstrate unity and resolve without taking the awful step of killing thousands, perhaps millions, of people. (The idea of such a warning shot first emerged in 1945, when some of President Truman's advisers had suggested that this might be all that was required to force the Japanese to surrender; in the event, because the United States only possessed two bombs, and because a warning shot might fail to have the desired effect, the idea was rejected.)

Firing a pure demonstration shot was heavily debated as a possible option for NATO. But it was hard to see how it would help. After all, if the United States exploded a weapon over the Baltic, what was to stop the Soviets from doing the same? If they did, wouldn't NATO be left in exactly the same position as it had been before pressing the button? And might not a pure demonstration shot show *weakness* rather than strength, *cowardice* rather than courage? By blowing up nothing, NATO might give the impression it lacked the nerve to go through with a real attack, and instead of deterring further aggression from the Russians, it might actually *encourage* swift and terrible retaliation. The Americans argued strongly and successfully against purely demonstrative use in the Nuclear Planning Group. Indeed, one of the few positive conclusions from the series of NATO studies was that "purely demonstrative use would demonstrate only inadequate resolve."

The compromise NATO came up with was a demonstration shot (or shots) that nonetheless inflicted damage on the enemy. A strike against a military target, in other words, executed not in the hope of securing military advantage so much as to convince the enemy to back off. Through this "militarily meaningful demonstration of resolve," NATO would try to walk the tightrope between the danger of rapid escalation and the need to avoid defeat. It was not a very happy compromise, but if flexible responses were to be credible at all, then the alliance, as one NATO official has put it, would simply have to attempt "the balancing act between the need to convey an adequate signal while limiting the risks of escalation."

The studies of the late 1960s and early 1970s (they were concluded in 1974) remain the basis of NATO's battlefield nuclear doctrine. They represent an exhaustive but ultimately unsatisfactory attempt by the alliance to come to grips with the problem of nuclear use.

It may be worthwhile, at this point, to make my own position clear. I do not advocate that all battlefield nuclear weapons be withdrawn from Europe. It is at least arguable that during peacetime they boost deterrence; that if they were all to be removed, the Russians would probably become *more* rather than *less* confident that they could get away with an attack on Western Europe. Equally, a limited number of battlefield systems help tie America into the defense of Europe and increase the "hostage effect" of the 300,000 U.S. troops stationed on the central front. But in the light of the NATO studies, it seems unnecessary to have the potential battlefield so chock-full of nuclear weapons, and though there are now fewer than there were when the arsenal reached its peak in the late 1960s—some 5,000 compared with 7,000—there are still more than can conceivably be justified for the purposes of deterrence or very limited use. The NATO studies showed all too clearly that nuclear war fighting would be both futile and suicidal. (Indeed, when, in the mid-1970s, the Pentagon began to suggest that developments in technology—smaller, "cleaner" warheads, precision-guided munitions, etc.—might change the picture, the Europeans argued, forcefully, that these developments did nothing of the kind.)

The vital point to be made concerns nuclear first use. I see little purpose in NATO declaring outright that it would *not* go nuclear first —a policy now advocated by some eminent former officials, among them the Americans McNamara, McGeorge Bundy, George Kennan, and Gerard Smith, as well as Britain's Lord Carver. The Russians would be unlikely to believe such a pledge, and though it might reassure the Western public, it would also undermine deterrence. I accept, too, that if you *do* have nuclear weapons on the battlefield, you have to have some sort of idea as to how and when you might use them. Deterrence, after all, implies a concept of possible use—and to that extent, the NATO studies in the early 1970s were clearly useful.

The fact is, however, that trying to compensate for conventional weakness with battlefield weapons—and planning to go nuclear *first*—is steadily coming to seem more and more incredible.

Consider, for a moment, the idea of "demonstrating resolve." Defenders of flexible response argue that this remains plausible. An automatic escalation to all-out war is by no means certain, they say, and the initial use of nuclear weapons, breaching a barrier that has held since 1945, might so horrify both sides that they would recognize an overwhelming common interest in composing their differences. According to the private assessment of one official who has played a key role in developing NATO strategy, the human reaction would be to do everything to avoid escalation. Neither side, he says, would want it; both would be appalled at what was going on, both would be desperately looking for signs that the other was ready to call a halt. Besides, it is argued, the Soviet Union would have attacked Western Europe on the assumption that NATO would *not* go nuclear. If NATO did, then that judgment would of course be shown to be flawed. The Soviet Union would know that if it responded to Western first use, it too would have to worry about escalation. It might decide that, after all, it was running too great a risk, and that retreat might make more sense than risking the consequences of further advance. The stake the two sides had in the conflict, after all, would not be equal. The West would be defending its homeland, its very existence, and everything vital to it; the Russians would not. They might, thus, have less resolve to continue upping the stakes than the West.

I may not be doing full justice to those who make this case. But this is the gist of it: you can't fight wars with nuclear weapons, but you can use them to stop yourself from losing—and if Europe is threatened by invasion, it must be prepared to do that, or to accept defeat.

The argument, however, makes some heroic assumptions. A conscious decision to initiate nuclear use would take extraordinarily strong nerves. It would also require a brave guess about what the Soviets might do in return. For if they did decide to decimate Europe, where would that leave NATO? If, amid the confusion of war, with its stresses, anger, and desire for revenge, the Soviets decided to respond to Western first use *in a limited way,* then, as we have seen, NATO would be worse off than it had been before going nuclear. And having taken the awful gamble of invading Europe in the first place, the chances would seem to be at least even that this is just what the Soviets would do. In the light of this, it would seem a risk that European governments would not wish to run—for fear of losing their continent.[4] Indeed, Lord Carver, former chief of Britain's defense staff, argues that "it would be criminally irresponsible for any Western leader to initiate a nuclear strike on the assumption that the Soviet Union either would not answer back in kind or would do so to such a limited degree that we could regard it as acceptable within whatever were our war aims."

With some justice, therefore, NATO's strategy has been likened to contemplating burning down your house to get rid of a burglar.

The struggle to make flexible response credible has continued, however. Analysts such as Colin Gray, an expatriate Englishman who advises the Pentagon, argue that NATO needs to develop a more serious "war fighting" posture. They believe that with better civil defense and much stronger, larger, and better-protected nuclear forces, the alliance could hope to call the shots in a nuclear battle with the Warsaw Pact. But the West was in a position to call the shots in the early 1960s, when it was clearly superior to the Pact, and even then it could not have saved Europe from destruction in a nuclear war. Moreover, any beefing up of the Western battlefield arsenal would instantly be matched by the Russians. And plans for waging a nuclear battle in Europe are unlikely ever to command much favor among the people who live there.

Yet the Pentagon has attempted to make battlefield weapons more accurate and more "controllable" in the hope of making bat-

---

[4]It might be argued, of course, that NATO would be losing it anyway. Conventional defeat, however, might not be irrevocable; nuclear defeat almost certainly would be.

tlefield nuclear use seem more plausible. A classic example is the neutron bomb.

The neutron bomb is tailored for use on the central front. It is designed to cause less "collateral" damage than a traditional nuclear explosion, and to be more effective in the builtup environment of the central front.[5] In a traditional nuclear device, the neutrons released by the original explosion are "checked" by a layer of uranium; it is the interaction between neutrons and uranium that generates the enormous destructive power. In the neutron bomb, the neutrons, instead of being checked by the uranium, are simply allowed to escape. The resulting blast and heat, though fearsome, are reduced by a factor on the order of two and a half. Within a limited radius, however, the neutron radiation effect is ten times as strong, making it just as deadly to life. Thus a 1-kiloton neutron bomb would kill people over as wide a radius as a 10-kiloton fusion weapon, though there would be far less blast, heat, and radioactive fallout. In a nutshell, the effect on human life (per kiloton) would be more lethal; the effect on buildings and other hardened structures, less so.

The neutron bomb has had a controversial history. It was given the go-ahead by President Gerald Ford; then, after its existence became known and widely publicized in 1977, President Jimmy Carter suspended production. Four years later, Carter's decision was overturned by Ronald Reagan. The neutron bomb, however, is not likely to make nuclear war fighting in Europe seem any more plausible than it is now. The Pentagon argues that in case NATO ever reaches the point where nuclear weapons have to be used, it is better to be armed with modern effective weapons rather than with products of the 1950s. Critics, however, question the potential effectiveness of the neutron bomb. Given that it would not destroy tanks themselves, how could you be sure that their crews had been killed, rather than just temporarily stunned or blinded? In any case, wouldn't the neutron bomb make it easier to cross the nuclear threshold, thus paving the way for the very "dirty" weapons everyone fears using?

---

[5]In particular, it is designed to kill military personnel in armored vehicles. Except at close range, radiation is much more effective against armor than heat and blast.

But whether or not these argument are convincing, the real problem with the neutron bomb is the problem facing anyone contemplating nuclear use in Europe. As fast as scientists develop supposedly more "usable" weapons, so the battlefield on which they would be used becomes more crowded. Every year the area suitable for armored combat in Germany gets smaller. The area between Bonn and the Hook of Holland, for example, has almost become one gigantic urban region, 250 miles long, and if a war broke out, much of the combat in open spaces would take place in West Germany's national parks. Even the Fulda Gap, scene of hundreds of simulated Warsaw Pact invasions, is no longer a gap at all; it has been all but filled by the sprawling city of Fulda.

Undoubtedly, in a war, the Soviets would seek to exploit this. Simply by advancing along main roads, and keeping close to cities, they would make it especially hard for NATO to use nuclear weapons against them. The main routes of advance would inevitably run through the main suburban sprawl of West Germany and past its major cities. Thus, the least provocative kind of nuclear use NATO could imagine—striking Warsaw Pact targets on the actual battlefield (that is, on West German soil)—would be next to impossible. Even a neutron bomb used close to a city might save the buildings, but it would not spare the inhabitants.

Not for nothing, then, has it been said that using nuclear weapons first on the battlefield would be potentially suicidal. Yet military planners continue to devise scenarios for it. Indeed, in trying to assess the results of a nuclear conflict in Europe, the Pentagon has come to depend more and more on computer simulations; the results of these, according to one Pentagon adviser, suggest that the level of casualties could be contained to a far lower level than the millions who "died" during the Carte Blanche exercise in 1955. But, as this source also points out, the computer simulations are utterly unrealistic.

"Were NATO to engage a conventional attack with nuclear fire," he says, "it would have to drop the warheads so as not to destroy its own armies, and 'in between' moving refugee columns and cities in West Germany, amidst an environment of false target location reports, mistakes, human fatigue, and command authorization breakdowns on both sides." The computer simulations, however, "treat Soviet forces as automata who cross into West Germany and advance directly into NATO nuclear killing zones. Here they are detected and destroyed by the lowest-yield nuclear weapon capable of doing the job. Command and control difficulties, confusion, false targeting, and other problems are simply assumed away." The Red Army, in other words, becomes a strategic dummy that allows military planners to justify an implausible strategy.

So much for the theory. What would happen in practice? Suppose the Russians attacked Western Europe, and NATO began to lose. Would an American president "push the button"? Or would he decide the risks were simply too great?

General Bernard Rogers, in his role as NATO's supreme commander, has said that he might need to seek "release authority" for nuclear weapons on the central front within forty-eight hours of a Soviet attack. Within that short space of time, he believes, NATO might have "its back to the nuclear wall."

What he means is this. Within two days, the Red Army might be poised for a critical breakthrough on at least one point in the NATO front line. Precisely where would depend on where the Russians chose to concentrate their forces. From that point on, Rogers would wish to have at least the *option* of using nuclear weapons to stop them.

The mechanism for "going nuclear" is complicated. In theory, all NATO states must be consulted—not easy, given the problems of communicating with fifteen or so governments in their capitals or bunkers in the high confusion of battle. The communication would be channeled through the NATO council, composed of permanent representatives, or ambassadors, meeting in permanent session in a secret site, probably in Belgium. But in practice, the decision would come down to the nation supplying the nuclear weapons (almost certainly the United States), and the nation in which they would be exploded (almost certainly West Germany).

The recommendation to "go nuclear" might come first from a divisional headquarters unable to hold a strategically vital gap in the hills. It would then pass up the NATO military chain to the supreme allied commander. If he endorsed it, the final authorization—and precise target or targets—would probably be agreed jointly by three men:

SACEUR, the American president, and the German chancellor. But in reality, even if the German chancellor objected, the American president would still be able to go ahead if he so decided.

So what would an American president decide? Almost certainly, he would receive conflicting advice from his aides. On the one hand, he would be under enormous pressure to use nuclear weapons because thousands, probably tens of thousands, of American soldiers would be dying in Europe, and because the loss of Western Europe would constitute, to put it mildly, the most staggering foreign policy defeat ever inflicted on America. (As one official put it, losing Europe would scarcely help him get reelected.) On the other hand, any president would be acutely conscious of the dangers of escalation—and that going nuclear in Europe might lead inevitably to the destruction, not just of Europe, but of America and the rest of Western civilization as well. As the Australian nuclear expert Desmond Ball and others have shown, no one knows how a nuclear war might be stopped once started. So the pressures on a president to be cautious—and avoid nuclear use —would be considerable, perhaps overwhelming. In the view of one Pentagon official well versed in these matters, the president might seek to compromise, using the "hot line" to warn the Soviet leader that unless the Warsaw Pact ceased its aggression—and ceased killing American soldiers—he would be forced to use nuclear weapons. He would stress, however, that he would use these only in Europe—providing the Russians did not strike America, he would authorize no strikes on the USSR. But even this option would leave open the danger of escalation and would hardly be a comforting one for the West Europeans.

Yet there is a chance that a nuclear war might start in Europe whether or not the U.S. president wanted it to. The argument, it must be stressed, is highly controversial and fiercely disputed by many in the Pentagon. But some nuclear experts, in and out of government, believe the current organizational arrangements that underpin flexible response make it fairly likely in themselves that, if a conflict began in Europe, nuclear weapons would be used.

The warheads for battlefield nuclear weapons are stored at special sites in Western Europe, known as "igloos." There are about a hundred in all, scattered across the Continent, though mainly in West Germany. Before any nuclear device can be fired, it has to be "married up" to its warhead, so before the West could use battlefield weapons, the warheads would have to be distributed from their igloos to field commanders. Some of these would go to American commanders, others to European ones, under a "dual key" arrangement (the Americans possessing the warheads, the Europeans the means of delivery).

The question of when this distribution should take place would be bitterly debated within the alliance. The act would undoubtedly be spotted by the Russians, and an early decision to undertake it might provoke the very crisis everyone was desperately seeking to avoid. Nevertheless, it would probably happen. During the Polish crisis in 1980, when it seemed as if the Russians were poised to invade Poland, Bernard Rogers sought and got the predelegated authority to distribute the warheads if he believed the situation serious enough to warrant it. That authority, apparently, has never been rescinded. And Rogers would want to distribute the warheads early. The storage igloos would be prime targets during a war, and the Soviets would clearly wish to destroy them (conventionally) before the warheads were moved. SACEUR would be intent on ensuring that did not happen.

The possession of warheads is not in itself enough, however, to permit a nuclear strike. Modern battlefield weapons are controlled by an electrical device known as a Permissive Action Link (PAL). Essentially, this is a means of activating an individual warhead by punching into it a special code. The codes are different for each system and are naturally kept closely guarded. But though tight control of the codes is clearly a sensible precaution in peacetime—it lessens the chances of terrorists being able to use nuclear weapons and of commanders being able to launch World War III on their own—it would pose horrendous problems in war. As former Pentagon adviser Paul Bracken has shown in a detailed study, the difficulties of relaying the right code to the right field commander in war might prove insuperable. Bracken believes, therefore, though the Pentagon denies it, that the codes would probably be distributed along with the warheads—thus making it theoretically possible for commanders in the field to launch their weapons once a war had started. The field commanders, of course, would not have the predelegation to fire, only the means of doing so. They would be told that their weapons were not to be used until they were given specific verbal instructions.

Those launch instructions might never come. Nonetheless, the danger of nuclear war would be intensified. With their communications network disrupted, and NATO forces split into "islands of force" —separated from each other and unaware of the broader picture around them—NATO commanders might assume that their colleagues were dead (not to mention their families) and simply decide to press the button. Once one weapon was fired, the situation could quickly escalate and get irretrievably out of hand. As Bracken puts it: "If there is an ambiguous or even a rumored delegation of authority, the likelihood of a frenzied orgy of pulling every trigger possible should not be discounted."

The dangers of NATO's current strategy are thus clear. Even if politicians decide, in a crisis, that the risks of first use are too great to run, the arrangements regarding distribution and release of nuclear weapons are deeply unsatisfactory, and could provoke decisions that would make first use extremely likely. And while there may be little point in NATO declaring, outright, that it would *not* go nuclear first in a war, basing an entire strategy around first use—planning for it, and filling the battlefield with weapons that might make it hard to avoid —is foolhardy. It is, however, the price that NATO has elected to pay by failing to provide itself with an effective conventional defense. Indeed, conventional weakness has led the West to some extraordinary contortions in the effort to make the nuclear threat continue to seem credible, as we shall see in the next three chapters.

8

Strategic Weapons

America's strategic nuclear weapons are the foundation stones of alliance security. They now constitute an arsenal of colossal power, able to blow up the Soviet Union and its satellites not once, or even twice, but several times over. They come in a variety of guises: bombs carried on some 300 intercontinental bombers; land- and sea-based missiles, which carry between them over 7,000 warheads; and since the early 1980s, a rapidly growing arsenal of air- and sea-launched cruise missiles.

It is not easy for the lay observer to understand why so many bombs are needed, still less to follow the twists and turns of modern nuclear strategy, with its baffling worst-case scenarios and impenetrable jargon. At times, the logic of modern nuclear planners would do credit to the theologians of the Middle Ages, with their proverbial tortuous debates about how many angels could fit on the head of a pin.

I believe that much of this logic is based on a false premise, that the nuclear debate is in danger of losing touch with reality, and that much of the pressure producing the West's swollen strategic nuclear arsenal in fact stems from the basic flaw in NATO's posture: its conventional weakness. With robust forces on the central front, it would be much harder to justify the degree of "overkill" currently present in the U.S. nuclear arsenal.

Broadly, what has happened is that American nuclear strategy has moved away from the notion of "pure" deterrence—in which the presumption was that a strike on the American mainland would result in the destruction of Russian civilization—toward infinitely more sophisticated notions of nuclear war fighting. The movement began under Robert McNamara in the 1960s. McNamara wondered whether it was either sensible or moral to target Russian cities: doing that, he reasoned, would simply invite a strike against *American* cities. But though he was the first to publicize the idea of a limited nuclear war, McNamara, as I have noted, shrank from its implications. He eventually settled for the concept of "assured destruction": if a war broke out, neither side be able to gain an advantage, and each would be able to destroy the other. We had become, as J. Robert Oppenheimer had anticipated, like "two scorpions in a bottle, each able to destroy the other, but only at the risk of losing his own life." In McNamara's judgment, the United States would be safe as long as it was capable of destroying, in retaliation to a Soviet strike, 20 to 25 percent of the Soviet population and 50 percent of its industrial capacity. If that could be achieved, the Soviet Union would simply cease to exist as a state. It would therefore have little incentive to start a nuclear war.

But since McNamara's day, plans for fighting a nuclear war have been steadily refined. The idea of "counterforce"—striking hardened targets (nuclear forces, leadership bunkers, and the like) rather than relatively "soft" ones, such as cities and industry—has gradually come to dominate American nuclear doctrine. It was boosted by two technological developments. The first was increased accuracy. With the development of inertial guidance systems for rockets in the 1960s and early 1970s, it became theoretically possible to deposit nuclear weapons very close to the spots at which they were aimed, thus making the destruction of hardened targets such as concrete missile silos seem a plausible goal.

The second crucial development was the advent of "MIRVing." MIRVs ("multiple independently targetable reentry vehicles") constituted a way of enormously multiplying the potency of strategic rocket forces. Instead of being able to deliver only one warhead with an individual rocket, MIRVing, begun in the early 1970s, made it possible to deliver several; the bus (or front end) of the rocket would release at precisely calculated intervals a series of MIRVs, each carrying a bomb, and each theoretically capable of falling on a predesignated target with an accuracy measured to a few hundred feet.

Thanks to heightened accuracy and MIRVing, strategic planners could develop targeting options that would have been unimaginable in the days of the old intercontinental bombers and crude first-generation rockets. Thus, James Schlesinger, the defense secretary in the early 1970s, developed a set of "limited nuclear options" for waging nuclear war—ways that the United States might attack the USSR, or respond to a limited Russian strike, that stopped short of the kind of all-out response that would invite all-out retaliation.

President Carter took this a step further, with his heavily leaked PD (presidential directive) 59, which required "American forces to be able to undertake the precise, limited nuclear strikes against military facilities in the Soviet Union, including missile bases and troop concentrations . . . [and] to develop the capacity to threaten Soviet political leaders in their underground shelters in a time of war." Finally, in 1982, it emerged that the Pentagon was planning for a "protracted" nuclear war, and that the purpose of the nuclear arms buildup was to put America into a position where, according to the *New York Times,* it could "prevail and be able to force the Soviet Union to seek the earliest termination of hostilities on terms favorable to the United States."

The notion of counterforce had been taken to ludicrous lengths and the idea of "prevailing" in a protracted nuclear war is nonsensical. To understand the thinking behind it we must glance first at the Russians. For the theories developed in the Pentagon have been developed in the name of deterrence, and the argument is often made that whatever Western planners may feel about nuclear war, the Russians take the idea of fighting one very seriously—and believe they can reach a position where they would be able to win.

*   *   *

It is true that Soviet military thinkers have indulged in some strange fantasies about nuclear war. The Soviet Union is a more militaristic society than the United States; some of its strategists appear to see nuclear war as no more than an extension of conventional war. Thus, it would appear that the Russians intend to go on fighting even after they have turned America into a radioactive desert. "Combat operations will continue for the purpose of the final defeat of the enemy on his own territory," reads one Soviet military manual, because "that side which manages during the first days of the war to penetrate more deeply into enemy territory naturally acquires the capability for more effectively using the results of its nuclear attacks and disrupting the mobilization of the enemy."

Soviet military manuals abound with nonsense like this, and military analysts have a point when they say that the Soviet Union does not think about deterrence in the way the West does. "There is profound error and harm," wrote Soviet General A. S. Milovidov in 1974, "in the disorienting claims of bourgeois ideologies that there will be no victor in a nuclear war."

But how seriously should we take this sort of thing? And how seriously should we take the huge Soviet missile buildup, and the concomitant emphasis on air and civil defense, which suggests to some that the Soviet Union is making plans to wage a protracted nuclear war and that it is only prudent for us to do the same? Was President Reagan right when he asserted that the Soviet Union believes it can fight and win a nuclear war?

Common sense alone suggests that the answer is no. If some senior Soviet military figures are as silly as Milovidov, there is no evidence that Soviet politicians are. As Leonid Brezhnev put it, rather self-righteously, in October 1981: "It is a dangerous madness to try and defeat each other in the arms race and to count on victory in nuclear war. I shall add that only he who has decided to commit suicide can start a nuclear war in the hope of emerging a victor from it. No matter what the attacker might possess, no matter what method of unleashing nuclear war he chooses, he will not attain his aims. Retribution will ensue ineluctably."

There is, of course, no sound reason for believing Brezhnev, any more than there is for believing General Milovidov. Except this: Brezh-nev is speaking the truth. Milovidov is not.

Besides, even if Soviet leaders once believed they could get into a position to fight and win a nuclear war, high-level Kremlin state-ments, at least since the late 1970s, suggest they now see things differ-ently. This could, of course, be propaganda. Without doubt there are still Soviet generals who believe in winning, just as there are American generals at the Strategic Air Command in Omaha who believe in winning, too. But many Soviet scholars are convinced that there is more to the change than propaganda. The Soviet leaders accept "a strategic nuclear balance between the Soviet Union and the United States as a fact," says Raymond Gartoff of the Brookings Institution, "and as the probable and desirable prospect for the foreseeable future."

It is not hard to see why. As Leon Wieseltier has pointed out in an excellent book called *Nuclear War, Nuclear Peace,* the Soviet Union may not like the notion of deterrence, but it acts on it. And it acts on it because it has no choice:

> Some of the Soviet Union's nuclear notions are evil, yes; but they are also absurd. What does it matter if they are making plans for after the apocalypse? The fantasies of seizing smoldering radio stations are fearful, but they are of no consequence. Nor is the fantasy of civilian defense. Shelters will not work wherever they are. They will save no one from a direct hit, or from the fallout of a direct hit, in Moscow or in Manhattan.

Russia's political leaders live in the real world. Whatever their generals tell them, they know that any kind of nuclear strike against America would almost certainly unleash a massive counterstrike that would not just kill them but blast their entire nation back to the Stone Age. Against that prospect, precise plans for limited counterforce strikes and protracted wars are meaningless.

To understand the kind of thinking that drives current nuclear strategy, and the extent to which it has drifted away from reality, we must look at one classic example of it, the idea of the "window of vulnerability," and the missile that idea spawned: the MX.

* * *

In the autumn of 1977, the Soviets began a series of missile tests at Tyuratam, a remote spot in the desert, west of the Aral Sea. The missiles were aimed at the lonely Kamchatka peninsula, 4,000 miles to the east, in the Pacific.

The United States was able to follow these tests closely. A satellite equipped with an infrared telescope and light sensor attuned to rocket firings monitored the take-offs; a network of radar stations, including two in Iran, followed the missiles in flight; and an air force Key Hole satellite (supposedly capable of detecting objects 8 inches long) photographed the dummy warheads as they landed. U.S. intelligence analysts, studying the data from the tests, concluded that the Soviets had made great strides in improving the accuracy of their missiles. In light of this, the CIA decided in mid-1978 that the U.S. land-based missile force could become vulnerable to a Soviet preemptive strike by as early as 1982. The development, said William J. Perry, a San Francisco businessman who served as the Pentagon's research-and-development chief during the Carter administration, "gave us a new sense of urgency, told us we were caught short."

At its baldest, the vision that had come to haunt Perry and the CIA was this: the Soviet Union was approaching a point where, by using a proportion of its own land-based missiles, it might be able to destroy as many as 90 percent of America's. This, it was thought, could put a U.S. president in an invidious position. The Americans, to be sure, would probably still have many, if not all, of their bombers (though bomber bases, too, might be struck in a crippling preemptive blow), and they would certainly have their submarines—the largest and most powerful part of the U.S. deterrent. But bombs and submarine-launched missiles, the theory went, would not be accurate enough to strike hardened military targets. Moreover, the Soviets would still have enough missiles left in reserve to discourage the United States from retaliating. Thus, according to the nightmare scenario, a U.S. president might face an awful choice: either retaliate—against Soviet cities—and thus invite a second devastating attack against his own, or surrender. That, in the fearful calculus of the nuclear planner, was the window of vulnerability that the new Soviet weaponry had opened.

It is important to grasp just what was being contemplated here. In the early 1980s, America's land-based missile force consisted of 52 aging liquid-fueled Titan rockets and 1,000 of the more modern solid-fuel Minutemen. Planners assumed that the Russians would have to target two warheads on each silo to be confident of success, meaning that a preemptive Soviet strike would have to involve hundreds of MIRVed missiles, each of which would have to work perfectly, depositing its warheads with pinpoint accuracy. Moreover, the Soviets would have to launch their attack knowing that the price of failure—and probably, as I will show, of success as well—would be the destruction of tens of millions of Russians. One only has to look at each step in the sequence to realize how unrealistic it is.

In the first place, Western intelligence has at best an imperfect idea of how accurate Soviet missiles are. Despite the sophisticated devices with which the CIA monitored the tests in 1977 and 1978, for example, they were unable to establish precisely what the missiles were being aimed at. Besides, Soviet missiles, in a war, would follow a very different trajectory than the one they follow during tests, exposing them to quite different geodetic, gravitational, and meteorological forces. Some Pentagon analysts deny that this would make a difference. The Russians, they say, put satellites in orbit over the pole, measure the geodetic forces, and then program their missiles accordingly (precisely what the United States does to complement its own east-to-west test shots from Vandenberg Air Force Base in California to Kwajalein atoll in the Marshall Islands). Moreover, say these analysts, the sheer size of the Russian warheads makes them "less sensitive" to this phenomenon, known as "bias." (The Russians go in for bigger warheads than the Americans, and would therefore, in the CIA's view, be able to make up in destructive power what they lack in accuracy.) Finally, it is said that both sides have carried out enough space flights to understand the magnetic bias of the poles.

This analysis, however, takes a decidedly optimistic view of Soviet capabilities. Even Soviet ICBM warheads would have to come within 400 to 600 feet of missile silos to destroy them, and scientists who study the upper layers of the atmosphere think bias could throw the Soviet warheads off by two or three times that distance. "It's our universal feeling that it's nearly impossible to have a passive object land a few hundred meters from the target," says Professor James Walker of the Atmospheric and Oceanic Studies Department at the University of

Michigan. "The Pentagon may not know how little we know about the upper atmosphere. The densities vary so radically and change so frequently that there is no way of knowing with any confidence how it will affect the trajectory of a reentry vehicle."

The Soviet warheads, in other words, would approach totally new targets on a totally untested flight path, be buffeted about in the multiple layers of the upper atmosphere, each layer having radically different densities and wind velocities—and yet still be expected to land within 400 feet of their target.

What's more, there seems little substance in the American claim that the "bias problem" has been solved. According to one weapons analyst who has seen the secret data from the American missile tests, "we just can't make it for counterforce. I've plotted the fall of the warheads, and few fall within the required radius." Like the Russians, the Americans would in wartime have to fire their missiles on a totally different trajectory than the one they use in peacetime tests. And even if, during a war, as one joke has it, the United States could blast the living daylights out of the Kwajalein atoll, their test target, that would be very different from striking precise targets in the Soviet Union.

But the great preemptive strike the Russians are thought capable of presumes something even more basic: it presumes that all, or at least most, of the actual rockets being used will *work*. That means (in each case) not just the fuses in the warheads, the computers and gyroscopes on the MIRVs, the release mechanism of the bus, and the delicate machinery in each stage of the rocket, but all the complicated electronic gear in the silo that monitors the status of the rocket, keeps it aligned on its target, and insures that it cannot be fired accidentally or without proper authorization. All this must function—perfectly—hundreds of times over, in perfect sequence. The unreliability of modern computer-controlled conventional weapons suggests this is unlikely.

In the 1970s, the U.S. Air Force tried four times to launch a Minuteman missile from an operational silo. On three occasions the missile didn't even manage to get above ground; on the fourth, it blew up shortly after takeoff. After these debacles, which the Pentagon says can be explained by modifications made to the missiles for test purposes, the air force decided to cut losses and chose to carry out all its tests from a launch pad at Vandenberg Air Force Base—a very differ-

ent proposition, and a good deal easier than launching from an underground silo. Even then, success was hardly guaranteed. "We had one
Minuteman we tried to launch every night for a year," Major Ron Peck
of the air force told the *Los Angeles Times* in 1984. And it is not just
warhead-carrying rockets that have problems. Weather and technical
difficulties force frequent postponements in all kinds of rocket launches, from the Atlases, which take satellites into space, to the shuttle.
"I'm always amazed when we launch anything at all," says Major Peck.

He noted that 100 people monitored a rocket launch, any one of
whom could cancel it. When controllers were less fussy about their
rockets, "a lot of them blew up." (The consequences of failing to take
adequate precautions appear to have been startlingly demonstrated in
the disaster that befell the Shuttle Challenger in January 1986.)

It is impossible to predict what would happen if America tried to
launch all its Minutemen in one carefully coordinated sequence. But
it is a fair bet that some would not get out of their silos, some would
blow up, and some would be plagued by mechanical problems en route
to their targets, which would cause their warheads to fall in quite
different patterns to the ones intended. In the 1970s, for example, it
was discovered that the electronic chips on which missile launches
depend tended to "burn out" after a few years of sitting in silos.
According to a technician in Silicon Valley, it took years before the
military understood this phenomenon, known as "purple plague." But
though purple plague has apparently since been cured, other circuitry
problems remain; one involves radiation given off by electronic packages inside the missile, which can "zap" the memory of the guidance
or communications systems. Others involve the computer software,
which is so complex that the only reliable way of "getting the bugs out"
is to test each individual package. For missiles sitting in their silos,
waiting for war, this is of course impossible. And in a massive launch
of ICBMs, new problems would almost certainly show up which no one
could possibly anticipate.

In the light of this, the chances of the United States being able
to execute a perfectly synchronized preemptive strike—supposing it
ever wished to do so—are very remote.

And if that is true for the United States, it is even more so for
the Soviets. Most Soviet rockets are still powered by liquid fuel, which

is both unreliable and dangerous. The old American Titan rockets, now virtual antiques, use liquid fuel, and they keep leaking or blowing up their silos. As the *New York Times* put it in December 1984: "Guaranteeing to launch even one of those on time, let alone a salvo, must give an engineer heartburn." In the 1960s, the Americans mastered the technology of solid fuel, whereby the fuel is inserted into the rockets in tightly compressed "blocks," and now the Soviets are catching up. Moreover, the liquid fuel they use in their huge SS-18 and SS-19 missiles is said to be less dangerous and more reliable than the type used in many of their older rockets. But the Soviets still lag behind the Americans in computer software, and will face the same problems as the United States in ironing out the bugs.

The more one examines the plausibility of a Soviet preemptive strike on U.S. missile silos—a kind of nuclear Pearl Harbor—the more fantastic it seems. Not only would the Soviets have to be sure they had solved the problem of bias (which they would not—and could not—be), and not only would they have to be sure that all their missiles would work (again, utterly impossible), but they would have to execute their strike with split-second timing so that incoming warheads did not blow each other up (a hazard known as fratricide). Moreover, they would have to do this without any kind of practice first. For the sake of argument, however, let us assume that a Soviet premier did consider the operation feasible. He would still be taking a greater gamble than any statesman in history had ever taken to order it carried out.

In the first place, how could he be confident that the United States would not "launch on warning"—that is, retaliate as soon as American spy satellites relayed to NORAD (the North American Air Defense Command at Colorado Springs) that Soviet missiles were on the way? After all, a preemptive strike would be a massively complex operation—and an American president would almost certainly get some warning of it (Soviet submarines putting to sea, intensified radio traffic, hectic activity at Soviet missile fields, movement of civilians, and so on). And if an American president suspected that his country was about to be struck, he could, after all, launch his own missiles immediately after the Russians had launched theirs. This would mean that the Russians would actually be disarming themselves by firing first, since their warheads would be on their way to hit, or miss, what by then would merely be empty holes in the ground. The Russian first strike would thus constitute a waste of warheads, while the American counterstrike could be directed so as to do damage to a whole range of more vulnerable Soviet military targets.

Admittedly, the president might only have about twenty minutes in which to make a terrifying decision, and U.S. policy, sensibly, is designed to avoid making the president dependent on having to "launch on warning"—a dangerous notion because it means going to war on the advice of a computer. But faced with such a dire contingency, "launch on warning" would be feasible—and perhaps likely. And the president would not even have to launch on warning. Almost 75 percent of American nuclear warheads, some 6,500 altogether, are not based on land at all but in submarines. These submarines, at least half of which are constantly on patrol, are invulnerable to a Soviet preemptive strike and would themselves be able to wipe out the Soviet Union several times over. A single modern Trident submarine, for example, carries 24 missiles with a total of 192 warheads, each one considerably more powerful than the bombs dropped on Hiroshima and Nagasaki. The theorists of the window of vulnerability say that submarine-launched missiles are relatively inaccurate (though this is also becoming less true), and that a president might be deterred from launching them by the prospect of a second Soviet strike. But even in a so-called surgical preemptive strike the Soviets would have killed millions of Americans. Some of America's missile fields are close to centers of population, and an attack on missile silos would cause considerable "fallout." Fallout occurs when the dust and debris thrown up by the blast is swept high into the air and carried by the prevailing winds until it descends as highly radioactive particles. Since an attack on missile silos would have to involve ground bursts—in order to cause maximum destruction—there would be considerable fallout.

Yet though 20 million or more Americans, in at least six states, might die from an attack on America's missile silos, the "window of vulnerability" scenario holds that a Soviet premier is expected to consider this insufficient provocation to persuade an American president to strike back. Only in the rarefied world of nuclear strategy, a world unencumbered by faulty valves, imperfect software, changeable weather, or human reaction, could such a scenario survive for long. For such a strike to become plausible, the Soviet Union would have to have fallen into the hands of desperate fanatics, who would be beyond deterrence. And were that situation to arise there is nothing the West could do that would be likely to make much difference.

There is one further, though more controversial, reason the window of vulnerability theory is absurd. No one knows what the effect on the planet would be of thousands of nuclear explosions occurring almost simultaneously, though recently some scientists have begun to speculate that it could be more dire than previously imagined. The reason is not so much the spread of nuclear fallout across the globe— as imagined by Nevil Shute in his 1960s essay in pessimism, the novel *On the Beach*—as of one of the simplest though often forgotten byproducts of nuclear weapons: smoke.

A nuclear holocaust would create firestorms ten, twenty, a hundred times worse than those that consumed Dresden and Hamburg in World War II, and these firestorms would create huge funeral pyres of smoke, billowing upward into the atmosphere. According to some scientists, the absorption into the atmosphere of billions of smoke particles could lead to the onset of a "nuclear winter" in which the light of the sun would be largely blotted out. Mankind, or what remained of it, would be condemned to live in permanent darkness, and temperatures, worldwide, would drop dramatically. So if the nuclear winter theory is correct—and no one knows whether it is or not—then the Soviet leaders who authorized a preemptive strike on the United States would at the same time probably be signing their own death warrants.

To be fair, plenty of U.S. politicians have pointed out the implausibility of the window of vulnerability. "It has never seemed realistic to me," testified Harold Brown, Jimmy Carter's defense secretary. The Soviets, he suggested, would have to be mad to risk their fate on such "a cosmic throw of the dice." Even the Joint Chiefs of Staff in 1980 acknowledged that "it does not seem likely that attainment of strategic parity or even an overall advantage by the Soviet Union foretells a realistic possibility of a Soviet 'bolt out of the blue' strategic attack."

But the Joint Chiefs of Staff continued to worry about the window of vulnerability. And the reason was not so much military as political: even if U.S. missiles were not vulnerable, the Soviets might *believe* they were. "A far more likely consequence [of the window of

vulnerability]," wrote the chiefs in 1980, "is that it will affect the
Soviet perception of the military balance in such a way that it will
embolden them to act with less restraint in international affairs . . .
and to exploit instability in the Third World when it occurs." This
view was to be echoed by Richard DeLauer, the research-and-
development chief in the Pentagon under Reagan, who told *Science*
magazine in April 1982: "The Soviets don't have to have a preemptive first strike. They just present the situation and say, look.
They marched into Afghanistan and what the hell was the best thing
we could do? We withdrew from their goddam Olympics. The last
time they tried to march in and put their missiles into Cuba, we got
their butt out of there. The Soviets don't have to pull the trigger.
They have superiority. They've got a deterrent and we don't, and
that's the window of vulnerability."

This, then, is the reason the fear of vulnerability has persisted so
long and runs so deep. The Soviets could not actually pull off a first strike,
but they could threaten to—and that's enough. The argument, however, makes little sense. Either the Soviets *are* able to mount a preemptive strike or they are *not*. If they *are*, then we are clearly in dire straits. If
they are *not*, then there would seem little point in fretting about the
consequences. It would seem clear from the evidence that they are not.
And if we can recognize the evidence, then it is fair to assume that the
Soviets are not so stupid as to be unable to do the same.

Underneath the tough talk from Richard DeLauer lies an appre-
hension that seems to stem more from an ideological fixation with
anti-communism than a sober assessment of the real world. How can
the Soviets "just present the situation and say, look" when there is no
"situation" to present? And how can DeLauer seriously compare Afghanistan to Cuba? The Soviet attempt to put missiles in Cuba directly
threatened U.S. national security; in the circumstances, Kennedy was
prepared to risk war to stop them, though even then the consequences
would have been devastating for both sides. In the case of Afghanistan,
there was no direct threat to U.S. security—as the Soviets knew. Besides, the Soviets could at least claim that Afghanistan fell into their
sphere of interest, and that their security was affected by the turbulence
just beyond their borders. This is not to justify the invasion. It is merely

to point out that the Soviets would probably have taken the same action in the 1960s if they had felt the situation demanded it—just as they defied the Yalta agreement to crush resistance in Eastern Europe in the 1940s and 1950s at a time when the United States had nuclear weapons and they did not.

The essential point is this: strategic nuclear weapons do not constitute usable units of force. They can have little value except to deter the use of other nuclear weapons and the notion that, at current levels, relatively small adjustments in the nuclear balance actually affect this is absurd. According to Stanley Hoffman, professor of history at Harvard University: "It is impossible to prove that the outcome of political conflict in the last thirty years has been determined by the exact ratio of strategic military forces. It is the relative importance of the stake to each side in every crisis which has been decisive."

Yet worries about the "political" effects of vulnerability, based on unreal calculations by strategic planners, have led the United States into a series of bizarre and ultimately futile attempts to "close" the window of vulnerability.

This effort amounted to a classic example of the Western habit of trying to find a technological "fix" that can't—and doesn't.

The hunt began in earnest, ironically enough, not under a hawkish administration, but during the presidency of Jimmy Carter, when the air force, alerted to the window of vulnerability, decided that the answer lay in a new missile with a "basing mode" which would insure against Soviet preemptive attack. The missile was the MX (for Missile Experimental), a rocket as tall as a six-story building, which would incorporate the latest in guidance systems and MIRV technology, and which would theoretically be able to fly from the American Midwest to, say, Vladivostok in a little under thirty minutes, and deliver nuclear warheads with an accuracy pinpointed to a few hundred feet.

The missile initially got the go-ahead under President Ford, but the problem was: how should it be based? Clearly, putting it in fixed silos would make no sense, since in the Pentagon's view these were now lined up like fish in a barrel. The idea was to find some form of basing mode that would remove the specter of vulnerability. This was easier said than done. But after examining over thirty schemes, the air force finally settled on one that they believed would work.

The scheme resembled a kind of space age version of hide and seek. It was a spectacularly ambitious enterprise. Had it come off, it would have been the greatest construction project ever, bigger than the Panama Canal, the Alaska pipeline, or the pyramids—bigger even than the Great Wall of China. It would have cost perhaps as much as $100 billion, and it would have transformed a sizable chunk of two western states—Utah and Nevada. Now in order to understand why Carter— a peaceful, essentially antinuclear president—came to bless a scheme he had once called the dumbest thing he had ever heard, it is necessary to embark on a brief digression.

In the early 1960s, after the crises over Cuba and Berlin had fueled concerns about nuclear war, the superpowers concluded a series of modest arms control agreements. These sought, among other things, to limit the spread of nuclear know-how to countries that did not already possess it, to prevent the placement of nuclear weapons in the Arctic or on the seabed, and to ban nuclear testing in the atmosphere. In the late 1960s, the superpowers began negotiations aimed at a more ambitious end—restricting the size and shape of each other's arsenals.

In 1972, these negotiations yielded two treaties, one of which restricted the deployment of so-called "antiballistic missile systems" (ABMs)—systems that would be able to shoot down offensive missiles —on the grounds that a defensive race would be costly, futile, and encourage an even faster offensive race. The second (the SALT I arms limitation treaty) set limits on the number of missiles each side could deploy. They were very high limits and they did little to slow down the arms race since both sides, by then, were busy MIRVing their missiles and the treaty did not restrict warhead numbers. But SALT I was intended simply as an interim measure, and once the negotiations were concluded both sides began another set of talks aimed at producing a second agreement.

It was the successful completion of a SALT II agreement that Jimmy Carter devoted considerable efforts to obtaining. By early 1980 it was complete, and the president went to Vienna to sign it with

Leonid Brezhnev. Unlike SALT I, SALT II *did* set limits on the number of warheads. Carter, however, was not popular in the Senate; his treaty came under fire from powerful politicians; and there was considerable pressure on him to respond to the window of vulnerability —which many thought the treaty did nothing to correct, allowing the Russians to build more than enough warheads plausibly to threaten a "first strike."

Carter had given added ammunition to his critics by canceling the B-1 nuclear bomber. He knew that he would have a much better chance of getting SALT II ratified by the Senate if he agreed to the air force plan for MX. In the end, it was to no avail; after the Russians invaded Afghanistan on December 24, 1979, Carter withdrew the treaty from the Senate, knowing there was now no hope of getting it passed. In the meantime, however, he had agreed to a basing mode for MX specifically tailored to fit in with the requirements of the SALT II treaty.

The plan involved stationing 200 MX missiles—at a cost officially estimated at $34 billion (skeptics put it at closer to $100 billion)— among 4,600 reinforced shelters in some of the most starkly beautiful terrain in the western United States. The shelters, to be dug in a vast area of sagebrush-covered valleys in Utah and Nevada, an area bounded by the neon lights of Las Vegas to the south and the Mormon spires of Salt Lake City to the north, were to be linked by 8,500 miles of road —almost a quarter of the length of the entire U.S. federal interstate highway system. Gargantuan 28-wheeled trucks would shuttle between the shelters, carrying not only the 200 MX missiles, but also 4,400 identical-looking dummies, good enough to be indistinguishable from the real thing to Russia's spy satellites (which can pick up details of weight, heat, and magnetic impulse, even if the rockets themselves are kept out of sight).

Nothing would be left to chance. In order to ascertain the reliability of this basing mode, the Pentagon would employ its own "spies," who would be given a free hand to try and crack the system and identify which shelters housed the real missiles.

In theory, therefore, the Soviet Union would only be able to eliminate America's land-based ICBMs by hitting all 4,600 shelters. Since it was reckoned, as we have noted, that you would need to target two warheads on each missile silo to be "confident" of destroying it, this would mean the Soviets would have to expend a total of 9,200 warheads to execute a first strike. And the beauty of the scheme—from the administration's point of view—was that SALT II would have limited both sides to a total of 9,200 warheads. So the Kremlin would have to exhaust its entire supply just to destroy MX, leaving itself none left over to deter an attack from American submarines. (Not only that: at prearranged intervals, the hatches over individual missile silos would be opened and Russia's spy satellites would be able to ensure that America was sticking within the limits of the SALT treaty by deploying no more than two hundred real missiles.)

There was something Strangelovean about the whole scheme. Here was the air force proposing to spend tens of billions of dollars on the biggest construction project in history—an endeavor that would require 2 million tons of cement plus about 40 billion gallons of water (the most precious of commodities in a land where, as one local miner put it, "the trees chase the dogs because it's so dry"). Yet they were proposing to do all this to solve a problem that did not exist.

By the time Carter left office, however, things had been set firmly in motion. Congress had approved initial funding for the scheme; contractors had been lined up to do the work; a special office had been set up in Washington to handle public relations; glossy booklets showing what it would look like had been printed; and air force delegations had trooped out to Utah and Nevada to give lectures in rickety school halls and local Rotary Clubs, bringing with them slide shows depicting the Soviet threat and diagrams purporting to show that MX would not interfere with the cattle and reassuring words about the opportunities that would open up for local businessmen. Utah and Nevada remained unconvinced. But there was an air of resignation about the air force's power, as reflected in one letter to the *Salt Lake Tribune:* "Where does a nine hundred pound gorilla sit? . . . Any damn place he pleases."

In the end, however, common sense prevailed and the so-called "racetrack mode" of basing MX was canceled by President Reagan. But it was not canceled because it was felt to be unnecessary—quite the contrary. President Reagan arrived in the White House infinitely more worried about the window of vulnerability than Carter. Indeed, if Carter had been the reluctant bridegroom, Reagan couldn't wait to get to the altar. A major plank in his election campaign had been the notion that America had become "number two" in the strategic arms race, and a number of influential figures—many of whom were to become key Reagan advisers—had formed a pressure group called the Committee on the Present Danger, which told anyone who would listen that America had become weaker than the Soviet Union, that SALT II was a fatally flawed, indeed dangerous, treaty, and that the window of vulnerability was a real and urgent problem.

But to have gone ahead with the racetrack scheme would have made Reagan deeply unpopular in Nevada and Utah, the heartland of Reagan country, and not insignificantly, it would have aroused the fierce opposition of one of his oldest friends, Senator Paul Laxalt of Nevada. So Reagan's defense secretary, Caspar Weinberger, had to reopen Pandora's box. Leaving aside the racetrack mode, how could the window be closed?

The administration reviewed the options: launching missiles from trains, hovercraft, small submarines (called submersibles) stationed just off the coast, airships—even giant trucks that could cruise the interstate highways and, in the event of war, pull off the road and launch their missiles. Not the least of the objections to this particular scheme was the possibility that the missile carrier might get caught in a traffic jam. Meanwhile, less reverent commentators offered a variety of more imaginative MX sites, ranging from golf courses and obsolete steel plants to dormant volcanoes and the backs of migrating whales.

One scheme closely examined by Weinberger involved launching MXs from aircraft, dropping them on parachutes and having the rockets ignite in midair. Nearly a decade earlier, the air force had demonstrated this was feasible; in October 1974 a Minuteman missile was dropped from a giant Lockheed C-5A, drifted down on its parachute until its nose was vertical; then the engines fired. The air force in three separate studies had already rejected the so-called "air mobile" concept as seriously flawed; so too had three presidents: Nixon, Ford, and Carter. Yet in summer 1981 the hints that emerged from the White House suggested that "air mobile" was the scheme Reagan favored. Lockheed began trying to work out how long it would take to build a hundred new C-5As, specially modified to carry the giant MXs. And on the air force drawing board was a plane, code named Big Bird, designed to stay in the air, ready to release a missile, for up to a week at a time.

Air mobile, however, was never likely to get off the ground. John Tower, at the time the diminutive chairman of the Senate's powerful Armed Services Committee, pointed out that the concept had already been rejected as "too unreliable, too costly and of questionable survivability" and that it would be "difficult to get through Congress." For one thing, a preemptive strike, designed to neutralize an air mobile basing scheme would likely prove twice as lethal as one designed to take out the racetrack shelters. (To destroy the racetrack MX, the Soviets would have to concentrate their attack on Utah and Nevada—in the process, killing an estimated 5.9 million Americans. To eliminate the threat posed by an air-based MX, they would be obliged to hit targets —mainly air bases—scattered throughout the United States. The estimated toll in that event would be 11.3 million.)

Thus, Weinberger was forced to think again. And in December 1982, he came up with another scheme, called "dense pack." Dense pack had the virtue of working in precisely the opposite way to Carter's racetrack mode. Instead of scattering the missiles over a wide area, the new idea was to deploy them very close together, in clusters. This density would ostensibly make them very difficult targets for a preemptive strike because though the first Soviet warheads to arrive would assuredly hit their targets, the blast, radiation, and debris from the initial explosions would deflect or destroy the warheads that followed (the phenomenon known as fratricide). Since it would take virtually a direct hit to destroy the specially hardened MX silos, a portion of the missile force would be bound to survive and be able to mount a retaliatory strike.

This scheme was in truth a good deal less outlandish than Jimmy Carter's, and it envisaged wasting considerably less space, but Congress was now becoming collectively weary of MX and gave it the thumbs down. The eventual result of this was that the administration, thwarted in its effort to close the window of vulnerability, whose dangers it had trumpeted to the world, and after having the whole matter reviewed by a bipartisan commission, elected simply to place the MX in fixed, land-based silos. Understandably, Congress didn't think much of this either. The whole justification for the MX in the first place had been the fear that land-based missiles in fixed silos were becoming vulnerable. Now the administration was proposing to spend money on missiles that were not going to solve that problem, but *add* to it. If the Soviets really were disposed to launch a preemptive strike, then the presence of the MXs would presumably make the option even more tempting. Steadily, therefore, Congress cut funds for MX, and by early 1985 the Reagan administration was in an ironic position: having inherited from Carter a plan to place 200 missiles in a supposedly invulnerable basing mode, it now looked as if it would be able to deploy no more than 50 in fixed vulnerable silos.

There was one consolation, however. The bipartisan commission to which the administration had turned for advice recommended the development of a new, smaller missile, mobile and with a single warhead. The logic behind Midgetman, as it was christened, was more sensible than that behind MX. The fear of first strikes, after all, had arisen because of developments in missile guidance and MIRVing; it was MIRVing that made it theoretically possible for a relatively smaller number of rockets to take out a much larger number—a danger that would be less likely if both sides moved to single-warhead missiles. Among those who recognized the virtues of this, albeit belatedly, was Henry Kissinger. Though as secretary of state in the early 1970s he had played a key role in the United States' decision to develop MIRVs, he later admitted: "If only I had thought through the implications of a MIRVed world.")

Even more important than the fact that the Midgetman would have only one warhead was the fact that it would be mobile—meaning it would be much harder to shoot at than fixed missiles in vulnerable silos. There were, however, a number of snags. The danger raised by Midgetman was of a Soviet "barrage" attack: the explosion of nuclear weapons in the air over potential Midgetman bases could knock over the launch trucks, kill the crews, and fracture communications so as to make contact impossible between the air force and any crews that survived.

Obviously, the aim would have to be to force the Soviets to barrage as large an area as possible—the larger the area, the less confidence they could have in their chances of disabling the entire Midget-man force. Ideally, this would mean keeping Midgetman in what is termed a "state of continuous dispersal," meaning constantly on the move. But since this would mean that the missiles would have to be trundling regularly around America's highways—not a prospect likely to appeal to most Americans (what would happen if one turned over in an accident, or, worse, was hijacked by terrorists?)—it quickly be-came clear that the military would almost have to keep Midgetman on its own turf. This is sizable—the ten largest military reservations alone give the air force some 12,500 square miles to work with—and in a crisis, the area would effectively become even larger because missiles would be able to dash in all directions to their firing positions.

Such a requirement, however, called for an ambitious new system: a launch truck not just able to move swiftly but stable enough to withstand the blast from all but a very close nuclear explosion. One vehicle on the drawing board, nicknamed Armadillo, is a squat truck, weighing about 45 tons, which, while hardly elegant, is intended to be sturdy. At its firing position, its crew would make it "safe" by several methods. First, heavy metal skirts would descend round the wheels to strike the ground on all sides, increasing stability. Second, metal bolts would be fired by explosive charges from underneath the vehicle into the ground, to act like a ship's anchors. Finally, the Armadillo might have hydraulic "legs" or "suckers" to give it yet more stability.

Thus ensconced, say those contemplating the Armadillo design, it would be able to withstand phenomenal pressure—perhaps as much as 30 pounds per square inch, six times what it would take to knock down an average house. In theory, then, a good number of Armadillos should be able to ride out a Soviet attack and still be able to launch a retaliatory strike.

The debate over Midgetman, as I write, is still in its infancy. But even if all the technical difficulties can be overcome to the satis-faction of Congress, there is another problem. Midgetman will be very expensive. One early estimate put the cost of a thousand Midg-etman missiles mounted on Armadillos at $70 billion. And the Midg-etman is part of an air force modernization program that includes not only MX, but the B-1, the "advanced technology bomber" (also known as Stealth, the ATB is intended to be virtually undetectable by Soviet radar), and a new generation of Stealth cruise missiles.[1] What this means is that Midgetman will face stiff competition for funds. Even so, the Midgetman program makes more sense than MX ever has, or does, or could.

I have reviewed in detail the notion of the window of vulnerability —and the efforts to close it—because they go to the heart of U.S. strategic thinking.

What happened in the late 1970s and early 1980s was that U.S. strategic planners identified a problem that did not exist, tried to find a "solution" to it, and couldn't. In the meantime, however, the pressure to find a solution had become intense because it was claimed that the Soviets might otherwise "perceive" their advantage and feel freer to exercise political and military muscle when they chose. As George Rathjens of the Massachusetts Institute of Technology said in testimony to Congress: " . . . to the degree there is a problem, it is largely of our own making. We exaggerate the growth of Soviet nuclear capabilities in order to gain support for our own prospective nuclear programs. Having done so, it is hardly surprising that others expect us to remedy what we have identified as critical deficiencies. Failure to do so would indeed make us appear irresolute by our own standards." Even William Perry, who as Pentagon research-and-development chief under Carter was one of the first to publicize the vulnerability problem, admitted in a 1982 interview in *Science* magazine that "to a certain extent, we have shot ourselves in the foot. We have inflicted these problems on ourselves by the way we have advertised them."

The alternative to advertising the "problems" would have been to discount them: to make it clear to the Soviets that any benefits they might think they could gain from theoretical notions of vulnerability would be purely illusory and that any belief that America's resolve had

---

[1]Stealth technology involves the use of nonmetallic composite materials and special techniques for masking the heat signature given off by aircraft or missile engines.

weakened would be both extraordinarily rash and horribly mistaken. No conceivable first strike would remove America's capacity to mount a devastating counterattack, and nothing in the foreseeable future would change that. Instead, successive administrations claimed, in effect, that America had become weaker than the Soviet Union, which is rather like telling someone you suspect is about to rob your house that you don't think much of your burglar alarm. Luckily, most burglars make their own assessment before attempting break-ins; the Soviets have almost certainly remained more impressed by American nuclear forces than have American strategic planners.

Why, then, has there developed so intense an obsession with arcane theories of vulnerability? What causes the endless worrying about numerical discrepancies and the ceaseless search for better, more accurate nuclear systems? (Why, for example, does the U.S. Navy need 760 nuclear-armed cruise missiles?) Does it really make any difference? Henry Kissinger raised a similar question in 1974. "What in the name of God is strategic superiority?" he asked in a famous speech in Brussels. "What is the significance of it, politically, militarily, operationally, at these levels of numbers? What do you do with it?"

Kissinger has since appeared to change his mind, a not infrequent occurrence, but the questions remain valid, and the answers to them are (in order): that strategic superiority is meaningless, that it has no significance, and that you can do nothing with it. As McGeorge Bundy, once President Kennedy's national security adviser and one of the most thoughtful critics of nuclear weapons policy, put it in 1969:

> There is an enormous gulf between what political leaders really think about nuclear weapons and what is assumed in the complex calculations of relative "advantage" in simulated strategic war. Think tank analysts can set levels of "acceptable" damage well up in the hundreds of millions of lives. . . . They are in an unreal world. In the real world of real political leaders—whether here or in the Soviet Union—a decision that would bring even one hydrogen bomb on one city of one's own country would be recognized in advance as a catastrophic blunder; ten cities would be a disaster beyond history; and a hundred bombs on one hundred cities are unthinkable.

Many officials and military men, however, continue to live in the unreal world Bundy has described. There are various reasons for this. One is institutional pressure: there are many careers, and a lot of money, tied up in the development and production of nuclear weapons. Another is the dry, academic reasoning that Bundy identifies as the hallmark of U.S. nuclear thinking. A third is interservice rivalry—both the navy and air force prize their respective deterrents, and whatever the strategic arguments in favor of American moving more and more of its deterrent at sea, the air force is reluctant to give up the "land-based leg" of the nuclear force, which it owns and controls. A fourth reason is political pressures. In the late 1950s John Kennedy campaigned for the presidency on the notion that the Eisenhower administration had allowed a "missile gap" to develop in Russia's favor. It wasn't true, but it spurred a bigger, more ambitious U.S. program. Similarly, Jimmy Carter agreed to support the MX because of pressure from the Senate. And Reagan, having condemned Carter as a strategic weakling, could scarcely be expected to settle for a less ambitious plan.

But there is another source of pressure on Reagan, one that is often ignored. This is the pressure that stems from the West's conventional weakness and NATO's strategy of flexible response. Flexible response anticipates NATO being prepared to go nuclear first if it begins to lose a conventional battle on the central front. It also anticipates that NATO be able to raise the stakes; if limited use of nuclear weapons in Europe does not persuade the Russians to cease their aggression, it anticipates the United States being prepared ultimately to use its intercontinental weapons.

It is this contingency that has driven much of the thinking about counterforce and small, "selective" nuclear strikes. In an age of such huge and potentially destructive arsenals, no American president would wish to order an indiscriminate assault on the Soviet Union—this would certainly lead to Armageddon, and the mere *threat* to behave like this (in defense of *Europe*) would not be credible, either to the Europeans or to the Russians. Instead the American president, so the theory goes, would need to be able to make a more selective strike, using, say, a handful of intercontinental missiles, in an attempt to force the Russians to back down.

To be able to do this, however—it is argued—America would

need to feel utterly secure. It would need to know that having launched a small, selective strike, it might not then lose the rest of its missile force to a massive Soviet counterassault. And though the idea of the Russians launching a bolt from the blue might make no sense, the idea of a preemptive Soviet strike following an American decision to start nuclear war is more understandable.

Thus, the most plausible justification for the excessively large U.S. arsenal is the unrealistic demands of NATO strategy. It therefore follows that if NATO beefed up its conventional forces, the justification for American war fighting scenarios—with all the dangers they contain—would disappear.

These scenarios, as we have seen, have never made much sense. The warheads would not fall where they were supposed to; millions of people would die; and, as various NATO experts have pointed out, communications between U.S. leaders and U.S. nuclear forces would probably be totally disrupted after a relatively small strike. A "limited" nuclear war would be unlikely to stay limited for long; having once started, it could well prove impossible to stop.

Indeed, the "war termination" problem, as William Kaufman calls it, is "almost unexplored territory" in U.S. nuclear strategy. Ending a nuclear war would be vastly different from ending a conventional war, where things tend to move comparatively slowly, and both sides are likely to have a pretty good idea of the situation they face: how many forces they have left, how they are disposed, what damage has been done to the enemy, and so on. Even so, in World War II, when the Germans and the Japanese kept fighting long after the "balance of forces" had swung against them, and when it was clear to any detached observer that their predicament was hopeless, it took traumatic events to bring the fighting to an end. What would it take in a "protracted" nuclear war, when the horrors of Hiroshima and Nagasaki had become routine, and when, because of shattered communications, neither side would quite know what damage it had inflicted, or even how much it had suffered itself? How would the president, in his emergency "Kneecap" plane (supposing, that is, he was alive and it hadn't been shot down by the enemy or crashed because of worn ball bearings) bring the conflict to an orderly end? It is a question that defies the imagination.

If America had only to worry about using its strategic weapons if attacked by the Soviet Union—rather than using them first in response to the dictates of NATO strategy—then it could live with a much smaller arsenal. It would also need to worry less about the supposed vulnerability of its land-based missiles and come to depend more on its missile-carrying submarines—the one element of its deterrent that seems likely to remain utterly "invulnerable" for generations to come.

NATO, however, continues to try and make nuclear forces seem "usable" in the defense of Europe—not just in response to a Soviet nuclear attack, but in response to a Soviet conventional attack, too. And though European leaders, on the whole, have found the arguments about vulnerability overblown, they have helped encourage them. Not only that, but while America was worrying about the window of vulnerability and its land-based missile force, the Europeans were worrying about another aspect of the nuclear deterrent: medium-range missiles in Europe.

The decision that these worries produced, and its aftermath, constitute one of the more revealing episodes in the history of the alliance, one worth looking at in some detail.

9

The Ladder of Escalation

On December 12, 1979, NATO made a historic decision. It agreed, at a meeting in Brussels, to deploy 572 new intermediate-range missiles in five European countries unless the Soviet Union agreed—through arms control negotiations—to dramatic reductions in its own theater nuclear arsenal. Almost exactly four years later, in December 1983, a U.S. transport plane landed at the air force base at Greenham Common, England, bringing in its hold the first of those new missiles. During the intervening four years, the alliance had had to weather a storm of criticism. There had been moments when it seemed the decision might not hold and when the prospects for deployment looked, at best, uncertain. In August 1981, for example, one prominent defense expert, writing after lengthy conversation with allied politicians and officials, concluded that the odds were "no better than even" that the NATO decision would be put into effect. The assessment was by no means atypical.

In the end, such fears proved ill founded. The arrival of the first American missiles at Greenham Common in late 1983 was greeted by an almost audible sigh of relief in NATO circles. Some suggested that the successful implementation of the decision was a cause for pride; the fact that the decision had been seen through showed NATO to be more robust and healthy than its critics had believed. "The trouble with the West," one senior U.S. official remarked to a colleague, "is that we never know when we've won."

Maybe. Having made the decision to deploy new missiles, NATO clearly had to stick with it. To have done otherwise would have been to appear to cave in to Russian pressure and to show itself irresolute and weak. But the decision itself was a gamble. It constituted yet another attempt to prop up flexible response, but it did not really do that. It brought little extra deterrence or defense but exacted a heavy political cost. It gave Soviet propagandists a field day. It played a significant role in reawakening the so-called peace movement. Moreover, it was not—as some on the Left fondly imagined—an American plot to cram new nuclear weapons down reluctant European throats. It was almost entirely a "European" initiative.

The origins of the 1979 decision are complicated and controversial. Perhaps the best place to start is with an event that took place in the Soviet Union in September 1974—the first test of a new missile that came to be known as the SS-20. The test was closely monitored by America's surveillance networks, and intelligence analysts soon had a clear picture of the missile. Unlike older Soviet missiles, it was propelled by solid fuel. Its compact size and shape suggested it could be easily moved around on a trailer. It had three warheads, each with a 200-kiloton yield (though for the time being they would be filled with sand, or some such substitute for fissile material); and observations on how the warheads separated from the nose deep in space, and then reentered the atmosphere to land in different places, convinced analysts that it was MIRVed, meaning, as we have seen, that each warhead could be released independently and directed to a separate target.

The analysts had some indications, too, about the new missile's range. It had been fired from Kapustin Yar, 200 miles southeast of Moscow on the banks of the Volga River, where, on a fertile lowland plain, amid woodland and fields of melons and vegetables, stands a bewildering complex of launch pads, hangars, communications centers, and other buildings—rather like Cape Canaveral in Florida. The Americans knew that Kapustin Yar was traditionally used for testing intermediate- rather than strategic-range missiles. And indeed, unlike the ICBMs, which have a range close to 6,000 miles—enough to cross the Atlantic and wreak havoc on the United States—the new missile flew only about 4,000 miles in its test. It was quickly clear, therefore, that the SSX-20 (X for experimental) was an intermediate-range weapon.[1]

News of the SSX-20 began to filter through to America's allies at a meeting of the Nuclear Planning Group in November 1974. In June of the following year, at another NPG meeting in Monterey, overlooking the ocean in northern California, James Schlesinger, then America's defense secretary, distributed satellite photographs, one of which showed extensive preparations under way at an old missile base near Drovenayo in Siberia. This, apparently, was where the first SSX-20s were to be sited.

In January 1976, NATO was again briefed on the SSX-20, this time more fully, at a Nuclear Planning Group meeting in an old war college in the suburbs of Hamburg, West Germany. The Soviets were now well down the testing road with the SS-20, the Americans explained, and after some early mishaps it was proving remarkably successful. Of its twenty-five flights, the last twenty had gone well, an uncommonly good record in a process often plagued by failure. The missile was supposedly accurate; it was reported to have a CEP ("circular error of probability") of 1,320 feet, which meant that Western intelligence estimated it should be able to fall, at least half the time, within a circle whose radius was 1,320 feet. It also supposedly "wobbled" little in flight. And from the activity at the missile factories, it looked as if the Soviets meant business; it was expected that they would produce around 300 of the new missiles.

---

[1] Early on there was some concern that it might be another ICBM, and that the Russians were only testing the first two stages or "sections" of the rocket in order to deceive Washington about their intentions, but this fear soon faded. The proof came, eventually, not from the missile itself but from observation of the supporting equipment: the capsule in which the missile was stored and the "transporter erector launchers" in which it would be carried were neither big enough nor bulky enough for ICBMs.

The news was beginning to alarm European officials. But the first major public speech about the SS-20 was made not in Europe but in America, by Dr. Fred Iklé, then the head of the U.S. Arms Control and Disarmament Agency. Iklé, a Swiss, and the author of several provocative articles, including one entitled "Can Deterrence Last Out the Century?," subscribes to the view that the Soviet Union is bent on strategic superiority. And in September 1976 he addressed the grandly entitled World Affairs Council in Los Angeles on the subject of the SS-20, describing the "specter of such weapons" growing "like a towering cloud over Europe and Asia." The development, he pointed out, appeared to be unprovoked; its aim appeared to be to deny NATO "escalation dominance"—that is, the ability to threaten plausibly to raise the stakes because of superior strength or at least equality, at a particular level of armaments. Faced with an array of powerful new three-warheaded, mobile missiles aimed at Europe, NATO would have less than ever to gain by going nuclear first.

Iklé's bleak analysis rattled some dovecotes in Washington. He had not actually charged the Soviets with violating SALT, but he had strongly implied that they were breaking the *spirit*. And with détente and arms control squarely on the agenda, it was important not to spoil the "atmosphere." A systems analyst in the Pentagon, James Thomson, was instructed to write an internal paper putting the other side of the case.

This Thomson did. His argument, in essence, was that the SS-20 represented a straightforward piece of modernization. The Russians were replacing some older missiles with brand-new ones. What could be more natural than that? It was a case with much to recommend it.

The Russians, after all, had targeted Western Europe with SS-4 and SS-5 missiles since the late 1950s, to which at first, America had responded by stationing Thor and Jupiter missiles in Britain, Italy, and Turkey, eventually withdrawing them on the grounds that their targets could easily be covered by U.S. strategic weapons. The SS-4s and SS-5s remained, and by the mid-1970s they were old and—powered by the volatile liquid fuel—in some cases unreliable and dangerous to handle. The SS-4, the older of the two, had to be towed to its launching pad by twelve tractors; once aloft, it relied on external fins to guide its flight path. The SS-5 was a bit more sophisticated, and had double the range. But both were overdue for replacement.

That the Soviets had now decided to replace their SS-4s and SS-5s, Thomson argued in his paper, need not be construed with alarm. And though, to be sure, the SS-20 was *qualitatively* superior to the SS-4 and SS-5—it was mobile, more accurate, more difficult to target, and certain to bring more warheads to bear on Western Europe—it did not mark a radical new departure. In terms of overall warheads, the West was still comfortably ahead. Besides, it had long been assumed that a significant number of Soviet ICBMs, though capable of crossing the Atlantic, had in fact been targeted on Europe. The evidence for this was circumstantial but compelling. In three major missile fields in the western USSR, the intermediate-range SS-5s stood shoulder to shoulder with intercontinental SS-11s. The back-up equipment in these fields, particularly command and control gear, suggested that these particular SS-11s—in all, some 150 to 200 of them—might be targeted on Europe.

The point was that the Soviets had so comprehensively targeted the cities and military installations of Europe with nuclear weapons of every kind—short- and long-range—that the addition of extra SS-20 warheads was going to have precious little real effect on the overall balance. But the Europeans were becoming jittery about the SS-20. Ripples of concern were beginning to spread through defense and foreign ministries, especially in Bonn and London. This concern was heightened by two other, linked developments. The first was the direction of the SALT talks. The second was the emergence of the cruise missile.

The "European" worry about SALT was a simple one. The aim of the SALT process was, in effect, to create a situation in which both sides would have strategic arsenals of equal power—the idea being that if this could be agreed, then neither side would be able to forge ahead, developing weapons in a destabilizing quest for "superiority." The old notion of mutually assured destruction, by which both sides would mean that if they started a war they simultaneously risked destroying the planet, would be reinforced—in effect, codified.

To some European officials, however, there was a danger in this.

It served to underscore the existence of a nuclear stalemate. If the superpowers actually agreed (implicitly at least) that neither could strike the other, where did that leave Western Europe? Didn't it puncture a gaping hole in the nuclear umbrella? What possible incentive would the United States have to put its cities at risk and come to Europe's rescue in the event that deterrence broke down and war broke out? The fear was especially potent in the German defense establishment, since, at heart, NATO is a code for American involvement in the defense of West Germany. With an accepted strategic balance, and the Soviets allowed an unimpeded buildup of missiles targeted on Europe, might not the code be broken?

However illogical, this fear came to absorb Helmut Schmidt and his defense advisers in Bonn. Schmidt, himself a former defense minister, had long worried about the effects of nuclear parity between the superpowers. Now, it seemed to him, things were getting worse. And one particular facet of the SALT negotiations caused him particular concern. This was the attitude the American administration took toward a new *Western* wonder weapon called cruise.

As nuclear weapons go, the cruise missile is a modest affair. In an age in which ICBMs the height of skyscrapers can theoretically deliver ten or more warheads, each capable of destroying a medium-sized city with pinpoint accuracy 6,000 miles or so away, the cruise, a mere 21 inches in diameter, and carrying only one warhead, seems almost anticlimatic. It is slow, too. While modern ICBMs can cross half the world in half an hour, the cruise is subsonic, traveling 500 miles per hour. But it has two advantages: it is cheap, and because it flies at hedge-hopping height, it is difficult to track by radar. It is, in fact, a small, pilotless aircraft, a direct descendent of the V-1 buzz bombs that the Germans used to deadly effect against London in the early 1940s. But it was not until the late 1960s, spurred by new breakthroughs in microelectronics and jet engines, that the American armaments industry began to develop the new missile. At first, it was envisaged for a very specific and limited role. The backbone of America's nuclear bomber force (300 B-52s) was aging: many older than the pilots who flew them. There was concern that against increasingly sophisticated air defense in Europe, an area in which the Soviets had invested heavily, the B-52s would have trouble carrying out their wartime mission. Cruise missiles seemed the ideal answer. They could be fired from an aircraft while still some 1,500 miles from the target, thus drastically reducing the need for pilots to penetrate hostile air space and risk getting shot down. Cruise missiles, the Pentagon reasoned, could at least considerably extend the life of the B-52.

But once the cruise genie was out of the bottle, it was hard to contain. For it began to dawn on defense planners that it was a remarkably versatile genie. It seemed to some that—given its cheapness—it could perform a number of functions, nuclear and conventional, on land and at sea, as well as in the air, to ease the burdens of European defense. It could also complicate Moscow's task of defending Mother Russia—and that, the argument went, would enhance deterrence. "Perhaps the most significant weapon development of the decade," a Pentagon director of research and engineering later enthused. The Defense Science Board estimated that it would take the Soviets ten years to "catch up" and achieve a similiar cruise missile program; in the meantime, it would cost them billions of rubles attempting to upgrade their air defenses to meet the new threat.

But the cruise missile, though popular among civilian planners in the Pentagon, had few fans in the White House. A number of officials and defense experts believed that it would become an arms controller's nightmare—small, mobile, and horribly difficult to check up on or verify. This would become even more true if the Pentagon developed, as many felt it should, *conventional* cruise missiles as well as nuclear ones. Short of using a Geiger counter, it would be impossible to tell the two types apart.

The argument, however, was still in its infancy. In late 1976, the Soviets deployed the first SS-20—at Drovenayo in Siberia—and though the issue got lost during the 1976 presidential campaign, it was squarely on the agenda when Jimmy Carter, the former peanut farmer and one-time nuclear submarine officer from Georgia, entered the White House in January 1977.

From the beginning, Carter's stance on nuclear weapons was viewed with suspicion in Europe. This increased when word reached European defense ministries that Carter had asked the Joint Chiefs of Staff if they could live with a drastic cut in the American missile force.

Then came the ill-fated trip to Moscow by Secretary of State Cyrus Vance, during which he proposed that both superpowers cut their arsenals in half, a proposal that prompted the Soviet foreign minister, Andrei Gromyko, to take the unusual step of calling a press conference to denounce it. And when in the spring of 1977, the State Department's director of politico-military affairs, Leslie Gelb, traveled to Europe to brief the allies on the American cruise missile program, the West Germans, in particular, found further cause for concern. Gelb's report simply outlined the advantages and disadvantages of cruise, but Schmidt's defense advisers worried that the Carter administration was preparing to sacrifice what they believed might be a potentially useful weapon on the altar of SALT.[2]

The arrival of the Carter administration added to European worries for another reason. Defense secretary Harold Brown and his deputy, Robert Komer, pursued an energetic campaign aimed at persuading America's allies to bolster their conventional forces. European governments have always been ambivalent about doing this, and not just because of what it would cost. They fear that if Europe ever became strong enough to resist a Soviet attack *on its own,* the United States might seize on this as an excuse to leave Europe. They might take the opportunity to withdraw their 330,000 troops—for years the glue that has held the alliance together—and adopt a more isolationist policy. Thus the Carter administration's zeal on the conventional forces issue (Robert Komer earned himself the nickname "NATO's Billy Graham") reinforced the dreaded specter of "decoupling"—the severance of Europe from America—that the emergence of the SS-20 and the progress of SALT had already raised among European officials.

At the London summit in May 1977, the Carter administration presented a long-range development plan for NATO. It called for the setting up of nine so-called task forces to examine different aspects of conventional defense (reinforcements, reserves, electronic warfare, readiness, etc.). But in deference to European concerns about the

---

[2]Indeed, in April 1977, the Carter administration did decide to offer the Soviets, as part of SALT II, a protocol that would restrict the development and deployment of cruise missiles until 1981.

SS-20 and a possible nuclear imbalance, a tenth task force was added to look at the nuclear problem. And European concerns were growing. A month after the London summit, NATO's Nuclear Planning Group met in Ottawa. During the meeting, U.S. Defense Secretary Brown held a private discussion with his British counterpart, Fred Mulley, about Europe's intermediate-range nuclear force. At the time, this consisted principally of aircraft: nuclear-capable Phantoms and Lightnings (the latter due to be replaced by nuclear-capable Tornados), and more importantly, the longer-range Vulcans and the 220 American F-111s based at airfields in Britain. The Vulcans, however, were old and unlikely to prove much of a match for modern Soviet air defenses. And though the F-111 was relatively modern—a small, fast, low-flying precursor of the B-1 bomber—aircraft as a whole were becoming increasingly vulnerable. More important, it was argued, so were the airfields on which they were stationed. In any case, the United States wanted to free up more "dual capable" aircraft like the F-111 for an exclusively conventional role.

But as well as strike aircraft, a total of over 400 warheads on U.S. Poseidon submarines had been specifically allocated to NATO (falling, in other words, under the operational control of SACEUR, rather than the Joint Chiefs of Staff in the Pentagon). This force had been increased after the appearance of the SS-20, and it also filled the role of an intermediate nuclear force. What Brown wanted to know was: would it be sufficient? Did Fred Mulley think NATO could rely simply on American submarines for its intermediate-range deterrent? Mulley did not reply immediately. He returned to London and consulted the recently appointed director of policy and programs at the Ministry of Defence, Michael Quinlan.

At forty-seven, Quinlan was a rising star in Whitehall. A brilliant though controversial figure, his attitude did much to influence Mulley's eventual reply to Brown. Basically, Quinlan believed that the Poseidon submarines would not, in themselves, constitute a sufficient deterrent. In the light of the added threat posed by the SS-20, something else would be needed, too. Put simply, Quinlan's belief was this: a potential aggressor must be able to spot no chinks in NATO's armor; deterrence must be a "seamless robe"; at the moment, there was a gap in this robe, and it needed to be filled.

Thus, under the standard scenario, a Warsaw Pact invasion of Western Europe would be met by conventional forces. If these failed, NATO would have to be able (or at least be seen to be able) to go nuclear—probably with battlefield weapons. But suppose the Pact replied in kind? Then NATO would have to be able (or be seen to be able) to raise the stakes again. But without a proper intermediate-range arsenal, NATO would have to move all the way from battlefield weapons to strategic weapons in one giant step. There would be nothing in between. And such a step might not seem credible to Soviet leaders. Faced with defeat in Central Europe, the Americans might decide that the risks of escalation all the way up to strategic weapons were too great —and NATO might have to surrender. Or, to put it another way, the Soviets might *believe* that NATO would simply not take the risk.

More specifically, Quinlan felt the Poseidon missiles, though officially assigned to NATO as intermediate-range weapons, were in fact *strategic* weapons. And submarines, Quinlan argued, pose technical problems: command and control are more difficult than with land-based systems; the missiles are less accurate; they are less easy to use in a "selective" strike because once a submarine gives a salvo it risks revealing its position. It is therefore more suited to an "all-or-nothing" strike, which makes it an indiscriminate weapon and gives it, in the calculation of war planners, a different role than the one Quinlan believes nuclear weapons should play in Europe.

Quinlan argued from a broader political perspective, too. It was vital, he said, that the Soviet Union see Europe as *involved*—sharing the alliance's nuclear burden, if only by providing its soil for the purpose. To position nuclear weapons in European countries would demonstrate precisely this. It would be a display of collective alliance resolve.

Mulley was persuaded. He sent a letter to Harold Brown in late summer 1977. No, he said, he did not think NATO's nuclear deterrent should be moved offshore. Furthermore, since the SS-20s were now plainly putting airfields at risk—meaning Europe might have to take new missiles rather than aircraft—he urged the administration to be careful not to "give away" cruise missiles in the SALT negotiations.

The letter did not go down well in Washington. But barely had it arrived than the Americans were given another, more significant, warning. This one was delivered in public—in the form of a gnomic speech by the West German leader, Helmut Schmidt. His speech, to the International Institute of Strategic Studies (IISS) in London, is often regarded as the first crucial step on the road that ultimately led to the December 1979 decision to deploy cruise and Pershing missiles in Europe. Given as the second Alastair Buchan memorial lecture (Buchan was a prominent British strategist who died in 1975), it was a profound, though veiled, expression of the unease he felt at the direction events were taking in the United States. Schmidt's feelings were compounded by his personal dislike of Carter, whom he felt to be an innocent in the turbulent sea of East-West relations. (The dislike was mutual.) It must be added that many of those unhappy with Carter in Washington had had occasion to bend Schmidt's ear on the subject. They warned him to watch Carter: the president, they said, was trying to sell European interests down the river.

In his lecture to the IISS, Schmidt talked at length about the economic aspects of defense and touched on the problems of terrorism. But the key section of his speech (though almost entirely ignored by the press) dealt with the nuclear issue. "SALT," he said, "codifies the nuclear strategic balance between the Soviet Union and the U.S. To put it another way, SALT neutralizes their strategic nuclear capabilities. In Europe, this magnifies the significance of the disparities between East and West in nuclear tactical and conventional weapons."

The White House, of course, already knew what Schmidt felt. But by going public the chancellor was dramatically increasing the pressure to find a solution. That autumn, a succession of high-powered American officials from the National Security Council and the State Department crisscrossed the Atlantic seeking to defuse the issue. The SS-20, they argued, as James Thomson had a year before, constituted no dramatic change in the strategic balance, and the restraints on cruise deployment would only last until 1981—by which time SALT III should take care of the SS-20. The American nuclear umbrella, they in effect declared, was as watertight as ever.

But like Cassandra, the White House was now doomed not to be heard. The whole fuss, it seemed to some officials, was unnecessary and irrelevant. Europeans had lived for years with a nuclear imbalance on the Continent, and, what is more, with aircraft in Britain as their only land-based, intermediate-range nuclear force. As everyone knew, these could if necessary be quietly upgraded when the time came—and not converted to a purely conventional role—thus fulfilling Quinlan and Mulley's demand that the whole intermediate-range missile force dedicated to Europe not be at sea. As to the argument that airfields were vulnerable: well, said the skeptics, so were missile bases. In the meantime, the White House believed, the priorities were to try both to create a stronger conventional defense and to keep a handle on the Soviet strategic threat through arms control. What Europe seemed to be moving toward—pressure for the deployment of a set of hard-to-verify new weapons—was going to work against both those goals, making one more difficult, and distracting attention away from the other. Moreover, there were those in the White House who even then were wondering whether the Europeans like Schmidt who were applying the pressure were not in danger of causing a political storm in their own countries that they would be quite unable to deal with.

But things were now moving quickly. On October 26, at a NATO Nuclear Planning Group meeting in Bari, Italy, the Americans took a step intended to ease European worries. They had set up, as the tenth task force provided for under the long-term defense plan, a new committee, called the High Level Group, and almost before they knew it the Europeans had seized the initiative.

10

Cruise and Pershing

The group of fifty or so NATO offi-
cials who arrived at the one and only motel in Los Alamos, New
Mexico, on February 22, 1978, had little opportunity to admire the
stunning view across the Rockies. It snowed constantly during their
two-day visit, blotting out the surrounding mountains. More significant, their meeting—the second of the newly formed High Level
Group—was one of the most crucial in NATO's history.

The men (and one woman—a member of the U.S. delegation)
who made the trip to Los Alamos, flying from Washington to Albuquerque before being driven in two sturdy green school buses up to
the hourglass–shaped plateau on which the town is perched, were all
senior defense officials (assistant secretaries, in American terms) with
backup from other defense and foreign ministry staff. Their allotted
brief as members of the tenth task force set up under Jimmy Carter's
Long-Term Defense Plan was to take a broad look at NATO's nuclear
arsenal. At their first meeting, in Brussels the previous December, the

officials had decided that they should concentrate first on intermediate-range, or theater, nuclear weapons.

But whereas the Brussels meeting had produced little of substance, Los Alamos quickly yielded a breakthrough.

In a modern conference center close by the still busy nuclear-weapons laboratories and the remnants of the chalet-style boys' school which, thirty-six years earlier, had been used by J. Robert Oppenheimer and his fellow scientists working on the Manhattan Project, the various delegations assembled around a U-shaped table. Down either side sat the Europeans, two from each country, with others sitting round the room against the walls. Between them, at the end of the U, flanked by his fellow Americans, sat the chairman, David McGiffert, assistant undersecretary of defense for international security policy at the Pentagon. McGiffert's instructions were clear. He was to find out what the Europeans felt, while committing himself (and the U.S. government) to nothing. A soft-spoken lawyer who specialized in arbitration cases, McGiffert listened to each delegation in turn. The British (represented by Michael Quinlan) and the Germans (through Wolfgang Altenburg, then a major general and now inspector general of the Bundeswehr) took the lead. Many of the arguments made in the Quinlan/Mulley letter to Harold Brown were repeated and both delegations, it was clear, believed that there was now a need to station new missiles in Europe capable of striking the USSR.

The key question, however, was how the other European countries would react. To an extent, NATO has always been a two-tier alliance, with the United States, West Germany, and Britain in division one, and the other European members playing a less prominent role. Still, no vital decision could be made without the consent of all members, and therefore McGiffert listened with a keen interest when the Belgian representative, Pierre Champenois, began to give his view.

Afterward, Champenois' contribution was seen by at least one member of the American delegation as the turning point of the meeting. While careful to emphasize that he wasn't speaking for his government, the Belgian stressed the need for what he called a more "visible coupling" between the United States and Europe. This, he made clear, meant the introduction of new missiles capable of striking the Soviet

Union—though not, he was careful to add, Moscow. That would be too provocative. Later, during a coffee break, Champenois was to underline his view. "We must remember," he said, "that the Poles are victims too." That was the point: NATO had a host of short-range systems that could devastate Eastern Europe, but none (except, of course, for bombers) that could reach Russia itself. And this despite what was seen as the intolerable provocation of the SS-20. With the SS-20, the Soviets might feel they could launch devastating strikes against Western Europe from Eastern Europe, and yet preserve the Soviet Union itself as a sanctuary. They might, therefore, feel they could confine a nuclear war to Europe.

Champenois' view was supported by the Dutch and, though the Greeks kept silent, by almost everyone else at the table. It dawned on McGiffert that there was a consensus—and the United States was on the point of being pressed to make a decision. The High Level Group was composed of officials not ministers. But the officials it comprised were all people close to ministers, people, as one observer put it, with "short lines of communication" to their respective governments. So McGiffert was being pushed into a corner. Faithful to his role as chairman, he summed up the meeting by concluding that the HLG believed there should be some "upward evolutionary adjustment" in NATO's nuclear posture.

The phrase was loaded with bureaucratic vagueness, but the White House, when McGiffert reported back, had not the slightest doubt what was meant. "They want cruise missiles, don't they?" said one official. Senior policy makers were furious. David Aaron, Carter's deputy national security adviser, remembered the agonized attempt to launch the "multilateral force" in the early 1960s, and believing the consensus to be a recipe for trouble and European backsliding, thought the initiative would have to be stopped.

James Thomson, the former Pentagon official who was now a staffer on the National Security Council, was appointed to the High Level Group for its next meeting to try and stop the idea of an "upward evolutionary adjustment" from becoming a second multilateral force. Like a policeman sent in to restore order after a breach of the peace, he dutifully traveled to Brussels in the spring of 1978 for the brief meeting of the HLG summoned to translate the Los Alamos consensus into a statement for ministers. McGiffert, too, fought to overturn the original consensus. But they failed. Things had gone too far to be stopped. Albeit "hung with qualifiers," as one source put it, the consensus went to ministers at their full Nuclear Planning Group meeting in Frederikshavn, Denmark, in April 1978, and the HLG was authorized to take the process a step further. What kind of weapons should be deployed? How many? And where?

Simultaneously, the National Security Council in Washington decided to organize a study group under the leadership of James Thomson to look at the implications of the whole business. By this stage Thomson and other U.S. officials had become persuaded by the force of the political and strategic concerns raised in Europe that something would have to be done, and in late summer the study group produced a document, called PRM (Presidential Review Memorandum) 38, which concluded that new weapons might be necessary.

Still, Jimmy Carter might never have backed the idea—and the decision to deploy cruise and Pershing missiles in Europe might never have been taken—had it not been for an occurrence quite separate from all the technical and doctrinal arguments that were absorbing the HLG. This was the fallout from one of the most damaging episodes in the history of the alliance.

Walter Pincus is a diligent reporter. Unlike most of his kind in Washington, he troubles to spend long, painstaking hours reading congressional testimony. And it was because of this habit that, in early June 1977, Pincus was reading the testimony of a hearing held by the Subcommittee on Energy and Water Power of the House Appropriation Committee. It did not sound promising, but Carter was engaged in chopping the water budget and Pincus was looking for evidence of new cuts. What he found was something very different. By one of the quirks of Washington bureaucracy, the energy subcommittee also handles the budget for nuclear weapons building, and amidst the testimony was one line stating that funds had been approved for an "enhanced-radiation" warhead for the Lance missile (a short-range battlefield system deployed in Europe). Pincus began calling his contacts in the army and on Capitol Hill and they confirmed that the Pentagon was planning to build an Enhanced Radiation warhead. On June 6, Pincus published his story. It appeared in the *Washington Post* under the headline "NEUTRON KILLER WARHEAD BURIED IN ERDA BUDGET." The reaction was swift and dramatic.

In all honesty, there was nothing especially sinister about the neutron bomb. Its ability to kill people without destroying buildings was simply the result of one more rather pointless attempt to shore up NATO's "battlefield" nuclear arsenal. When in January 1976 the then Defense Secretary, Donald Rumsfeld, had briefed the allies on U.S. thinking about intermediate nuclear forces, the neutron bomb had been but one item on his agenda. None of the ministers present had seen any cause for concern, nor had NATO's "permanent representatives" in Brussels, nor had a special team then studying new technologies for NATO. A total of $43 million had been included in President Ford's last defense budget in 1976 for production of the warhead. And at the time of Pincus's article, Jimmy Carter had probably never heard of the weapon. Since, at any one time, the Pentagon has a considerable array of exotic weaponry in one form or another—as raw ideas, at the research stage, or in full-scale development—there was no particular reason he should.

But if Carter's grasp of the subject, on June 6, 1977, was sketchy, he soon got a crash course in the theories of enhanced radiation. Pincus's article was the springboard for an immediate and massive Soviet propaganda campaign against the "killer warhead" and "the weapon that kills people but spares property." It was just the kind of issue to strike a chord with the European Left. In Holland, traditionally the most pacifist of NATO's members, new life was breathed, almost overnight, into a long-dormant peace movement, the Communist party, and the Catholic church (notably left wing and looking for an issue with which to revive its apathetic flock) leading the way. The Soviet phrase "the capitalist bomb" proved a useful slogan, and a petition against deployment of the neutron bomb quickly collected a million signatures. There were protests in West Germany, where Egon Bahr, executive secretary of the ruling SPD party, and Schmidt's most troublesome left winger, pronounced the neutron bomb to be "the symbol of mental perversion." And in Britain, too, the antinuclear movement, fueled by the propaganda barrage from the Soviet Union, began to grow.

It was all a little absurd. Jimmy Carter, the "peace-loving" president, was being seen as betraying many of his supporters, "secretly" developing a "capitalist" weapon, and giving another sinister twist to the arms race. Yet there was nothing new in "burying" the neutron bomb in the energy subcommittee's budget. It was standard practice, a quirk of Washington bureacracy, for such new nuclear projects to be listed in this manner.

Besides, the neutron bomb had not been dreamed up by the Carter administration. Far from it. The technology, in fact, had existed since the 1950s; all that had held back development were doubts about its military utility. But now Jimmy Carter faced one of the most testing decisions of his presidency. Should he proceed with development, and risk damage to his peace-loving image and trouble from Europe? Or should he follow his conscience and call a halt to the whole thing, at the risk of giving more ammunition to those who were already writing him off as a weak and indecisive president who was afraid of nuclear weapons?

By the spring of 1978, after several months of agonizing on both sides of the Atlantic, and a good deal of confusion, Schmidt appeared to have persuaded his Social Democratic party that the neutron bomb made sense. But no sooner had Schmidt indicated his readiness to go along with Carter's wishes and formally back the weapons than Carter suddenly pulled the rug out from under him. He abruptly decided to defer production of the neutron bomb, and though he left open the possibility of a resumption (depending on "the degree to which the Soviet Union shows restraint in its conventional and nuclear arms programs"), it was a fatuous presumption. No one was fooled. It was said that Andrew Young, U.N. ambassador at the time, had a lot to do with Carter's change of heart. Whatever happened, the president informed his horrified advisers that the price of going ahead was more than he was prepared to pay: "His administration," one of them later wrote, "would be stamped forever as the administration which introduced bombs that kill people but leave buildings intact." Suddenly, as one adviser put it, "after a year of twisting arms, the American president cried 'April Fool.' "

It was scarcely an inspiring spectacle, and in Europe, confidence in Carter slid even further. Schmidt, of course, was already fuming to his advisers that the president didn't know what he was doing.

(Schmidt was a difficult man to please. Once asked whom Schmidt would prefer as U.S. president, one of his aides thought for a moment and then said: "Helmut Schmidt.") Nor did Carter's decision please the defense community, which regarded it as the worst kind of error that could be made. In its view, Carter had set a precedent: the Soviets had been given a veto over a NATO deployment decision and, from now on, the Kremlin would feel confident of having a powerful say over what U.S. weapons could and could not be sent to Europe. The neutron bomb may have been an unnecessary weapon, and of no military value, but Carter's mishandling of it was to have far-reaching and damaging consequences.

Throughout the neutron bomb affair, the Europeans had kept up the pressure for deploying new intermediate-range weapons on the Continent. The SS-20 was now being deployed at the rate of one a week, which strengthened their hand, and Carter was now uniquely vulnerable. He knew that if he failed to respond firmly to the new NATO initiative he would invite further scorn. The image of him as a weak president would be reinforced; he had to *prove* that he was an effective leader of the alliance. If he wanted to secure European support for his SALT II treaty, the negotiations for which were then reaching fruition, he would be well advised to heed European security concerns. So by the autumn of 1978, aware of the conclusions of the High Level Group, and informed by his advisers that he could no longer ignore the problem, Carter was reluctantly persuaded of the need to deploy new intermediate-range missiles in Europe. But having made up his mind, he was determined that there should be no hitch.

The pressure for the new missiles, as his advisers were keenly aware, was coming from left-of-center governments—principally Schmidt's in Germany and James Callaghan's in Britain. The knowledge that these two men faced fierce opposition from substantial sections of their respective political parties had worried Washington from the beginning. Had the two leaders correctly gauged the amount of political fallout there would be? Would they be able to handle the inevitable rallies, the Soviet agitprop, the threats, the blandishments, the diplomatic blackmail?

With all this in mind, Carter sent his national security adviser,

Zbigniew Brzezinski, to Europe in October 1978 to assess the situation. Brzezinski came away satisfied that Callaghan and Schmidt would be able to handle their opposition. In January 1979 Carter brought matters to a head. At what the world was told, 95 percent truthfully, was an "economic" summit on the French Caribbean island of Guadeloupe, Carter, Callaghan, Schmidt, and Giscard d'Estaing, the French president, met in a small, open-sided beach hut, fringed by palm trees, bathed in sunshine, and within earshot of the surf. The most sensitive topic on the agenda, however, was not economic but nuclear. The four men and their closest advisers assembled to discuss the plan for new missiles in Europe.

Carter's own attitude was no longer in doubt. His conversion on the road to this nuclear Damascus may have owed less to strategic logic than to guilt over his mishandling of the neutron bomb affair, but he was now anxious to show resolve. Europe might have launched the project, but with the phantom vessels of the Multilateral Force still haunting Washington, America must now set the course. The deployment program, said Carter, must go ahead, and as speedily as possible, although an effort should simultaneously be made to tackle the SS-20s via arms control.

Carter got less than ringing endorsement from all sides: the tetchy, heavy-smoking German chancellor was beginning to worry about his left wing. Perhaps, he wondered, there should be more negotiations with Moscow. Callaghan, too, though he believed the West should be resolute if the Soviets would not budge, stressed the need for new talks. The strongest line came from Giscard, who was solidly behind Carter. France, of course, had no intention of taking any of the new missiles; since 1966, the only nuclear weapons on French soil had been French. But, at the same time Giscard, like his predecessor de Gaulle, knew that the stronger NATO was, the safer France would be too. So it fell to the French, who have never shirked telling their allies to do things they themselves have no intention of doing, to point out that there was little chance of the Soviets reducing their SS-20 force while the West had nothing to bargain with. Eventually, Carter carried the day. And after the summit, officials in both Washington and European capitals had the sense that a Rubicon had been crossed. There was no going back.

What remained to be settled were the details: how many missiles and of what types—and how to deal with the general wish for "an arms control solution." Much of the analytic work on numbers and types had already been done. Washington and the High Level Group had considered several weapons options: a new medium-range ballistic missile code-named Long Bow; the F-111H, an update of the American F-111 fighter bomber then (and now) stationed in Britain; the Pershing II missile; and cruise missiles in all three varieties—ground-, air-, and sea-launched. Long Bow quickly fell by the wayside (it was only at the feasibility study stage). So, because of general worries about aircraft vulnerability, did the F-111H. That left Pershing II and the three kinds of cruise missile.

Pershing II was an easy choice. There were already 108 Pershing 1A missiles in place in West Germany and replacing these with a similar *type* of weapon seemed to make more political sense than introducing a new device no one had ever heard of. In fact, the new Pershing would be considerably more formidable than the old. It would be moved into the same trio of homes—at Neckarsulm, Schwabisch-Gmund and Neu-Ulm, near the city of Stuttgart in Baden-Württemberg—where the Pershing Is had been held in operational readiness by the U.S. Army's Fifty-sixth Field Artillery Brigade. And the Pershing II would be made by the same company—Martin Marietta, in Orlando, Florida. But there the resemblance ended. Where the Pershing IA, with its maximum range of 460 miles, could carry its up-to-490-kiloton warheads no farther than Hungary, Poland, East Germany, or Czechoslovakia, with little expectation of hitting anything but sprawling, vulnerable targets when it got there, the Pershing II, traveling at 5,000 miles per hour, with its RADAG (radar area terminal guidance) system, would be *theoretically* capable of placing its less-than-20-kiloton payload within 25 yards of its chosen destination—thus putting a huge swath of Soviet territory west of Moscow at risk, and satisfying the condition that Russia itself should become vulnerable to European-based weapons. (Martin Marietta had initially planned a range more akin to the IAs, but they assured the Pentagon that the extra distance could be achieved by simply adding a third "stage" to the rocket.)

The Pershing II, therefore, while unable to hit Moscow (except with a very light payload), would be able to threaten all of the key

Warsaw Pact military nerve centers (and the military command and control facilities just west of Moscow) within its 1,000-mile range. Carried on Transporter Erector Launchers (one to each), the missiles would be able to travel on road or across country and would be capable, because of the Automatic Reference System built into the navigation equipment, of firing not just from presurveyed sites but from any convenient spot. Equally, the last-minute course correction capacity, based on radar-comparison of the target area with a computer-stored radar map of the known surroundings, would make the Pershing II hard to deceive by camouflage. All this high technology, however, was not to prove quite so effective when actually tested. Martin Marietta had to contend with a series of embarrassing flops, with the missile consistently missing its target—often by large distances—almost to the eve of the first deployment. Indeed, so bad was the new Pershing's test performance that Congress came close, on several occasions, to canceling the whole program. But this was all in the future. For now, the Pershing II seemed admirably suited to the HLG's needs.

But its 1,000-mile range, while adequate for a weapon to be stationed near the front line in West Germany, ruled out the Pershing as an option for other European countries. Schmidt had made it clear that Germany would only take new weapons if other countries on the Continent (i.e., not just Britain) shared the burden and the risks. And cruise missiles seemed the answer to this requirement. They had a range almost twice that of the Pershing II, and their hedge-hopping flight path, it was believed, would constitute a nightmare for Soviet air defenses (one Pentagon estimate suggested Moscow might have to spend $50 billion to guard against cruise). Above all, cruise missiles were *comparatively* cheap.

The question was: should these missiles be ground- or sea-launched? At one point Schmidt pressed for the sea-launched variety: he argued that it would be less vulnerable to attack by the Soviets and would not cause as much political trouble as the ground-launched version. He was probably right. But the White House would have none of it; if Schmidt wanted sea-launched missiles, they countered, then what was wrong with the Poseidon missiles already allocated to the alliance? Had Schmidt been content with these, there would have been no need for the new plan in the first place. Besides, ground-launched cruise would be easier to verify in any future arms control agreement. They would be less costly to install. And the whole logic of the deployment plan called for the European countries to take the new weapons on their *soil*—to demonstrate visibly the coupling between America and its allies. In the end, Schmidt agreed to accept the decision: having done so much to press for it, it would have been hard for him to do otherwise.

Having decided on type—a mixture of Pershings and ground-launched cruise—the alliance had to fix on a number. The final figure of 572 was a compromise: there had to be enough missiles to ensure, first, that they could not all be wiped out easily in a preemptive strike and, second, that they could penetrate Soviet air defenses. There had to be enough, too, to spread among the five countries who eventually agreed to play host (making the packages too small would have been uneconomic). But there was a danger in having too many: a large force of intermediate-range missiles might, it was feared, make it possible for America to wage a "limited" war in Europe without ever having to use its strategic forces. And that was not the intention at all. The intention was to provide a link between the short-range systems on the battlefield and the last-resort strategic ones in America. From this reasoning came the final tally: 108 Pershing IIs to go to Germany, 464 cruise missiles to be spread (in "squadrons" of 16) among Belgium (48), Holland (48), Germany (96), Britain (160), and Italy (112).

Finally, there was the matter of arms control, and here again the alliance agreed on a compromise. NATO set up a new committee to handle this, comprising mainly officials from foreign rather than defense ministries, and the committee, which came to be called the Special Consultative Group, considered three possibilities: negotiate first and deploy the weapons, if necessary, later; deploy first and negotiate later; or do both at the same time.

The first possibility was quickly discounted. Without a definite weapons decision, Congress would be sure to block the necessary funds for cruise and Pershing, and the Soviets, busy deploying SS-20s at the rate of one a week, would have no incentive whatsoever to negotiate.

The second possibility was discounted, too. Though regarded as the most sensible one in Washington—after all, if the Europeans wanted the new weapons, they should install them; if they didn't, they shouldn't—it got the thumbs down in Europe. European governments believed that only if there was an arms control component in the package could it win the necessary public support.

Thus was the "dual track" decision born. NATO would not negotiate before deciding to deploy nor would it deploy before deciding to negotiate. Rather, it would declare its decision to modernize while at the same time offering the Soviet Union the chance to bring the whole spectrum of weapons—SS-20, cruise, and Pershing—under control through mutual agreement. However implausible the arrangement sounded, it was the only one that could satisfy both the United States and West Germany. And it was the one that was formally endorsed, on December 12, 1979, at a special meeting of NATO's foreign and defense ministers in Brussels.[1]

That, however, was only the beginning. Over the coming months and years, the alliance was to be buffeted by precisely the kind of political trouble Washington had feared and European politicians had all too blithely dismissed. Academic theories about coupling, in conjunction with misplaced alarm about SALT and Carter's political weakness after the debacle of the neutron bomb, had combined to produce a decision that was to damage the consensus behind Western defense policy.

As one official remembers it, the British government first came face to face with the peace movement on two pleasant summer days in June 1980. Having announced to a packed House of Commons the prospective sites of Britain's cruise missile bases (Greenham Common in Berkshire and Molesworth in Cambridgeshire), Francis Pym, the defense secretary, journeyed through the English countryside to both areas a week later to explain to local residents that the new bases would mean no disruption of their lives. But at both of the chosen sites for his meetings—Newbury (near Greenham Common) and Molesworth —he faced not polite questions about the effects of cruise missiles on local wildlife and of an influx of American military on local schools, but heckling crowds of demonstrators who pressed around his chauffeur-

---

[1]At the same time, NATO agreed to pull a variety of older battlefield nuclear systems *out* of Europe—and more than proportionately (some 1,000 in all).

driven car and waved placards demanding that cruise missiles be kept out of Britain. Pym, a mild-mannered, conciliatory figure, was shaken by the vehemence of the protests.

It was only a foretaste of what was to come. The peace movement, largely dormant since the early 1960s, was back. NATO had provided it with a catalyst in the shape of a new and controversial weapons program. The days were over when nuclear decision making had been of little concern outside official circles—a state that had prevailed throughout the 1970s.

Four months after Pym's visit to Molesworth and Newbury came Britain's first major anticruise demonstration: all told, some 50,000 people crowded into Hyde Park on a cold, gray October day to demand that the British government adopt a policy of unilateral disarmament. A year before, the Campaign for Nuclear Disarmament had barely been able to muster 1,000 at a similar rally.

Over the next three years scenes similar to the one in Hyde Park would become familiar in many European capitals. The pattern was different in each country. The least affected of those earmarked to receive cruise was Italy. The socialist government of Prime Minister Bettino Craxi accepted the new missiles with a readiness that surprised and delighted Washington. Clearly, there was in this an element of national pride—a desire to cut a "bella figura" in an alliance that sometimes showed signs of revolving purely on a U.S.-U.K.-German axis.

Elsewhere things were more difficult. In Holland, traditionally the most pacifist of NATO countries, the streets at weekends were soon heaving regularly with demonstrators, and the fragile Christian Democrat government was under threat from no fewer than 400 different pacifist organizations under the leadership of the Interchurch Peace Council and and the Communist-led Stop De N-Bom. Having proved the cradle of the new movement (during the neutron bomb affair), its organizers, with a little help from the Soviets, simply diverted the protest to the impending cruise deployment.

Similarly, in Belgium, a powerful amalgam of antinuclear religious and political groups influenced the shaky coalition government. As in Holland, the Catholic church was a central force in the burgeoning movement, and in Antwerp the Catholic peace organization, Pax

Christi, ran a clearinghouse for pacifist propaganda called the International Peace Information Center.

In both countries the peace movement soon gained political clout —as it did in West Germany, where Helmut Schmidt's SPD party was eventually to turn against the cruise decision (though not until it had lost power). In Britain, the Labour party, which had done all but give its formal blessing to cruise, turned even more vehemently against it. Having been swept from office in June 1979, it voted overwhelmingly for unilateral disarmament at its annual party conference just over a year later.

NATO's "dual track" decision was not the sole cause of the new peace movement. The brief, incendiary campaign against the neutron bomb in 1978 had first raised public consciousness of nuclear matters, and the general deterioration of East-West relations that followed the invasion of Afghanistan did not help. But the prospect of cruise and Pershing missiles arriving in Europe revived old fears about living next door to nuclear weapons and the vulnerability which resulted from that. The putative missile bases seemed to the disarmers to beg for Soviet preemption and to make more likely the prospect of a limited nuclear war, with the Soviets and the Americans fighting things out in Europe while, through fear of mutual obliteration, keeping their own homelands intact.

It was an ironic charge, since the whole aim of the plan was quite the opposite. It was intended to let the Russians know that if they attacked they would run the risk of having their homeland hit by U.S. nuclear weapons based in Europe. But the complicated nuclear theology involved in this was lost on (or knowingly distorted by) the disarmers. What the Americans were up to, in the view of the veteran unilateralist E. P. Thompson and his disciples, was sending new weapons into Europe in order to give them a better chance of fighting a nuclear war with impunity. Cruise missiles, Thompson said, "place us, with finality, within the game-plan of the Pentagon"—this plan, apparently, being to wipe out Europe, while leaving America intact.

The Kremlin, of course, lost no opportunity to encourage this kind of nonsense. Brezhnev personally decorated his former ambassador to Holland, Aleksandr Yosipovitch Romanov, for his success at marshaling "the resistance of the people of the Netherlands" against the neutron bomb. And now other ambassadors, plus Soviet newspapers and officials, rallied to try and repeat that success. The United States, said the Soviet ambassador to Paris, was seeking to "Europeanize" an envisaged nuclear war, and to attain strategic objectives without exposing the United States to the risk of total destruction. "Washington's design," intoned *Pravda* in April 1980, "as the West Europeans must increasingly be realizing, is to remove America itself from the line of fire and allocate to West Europe the role of forward 'nuclear opponent' of the USSR and the other Warsaw Pact countries, with all the fatal consequences that entails for the West European NATO countries."

Nonsense it might be. But as the protest movements expanded, and the Russians stepped up their propaganda, myths about the "dual track" decision flourished. After Ronald Reagan took office in January 1981, for example, it came to be widely believed that his administration, even though it had not come to power until fourteen months after the decision was made, was trying to force the new missiles on Europe. To be sure, Reagan's tough anti-Soviet rhetoric—with his description of the Russians as "godless monsters" and of the Soviet Union as "the focus of evil in the modern world"—was, it is true, scarcely calculated to soothe frayed nerves. But the suggestion that he was responsible for cruise and Pershing was ironic; in fact, the new civilian leaders in the Pentagon were highly skeptical about the "dual track" decision. Richard Perle, the hawkish assistant secretary for international security affairs, would gladly have canceled it. But it was felt in Europe and at the State Department that it must go ahead. To abandon it would have been tantamount to an expression of no confidence in NATO; worse, it would have looked like caving in under Soviet pressure. Rapidly, the decision had come to assume the status of a litmus test of NATO's resolve: was the alliance still able to implement difficult decisions, or was it not?

Having agreed to back the decision, the Reagan administration also began negotiations with the Soviets in order to satisfy the European hope for an arms control solution that would avert the need for the new missiles. Predictably, the talks got nowhere. Nothing in the history of arms control suggested that the Kremlin would be prepared to dismantle expensive new missiles that were already in place in return for a promise to scrap weapons that were not even deployed. Instead, as the Carter administration had feared, the Russians simply used the talks to try to divide the alliance and whip up public opinion against cruise and Pershing.

In the end, of course, the Russians, and the peace movement, failed. The new missiles began to arrive in Europe, on schedule, at the end of 1983. In the two key countries—West Germany and Britain— right-wing governments had been reelected in mid-1983, which was fortunate, since the main left-wing parties in both countries were now, as we have seen, opposed to the new missile deployments. But in both countries, too, public opinion polls suggested that the new missiles were not popular. Firm majorities were opposed to them. And a growing number of officials—including some who had been involved with the original decision—were beginning to wonder whether it had been wise. "If it had come down to a choice between having cruise and Pershing and having no peace movements, I think I'd have chosen no peace movements," one official confessed to me.

That, surely, was the point. For complicated doctrinal reasons NATO began to install 572 new missiles in Europe. But it proved quite unable to explain to its public why it was doing this, or why the missiles mattered so much. And now, in the shape of the peace movement, it faced a threat to the public consensus behind defense in Western Europe that had existed, more or less unbroken, since the war.

What, for all this trouble, was NATO getting? It was getting, at an estimated cost of $7 billion, 108 Pershing IIs and 464 cruise missiles. "A hell of a price tag," Richard Perle is reported to have said, "for a marginal military fix."

The 108 Pershings—if they worked—would undoubtedly prove formidable weapons. Accurate and fast-flying, they would be able to strike key military targets and command centers west of Moscow. But stationed near the front line, they would also be immediate and obvious targets for Soviet attack.

And if the Pershings are vulnerable, then the cruise missiles are even more so. In war, mounted four at a time on 30-foot-long, four-wheeled tractor-trailers known as Transporter Erector Launchers, a flight of sixteen cruise missiles would be moved in a quartet of TELs, accompanied by two similar-sized launch-control centers (one operational, one in reserve). Both launchers and control vehicles would be towed by 10-ton heavy-duty tractors, built in West Germany, capable of climbing hills, fording rivers, and moving across country independent of roads. With each missile flight would travel a miniature army of support troops—one flight commander, four launch officers, nineteen maintenance men, forty-four soldiers, and a doctor—carried in a convoy of sixteen armored trucks. Given sufficient warning, the whole caravan would move to one of a series of presurveyed firing points, anything up to 100 miles from the home base. But even though in an emergency—and one launcher in each flight is in a state of Quick Action Alert—it is theoretically possible to have action-readiness within fifteen minutes of the missiles being moved from their bunkers, the procedure is very cumbersome and the whole convoy of twenty-two vehicles would be easily spotted from the air (or by satellite). Cruise missiles, therefore, are extraordinarily vulnerable. They would clearly present the Soviets with a prime and large target, either for conventional or, if there were signs of their being moved, nuclear attack.

And unlike the Pershing, the cruise is not a good weapon, even in *theory*, for the kind of discriminate, selective strikes NATO had in mind when it made its 1979 decision. The difficulties it would pose to enemy radar by flying so low could backfire: if, say, one or more cruise missiles were spotted by the Soviets, how would they know how many had been fired? Obviously, they would find out when the warheads started exploding; but given the slow flight time of cruise, they might not choose to wait that long. And the fact that cruise missiles would take up to five hours to reach their destination (especially from Britain, from which the Soviet Union is virtually out of range) hardly makes them ideal for striking military targets. By the time they arrived, the target, even if fixed, might no longer matter.

Moreover, just as the Pershing II has been plagued by development problems, so too has cruise.[2] In a report published shortly before

---

[2]An investigation by ABC News in 1983 suggested that in three out of nine tests conducted over land, the army gave its test missile a better chance of proving accurate by placing radar corner reflectors around the target in order to help the warhead to zero in on it. The ABC News report cast doubt both on the Pershing's test record and on the realism of the tests themselves.

its deployment in Europe, the General Accounting Office complained that its "terrain contour matching" guidance system (Tercom for short) might prove ineffective against a "wide spectrum of high value targets." The main difficulty has been the production of sufficiently reliable radar maps of the terrain over which the missiles might have to fly. The maps, fed into the computers of individual missiles, and theoretically enabling them to identify their targets, are derived from satellite photographs, and the problem is that, given the changing seasons, the missile radars may "see" different images of the ground at different times, depending, for example, on whether the trees have dropped their leaves, or whether there is a covering of snow. According to *Skilnick's Radar Handbook*, a standard reference work, "radar altimeters used over forests, deep snow and deep ice can give erroneous readings. In fact aircraft have flown into the Greenland icecap while their radar altimeters were still registering their altitude just above sea level." The Soviet Union has many forests, and the Siberian steppes, over which cruise would have to fly, are covered with snow for much of the year.

Cruise missiles, then, promised precious little military advantage. But by the time of their first arrival, millions more people in Europe were worrying about nuclear matters, and about NATO strategy, than had been in 1979. And the peace movement, the most visible expression of this, had, in the view of Michael Howard, Regius professor of history at Oxford, sent "a signal both to Moscow and to the United States not simply that the people of Western Europe are not prepared to defend themselves with nuclear weapons, but that they are not prepared to defend themselves at all: a signal that could create a quite terrifying degree of instability by presenting the leaders of the Soviet Union with options that hitherto have been firmly closed to them."

The alliance was unlucky. It had to implement its decision in changed circumstances from those in which it had been conceived, though it must be said that by mid-1979, if not sooner, there were already plenty of signs that détente was crumbling. Nevertheless, the decision itself scarcely seemed worth the trouble. If the allies were so anxious for renewed evidence of U.S. commitment, then they would have done better simply to update, quietly and without fuss, the nuclear-capable aircraft stationed in Britain, rather than go through the song and dance of the "dual track" decision, with its implicit invitation to the Soviets to meddle in the affairs of Europe, stir up trouble, and try to gainsay a weapons decision that was none of their business.

What the cruise and Pershing decision made plain was the kind of thinking that drives so many NATO decisions. To quote Michael Howard again:

> The belief of some strategic analysts that the Russians can only be deterred from attacking us by the installation of precisely matching systems—"ground launched missiles must be matched by ground launched missiles"—is politically naive to the point of absurdity. The United States is "coupled" to Europe, not by one system rather than another but by a vast web of military installations and personnel, to say nothing of the innumerable economic, social and financial links that tie us together into a single coherent system. To satisfy these pedantic analysts, who require still further guarantees, the Americans, whose patience seems inexhaustible, have already allocated NATO a submarine-based force of immense destructive power.
>
> If all this is insufficient to deter the Soviet Union from a course that they are in any case likely to contemplate only in the direst of extremities, what difference will be made by the installation of Pershings and cruise missiles, particularly if these remain under sole American control?

"Coupling," in short, depends ultimately as much on leadership, will, and faith as it does on weapons. The credibility of guarantees in any alliance, especially NATO, is a political problem: nothing will force the Americans to come to Europe's assistance. And the imposition of meretricious technical solutions is more often an illustration of weakness than of strength.

PART THREE

THE SEARCH
FOR A WAY OUT

"O Hercules, the valor of men is at an end."
—Archidamus, king of Sparta, on seeing a dart fired
from a machine brought from Sicily, c. 55 B.C.

11

Star Wars: The Dream

Not least of the drawbacks of the plan to deploy new cruise and Pershing missiles in Western Europe was that for four years or more, from December 1979 until at least December 1983, the controversy over deployment distracted NATO from the task of real importance: improving its conventional forces. As alliance politicians and officials wrestled with the problems of impending deployment, other issues were overshadowed.

Distractions like that caused by cruise and Pershing have become endemic in an alliance unwilling—perhaps unable—to face up to its most serious weakness. Even before the first missiles were installed in the bunkers of Greenham Common, NATO was beginning to grapple with another all-consuming initiative, this one on a scale that promised to make cruise and Pershing look like a sideshow. If the "dual track" decision of December 1979 constituted yet another attempt to bolster flexible response, the so-called "strategic defense initiative" launched by President Reagan in March 1983 envisioned nothing less than a transformation of the whole basis of the alliance. What Reagan wanted to do was eliminate, once and for all, the threat of nuclear war.

"Let me share with you a vision of the future which offers hope . . . ," he said in his televised speech of March 23, 1983. "What if free people could live secure in the knowledge that their security did not rest upon the threat of instant retaliation to deter a Soviet attack? That we could intercept and destroy strategic ballistic missiles before they reached our own soil or that of our allies? . . . I call upon the scientific community in our country, those who gave us nuclear weapons, to turn their great talents now to the cause of mankind and world peace: to give us the means of rendering these nuclear weapons impotent and obsolete."

The strategic defense initiative, or SDI, quickly became the subject of heated debate. Ardently backed by some, excoriated by others, it was featured in a flood of newspaper articles, television programs, scientific treatises, and official documents. Its futuristic new technologies of death rays, orbiting battle stations, and breathtakingly sophisticated computers gave graphic artists a field day and brought what had once been regarded as the exclusive province of science fiction into countless living rooms. Experts debated the plan in exquisite detail, arguing passionately over how many battle stations it would take to cope with the Soviet nuclear threat and how many megajoules of power would be needed to maintain space-based defenses. Meanwhile, the tantalizing vision Reagan had conjured up—of a world free from the terrifying destructive power of nuclear weapons—caught the imagination of millions of people, not just in America, but throughout the West. After all, who could not be *for* a strategy that rescued mankind from the shadow of nuclear holocaust, which has lain over it for forty years? Who could disagree with Reagan's assertion that it is "better to save lives than to avenge them"?

Unfortunately, the president's vision was as flawed as many of the arguments used to support it. As far into the future as we are capable of seeing, and probably forever, there will be no effective Star Wars defense against nuclear weapons. The world will continue to be held hostage to the threat of a holocaust. And the pretense that it might be otherwise is a dangerous, even reckless, one, for it builds up hopes that can never be fulfilled. At best, Star Wars could provide, at mind-boggling cost, a partly effective defense that might conceivably boost deterrence—but would be more likely to do the opposite.

Star Wars, in short, is the latest and most extreme embodiment of the boundless faith in high technology that has characterized Western defense since World War II. As popularly conceived, it is the technological fix to end all technological fixes. It is based on a dream of achieving perfect defense, a defense *without risk.* It threatens to suck away vast resources from less glamorous, less dramatic, but more feasible projects—from *usable* weapons—and to provide a bonanza of undreamt-of proportions for the defense industry. It threatens to spark a new and intensive round in the arms race, in the development of all kinds of weapons, exotic and otherwise, for the Russians do not see Star Wars as defensive, and never will. And it threatens to kill arms control. All in all, it is likely, if pursued, to lead to a vastly more unstable world than the one we currently inhabit. Instead of being offered the nuclear-free future that Ronald Reagan fondly imagines, our children or our children's children are likely to find themselves living amidst greater danger than we do.

Star Wars is the quintessence of the new Maginot line.

When Ronald Reagan arrived in the White House he pretended to no great expertise in nuclear matters. The arcane details of MIRVing, throw-weight, and fallout were beyond his ken, and seemingly beyond his interest. By his own admission, he was president for two and a half years before he realized that the majority of Soviet nuclear weapons are based on land. (He once shocked a group of congressional leaders who had come to discuss the MX by saying: we've got to worry about the land-based missiles and not the submarine missiles, because they are not nuclear.) But for all his lack of knowledge, Reagan came to office bearing one stout conviction: the notion of mutually assured destruction, he felt, was as mad as the acronym it gave rise to. It was like two men pointing cocked pistols at each other's heads.

Underlying President Reagan's conviction was a deeply moral view of the world. "He is a child of the 1920s," as one European ambassador put it. "He still believes America is the shining city on the hill." On several occasions, both before and after he became president,

Reagan was reported saying that he believed literally in scriptural forecasts of a climactic war between the forces of light and darkness —the New Testament prophecies of Armageddon, predicted as likely to follow after the Beast and the Antichrist have appeared and gathered together the heathen nations. (There will be a period of Tribulations, the prophecy suggests, and then there will be a world war between the heathen hordes and Christ's army, paving the way, after Armageddon, for the return of Christ for a thousand-year reign on earth.)

In 1985 James R. Mills, a California state legislator, wrote in *San Diego* magazine about a conversation he had had with Reagan fourteen years earlier. Reagan was then governor of California. Just before tucking into a flaming dessert of cherries jubilee, according to Mills, he brought up the subject of Armageddon.

> With firelit intensity he said, "In the thirty-eighth chapter of Ezekiel, it says that the land of Israel will come under attack by the armies of the ungodly nations, and it says Libya will be among them. Do you understand the significance of that? Libya has now gone Communist, and that's a sign the day of Armageddon isn't far off.
>
> ". . . Ezekiel said that fire and brimstone will be rained upon the enemies of God's people. That must mean they'll be destroyed by nuclear weapons. They exist now, and they never did in the past. . . .
>
> "Ezekiel tells us that Gog, the nation that will lead all of the powers of darkness against Israel, will come out of the north. Biblical scholars have been saying for generations that Gog must be Russia. . . . It didn't seem to make sense before the Russian revolution, when Russia was a Christian country. Now it does, now that Russia has set itself against God. Now it fits the description of Gog perfectly."

Mills pointed out, he says, that according to Ezekiel, Ethiopia would also be among the "evil powers," and that at the time it was not Communist. (But soon afterward, as he says in his article, that changed when Emperor Haile Selassie was deposed, presumably reinforcing the Christian fundamentalist world-view.)

There have been various efforts, following the president's Star

Wars speech, to reconstruct how it came about, but what must always be borne in mind is Reagan's own view of the world, his profound belief that it was, and is, intolerable for America and other Christian nations to be eternally vulnerable to the whims of an "evil empire." To Reagan, American technology is the West's natural and God-given ally against an unacceptable threat.

When he was governor of California, Reagen apparently discussed his dissatisfaction with traditional deterrence theory with some of the rich and influential West Coast conservatives who shaped and financed his political rise. This group, sometimes called his "kitchen cabinet," included in its number Joseph Coors, the brewing magnate from Colorado, and the late Justin Dart, the industrial multimillionaire who liked to describe himself as a "big issues guy." ("I'm interested in the national economy and our defense ability, not all these crappy little issues like equal rights or abortion," he once told an interviewer.)

Once Reagan was in the White House, there was no shortage of people ready and eager to press upon his advisers what they saw as the urgent need to develop defenses. Among the major lobbyists were two retired military men, General George Keegan of the air force and Lieutenant General Daniel Graham of the army. Graham, a small, energetic man with a shock of white hair, was an especially ardent enthusiast. Head of a pressure group called High Frontier (founded by the Heritage Foundation, the conservative think tank), he had lobbied hard against the 1972 ABM treaty that drastically constrained the deployment of ground-based defenses and outlawed the testing and deployment of space weapons. Graham had traveled all over America and Europe, extolling the virtues of strategic defense. He had even written a book on the subject, in which he held out the possibility of America rendering itself safe and performing a "technological end run on the Soviets" through a Star Wars effort. "The kind of superiority we should seek," Graham explained in a 1980 interview, "is technological superiority—that is, to have some of our military capabilities in an area where the Soviets, with inadequate technology, cannot challenge us. . . . If we challenge them in a technical way—such as with a space-borne defense system— . . . we can quickly restore the balance."

More influential than either Keegan or Graham, however, was Edward Teller, the hawkish physicist who had worked with J. Robert

Oppenheimer on the Manhattan Project to develop the atomic bomb, and later became known as "the father of the hydrogen bomb," the atom bomb's younger and vastly more powerful cousin. Teller, also a long-standing opponent of the ABM treaty, was, at seventy-five, a passionate Star Wars enthusiast. On September 14, 1982, and apparently on three other occasions, he obtained an audience in the White House with President Reagan. His contributions may not have been decisive, but in Reagan, for the first time, he had a president disposed to be sympathetic. For years, strategic defense had been a political orphan. Although research into its potential had proceeded, in a haphazard way, it had been funded by Congress largely as a "hedge" against any possible breakthrough the Russians might make rather than because of any serious intent to deploy. With the signing of the ABM treaty in 1972, the superpowers had formally renounced space-based defenses, opting to base their security—explicitly in the American case, and effectively in the Russian case—on the notion of "mutually assured destruction." An attempt by either side to build defenses, it had been felt, would do more than intensify the arms race. Those, like Teller, Graham, and Keegan, who argued that MAD *was* mad were a lonely and largely ignored minority.

Just as the military men anxious for Britain to develop the tank in the early years of World War I needed a political champion, so did the star warriors. The tank got Winston Churchill. And after the presidential election of 1980, Star Wars got Ronald Reagan.

According to George Keyworth II, Reagan's scientific adviser until mid-1985, and a protégé of Teller's, there were three "primary motivations" that caused the president to launch the Star Wars initiative: "Those motivations were, first, the inherent unacceptability—or immorality, if you will—of mutual assured destruction as the guarantor of the world's future; second, the lack of options for future presidents to maintain a secure offensive deterrent; and third, the utter failure of the mechanisms of arms control, as practiced over decades, to halt the buildup of enormous stockpiles of nuclear weapons."

If we are to accept Keyworth's account (and in offering a *post-hoc* explanation he makes the president's position sound more carefully thought out than the evidence suggests it was), what Reagan feared was the extent to which the massive Soviet military buildup of the 1970s, persisting into the 1980s, was threatening strategic stability. With nuclear delivery systems getting more accurate, the specter of a crippling preemptive strike was going to grow. The future brought with it the possibility, in Keyworth's words, "that many, many thousands of highly accurate nuclear warheads could suddenly rain down on our own retaliatory forces." Put another way (in the words of a second official), the balance between the superpowers of second-strike or retaliatory forces (clumsy, inaccurate, able only to hit "soft" targets, such as cities) was being replaced by a balance of first-strike forces (precise, accurate, and able to strike "hard" targets, such as missile silos and command centers). This, it was thought, was putting both sides on a "hair trigger" in which the incentive, in a crisis, would be to strike first.

It was, of course, an old fear. The risk of either side making a preemptive strike has always been exaggerated: the imperfections of technology, now and in the foreseeable future, mean that to launch a first strike would be a terrible, probably suicidal gamble. But, in some quarters, the fear remained potent, and the failure of the Reagan administration to find a "survivable" basing mode for the MX missile —indeed, its difficulties in getting any funding at all for the MX— spurred the effort to find a new solution to the problem of vulnerability.

Reagan feared that without strategic defense the West might prove increasingly unable to cope with the menacing Soviet buildup. Like all presidents, he had come, once in office, to appreciate the awesome responsibility of having a finger on the nuclear button. But unlike most presidents, Reagan—a moralist who tended to see the world in black and white, and an optimist with a boundless faith in Yankee ingenuity—felt that there had to be a better way.

In late 1982 and early 1983, the political advantages to be gained from a new departure came to intrigue a small group of Reagan's key advisers, and especially Robert McFarlane, at the time the president's deputy national security adviser. With fears of nuclear war rising in America as well as in Europe, sparked by the prospect of new missile deployments (MX, Trident, cruise, and Pershing)—and helped along, incidentally, by some of the president's own early rhetoric—the nuclear freeze movement was gaining ground in Congress, and the nation's influential Catholic bishops appeared to be on the point of issuing a militantly antinuclear pastoral letter. The arms reduction talks in Geneva were stalled; the Soviet missile buildup was proceeding apace. The idea of a bold new initiative, designed to undercut the peace movement, seize the moral high ground, and challenge the Russians to change their ways, had undoubted appeal. The opportunity seemed tailor-made for a president with Reagan's remarkable communications skills, and it should be said that for this purpose—as a rhetorical tool —Star Wars has had a certain success.

The clinching factor was the attitude of the Joint Chiefs of Staff, and above all of the chief of naval operations, Admiral James Watkins. A devout Roman Catholic, Watkins had long shared Reagan's doubts about mutually assured destruction. Indeed, according to Pentagon sources, he had more than once caused alarm by talking as if he believed nuclear deterrence to be morally dubious, and, perhaps, over the long term, unsustainable. (He even developed a habit of inserting remarks to this effect into his speeches, though on the insistence of officials they were always excised before the speeches were given, since they ran quite contrary to and threatened to undermine existing NATO strategy.)

In February 1983, according to the *Philadelphia Inquirer*, the then chairman of the Joint Chiefs of Staff, General John Vessey, faced a dilemma.

> He and Reagan got on so well that the President had recently instituted monthly meetings with the Joint Chiefs. Now the problem was, Vessey couldn't decide what to talk about. He called the chiefs to his office on a Saturday morning.
> "We decided we didn't want to just tell him readiness was up and so forth," a participant recalled. . . . "We wanted to bring the President something new, different and exciting."

Admiral Watkins came to the rescue. Over the previous few months he had spoken several times to Edward Teller. Now he proposed that the time had come for a more serious look at the new technologies that might make it possible to defend against a Soviet missile attack.

By now, things were moving swiftly. McFarlane, increasingly

struck by the political possibilities of such a new initiative, talked at length to Watkins. And on February 11, 1982, at a meeting in the elegant Roosevelt Room, opposite the Oval Office, Watkins made a powerful presentation suggesting that the president throw his weight behind a major research effort. According to one well-placed White House correspondent: "McFarlane interjected: Are you saying that over time this could lead to deployable systems? Exactly, Watkins replied. McFarlane then polled the other four military leaders around the table. None dissented." (There is some doubt about the extent of the chiefs' enthusiasm. It is fair to say that none of them, with the possible exception of Watkins, believed that the strategic defense initiative would achieve quite the prominence it did. In the context of the defense budget, it was seen more as an extra than as a high priority. No one wanted to sacrifice other conventional or strategic programs to fund it.)

Watkins had helped provide Reagan with the ammunition he wanted. Collectively, the president and a handful of aides, a report on NBC Television later put it, were "dazzled" by the new technologies they had heard about: "lasers, particle beams, and other exotic weapons —in their view, America's natural ally against the Soviet military threat."

Yet it was to be another six weeks before the seminal speech was made. McFarlane and his boss, national security adviser William Clark, limited discussions on the forthcoming initiative to a very small group; they knew that running it through the usual interagency process, and involving the Departments of Defense and State, would be a recipe for delays, objections, and probably unfavorable leaks. Keyworth, though a true believer, was himself excluded from the detailed planning until about a week before the speech. So was Secretary of State George Shultz. Indeed, Shultz had not even attended the crucial February 11 meeting on Star Wars; there had been a violent snowstorm that morning, and he had been unable to get to the White House from the State Department. The Joint Chiefs of Staff had been brought from the Pentagon by helicopter. Inevitably, the meeting became known as "the snow job." Over the belated objections of the secretary of state, and without consulting any of the experts in the State or Defense departments who handled the day-to-day business of arms control and nuclear policy, Reagan and a few advisers made one of the most momentous decisions of his presidency. Not even Defense Secretary Caspar Weinberger was fully in the know. At a Nuclear Planning Group meeting only two days before the speech, neither he nor his key lieutenant, Richard Perle, was able to tell his colleagues anything. (Poor Weinberger, in fact, had to start ringing them up to pass on the news the moment he got back to Washington.) And even Edward Teller had no idea what was coming until, on the day of the speech, he was invited to the White House with other scientists and national security experts to have a preview of the speech and be told: "Edward, you're going to like it."

The speech thus came as an almost total surprise to officials in Washington, to America's allies in Europe, and to the Kremlin alike. Virtually no briefings had been prepared on what the president had in mind or where he thought the abrupt change of emphasis might lead, and the ensuing confusion was considerable. "Don't worry, gentlemen, it's just another of the president's fireball speeches," former Secretary of State Alexander Haig joked the next morning to his colleagues on the presidential commission set up to examine America's strategic forces. But it soon became clear that it was much, much more than that.

Immediately after the speech, National Security Decision Directive 6-83 mandated an examination of the available and potential technology. Three investigation teams were set up. One, under former NASA administrator James C. Fletcher, looked into nuts and bolts. The second, under Fred Hoffman, who runs a defense consulting firm called Pan Heuristics, reported on policy implications. The third, an interagency team led by Frank Miller, the Pentagon's director of strategic forces policy, was charged with pulling together the results of the first two. The conclusion of the Fletcher panel was, essentially, that "a robust, multi-tiered ballistic missile defense system" could "eventually be made to work." Although hedged with qualifications, the tone of the top-secret report to the president was upbeat. According to Pentagon sources, it urged that "a vigorous research-and-development program be pursued. This," it continued, "would permit informed decision on whether to initiate, in the early 1990s, an engineering validation phase leading to a deployed defensive capability after the year 2000."[1]

The Hoffman report was also upbeat. "They made the same mistake we made with MIRVs," one official, a skeptic of Star Wars, told me. "They looked at it mainly from the blue side [i.e., the Western side] and asked, 'What good can it do for *us?*' They didn't look properly at what would happen if the Soviets did it too."

The efforts of Fletcher and Hoffman were pulled together by the interagency team led by Frank Miller. Their report, much more cautious than Hoffman's, nevertheless recommended that work on Star Wars go ahead, and that a very thorough assessment should be made of the potential risks and benefits.

The three studies led, first, to the president's National Security Directive 119, seeking funding for a strategic defense initiative; second, to a recommendation for a five-year technology development policy, to run between 1985 and 1989. Finally, a special office was set up and a key appointment made. Lieutenant General James Abrahamson, an air force man and former director of the space shuttle program, was brought in to head the project.

So the ground was laid. What had hitherto been a collection of low-key and rather haphazard research efforts into the potential of defensive weapons had suddenly been transformed into a very high-profile and ambitious program. Once a futuristic dream embraced by a handful of true believers, Star Wars had become serious business. So what were the implications? Were Reagan and his advisers right to be dazzled by the new technologies? What, if anything, could be achieved?

A little more than a year after Reagan's Star Wars speech, the Pentagon staged a remarkable demonstration over the Pacific. Shortly before six (local time) on a June morning, a Minuteman 1 interconti-

---

[1]Actually, the members of the Fletcher panel were almost evenly divided about the feasibility of strategic defense: the optimistic view prevailed, but not as forthrightly as some of the more committed members wished.

nental ballistic missile blasted off from a complex of launch pads on the test range at Vandenberg Air Force Base in Southern california. As the missile soared upward, out of the earth's atmosphere, it released a single dummy nuclear warhead. The target: Kwajalein atoll, 4,800 miles away in the middle of the Pacific. It was the sort of test firing that to the Pentagon, over the last twenty years, had become virtually routine.

What happened next, however, was anything but routine. Twenty minutes after the launch, another rocket (also a Minuteman) lifted off from Kwajalein atoll itself. The aim of the second missile was to find, intercept, and destroy the dummy warhead as it streaked through space at 11,000 miles per hour. The nose cone of this interceptor rocket was a minor miracle of engineering. The crucial part of a project called "homing overlay experiment" (HOE), it contained within its squat cylindrical shape eight infrared telescopes, a laser gyroscope, a computer, and fifty-six thruster rockets. A hundred miles above the ocean, thanks to all this technology, the miniature homing vehicle made split-second adjustments to its course, its telescope sensors feeding information to the onboard computers, which in turn passed it on to the propulsion system. Then a web of high-tension aluminum spokes, wound tightly around its body in a series of spirals like a closed umbrella, sprang open as the vehicle closed with the dummy warhead. Fifteen feet in diameter, this whirling umbrella was designed to catch the warhead in case of a near miss. In the event it was not needed. The HOE vehicle scored a bull's-eye. A hundred miles above the Pacific, two tiny objects, each barely a yard long and eighteen inches across, met head-on at a combined speed of 22,000 miles per hour and shattered into a cloud of metal dust that quickly burned itself out in the earth's upper atmosphere.

It was a staggering technical triumph. Back in the Pentagon, the top brass could not conceal its delight. "It was an absolutely tremendous success," declared Major General Elvin R. Heiberg II, who headed the army program responsible for the project. For the first time, the Americans had proved they could "hit a bullet with a bullet" in outer space. Whatever else, the demonstration revealed that technology had made possible something that would not have been possible ten years earlier.

But as a multitude of critics were quick to point out, shooting down one warhead, with one interceptor, in one carefully staged test, scarcely provided grounds for believing that an impregnable missile shield would ever become possible. As one Pentagon official put it to me at the time: "Anyone who believes that must be on hallucinatory drugs of some kind." Even if it becomes possible to mass-produce a miniature homing vehicle—which would have to be a hundredth the size of the HOE vehicle—and make it work as well as the test model, the difference would be between keeping out one drop of water and keeping out a deluge. In a full-scale Soviet missile assault on the United States, hundreds of missiles would release 9,000 or perhaps, by the 1990s, 20,000 warheads, mixed with tens of thousands of decoys—a huge multitude of tiny objects rushing through space. A mere handful of warheads getting through would be enough to destroy America's major cities; even the penetration of one Hiroshima-sized bomb (and most Soviet warheads are much bigger than that) would mean the deaths of hundreds of thousands of people. Preventing, say, 90 percent of the Russian warheads from getting through would require a technological feat of quite astonishing proportions, but it would still permit 900 or more warheads to find their targets.

The hypothetical journey of a Soviet ICBM from liftoff out of a Siberian silo to detonation of the warheads over American civilian or military targets takes approximately thirty minutes. This period can be divided into four distinct phases:

1. *Boost*, which lasts about five minutes, during which the rocket rises out of its silo and up through the earth's atmosphere.
2. *Postboost*, also lasting about five minutes. The bulky sections (or stages) of the rocket that powered it into space fall away, and the front end (bus) detaches itself and disgorges up to ten (and maybe, if the current arms limitation agreements break down, up to twenty) independently targeted warheads and "penetration aids," such as aluminum foil balloons.
3. *Midcourse*, the longest phase, lasting ten to fifteen minutes, during which warheads and decoys travel halfway around the earth, speeding through the emptiness of space toward their destinations.

4. *Terminal,* the final few minutes as the warheads and penetration
aids reenter the earth's atmosphere; at this point, atmospheric
drag slows down the warheads, while the searing heat of reentry
causes most of the penetration aids to burn up.

To the would-be defender, each of these phases poses special
opportunities—and special problems. The arithmetic of Star Wars
varies, depending on whom you listen to, but anything like a "robust"
defense will have to be multi-tiered—that is, it will have to entail an
effort to strike the attacker in at least three, and possibly all four, phases
of flight. Thus if 80 percent of ascending missiles can be downed in
the boost phase, 80 percent of the remainder in postboost, 80 percent
of surviving warheads in midcourse, and 80 percent of those that make
it through the first three tiers in terminal, then the cumulative effect
will be that virtually no warheads will get through.

Almost everyone—proponents of SDI and critics alike—agrees
that the key to a successful defense lies in "boost-phase kill." Unless
America can "thin out" hundreds of Soviet missiles in the first few
minutes after launch, it will have no realistic hope of stopping a massive
attack. The problems facing the "midcourse" and "terminal" defenses
—identifying, tracking, and striking thousands of tiny individual warheads hurtling through space—will be insuperable. Boost-phase kill, on
the other hand, offers two advantages. First, all the warheads and
decoys carried by a rocket are destroted *before* they are released into
space (like destroying a beehive before it releases a swarm of bees), and
second, rising rockets are readily identifiable targets. They are large,
and they blast out flames and hot gases, so that any heat-sensing device
can spot them. In the words of the anti-SDI Union of Concerned
Scientists, the flaming afterburn stands out "like a firefly in a darkened
room."

The problems of boost-phase kill, however, start with those posed
by geography and the inexorable laws of motion. There are *at most* four
minutes in which to strike— and probably considerably less, since both
the United States and the USSR are becoming capable of developing
rockets with a boost phase of only *fifty seconds.* And no purely ground-
based system could get near enough to do the job without encroaching

on Soviet territory. So the United States will have to rely on hardware in space, and this presents some tricky problems.

In the postboost and midcourse phases, when the initial stages of the rocket have fallen away, the advantages the defender has are time —twenty minutes or so in which to strike—and the fact that individual warheads are likely to remain on a predictable path because, as the SDI director, General Abrahamson, puts it: "They have to go after specific targets and, thus, because of natural law, don't have the luxury of evasive action." But the problems, by then, have multiplied. Now hundreds of relatively large targets have been replaced by thousands, or tens, even hundreds of thousands of relatively tiny ones—nuclear and fake-nuclear bullets—hurtling through space. Either they *all* have to be targeted, or the intercepting weapons have to be clever enough to discriminate between real warheads and phony ones, a task whose magnitude can be imagined.

In the terminal phase, as they enter the earth's atmosphere, most of the decoys frizzle up in the heat or get separated from the warheads by a process known as "atmospheric sorting" (they are lighter, so fall more slowly). Meanwhile, the warheads themselves have slowed to about 2 miles a second and can now be shot at with ground-based weapons—guided missiles, artillery, etc. But the warheads by now are also dangerously close, and if primed to explode when hit, could still cause terrible destruction even if struck 20 miles above their targets. Besides, since it would be impossible to predict which warheads would get through the outer defenses, it would also be impossible to predict which targets should have terminal defenses: *every* city, *every* military base, and *every* missile field would have to be guarded. In the kind of missile shield envisaged by President Reagan, therefore, terminal defenses make little sense.

None of the technologies currently under scrutiny looks likely to be able to do even a fraction of what would be needed to make a full-scale defense conceivable. The Pentagon's own director of research and engineering, Richard DeLauer, has described the prospects for success as dependent on breakthroughs in an array of key technologies, each "equivalent to or greater than the Manhattan Project."

Kinetic Energy Weapons

The bull's-eye in space scored by the Pentagon on June 11, 1984, was achieved under a project code-named Homing Overlay. Run by the U.S. Army, it long predated Reagan's initiative (having been conceived in 1978) and was deliberately designed within the constraints of the ABM treaty (which allows for experimental development and testing of defensive systems, so long as it is carried out using recognizable missile ranges).

The "homing overlay vehicle" that destroyed the dummy warhead did so by *kinetic energy;* that is, by sheer force of impact. Kinetic energy weapons, in the words of Dr. Gerold Yonas, SDI's chief scientist, are "smart rocks," and they don't have to be all that hard: on Yonas's desk is a 3-inch-thick sheet of steel with a hole in it made by a plastic pellet fired at 800 miles per hour.

At least kinetic energy weapons *exist,* which is more than can be said for most of the hardware being contemplated for Star Wars. But they have a number of drawbacks, the most serious of which is their speed. Compared with laser beams, which travel at the speed of light, they are disappointingly slow. They may get faster—those powered by chemical propellants may eventually, if the optimists are to be believed, achieve speeds of more than 17,000 miles per hour, and those powered by electricity speeds in excess of 50,000 miles per hour. (An electromagnetic rail gun, which works like a slingshot powered by electric current, is, for example, being tested at the University of Texas.) But they will always be thousands of times slower than lasers, and they will never be fast enough to hit Soviet boosters from Western territory.

This means that the only hope of using them for boost-phase kill is to have them mounted on satellites. The satellites will contain rockets in pods, and these rockets will be armed with miniature homing vehicles. Theoretically, if so mounted, they will be able to strike ICBMs at the top of their boost phase or in the postboost phase. But the infrared telescopes on which kinetic energy weapons depend do not work well in the atmosphere, and their effectiveness would be dramatically reduced if the Soviets shortened the boost phase of their missiles so that they burned out about 50 miles above the earth (instead of the present 200–250 miles). Also, as the Union of Concerned Scientists has pointed out, the Soviets may eventually be able to design missiles without buses (the warheads and decoys spinning off the instant the rocket burns out), thus making it very hard for kinetic energy weapons to strike in the postboost phase.

But the most serious headache posed by kinetic energy weapons is that, because of their slowness and their restricted range, they will have to be mounted on satellites in *low orbit.*

Such satellites will only be over their "target areas" for only about five of the ninety-four or so minutes it takes them to orbit the earth. For that reason, and because each satellite will only be able to hold a limited number of interceptors, a veritable galaxy of satellites will be required to ensure that that targets are always covered. Precisely how many has been the subject of fierce dispute, but inevitably, at this stage, the calculations have a back-of-the-envelope quality: they depend on all kinds of assumptions, such as the speed with which weapons can be re-aimed.[2] But most scientists believe the number will run into hundreds, if not thousands. Just lifting all that weight into orbit will be enormously expensive ($6 million a ton at current prices), not to mention the expense of the satellites themselves (perhaps up to $500 million each—the price of two destroyers) or the problems of protecting them against Soviet attack.

Not surprisingly, then, many star warriors, including one of the

---

[2]The most optimistic estimate of the number of satellites I have come across is 100, each holding 150 interceptors. This was supplied by former national security adviser Zbigniew Brzezinski, physicist and Star Wars enthusiast Robert Jastrow, and Max Kampelman, a Washington lawyer subsequently appointed head of the U.S. delegation to the Geneva arms control talks. They suggested, in an article in the *New York Times Magazine,* that such a "boost phase defense" could be in place by the early 1990s, that it would be "sufficient to counter a mass Soviet attack from all their 1,400 [land-based] silos" (submarines are left out, so is any possible expansion of land-based forces), and that it could be accommodated easily within a $45 billion price tag. Many experts find this wildly optimistic and believe that to keep enough kinetic energy weapons within range of Soviet launch sites at all times, the United States would need many more satellites and perhaps as many as 20,000 interceptors.

project's leading lights, George Keyworth, are skeptical about the potential of kinetic energy weapons as boost-phase killers. Apart from everything else, Keyworth points out, satellites firing kinetic energy weapons might not be able to re-aim and fire again quickly enough if they missed with their first shots.

Keyworth, however, does believe that kinetic energy weapons could be used in the midcourse phase. The homing vehicle that brought down the warhead over the Pacific in June 1984 did so (in effect) in "late midcourse," and certainly kinetic energy weapons could be fired, as happened then, from ground-launched missiles, or from satellites. But the problem would be sheer numbers. To distinguish between real warheads and decoys the "smart rocks" would have to be "intellectual giants," as one analyst put it, and if they were unable to distinguish the difference, they would have to go after everything—warheads, chaff, decoys, aluminum balloons, the lot. Since one would have to anticipate a high failure rate, the number of weapons needed to do this would be simply staggering.

Lasers

Military planners have dreamed of laser weapons since the 1950s, when scientists first learned the trick of producing amplified beams of coherent light. Unlike ordinary light, a helter-skelter mixture of light waves of different frequencies scattering in every direction, laser beams consist of light waves of identical frequency, marching in perfect step with one another and finely focused, diffusing little over great distances. (They travel, of course, at the speed of light—186,000 miles per second.) By the time Reagan unveiled his Star Wars initiative lasers were already being widely used in medicine, industry, and in the military for range finding, missile guidance, and, increasingly, as high-speed, short-range weapons. In May 1983, the U.S. Air Force destroyed five air-launched Sidewinder AIM9-L missiles fired in rapid succession with a 10.6 micron carbon dioxide laser mounted in a large jet transport. But the use to which the star warriors wish to push them is altogether more demanding; what they have in mind are laser beams that can be focused over thousands of miles of space while still remaining powerful enough to burn holes in the skins of Russian missiles.

The most basic and "mature" form of laser currently in use is the chemical laser, powered by the violent chemical reaction of hydrogen and fluorine. But scientists have reason to be dubious about the potential of chemical lasers.

First, they consist of long wavelengths of light. This makes it hard to focus them across vast distances. A chemical laser beam might have to spend up to seven seconds "dwell time" on a missile's skin in order to burn a hole in it, and the problems of keeping the beam focused on precisely the same spot during that time—while the missile travels, say, twenty miles—can be imagined. To be effective, chemical lasers would require immensely complicated and delicate optical systems for aiming their beams.

Another problem would be power. Pumping a chemical laser through the emptiness of space would require a considerable quantity of fuel. The generating equipment would have to be in space, mounted on a fleet of satellites in low orbit. As with kinetic energy platforms, the number required is a matter of fierce debate among scientists— estimates range from 100 or 200 all the way up to 1,600 (which is probably overly pessimistic).[3] But the satellites would have to be huge, weighing a hundred tons or more, and just getting them into space, let alone defending them, would pose momentous problems. Many scientists involved in Star Wars therefore discount chemical lasers. They believe the problems will never be overcome.

More promising, though also fraught with snags, is the technology

---

[3] The Union of Concerned Scientists began by estimating the figure at 2,400. One of the SDI scientists, Gregory Canavan, did some calculations of his own, revealing flaws in the UCS figure. But his own calculations have also been challenged. So have those of a paper written at the Lawrence Livermore laboratory, suggesting that only 90 satellites would be needed. This, says the British scientist R. V. Jones, contains "some fantastic assumptions: the laser satellites would be in 6 orbits at 300 kilometers altitude; against the simultaneous launch of 1,400 Russian ICBMs, no more than 8 satellites could be engaged, and 4 of them would be expected to destroy some 1,200 missiles, or 300 per satellite, each satellite killing 10 ICBMs per second!"

of excimer and free-electron lasers, both of which emit their energy in shorter wavelengths, or pulses. Capable of concentrating greater energy over greater distances than their long-wavelength cousins, they would in theory require much less "dwell time"—only a second or so. (Though this is still not good enough, says General Abrahamson: he believes that lasers will have to be able to do their job in "perhaps one-tenth of a second" to be effective, a tall order indeed.) The star warriors are excited about the potential of free-electron lasers. In an interview with me, in September 1985, George Keyworth singled them out as an area of rapid advance. What had merely been a "good idea" when SDI was launched had become, thanks to work at top-secret laboratories like Lawrence Livermore in California and Los Alamos in New Mexico, he told me, "one of the most promising areas of technology, a front contender." The key breakthrough, Keyworth said, had been finding a more efficient way of turning raw electrical power into laser energy.

The hope, then, is that free-electron laser weapons will eventually be able to flash lethal rays over tens of thousands of miles. Where might such weapons be based? One answer is 22,000 miles up in space. Satellites there would be in "geostationary orbit," moving at the same speed as the earth's rotation, and therefore hovering always above the same spot on the earth's surface. This would remove the need for vast numbers of satellites, but aiming and firing at Soviet rockets from such an enormous distance will not be easy. The accuracy required will be of the order of one in 350 million, according to the conservative British scientist Professor R. V. Jones, who says it will be comparable "with having to check in advance that the sights of a rifle are aligned so accurately with the barrel that the aiming error would be no more than one bullet diameter at a range of 1,000 miles, without having a chance to fire a trial shot and with the rifle more than 20,000 miles away in space." And even if a trial shot could be fired—against a "friendly target" (i.e., a missile rising from an American silo)—the aiming problem would still be horrendous. Not only that: free-electron lasers would require even greater supplies of power than chemical ones, and their generators might prove so bulky as to rule out any hope of hoisting them into space. Thus neither Keyworth nor his mentor, Edward

Teller, appears overly enthusiastic about the idea of laser battle stations in space. They "won't fit the bill," says Teller. "They must be deployed in great numbers at terrible cost, and could be destroyed in advance of an attack."

There is an alternative solution: putting the lasers themselves on the ground and bouncing their beams off mirrors in space. Since lasers do not work well in the atmosphere—its different layers distort their beams and cause them to shimmer, just as the stars, observed from the earth, appear to twinkle—the battle stations will have to be sited on mountaintops. That way, the beams fired upward will only have to cope with the thin upper layers of the atmosphere. But if the Soviets are unsporting enough to attack in bad weather, the defense will be in trouble, since laser beams cannot effectively penetrate clouds. And whether the laser beams are bounced off mirrors in geostationary orbit down to "battle" mirrors in lower orbit, which in turn "aim" them at the Russian rockets or their nuclear cargo, or whether the beams are leapfrogged across a whole series of battle mirrors in low orbit, the mirrors will have to be gigantic, cheap enough to be deployed in large numbers, and almost unimaginably perfect. They will have to be able to prevent a phenomenon known as "spherical spreading" (the beam from a laser, like the beam from a flashlight, tends to widen out with distance), and they will have to be tremendously robust to withstand and redirect the powerful beams fired at them. The mirror, perhaps 45 to 90 feet in diameter, may be too large to be hoisted into space in one piece, and might have to be assembled in orbit. The star warriors are counting on breakthroughs in the technology of "adaptive optics"— the ability to build very thin and flexible mirrors that can change their shape. But at the time of writing the largest example of adaptive optics is a mirror 10 inches in diameter, and what is envisaged would require something two or three orders of magnitude larger.

All in all, the deployment of a mirror-based defense would be a fantastically elaborate and precise operation, and not surprisingly many scientists dismiss it as expensive and impractical. But if Star Wars is to work, the fantastic will become commonplace. Consider the most controversial, and to some, the most plausible form of directed-energy weapon: the X-ray laser. Potentially the most deadly member of the laser family, it will require no dwell time whatsoever and be capable of explosively vaporizing a missile's skin in a fraction of a second. It would not need to be as carefully aimed as chemical, excimer, or free-electron lasers; its "beam" could be thirty yards or more in diameter.

Edward Teller and his disciples like to put it about that systems like the X-ray laser are the ones that contain real promise. Chemical lasers and the like are more of a sideshow, discussed in public precisely because their potential is limited. It is a convenient argument, but not wholly convincing; because for Reagan, with his dream of nonnuclear defenses, the X-ray laser has one drawback: it derives its colossal power not from chemicals or electricity, but from a *nuclear explosion.* Partly for this reason, its development has always been shrouded in secrecy. In February 1981, *Aviation Week and Space Technology* reported that the Lawrence Livermore laboratory in California had tested an X-ray laser pumped by a bomb (as part of a top-secret program called Dauphin). The administration subsequently acknowledged the testing program, which takes place under the desert in Nevada, but it remains highly classified. However, the basic principles of the Dauphin—now renamed Excalibur, after the magical sword that King Arthur pulled from the stone—are clear. The X-ray laser is a nuclear bomb surrounded by a parallel bundle of very thin metallic rods. These rods are gimbaled so that they can be aimed at individual enemy missiles. In theory, when the bomb explodes it causes temperatures found in nature only in the interior of stars, floods the rods with radiation, and fires them an instant before the whole device is consumed by the nuclear fireball.

X-ray lasers would have to be fired from space, and Congress in unlikely ever to welcome the idea of keeping, say, 1,400 nuclear bombs circling permanently around the earth in low orbit (even if the treaties that forbid the deployment of nuclear weapons in space were revoked). So how would the X-ray laser work? "You obviously have to get your weapons up *after* the enemy has launched his first salvo, not *before,*" says one Livermore scientist. "I'm not saying how this would work, but you might do it by sending up your weapon on a missile of your own" (my italics).

Thus the X-ray laser would be a "pop-up" defense. And coordinating a pop-up defense would not be child's play. Seconds after the warning of a Soviet missile attack, America would have to launch its own defensive missiles, carrying the X-ray laser bombs in their nose cones. The defensive missiles would have to rise fast enough and high enough to fire off and explode their X-ray bombs at the exact moment when the Russian missiles reached the top of their boost phase or conceivably had entered their postboost phase (X-ray lasers do not work in the atmosphere). To have any chance of accomplishing this, submarines would have to be used, and they would have to be stationed perilously close to the Soviet coastline—probably in the Arabian Sea just south of Pakistan, about the closest they could get to the major Soviet missile silos strung out along the trans-Siberian railway. Flashing instructions to submarines in the first moments of nuclear war would be very difficult, assuming of course that the submarines had not already been found and sunk. Even that does not do justice to the problem. Submarines take around thirty minutes to fire off all their missiles, but they give away their position the instant they fire their first salvo. It is likely that, if not found and sunk before they began firing, they would be found and sunk before they finished. What is more, the submarines would have to be specially built, because the Pentagon would not wish to risk its existing ballistic missile submarine fleet, which forms the backbone of the U.S. nuclear deterrent.

Finally, even were everything to work perfectly, it would take about three minutes to get the rockets carrying the pop-up lasers into position to fire. Since the ICBMs under attack would be ending their boost phase after, at most, *four* minutes, this could pose quite a task. For the three minutes it would take to get the pop-up laser in place do *not* include the time it would take to process and verify information from early warning satellites about the Soviet attack (and currently that takes two minutes), nor do they include the time it would take to get authorization to fire what would be a nuclear weapon into space. Unless it is assumed that both these things could happen *instantly*, the West would be wasting billions on a weapon that could not possibly work. In sum, the whole operation would call for a command and control system well beyond anything that has so far seemed possible. The X-ray laser would be a "single-shot" device; if it missed, there would be no second chance. And the Russians would almost certainly find it much easier to build missiles that burn out after fifty seconds than the Americans would to build pop-up missiles.

Particle Beam Weapons

In addition to lasers, there is one other type of directed energy weapon whose potential is being examined by the star warriors. Instead of flashing a beam of light at its target, this would project a stream of atoms or subatomic particles, which would penetrate deep into the structure of the target—i.e., missile or warhead—causing implosions, and destroying its innards and other essential components. The effect would be like that of a lightning bolt, which indeed a particle beam closely resembles. The attraction of such a weapon would be its lethality—no worries over dwell time; destruction would be instant—but the drawbacks would be considerable.

Like X-ray lasers, particle beams are quite ineffective in the atmosphere, so their usefulness, providing the generating equipment could be got into space, would be for postboost and midcourse kill (the attacking rockets would be immune from attack during the crucial boost phase). But even if that was judged to be worth the effort there would remain the problem of getting the generating equipment into orbit. Particle beams require colossal amounts of energy, and a single particle beam battle station might have to weigh as much as 500 tons. Finally, particle beams travel more slowly than laser beams. To make them reach more than half the speed of light you might need even bigger battle stations.

(There is one special type of particle beam that can operate in the atmosphere. Built into a remote hillside at Lawrence Livermore is a tunnellike laboratory being used for tests of a particle beam weapon that might eventually be adapted so that it can ram its subatomic particles up through the atmosphere, the ultimate aim being to destroy incoming warheads in the terminal phase. The problem at the moment, says William Barletta, a particle beam expert at the lab, is stopping the particle beams from "kinking" in the atmosphere like garden hoses. With the help of Livermore's Advanced Test Accelerator, he thinks this may eventually be solved.)

The technologies available to star warriors are undoubtedly dazzling. Some may even be ready for systems-level development by the

1990s. But a cursory glance, such as the one above, suggests that the problems of making them effective are legion. Still, let us concede for the moment that at some stage it may be possible to design lasers, particle beam accelerators, and kinetic energy weapons that are able to burn through the skins, fry the innards, or destroy by impact existing ballistic missiles. For as yet we have scarcely touched on the *real* problems. The fact is that Star Wars would depend not so much on whether individual gadgets would work but on whether a system could be created that *as a whole* could function reliably, cope with Soviet countermeasures, *and* do both these things while leaving America on the right side of bankruptcy. The evidence suggests that in an even vaguely utopian form (such as the provision of a semieffective defense of "soft targets," i.e., people) it will be possible to do none of these things.

When interviewed about Star Wars, SDI's rather engaging director, General Abrahamson, likes to point out that "the long pole of the tent is not the weapons . . . it is the infrastructure [and] the command-and-control system." This would seem sensible enough. At least as much money is being, and will be, spent on this "battle management" side of Star Wars as on the weapons themselves. After all, before you think about knocking missiles out of the sky you have to consider all sorts of other things: tracking them from the moment they take off, tracking the bus and then the warheads once the boosters have fallen away (much harder, because there is no bright plume of fire to act as a beacon, and warheads are comparatively tiny), sorting warheads from decoys, coordinating your tracking satellites with your weapons-firing devices, enabling each of your weapons to fire at precisely the right moment and at precisely the right target, monitoring what is destroyed and what is not so that you don't waste valuable shots on shattered warheads, and creating a system of command and control that would be resilient and complex enough to cope with this fantastic operation.

Difficulties proliferate in every corner of the project, and the task of "managing" a defense against hundreds of missiles is far beyond anything the human brain is capable of. Only computers will be able to absorb and process the billions of bits of information quickly enough to provide any realistic chance of success, and the computers themselves will have to be breathtakingly sophisticated, far more so than anything likely to be available in the 1980s. "The computers would require 10 million lines of error-free code," says Richard Garwin, a top missile scientist (and an opponent of Star Wars).[4] "I don't know anyone who knows that this is possible."

Certainly no human being could design the software program for a "battle management" Star Wars computer. That would have to be done with the aid of computers, too. (A typical programmer can produce about 3,000 lines of documented debugged code per year. Producing 10 million lines of code, therefore, might take 1,000 programmers three years, or 300 programmers ten years. But these 1,000—or 300—programmers would have to work as closely together as a well-trained orchestra for an extraordinarily long time, a feat of human cooperation without parallel in human history.) And supposing you *could* design the software, how on earth could you check it for errors? According to General Abrahamson, you would have to put it through "debugging runs"—perhaps as many as 50 million. But even then there would be no guarantee that it would work properly. Redundancy, of course, might be built in as a hedge against failure. Keyworth, for example, is fond of pointing out that the AT&T telephone system seldom breaks down and contains 10 million lines of code. But the AT&T system was developed over many years, with a lot of trial and error, and no one is proposing to bet the security of the Western world on it.

The only way of *guaranteeing* that the system would work in a crisis would be to test it under the actual conditions in which you intended to use it. This, however, would involve starting the third and probably last world war. So you would simply have to hope that the computer would function perfectly in conditions far more strenuous than it would ever have encountered in tests or debugging runs.

Thus, even if the technological problems could be solved, and the vast amounts of money found, *any* Star Wars system would still be an enormous gamble. We have already noted that most modern weapons work less well in practice than they do in theory, but whereas conventional weapons can be tested in conditions roughly approximating those of war, and even nuclear missiles can be tested sufficiently to ensure

---

[4]The launch sequence for America's space shuttle, by comparison, requires a modest 10,000 lines.

that enough would get through to cause horrendous damage, the delicate architecture of Star Wars would be another matter. Not until it was too late would anyone know whether it would work or not. Yet despite this, the search for a means of creating an "autonomous" Star Wars system is proceeding apace.

In October 1983, seven months after President Reagan's speech, the Pentagon announced the launch of a five-year, $600 million research project called the Strategic Computer Program. It does not fall under the aegis of General Abrahamson and his staff, though they will be the prime beneficiaries if the project is successful. Instead, the program is being run by the Pentagon's Defense Advanced Research Projects Agency (DARPA), which has described its goal in a little-known report entitled *Strategic Computing, New-Generation Computing Technology: A Strategic Plan for Its Development and Application to Critical Problems in Defense.* If DARPA ever achieves this goal, noted one Washington computer expert in the *Atlantic,* "future historians might rank this remarkable document with Albert Einstein's 1939 letter to President Roosevelt recommending development of the atomic bomb." The goal is nothing less than the creation of computers capable of exhibiting "artificial intelligence":

> Instead of fielding simple guided missiles or remotely piloted vehicles, we might launch completely autonomous land, sea and air vehicles capable of complex, far-ranging reconnaissance and attack missions. . . . In contrast with previous computers, the new generation will exhibit human-like, "intelligent" capabilities for planning and reasoning. . . . Using this new technology, machines will perform complex tasks with little human intervention, or even with complete autonomy. . . . Our leaders will employ intelligent computers as active assistants in the management of complex enterprises.

Among the gizmos listed for study in this astonishing report are an "unmanned robot tank" that would be able to fight the Russians all on its own, and for the air force a "pilot's associate"—a silicon co-pilot that would be able to assist the human being in the pilot's seat operate the electronic warfare equipment of complex modern aircraft. But the biggest and most dramatic role the new so-called fifth-generation computers might be called upon to perform, of course, would be to assist Star Wars. And the envisaged Star Wars computers would not only have to cope with a huge amount of data very, very fast, they would have to *function automatically.* Not just the processing of data, but the decision to fire would be made by computer. There would be no time for human beings to be involved, no time for anyone to telephone the president.

Those who are pushing SDI have more or less accepted this. "It seems clear," concluded the panel of scientists that looked into the nuts and bolts of Star Wars after the president's speech, ". . . that some degree of automation in the decision to commit weapons is inevitable if a ballistic missile system is to be at all credible." In April 1984, in a hearing of the Senate Foreign Relations Committee, George Keyworth was asked by Senator Paul Tsongas of Massachusetts who would make the decision to activate Star Wars. "We don't know," replied the president's scientific adviser. "By the year 1990, it may be done automatically." Would the system be "switched on" all the time? Not necessarily. In separate testimony to the House Appropriations Committee, General Abrahamson indicated that when the situation was calm ". . . many of the automatic features would be shut down and turned off. But were a crisis to build, the president would make those decisions ahead of time, and he would probably tell the Russians, 'Okay, now I am activating an important part of our system,' which means that it is automatic. Hopefully, that would begin to reduce the crisis."

One hopes we will never find out, for some believe that "activating" the system would have precisely the opposite effect. Indeed, as computer expert Jonathan Jacky has observed, the testimony underlines just how vulnerable the idea of computer control is:

> Keyworth's and Abrahamson's suggestions that the system would be activated only during crises strongly imply that even they do not believe that the system could be made very reliable: if we leave it turned off most of the time, we might reduce the chance of an accident. But many analysts have observed that *a crisis is exactly*

the worst time to delegate control to an unstable system. The
chances that there will be some incident that triggers a false alert
are probably greater then, and the consequences of responding to
a false alert could be much worse.

One of the most complicated computer networks currently in use
resides at NORAD, the North American Air Defense Command. The
air force technicians at NORAD, whose headquarters is buried deep
in the granite heart of Cheyenne Mountain, at the edge of the Rockies,
would be the first to know if a Soviet missile attack was launched on
America. The consoles that would register blips showing Soviet missiles
rising out of their silos are linked to computers, which are in turn linked
to a worldwide early warning network of tremendous sophistication.

In November 1979, a training tape containing a simulation of a
Soviet attack was somehow played through NORAD's "live" warning
system, creating a false alert. The error was quickly spotted, and there
was no more than a brief panic. Seven months later, in June 1980, a
46-cent computer chip in a microcomputer failed, again leading to the
transmission of an erroneous message that the United States was under
attack. About a hundred B-52 bombers were readied for takeoff, as was
the president's emergency plane, the National Alternative Airborne
Command Post, nicknamed "Kneecap." As in 1979, the fault was
swiftly identified and the readied aircraft were "stood down." On both
these occasions, however, the world was relatively calm: it simply did
not seem likely that the Russians were preparing to launch a "bolt from
the blue." And at NORAD there is time to make checks, there are
human beings "in the loop," and there have been enough false alarms
to instill considerable caution about total reliance on microchips or
software. No one, as has been said often enough, "wants to go to war
on the basis of a computer."

But what if a computer failure at NORAD were to occur during
a crisis? Defense analyst Paul Bracken, who has done a detailed study
of the command and control of nuclear forces, points out that it would
then be much easier for things to get out of hand. Everyone would be
jumpy; the Soviets would see the B-52s being readied for takeoff, and
might respond by scrambling their own bomber forces. Even if the
computer failure was detected, a series of "corresponding alerts" might

begin in a kind of high-tech version of the mobilization/countermobili-
zation process that led up to World War I.

With luck, this will never happen. But given the complexity of
Star Wars, computer errors seem almost inevitable. After all, many of
the most serious problems in modern conventional weapons are caused
by bugs in the software. Take the ill-fated Divad gun. Most of the basic
hardware components—the chassis, the radar, the gun, and so on—
worked well enough *separately*, but Ford Aerospace could never solve
the software problems involved in making them work smoothly together. (It was this that on one celebrated occasion caused the gun to
take aim at a latrine rather than its designated target.)

The Star Wars computers would be thousands—if not millions—
of times more complicated than the computers used in Divad, and
unlike the Divad's they could never be properly tested. Unless the star
warriors find a way of repealing Murphy's Law—the one that holds that
if something *can* go wrong, it will—computers, like everything else
built by human beings, will always be capable of breaking down, and
the more complicated they are, the more likely it is to happen. Thus
one could never have confidence in a Star Wars computer, and the
notion that SDI would have to be fully automatic is perhaps the most
troubling aspect of the whole project. "No one who knows about
missile defense systems would put the survivability of such systems in
the hands of computers," says Richard Garwin. "It's like a whole bunch
of sparking switches in a gasoline-filled room. The least error in that
computer system would launch a nuclear war."

Even if that is an exaggeration—and, to be fair, many analysts
believe it is—and even if the worst that could result from a malfunction
of the system would be some bangs and flashes in space and a harmless
waste of Star Wars ammunition, the danger of entrusting Western
security to a computer-controlled system would still be considerable.

"An accident is not really the problem," one of those involved in
SDI research told me. "Your lasers might burn a few holes in the
Siberian snow, but who cares if that happens? And kinetic energy
weapons, if they were fired, would burn out on reentry, like meteors.
They would become ash, molecules distributed in the air, long before

they hit the ground. Remember, none of these weapons are weapons of mass destruction."

This particular scientist, who started out hopeful about the potential of SDI, and has since become more pessimistic, made it clear as we talked that he has no objection, in principle, to "militarizing space." "Why not take war to the heavens? It's the best place for it." Yet despite this, and despite the fact that he worries little about accidents, "taking the control of mighty weapons out of the hands of politicians" would constitute a grave risk. The system, because of worries about its reliability, and because the Russians would presumably wish to be allowed to send missiles into space during peacetime (on tests and space missions), would have to be switched off most of the time. The problem, therefore, would come during a crisis: Moscow, after all, does not believe that the American Star Wars program is defensive in nature. It believes that the United States is intent on building defenses so that it can be free to launch a preemptive strike with impunity. And an American announcement that SDI had been turned on might cause the Russians to fear that they were about to be struck. They might then say: "We'd better go first, while we can." The decision to switch on could actually trigger a nuclear strike. Leaving the system unarmed and only arming it in a time of crisis could thus give the Russians a wrong signal that the United States was preparing for a preemptive strike and was arming its defense system to scale up the counterattack from submarine-launched missiles.

So much for the initial problems. We have seen that *any* system America might build, supposing that the technological difficulties could be overcome and the vast amounts of money found, would be an enormous gamble, and a dangerous one. We have, as yet, scarcely glanced at what the Russians might do. For during the years it would take America to build a defensive system, the Soviet Union would almost certainly be working flat out to render it useless. Let us glance at the countermeasures the Kremlin could take—many of them, unlike Star Wars itself, easily achievable through existing, not futuristic, technology.

"If you start to build Star Wars, we will be obliged to build new nuclear weapons, and more of them, which can penetrate your defen-

sive shield," says Georgi Arbatov, director of the Kremlin's Institute of
U.S. and Canadian Studies. That, of course, would be the simplest
thing the Russians could do. According to U.S. intelligence, they already have "extra" missiles at many of their missile sites, enabling them
to reload individual silos once an initial salvo has been fired. (One
estimate puts the number of "extras" at 1,000.) They could add to
these, deploy new silos, increase the size of their ballistic submarine
fleet, and generally bolster an already swollen arsenal by doubling or
trebling their current total of 8,000 warheads. They could add countless
decoys. "Any defensive system," Richard DeLauer, undersecretary of
defense for research and engineering, has said, "can be overcome by
proliferation and decoys, decoys, decoys, decoys." The Russians could
also protect their missiles by giving them specially coated skins that
would be hard for lasers to penetrate, or by making their boosters
revolve, which would prevent lasers that require dwell time from accomplishing their task. Lowell Wood, a burly, bearded Livermore scientist and flamboyant Star Wars advocate, anticipates that this would
pose no real problems; the defense, he says, would be using "a submachine gun against a ballet dancer." But whereas this might conceivably
be true against the nuclear-pumped X-ray laser, it would certainly not
be true against chemical or excimer lasers.

Another improvement in missilery would be harder to counter:
making the boost phase shorter by creating powerful "fast burn" rockets that would rise swiftly out of the earth's atmosphere. These would
give the defense not four minutes, but as little as fifty seconds in which
to strike before the release of the bus. The Soviets could also design
rockets that would not require a bus, but that would release their
warheads and decoys the instant the boost phase was over.

All this, of course, would take time and money, but then so will
Star Wars; only the staunchest optimists believe anything like an effective defense could be in place before the end of the century. And the
countermeasures would almost certainly cost far less than the system
itself.

One of the more thoughtful critics of Star Wars is James Schlesinger, a tough former defense secretary who is in a good position to
assess the issue. In the 1960s Schlesinger worked for the Rand Corpora-

tion, the air force think tank based in Santa Monica, California, and in the early 1970s he moved to the White House to take a job in the Office of Management and Budget (as it is now called). In both these roles he became closely involved in the debate over strategic defenses, at the time when the issue first came to the fore in American politics. It was an experience that taught him to be cautious.

In a speech on October 25, 1984, Schlesinger reminded his audience of the cost calculations that had been done in the 1960s. Back then, he said, it had been judged that it would take five times as much money to erect a defense as to neutralize it. By the 1980s, he conceded, that ratio might have modestly improved, but even that was doubtful. "It is suggested that the ratio is now on the order of three to one. But that judgment primarily rests on a single change: the belief that we can intercept Soviet missiles during the boost phase prior to separation of the reentry vehicles [warheads]. Nonetheless, it is clear that the ratio is still strongly weighted against defense and will remain so. . . ."

We have already noted that the Soviets could take a number of relatively cheap measures to protect their missiles during the boost phase. Yet Star Wars advocates believe (contrary to Schlesinger) that, in the end, the defense-offense spending ratio will not be five to one, or three to one, but *one to one*, or even better, and tilted in favor of the defense. That, indeed, is the critical assumption behind the whole initiative. If it costs more to build defenses than to counter them, then there is clearly no point in doing it. You are in a position where your opponent can force you, year after year, to spend more than he does just to maintain the status quo. And as we look at the sheer range of countermeasures available, the whole fanciful arithmetic of Star Wars begins to look more and more dubious.

Earlier in this book we examined the application of "emerging technology" to the central front in Europe—smart weapons linked to supersophisticated sensors and computers that might someday revolutionize conventional defense. ET would be a sequential system, and sequential systems, as we observed, rarely work in war. There is too much that can go wrong. All sorts of things have to happen in perfect sequence, and the whole system falters if you can disrupt just one element.

Star Wars would be the ultimate sequential system. However much redundancy you tried to build in, in terms of numbers of satellites, numbers of battle stations, and so on, a long chain of events would still have to happen perfectly to prevent devastating results. The Russians could use conventional weapons to go after ground-based terminals (during the conventional war that would probably precede nuclear war), or they could use sabotage. Teams of Spetznaz—Soviet special forces—who would infiltrate allied countries before or during an attack would clearly make Star Wars installations a high-priority target. Command and communications links would be vulnerable to bombing, blinding, jamming, and "spoofing"—that is, enemy attempts to break into the system and control it by transmitting on the same frequency —and the enemy would have a choice of different kinds of communications links to disrupt: satellite to satellite, satellite to ground, and so on. Besides, communications blackouts could be created over wide areas by the simple expedient of exploding nuclear weapons high in the atmosphere.

Indeed, nuclear weapons themselves would pose the single greatest headache to a defense system. Exploding a mere handful in space —and no conceivable system could prevent that—would wreak havoc with the fragile mechanisms of Star Wars. Take just one scenario, offered by a Livermore scientist. The Russians could "send a series of missiles strung out single file, each missile fused to detonate if it sensed that some defensive weapon was about to destroy it. The resulting fireballs would serve the attackers as blinds, through which successive missiles could penetrate closer to the target. By using enough missiles, the enemy could be certain of finally reaching the target."

But what of the satellites themselves? Boost-phase kill would require, if not a galaxy of orbiting battle stations, then certainly an array of prepositioned mirrors, communications and sensor platforms ready, at any instant, to begin flashing information to each other and back to earth about an impending Soviet attack. And supposing most of your weapons could be popped up into space just before use—a staggering supposition—then you would place even greater strain on command, control, and communications links, not to mention the problems you would have protecting launch submarines in hostile waters just off the Soviet coastline. But even then a good deal of hardware would have to be prepositioned in space—communications satellites, surveillance satellites, and the like—and protecting even *these* against nuclear weapons would be well nigh impossible. The X-ray laser that entrances Edward Teller, for example, might prove far more useful in *countering* a defensive system than in aiding it; if able to attack fast-moving rockets, it would *certainly* be able, in the hands of the Soviets, to attack satellites and battle stations moving through space in well-defined orbits. And in space, as on land, any development pioneered by the United States will eventually be imitated by the USSR. (A small number of nuclear explosions would be sufficient to cause havoc to a space-based defense. The Russians could achieve this by using a small number of missiles, each armed with one warhead specially hardened against laser beams.)

But there would be no need for weapons as powerful as nuclear bombs to knock out defensive satellites. They would present large and vulnerable targets. One possible kinetic energy weapon under study is the electromagnetic rail gun. This would use a burst of electric current to fire General Abrahamson's "smart rocks" (homing vehicles) along a rail and out across space to their targets. The snag is that such a rail gun might have to be 150 meters long with a bulky power generator at one end, and protecting this—the equivalent, as one skeptic put it, of "an aircraft carrier in space"—would be a nightmare. The same problem would apply to other forms of battle stations.

Scientists involved in Star Wars are well aware of the "vulnerability problem." At research labs like Los Alamos and Lawrence Livermore in the dusty heartland of California, they are exploring ways of providing SDI weapons with armor. "Some of the biggest challenges we face," acknowledges Gerold Yonas, "are making weapons not only lethal but survivable—survivable in the sense that boost-phase weapons will orbit over the Soviet Union and thus be subject to attack." One study done by Livermore suggests that the protection of battle stations in space might call for shielding by a million tons of protective material. But that raises another problem. The battle stations would be heavy enough without any protection, weighing perhaps 150 tons each; adding huge amounts of shielding would make them even heavier, and hoisting such weight into space would be phenomenally expensive. (At the moment it costs $3,000 to send just one *pound* of material into orbit on the space shuttle.) Officials have even suggested, somewhat fancifully, that it might be easier and cheaper to mine the vast amounts of shielding material required from the asteroids or the moon rather than trying to lift it from earth.

The coordinators of the SDI project in Washington remain confident that the problems can be solved. The price of shipping material to space may fall, they say, to perhaps $300 per pound. Bullet-proof vests, after all, have become steadily lighter, and lightweight armor, probably made from carbon fabrics, may be invented for space-based weapons. Besides, satellites do not need to be protected by armor alone; they can be designed to dodge and weave when attacked, or armed so they can automatically open fire at objects that get too close. But such measures may resemble Lowell Wood's ballet dancer faced with a submachine gun. The central dilemma for the star warriors is that most of the hardware being dreamed up would be much more effective against satellites and space-based battle stations than against missiles and warheads.

A determined opponent would have a host of available options. Innocent-looking commercial satellites could in fact disguise space mines, which, when a conflict threatened, could close in on defending satellites and explode (likely to be especially effective against hardware in high, geosynchronous orbit). Both the Soviet Union and the United States are developing antisatellite weapons, and antisatellite weapons have obvious anti–Star Wars potential. The existing Russian ASAT is pretty crude; a small ground-launched rocket, first tested in the 1960s, it has to orbit the globe twice before being in a position to strike its target. And even then, by all accounts, it is likely to miss. But America is developing a more sophisticated ASAT—a "half orbit" system to be fired from an F-15 fighter—and before the United States has even begun to begin think about Star Wars deployment, the Russians are likely to have followed suit and to have developed an ASAT with at least as good a chance of proving successful as the system it would seek to destroy.

Indeed, the Russian ASATs and space mines and killer satellites might not need to be supersophisticated. Mirrors stationed in geosynchronous orbit to deflect laser beams down toward Russian missiles, for example, would have to be almost indescribably perfect. The slightest blemish or warp or crack would render them useless, and a satellite that exploded nearby, scattering a substance as innocuous as sand, would transform their delicate architecture into orbiting debris.

Thus in the game of countermeasures and countercountermeasures that Star Wars would assuredly spark, the likelihood is that offense would continue to enjoy a huge advantage over defense. And that is putting it mildly. The difference between the two, as *Newsweek* has graphically put it, is "the difference between building a machine gun and building a computer-controlled defensive-weapons system that would protect soldiers by locating, tracking and destroying enemy machine-gun bullets in the chaos of an all-out battle." Nuclear weapons have to do *so little*—they are so crude, so imprecise, so unimaginably destructive—that only a few have to get through, and land roughly near a center of population, to cause unspeakable damage. (The bombs themselves are also surprisingly cheap—in America, about $1 million apiece, less than the price of an advanced antiaircraft missile like the Phoenix.) By contrast, Star Wars would have to be extraordinarily fragile and complex, and to give any credence at all to President Reagan's vision it would have to do *so much*. It is easier, as has often been observed, to break a fine watch than to mend one.

Faced with such skepticism, the star warriors have a stock response. "Many . . . scientists said a few years ago that we couldn't reach the moon; and many scientists said that you couldn't possibly put a missile in one continent and hit a target in another continent; and many scientists have said a great many things that have proven to be wrong once the work has been done," says Caspar Weinberger. All of which is true. But the moon, as others were quick to point out, does not shoot back. Unlike the Russians, it had neither the desire nor the capacity to devise endless ways of stopping the Apollo program. There was no one on the moon prepared to invest billions of rubles, and years of time, to stop space vehicles from landing. Besides, as the Union of Concerned Scientists has pointed out, it is simply not true to say that science can achieve everything. "The laws of thermodynamics tell us that one cannot build a perpetual motion machine, and the principle of relativity implies that it would be futile to try to design spaceships that move faster than the speed of light."

R. V. Jones made a similar point in his own report on Star Wars, published in 1985, when he commented that "American technological enthusiasm has not always been well founded." Recalling his own experience of working with the Americans on an attempt to develop a method of submarine detection relying on "infrared reconnaissance of the ocean surface," he pointed out that the British always had doubts about the project, whereas the Americans were always "confident and enthusiastic." In the end, British doubts were vindicated. Jones went on to warn of the danger of succumbing to the "emotional appeal" of Star Wars. "We need to remember the words Louis Pasteur said that he would like to see inscribed on the threshold of all the temples of science: 'The greatest derangement of the human mind is to believe in something because one wishes it to be so.' Or, in the words of Crow's Law: 'Do not think what you want to think until you know what you ought to know.'"

Nonetheless, it may be true that there is nothing in the laws of physics that makes Star Wars an impossible concept. Just as some of the weapons we examined earlier might work well enough on a dust-free battlefield with the enemy not fighting back, so Star Wars might succeed eventually—just in a limited way—if the Russians made no changes whatsoever in their current forces and opted to carry on forever more with what they have now, forswearing any new developments. I am not suggesting they will do this. But if they did—if they took *no* countermeasures, and American scientists managed to solve all the problems, and American engineers managed to construct a flawless system—the West would *still* face devastation in a war. It would be in a similar position, as one SDI analyst puts it, to "the foolish householder who padlocks his front door and stands guarding it with a shotgun while leaving his back door open."

Star Wars envisages a defense against ballistic missiles. The whole space-based array would be useless against bombers and cruise missiles, which fly relatively low and would be immune from an attack launched out of the heavens. Indeed, in the 1960s, when the Soviets opted to deliver the bulk of their nuclear bombs aboard intercontinental missiles, America let its once proficient air defense system slip. Now, in a war, it would have trouble coping with Soviet bombers; it has a hard enough time detecting and tackling drug-running aircraft. And though the United States led the way in the development of small, slow-flying, and relatively cheap cruise missiles, the Soviet Union has stolidly followed in its footsteps. In fact, cruise missiles, especially the sea-launched variety, may ultimately bestow more advantages on the Soviets than on the West. The Soviets have more submarines available for conversion into cruise missile platforms than the Americans; in addition, the best targets for slow-flying cruise missiles are coastal ones, and America has many more of these than the USSR. So Star Wars raises the prospect of, say, twenty or thirty Soviet cruise-missile-carrying submarines converging on the American coast in a time of war, ready and able—unless sunk—to rain nuclear devastation on the continent.[5]

James Schlesinger estimates that if the United States goes ahead with Star Wars it will have to spend a minimum of $50 billion a year on an accompanying effort to strengthen air defenses against the cruise and bomber threat. Even if it did, it would still be vulnerable to the "clandestine delivery" of nuclear weapons—suitcase bombs and the like, perhaps "wired up" so that they can be detonated by remote control. (In Europe, as we will see, the problems are worse; to take one slightly absurd example, the Russians could even send dogs armed with small bombs across the border into West Germany.)

The upshot of all this is that a Star Wars defense could never work without Soviet cooperation. Not only would the Russians have to agree dramatically to constrain their offensive forces, but they would have to agree to work toward a world in which both sides' defenses were given the best possible opportunity to work.

The Reagan administration, of course, had hopes that it might persuade the Russians to share in just such an effort. The president called on them to help create a "nuclear-free" world. He even suggested that America would be prepared to share the fruits of its Star

---

[5]The argument that cruise missiles are less dangerous than ballistic ones because they fly slower is at best dubious. They are, theoretically, very accurate; they are small and hard to detect; and once a new generation arrives, complete with Stealth counterradar technology, they will no longer even be "slow." Besides, launched from submarines just off the American coast, they will not have far to fly to many high-value targets.

Wars research, in the hope of helping bring this about. But this hope defies common sense. In the first place, the chances of a future American president agreeing to pass over highly sensitive technological secrets are slim to the point of being absurd. Throughout the arms race America has prized its technological lead, considering it the basis of its strength; the aim has been to stay one step ahead of the Russians and force them to spend money and effort catching up. American ingenuity has compensated for Russian numbers. True, the limits of this philosophy have been explored in this book, but is there really any likelihood of a future American president suddenly deciding to go to the lengths of free collaboration with the country once described by Reagan as "the focus of evil in the modern world"? To bestow upon the USSR the United States' most sensitive and secret information would be construed as unbelievably foolhardy, even treasonous; most technologies have more than one application, and a breakthrough that might help the Russians build Star Wars might also help them develop countermeasures against it, or worse, develop new offensive weapons. (The lasers and particle beam weapons currently being contemplated for use against missiles, for example, may eventually prove all too usable against people.) What guarantee would there be that the Russians would only use the secrets they were given for defensive purposes? The answer is that there would be none. The relationship between the United States and the Soviet Union is an antagonistic one: each has a diametrically opposed view of the world; neither trusts the other; if they did, there would be no need for huge conventional armies in Europe, for enormous arsenals of nuclear weapons, or for Star Wars. So to suggest that one side will start helping the other is ludicrous.

The same goes, without doubt, for the kind of all-embracing arms control regime that would be necessary to give Star Wars a chance. The chances of the Russians accepting such a regime are slim. There are some experts, such as the American Sovietologist David Rivkin, who argue that they might. The Russians have never been greatly enamored of nuclear weapons, says Rivkin. And whereas they may once have hankered after a theory of nuclear victory, they have appeared to become, in the early 1980s, more and more dubious about the idea of nuclear war fighting. Add to this the fact that Moscow has always been interested in the concept of "damage limitation"—in case nuclear war should occur—and you might have the circumstances in which the Kremlin would be prepared to join Washington in a "build-down" of offensive forces and a buildup of defensive ones. Indeed, Moscow's willingness to pursue such a course might be enhanced by the knowledge that, in a "Star Wars world," the Soviets would be free at last to exploit their conventional superiority over the West—one reason, of course, why many feel the West would be foolish even to attempt it.

But, as Rivkin acknowledges, achieving the kind of arms control that this vision implies would require not just a demonstration that Star Wars can work, and work highly effectively, but an extraordinarily subtle blend of diplomacy, defense buildup, and public relations—a blend that the nineteenth-century Austrian statesman Count Metternich might have been capable of but that NATO most certainly is not. And even were the West to design such an arms control strategy, I believe the Russians, whatever the arguments to the contrary, would be unlikely to stake everything on what would be at best an uncertain and monumentally expensive gamble. From the first, they have seen SDI not as defensive but as offensive; viewed from their perspective, it is part of an American defense program that includes a whole new generation of nuclear weapons, including the D-5 missile that will be based in Trident submarines, 760 prospective sea-launched cruise missiles, 3,000 air-launched cruise missiles, the B-1 bomber, and the MX.

Instead of arms control, the prospect is of an all-out race in offensive, defensive, and "defense suppression" systems. Consider past experience. The discovery by American intelligence in the 1960s that the Russians were constructing an antiballistic missile system around Moscow proved a crucial factor in triggering Washington's decision to MIRV its missiles. Enabling each missile to deliver a set of warheads rather than just one greatly increased the chances of the "offense" being able to defeat the "defense."

"Are the Soviets likely to be any less 'offensive conservative' than we were then?" asks James Schlesinger. "Given the Soviet Union's political ambitions, or its neurosis, or its quest for world domination, or its Marxist Leninist creed (depending upon whose eyes one is looking through), how likely is it that in the event of an American deployment of substantial strategic defense, the Soviets would agree to a constraint on offensive capabilities?"

And knowing that the Russians would be working on developing countermeasures to defeat Star Wars, the Americans, of course, would be obliged to do the same. Indeed they already are. In addition to the strategic programs I have mentioned, the air force is planning the Stealth bomber (intended to be virtually undetectable by Soviet radar), while the Defense Advanced Research Projects Agency is working on a cruise missile with similar attributes; it will use exotic fuels and high-performance engines that will enable it, if all goes as planned, to fly at more than three times the speed of sound. What Star Wars system could possibly cope with that?

Meanwhile, the Advanced Strategic Missile Systems program, headquartered at Norton Air Force Base in California, is busy examining ways of ensuring that American *ballistic* missiles never meet the kind of fate the star warriors want to provide for Russian ones. The program is secret, and small beer compared with Star Wars itself (it received only around $1 million in 1985), but more funds are planned, and the ideas being contemplated suggest what might be in store.

Most of the research, it seems, is into advanced penetration aids and decoys that would confuse defenses, making it harder for them to identify actual warheads. The penetration aids include chaff (clouds of tiny pieces of metal) and, according to the *New York Times*, "light-reflecting aerosols that confuse enemy sensors; decoys that present enemy defenses with a baffling multiplicity of targets; and 'defense suppression systems' that home in on enemy radars and destroy them to clear the way for nuclear missiles." One sophisticated decoy being developed by a research lab is apparently capable of reading the signals from enemy radar or infrared sensors and instantaneously devising a countersignal to fool the defenders into thinking the decoy is a real warhead. Another research project involves the creation of a new agile reentry vehicle for future American missiles that would be able to zigzag its way through space. Meanwhile, according to the Pentagon, another part of the Advanced Strategic Missile Systems program is studying ways of protecting missiles in the boost phase of their flight by, for example, disguising the exhaust plumes they emit when lifting off. "You can always beat the other guy's defenses if you know what he's got coming at you," Major Larry Skapin, an air force missile engineer who represents the program in the Pentagon, told the *New York Times* in February 1985.

The Russians undoubtedly have their own version of the Advanced Strategic Missile Systems program. But stopping the Americans even from *fielding* an SDI system would not prove difficult if they chose to do so. The weapons involved, after all, would have to orbit over the Soviet Union, and it would take years to get them aloft—a shuttle launch every two days for five years, according to one estimate. There is also the possibility that space-based weapons powerful enough to strike rockets just after they had risen out of their silos might be powerful enough to strike targets on the ground—a point raised by Mikhail Gorbachev, the Soviet premier, at the Geneva summit in November 1985. Neither superpower would be likely to welcome any kind of battle station orbiting above its soil if there was even the slightest chance that this might be able at a moment's notice to incinerate centers of population or key military sites.

"Suppose the Russians decided to dispute our right to fly weapons over their territory," said one man involved in SDI research, "and whatever we put up they promptly shot down, just as they shot down the U-2 and the Korean airliner? What could we do about it?" (At the moment, as this source points out, there are no actual weapons above the Soviet Union, only reconnaissance and spy satellites.) An alternative scenario has the Russians sending space mines into orbit close to pieces of American hardware as soon as they are sent up. The United States presumably would seek to declare an "exclusion zone" in space of, say, 70 miles in diameter around each orbiting battle station or mirror. But this would be like declaring huge exclusion zones around ships at sea; the chances are that the Russians would simply refuse to heed them.

12

Star Wars: The Reality

$\mathbf{R}$esearch projects, like wars, are sometimes easier to start than to stop. With the full weight of a presidential commitment behind it, Star Wars quickly gained considerable momentum. When first unveiled in March 1983 it provoked a good deal of incredulity and not a little mirth; as one former high-level defense official put it to me: "People giggled." Two years later people weren't giggling anymore. President Reagan appeared to have talked himself into an almost transcendental faith, believing, as one senior Republican put it, that Star Wars was "the Second Coming." The passions the subject evoked on all sides were striking, and the fierce denunciations of opponents seemed only to stir the star warriors into ever more determined, more grandiose expressions of support. The critics were dismissed as nay-sayers or Luddites, or worse. It was implied, in some quarters, that their disloyalty to the cause made them anti-American, even pro-Soviet, that their support of mutually assured destruction made them immoral.

That Star Wars should have such impact was scarcely surprising.

It had been launched by an extraordinarily popular president, and one who, in November 1984, was reelected by an overwhelming majority. It encouraged a generalized longing, felt by millions of people, for escape from the nuclear "box." Not the least significant of those who have "come out" for Star Wars, albeit with reservations, was the writer Jonathan Schell, who concluded in his pessimistic book *The Fate of the Earth* that man would have to "reinvent politics" if he was to escape the nuclear dilemma—a prescription no less apocalyptic, and fantastic, than the president's. The wish to *believe* reflected itself in the opinion polls; though, interestingly, the polls also showed that people harbored doubts about SDI's feasibility. In any case, polls on a subject like this are of limited value; so much depends on the way the questions are asked.[1]

Meanwhile, huge sums of money were at stake. The initial Star Wars program envisaged spending $26 billion in the first five years, and despite some trimming by Congress, by late 1985 a billion dollars worth of contracts had been allocated to universities, research firms, and defense contractors. To the scientists involved, it was an immediate and irresistible—perhaps the ultimate—challenge. "Is it any wonder that scientists have fallen in love with nuclear defense?" asked *Newsweek* in June 1985:

> Here are fantastic, cataclysmic energies—megavolts and ter-rawatts and gigajoules, rending the air in microsecond bursts; here is a chance to build the kind of lasers they can only dream about in other fields. Here is a chance to help break the world's precari-

---

[1] A February 1985 poll that asked, "Do you want the United States to defend Americans against Soviet missiles?" found 90 percent of its respondents saying yes; other pollsters who asked similar questions got similar responses. But a *Washington Post*–ABC News poll in August 1985 made its respondents think harder: "Supporters say such weapons could guarantee protection of the United States from nuclear attack and are worth whatever they cost. Opponents say such weapons will not work, will increase the arms race, and that the research will cost many billions of dollars. How about you: would you say you approve or disapprove of plans to develop such space-based weapons?" Here, 41 percent of respondents said they approved, and a majority—53 percent—said they disapproved.

ous dependence on the balance of terror, a chance for nuclear physics to do something for humanity in compensation for inventing the hydrogen bomb. Here is the greatest technological challenge in the world today, out of which may come the next generation of Nobel Prize winners and which may, in its very immensity, solve that most elusive of scientific quests, the search for lifetime funding. To almost everyone else, including Ronald Reagan, Star Wars is an abstraction—a promise of a distant millennium when nuclear weapons will no longer exist, a piece of the global chessboard, a budget line. To scientists, it is as real as lightning.

Not the least of the reasons it is real to scientists is that it means jobs: at a time when the demand for new types of nuclear warheads is ebbing and the challenges of nuclear technology have dimmed, SDI offers a promising new field of endeavor, one likely to offer employment at laboratories like Lawrence Livermore and Los Alamos for years to come. Not all scientists with opportunities to participate in SDI have been beguiled, however; most of the physics professors at the University of Illinois signed a statement saying that SDI was technically dubious and not worth investigating. They refused to accept funding from the SDI organization. And one of the computer world's most respected authorities on large-scale programming, David Parnas, had second thoughts in July 1984. Hired at $1,000 a day to sit on an advisory panel convened to study "computing in support of battle management," Parnas quit, saying he thought it would never be possible to construct a sufficiently reliable computer system to enable SDI to work.

SDI was becoming real enough, too, to defense contractors. Here was the prospect not just of megavolts and gigajoules, but of billions and billions of dollars worth of business, a bonanza beyond their wildest dreams. No wonder, then, that hundreds of firms wanted to become involved in the research: if experience was anything to go by, research eventually would lead to development, and development to producing hardware. There were clearly fortunes to be made from Star Wars.

From across the Atlantic, European governments watched developments with mounting alarm. During Reagan's first term most of

those involved in nuclear matters had not taken Star Wars very seriously. They seemed to see it, insofar as they saw it at all, as an American
craze that would have to run its course and then, with luck, would
simply go away. Only when Reagan was reelected by a landslide did it
become clear that it wasn't going to. And if allied governments were
slow to realize the implications of Star Wars, their "state of mind"
when they did, as John Newhouse observed in the *New Yorker*, became
what might fairly be described as "obsessive."

European officials had many and varied reasons for being unhappy
about Star Wars. Their unhappiness was rooted, first, in temperament.
Historically less inclined to believe in bold, sweeping initiatives than
their American counterparts, they were more disposed to be pessimistic
about this one. Whereas Star Wars appealed to something deep in the
American psyche, the dream of mastering space, the last frontier (not
for nothing is one of Washington's most popular tourist attractions its
impressive Air and Space Museum), Europe was collectively less dazzled. As one scholar of U.S.–European relations put it: "The Americans
are a problem-solving people. They still believe that there is a solution
to every problem. The Europeans tend to believe that solutions just
create new problems."

More specifically, Europeans had a host of different factors to
worry about—geographic, strategic, and political, as well as technical.
They were confused about the real *aim* of Star Wars and troubled by
the rhetoric. When officials visited Washington on fact-finding trips,
which they did quite often, they came back dissatisfied and, it seemed,
with precious few facts. The whole project, viewed from European
capitals, had not been thought through. The "technological band-
wagon," as one British official put it, seemed "in danger of running
away down the hill, leaving the horses behind."

Though the Americans protested that the Star Wars umbrella
would extend over Europe as well as America, Europe—from almost
every perspective—seemed to end up worse, not better off. For one
thing, as difficult as it will be to erect a defense over America, it will
be even harder to erect one over Europe. Faced with a growing array
of medium- and short-range Soviet missiles, the Europeans would have
not half an hour to destroy incoming warheads, but five to ten minutes.

(Space-based systems could be fairly effective against SS-20s, which have a steep trajectory and travel relatively slowly, but special ground-based antitactical ballistic missile systems would be required to provide any hope of stopping SS-21s, SS-22s, and SS-23s.)

But beyond the technical arguments that troubled European officials were a host of others: political, strategic, and financial. If the Americans spent vast fortunes on Star Wars, then they would have less money with which to defend Europe, or anywhere else. Would that not increase the pressure for the withdrawal of American troops from the central front? And what about doctrine? Flexible response, as we have seen, envisages NATO being able to make small, limited nuclear attacks on the enemy if it begins to lose a conventional war. Would not a half-effective Star Wars system, while unable to cope with larger attacks, be able to cope with small, discriminatory ones? And would not Star Wars, by making nuclear war harder, make conventional and chemical war easier to risk, and thus more likely to happen?

The Americans, it seemed, were bent on fundamentally changing NATO strategy. The last time that had happened, with the shift to flexible response in the 1960s, it had taken eight years and almost torn the alliance apart in the process. Yet here were the Americans, in the wake of a presidential speech about which no one had been consulted, and with no serious debate beforehand, proposing to change the strategy *unilaterally*, and much more dramatically than ever before, with no one having the least idea whether the replacement was going to work or not. Meanwhile, the strategic environment was likely to get more dangerous, the arms race was going to be jacked up another notch, and arms control was quite possibly going to be dealt a lethal blow. Despite a certain amount of misty-eyed public optimism about a brave new world of defenses (some of it perceived as fairly cynical), with the Russians coming round to recognize that nuclear weapons would be less effective and therefore deciding there was less point in building them, the principal casualty looked like being the antiballistic missile treaty —in the view of many, one of the most solid monuments on the arms control landscape. ("The keystone in the still shaky arch of security," the British foreign secretary, Sir Geoffrey Howe, has called it.) Meanwhile, like Trollope's Septimus Harding, Washington seemed to be suffering "persistent bouts of morality," in this case of a rather danger-ous kind. The constant suggestion that mutually assured destruction was somehow wrong presupposed that there was a better way; most European officials and politicians felt that there was not.

In some of this, to be sure, there was an element of carping. Flexible response, as we have seen, is scarcely a satisfactory doctrine; the notion of going nuclear first to check a losing conventional war has long seemed somewhat incredible. The Europeans themselves have come up with few constructive ideas for an alternative: and, arguably, the installation of cruise and Pershing, by stirring up concern about nuclear weapons, has increased the pressures for change. Resisting the need to improve their own conventional forces, the Europeans had helped create the conditions that prompted Reagan's radical step.

Still, in suggesting that Star Wars would solve nothing, they had history—and common sense—on their side. The European leaders, as one American opposed to Star Wars put it, feared that the emperor had no clothes. Faced with peace movements that lost no opportunity to denounce nuclear weapons, they could find little comfort in the rhetoric used to defend Star Wars. Politicians such as Margaret Thatcher in the United Kingdom and Helmut Kohl in West Germany, after all, had to contend with opposition parties only too happy to exploit the idea that nuclear deterrence was immoral—precisely the implication of SDI. The peace movement that backed those parties had, after all, believed that all along. (In Britain, for example, as one official pointed out, those who believed in unilateral disarmament vastly outnumbered those who believed in SDI. "You still see plenty of Volvos with CND stickers on them," commented the official in spring 1985, "but the faith in Star Wars is still confined virtually to the far Right.") The Europeans, having been assured throughout 1981 and 1982 that they must take new cruise and Pershing missiles on their soil, were now being told that these were immoral and soon to become obsolete. So the moral tone in the Reagan administration's rhetoric was likely, in the end, to do much more harm than good. And not just in Europe. As James Schlesinger put it: ". . . the justification for strategic defense should never be based on assertions regarding the immorality of deterrence. For the balance of our days the security of the Western

world will continue to rest on deterrence. Those were—and are—
reckless words."

The British and the French had special worries about Star Wars.
At the core of both nations' forces were small, "independent" nuclear
deterrents, and these—far more than the vast arsenals of the United
States and the Soviet Union—seemed likely to be threatened by a
half-effective Star Wars system. France's "minitriad" of nuclear forces
—its eighteen single-warhead missiles on the Plateau d'Albion, its four
nuclear submarines (each armed with sixteen missiles), and its Mirage
bombers—along with Britain's four Polaris boats, each carrying sixteen
missiles, constituted weapons of last resort. They existed simply to *deter
direct nuclear attacks on the soil of France and Britain.* Though neither
country could destroy the Soviet Union, each could "tear off an arm,"
in de Gaulle's phrase, and cause sufficient damage and loss of life to
make an attack seem a foolhardy act.

Naturally, therefore, both France and Britain prize their "minimum deterrents." France, with its explicitly Gaullist policy, may shelter willy-nilly under the American strategic umbrella, but it prefers to
put its faith in its own. ("However large may be the glass offered to
us, we prefer to drink from our own, while touching glasses round
about," said de Gaulle.) And Britain, which in wartime would be
NATO's "unsinkable aircraft carrier," and thus a prime target, believes
that an independent deterrent provides valuable extra insurance. In
1983, when Reagan launched Star Wars, both Britain and France were
modernizing their independent deterrents, Britain by buying the sophisticated American Trident system for around $10 billion—a hefty
price tag for a small country. Not surprisingly, Star Wars evoked little
enthusiasm in Whitehall or on the Quai d'Orsay. Here is what was
foreseen:

*America, at colossal expense, builds a half-adequate Star Wars
system; the Soviet Union, spurred on by this, does the same. Each
superpower, because it possesses a vast arsenal, is still able to threaten
the other with unimaginable destruction. But for Britain's and France's
deterrents the change is dramatic: they have been rendered impotent.
Not possessing the luxury of being able to overwhelm a defense with
sheer numbers, they know that if war comes, the Soviet Union's half-*

adequate Star Wars may be good enough to cope with their small forces.
Thus the money spent on these forces would turn out to be a waste;
worse, the central pillar of both French and British defense would have
collapsed. They would end up depending more and more heavily on
America at a time when such dependence would probably be more and
more ill advised and when the world, because of Star Wars, would seem
much more dangerous.

On December 22, 1984, British Prime Minister Margaret
Thatcher visited Ronald Reagan at Camp David. Mrs. Thatcher was
closer to the president than any other European leader, and a warm
admirer. The feeling was reciprocal. (Once, at an economic summit in
Versailles, the prime minister rang the president between sessions on
a matter she regarded as of great importance. Reagan listened to the
unquenchable flow for a few seconds, then held the telephone away
from his ear and said to an aide: "Isn't she wonderful?") During the
arms talks over intermediate nuclear weapons (cruise, Pershing, and the
SS-20), she had helped persuade the president to moderate the U.S.
negotiating position. Now, once again, she sought to use her influence.
For an hour and a half she made the case against Star Wars.

She covered a lot of ground. She discussed arms control, and the
danger to the ABM treaty, which she had read in its entirety. A former
research chemist, she went through the technical arguments in detail,
discoursing at length on possible Russian countermeasures, such as
"revolving boosters" and bombs in suitcases. Above all, she stressed the
dangers of continuing to say that nuclear deterrence was immoral and
that nuclear weapons could be rendered obsolete. It was, by all accounts, an impressive performance. At that stage, as the *New Yorker*
later observed, Mrs. Thatcher became "probably the only person" who
"told Reagan to his face what is wrong with Star Wars—from a European point of view, at least." Secretary of State Schultz and the national security adviser, Robert McFarlane, tried to answer her points.
So did Reagan himself. He spoke at one stage about the awfulness of
having a finger on the nuclear button and produced a letter from
Dwight Eisenhower written at Camp David making a similar point.
But it was Mrs. Thatcher who did most of the talking.

The British Foreign Office had been quicker than most European foreign ministries in grasping the implications of Star Wars. (When a team of U.S. officials visited key capitals early in 1984 to try and dispel "myths" about Star Wars, they reported back to Washington that Britain was the most hostile.) And by the time Mrs. Thatcher met Reagan—just after his massive reelection victory—European concern was growing. Only two weeks earlier, Mikhail Gorbachev, the prospective Soviet leader, had visited London, and impressed Mrs. Thatcher as a man she felt the West could "do business with." At the same time, however, Mrs. Thatcher and her advisers had been struck by the vehemence of Gorbachev's attacks on Star Wars and left in little doubt that if America pressed ahead, the USSR would respond by doing its best to undercut American defenses. Having just endured heavy political fallout over the deployment of cruise and Pershing missiles, neither the British prime minister nor any of her European counterparts wanted a return to the state of high tension with the Eastern bloc that Star Wars seemed to portend.

The upshot of the Camp David meeting was a four-point agreement, signed by both Mrs. Thatcher and Reagan. The four points were, in brief, that the West was seeking balance with Russia, not superiority over it; that Star Wars was a research program, with deployment subject to negotiation, taking into account existing agreements; that the purpose of the exercise was to enhance and not to undermine deterrence; and that the aim in arms control negotiations should be to seek lower levels of offensive forces.

The four points did, at least, stake out a European position on Star Wars. But in Washington, as most European officials knew, their significance was strictly limited: they did not affect the program one iota. Equally, when Paul Nitze, the president's special adviser on arms control, made a speech in March 1985 that seemingly echoed the cautious outlook of Camp David, the Europeans were scarcely reassured. Nitze suggested that any Star Wars system would have to be both cost-effective—meaning it would have to cost less to deploy than to counter—and survivable. European governments, of course, thought there was no chance of it ever being either. They suspected, moreover, despite Nitze's speech, that SDI was fast becoming *more* than a research program and that it might end up being deployed whether it was cost-effective and survivable or not.[2]

In Reagan's inner circle, as European officials knew, the issue had become like "a badge of loyalty"; you criticized it at your peril. Even defense consultants who did studies for the Pentagon knew that if they voiced skeptical views in public, their business might be curtailed. "The White House is in a 'them and us' mode on this," said one. "You're either for Star Wars or you're against it. They talk about research, but in reality they mean commitment."

As for whether Star Wars could ever be cost-effective or survivable, "they answer the question with assertions that it can be done," said this source, two years into the program. "They offer no *evidence* to back it up."

On October 31, 1986, Defense Secretary Weinberger told the Senate Foreign Relations Committee that he could not conceive "of strategic defense being more costly than the constant need to modernize and strengthen as each side makes a move to which the other side has to make a response." Asked if he would change his mind if Star Wars *did* prove more costly, he said: "No . . . I would not, because I would think the additional cost in protecting people's lives, in protecting this nation, would be . . . worth anything that it would cost."

In the White House, and in the makeshift offices occupied by SDI's coordinators a few blocks away in downtown Washington, the mood remained one of buoyant, almost nonchalant self-assurance. "I now feel entirely confident we can do it," George Keyworth told me

---

[2]Almost a year earlier, Frank Miller, the Pentagon official who had chaired the initial interagency study on SDI, foreshadowed Nitze's speech in testimony to Congress. Addressing the House Committee on Foreign Affairs on July 26, 1984, Miller said: "If at some point in the future, the end of this decade, the beginning of the next, the administration decided to come to the Congress to ask you to fund full-scale development and beginning deployment, that administration would have to convince you, as well as itself, that such a system would be effective; that it would be cost-effective; and that it would be survivable. . . ."

in September 1985. "What we need time for is to find the optimum way of doing it." With excusable hyperbole, one scientist in Washington who takes a different view described to me his feelings about the most committed star warriors:

> They are blinded by technological optimism. They believe that all they have to do is configure the right pieces of metal into the right shape and they have achieved their goal. . . . They think that international politics is subject to an engineering solution. It's as if the 1960s and 1970s never happened, as if these people are living in a time warp, or on another planet. . . . Star Wars is the defense equivalent of floating cities, or railway lines under the Atlantic. . . .

To be fair, many scientists involved in SDI research were uneasy about all the hype. They were disturbed by the showy tests and, in some cases, by what appeared to be manipulative, self-serving use of "classified information." They feared that the pressure for results might jeopardize their reputations, and perhaps the chances of the program yielding anything at all. In an interview with the *New York Times,* Dr. Roger L. Hagengruber, director of system studies at the Sandia National Laboratory in Albuquerque, talked of the general desire to "have very early demonstrations, to show lethality," adding that such tests could be "contrived." "These demonstrations have the potential to be what we call strap-down chicken tests, where you strap the chicken down, blow it apart with a shotgun and say shotguns kill chickens. But that's quite different from trying to kill a chicken in a dense forest while it's running away from you."

One clear example of this, though Dr. Hagengruber did not specifically cite it, was the September 1985 test of a chemical laser. The target was the second stage of an old Titan missile, and when it was struck it exploded, spectacularly. The missile, however, was stationary and on the ground. It was also held firmly in place by wires so tightly strung, apparently, that it was sure to come apart when struck by the laser beam.

Rather more serious was evidence that emerged in November 1985 about Edward Teller's pet project, the nuclear-pumped X-ray laser. Despite Teller's enthusiasm, it appeared that all was not as well with the program as he liked to imply. In one underground test in Nevada, a key "focusing element" had proved defective, and there were doubts, too, about the results of earlier tests. A group of scientists, angry about the way in which the X-ray laser program was being discussed, risked jail sentences by leaking details of the problems to *Science* magazine.

The question of how to handle Star Wars posed delicate problems for European leaders. The French, predictably, were the most openly hostile. Chancellor Helmut Kohl of West Germany, torn between his own doubts on the one hand, and his loyalty to Reagan on the other, shrank from being publicly critical of Star Wars. And Mrs. Thatcher, intent on preserving her "special relationship" with Reagan, judged it best to make her criticisms privately. Indeed, it was Mrs. Thatcher who became the first European leader to agree in principle to her country's participation in the Star Wars research program. The decision was made more out of the realism than rhapsody. The British clearly recognized that research was unstoppable with Reagan in the White House, and judged that if Britain did not participate it might "miss the boat" in the development of all kinds of "cutting edge" technologies, some of which might have a lucrative commercial spinoff. They also feared that some of the best and brightest British scientists might be lured across the Atlantic to work on the project in America. Another British motive was the belief that it might prove easier to exert influence from within rather than from without—especially in the light of the Camp David agreement.

In European foreign and defense ministries, there were fewer reservations about criticizing Star Wars. Michael Heseltine, Britain's defense secretary at the time, was a leading skeptic. (He had firsthand experience, as one official put it, "of how military-industrial complexes work.") And on March 15, 1985, Foreign Secretary Sir Geoffrey Howe made Star Wars the subject of a major critical address to the Royal United Services Institute in London.

Howe's speech was carefully phrased. He spoke of the dangers of ignoring the Soviet Star Wars effort, and he raised many of the major problems posed by SDI—financial, strategic, and technical. Might not

the money be better spent elsewhere? What would be the consequences for the alliance?

> In terms of NATO's policy of forward defense and flexible re-
> sponse, would we lose on the swings whatever might be gained on
> the roundabouts?
> The attractions of moving toward a more defensive strategy
> for the prevention of war are as apparent as are the risks. It would
> be wrong to rule out the possibility on the grounds that the
> questions it raises are too difficult.
> But the fact that there are no easy answers, that the risks may
> outweigh the benefits, that science may not be able to provide a
> safer solution to the nuclear dilemma of the past forty years—all
> these points underline the importance of proceeding with the
> utmost deliberation.

The danger of Star Wars, Sir Geoffrey suggested, might be that
we would end up by creating "a Maginot line in space." (The French
foreign minister, Claude Cheysson, had used a similar phrase a few
months earlier.)

Sir Geoffrey's speech occasioned a prompt and savage reaction. It
was attacked by Richard Perle, the U.S. assistant secretary of defense
for international security policy, who happened to be in London at the
time. And it was the subject of a lengthy editorial in the *Times* of
London that came close to accusing the mild-mannered Sir Geoffrey
of "appeasement." The piece showed, all too clearly, how much passion
Star Wars had stirred up. But for all the heat, there was not much light.
The London *Times* editorial writer, defiantly hopeful as he was, had
no more idea than anyone else whether Star Wars would eventually
work, or in what form.

That, of course, was the heart of the matter. What exactly *was*
Star Wars? Or rather, what, after two years, had it become? The
Europeans suspected that if $26 billion was spent on research some-
thing would come out of it, and most insiders in Washington agreed
with them. "You can't spend all that money without something coming
out the other end," as one put it. The question was what? If Reagan's

initial vision was fantasy, and most officials suspected that it was, then what was left? What did those involved in the program *really want?*

The answer to this was not at all clear. Basically, there appeared to be two schools of thought. The first—the one espoused by the president—was that the defenses he envisaged would lead the West away from its precarious dependence on nuclear deterrence into the promised land of mutually assured survival. The second, more realistic, view held that this was fantasy, at least for the foreseeable future, and that the real aim of SDI must not be to *replace* deterrence but to *boost* it, or as worst-case analysts would say, *restore* it. Those who believed this argued that a less than perfect shield would suffice, since the principal aim of the system would be to complicate Soviet plans of attack and deny the Kremlin the option of mounting a full-blooded first strike against American missile silos in the expectation that it might be successful.

The three advisory panels that reported to President Reagan on SDI's feasibility in 1983 provided an early preview of the division between the "get rid of deterrence" and the "boost deterrence" camps. Essentially, the Fletcher panel, which concentrated on the nuts and bolts, came out for mutually assured survival, concluding (albeit after much disagreement among its scientists) that "a robust, multi-tiered ballistic missile defense system" could eventually be made to work. The report stressed, however, that such a system would require cooperation from the Russians—and that its construction would have to be accompanied by reductions in the offensive arsenals of both sides.

The Hoffman panel, in its report on policy implications, laid more emphasis on the short-term aim of boosting deterrence. One small scenario it drew involved a Russian conventional attack on Europe in which, to prevent NATO from reinforcing its troops, the Kremlin authorized a small nuclear strike on a handful of major ports—say, five —on both sides of the Atlantic. Might not the Soviet Union now feel it could risk such a step without fear of drastic retaliation? the panel asked. If America had a defense in place, however, the Russians would not simply be able to drop five bombs on five ports; they might have to drop twenty or more to be sure of striking their targets. They would consequently have to worry that launching such a large salvo would be much more likely to provoke retaliation.

But the principal concern of the "boost deterrence" school was a broader one. As we have seen, there is, in America's strategic community, a growing anxiety about the vulnerability of America's land-based missiles, and the danger of preemptive strike posed by the Russian missile force, in particular the 5,000 warheads on the huge SS-18 and SS-19 missiles. In the mid-1980s, having failed, after enormous effort, to find a secure basing mode for the MX, the problem—if there was a problem—loomed as large as ever. And what attracted some people to Star Wars was the notion that an imperfect defense might help solve it. After all, faced even with *limited* defenses, the Russians would be less confident about the chances of launching a successful preemptive strike.

The simplest, fastest, and most modest way to achieve such a defense, of course, would be to erect ground-based defenses around missile sites and other vital military installations. More down to earth, literally, than anything envisioned under the Star Wars program, this might indeed prove feasible. The kinetic energy homing vehicle that shattered a dummy warhead in space over the Pacific in June 1984 had shown that modern weapons could—if made properly—destroy warheads. And since missile silos, unlike cities, are small targets, there would be no need to cover a huge area. Your aim would simply be to stop just one or perhaps two warheads from exploding *on the ground* at the silos you chose to defend. There would be no need to perform the series of scientific and military miracles required to effect boost-phase kill. There would not even be a need to defend *all* of your missiles. Since your aim would be to make clear to the Soviets that a first strike could not possibly work, you would simply have to protect enough of them to enable you to launch a devastating retaliatory strike. And it wouldn't even matter if your defenses did *not* work perfectly. The Soviets would still have to take them into account; they could no longer be confident of being able to execute a first strike. Nuclear deterrence, in the view of "missile defense" proponents, would thus not be replaced, it would be *enhanced*. This limited defense might, of course, incorporate some space-based elements, too. But the most cost-effective "architecture" would almost certainly involve keeping most of the hardware on the ground.

The notion of boosting deterrence is at least more plausible than the notion of rendering nuclear weapons obsolete. Unfortunately, however, it poses a number of problems, both political and strategic.

Take, first, the strategic problem. If America put up a limited defense on its own, and Russia did nothing, then deterrence would certainly be boosted, at least for the West. But the assumption, of course, would have to be that if America constructed any kind of a defense, the Russians would match it. And the uncomfortable truth is that if that happened—and both sides created equal but imperfect defenses—then deterrence would probably not be strengthened, but weakened.

The reason for this is complicated, but it has been set out, with mathematical precision, by a retired air force general named Glenn Kent. As a critic of Star Wars, Kent's credentials are hard to question —even, perhaps especially, among conservatives. Unlike many who have attacked the program, such as the Union of Concerned Scientists, he is a strong supporter of President Reagan and, in principle, a defender of military buildup. An adviser to successive defense secretaries during the 1960s and 1970s, Kent belongs to that curious clan characterized by Fred Kaplan as "the wizards of Armageddon," the systems analysts whose calculations form the basis for America's war plans. Paul Nitze, Reagan's special adviser on arms control and a founding member of the conservative pressure group the Committee on the Present Danger, calls him, simply, "one of the best mathematicians I have ever met."

Retired from the Pentagon by the time Reagan unveiled Star Wars, Kent, an engaging man with silver hair and a southern drawl, developed his position on Star Wars for the Rand Corporation. The case he makes is more sophisticated than most criticisms of the program, and is primarily strategic rather than technical. Deterrence, he points out, is measured by the number of warheads that could be delivered to Soviet targets *after* America has endured a Soviet preemptive strike. And it is by this measure that America loses out—dramatically—if both sides develop roughly equivalent defenses, the reason being the different structure of American and Soviet nuclear forces, and in particular the Soviet Union's substantial lead in land-based missiles.

The easiest way to illustrate Kent's calculations is with an example. If the Soviets launched their SS-18 and SS-19 heavy missiles (a total of 5,000 warheads) in a preemptive strike, they could *theoretically* destroy America's entire land-based missile force, based as it is in only 1,000 silos. But at the moment, in a world without defenses, America would be able to fire back 3,000 surviving submarine-based warheads —a plausible figure, given the number of submarines likely to be "on station."

Now let us assume that both superpowers have half-adequate defenses, each able to destroy 3,000 of the other side's warheads. The Soviet Union's preemptive strike becomes less devastating than it was, but given the sheer number of warheads involved, there is still the *theoretical* possibility that it could knock out most American land-based missiles. America's retaliatory blow, however, has been rendered almost impotent. The 3,000 warheads it was relying on to fire back a crushing counterstrike on the USSR are soaked up by Russian defenses.

Kent plots his calculations on a graph. They show that for a long time, while both sides are deploying space-based defenses, America will be at a grave disadvantage, and that the disadvantage will only disappear when—or rather if—both sides get into a position of having developed extremely robust and effective defenses. Until that moment, however—a moment that may never come—Kent's arithmetic suggests that America will have to *deploy its defenses at twice the rate of the USSR just to maintain an effective deterrent.* He points out, therefore, that if the United States is going to get into a Star Wars race with the Soviet Union it will have to run that race twice as fast as the Soviets do, and run it to the end. Will Congress, he asks, in an age of fiscal restraint when the prime worry will be cutting the huge federal deficit, really be prepared to do this? Or does the United States risk ending up with the worst of all possible worlds, in which both sides "break out" of the ABM treaty and the Soviets end up deploying a massive Star Wars defense while the United States does not?

Those who argue that Star Wars will boost deterrence thus rest their argument on a shaky foundation. They claim that limited defenses will complicate Soviet plans of attack and create more uncertainty for Soviet planners. But as Kent demonstrates, limited defenses will also complicate America's plans to retaliate. And what could be more uncertain for Soviet planners than the idea of a first strike in current circumstances? I have argued in this book that fears of vulnerability are desperately overblown and that even if the Soviets *could* make the kind of precisely coordinated surgical strike against land-based missiles that everyone fears, the United States would be able to wreak terrible havoc in retaliation by using its sea-based weapons and bombers.

But the idea of defending American missile silos falters for another reason. Those most intimately involved with Star Wars know that "selling" a defense of missiles is not easy. It does not have much of a constituency among the Right, which wants a full-blown system, nor among the Left, which thinks it unnecessary. The complex argument that SDI may boost deterrence and thus in the end save lives is one that previous experience has shown is likely to leave the American public cold, even if the argument were plausible. And consider, finally, the practical difficulties of actually constructing a ground-based defense and winning political support for planting interceptor rockets around missile fields, with all the complex of radars and command posts they would demand. As one insider put it: "There just aren't enough trucks in Washington to take all the environmental impact statements you'd get up to Capitol Hill."

Thus the catch-22 of Star Wars is that what seems politically possible—a defense of cities—is practically impossible; whereas what seems practically possible—a ground-based defense of some missile silos—is likely both to leave America worse off *and* be politically impossible. Reagan himself stressed on several occasions that an attempt to defend weapons might prove "destabilizing." He did so in his initial speech in 1983, and again in a speech to the National Space Club on March 29, 1985, when he said that Star Wars "is not, and should never be misconstrued as, just another method of protecting missile silos."

In the light of this, the administration was bound to sound confused. As James Schlesinger observed, Reagan's initial speech

> held out to American citizens the unqualified hope that they need not forever live with the nuclear threat over their heads. Through the vigor of American technology, someday—even if not until the twenty-first century—your cities would once again be safe from nuclear attack, as they have been for most of the nation's history. In that lay the political appeal of the speech—and we should

understand that its appeal is fundamentally political—for invulnerability to nuclear assault is what the American public believes is going to be achieved.[3]

Thus, whatever their reservations about space-based defense, officials knew that they had to emphasize this to keep the program going. Otherwise Star Wars might simply cease to be. A British official, asked what happened when he posed "hard questions," captured the flavor:

> The answer is always "We don't have the answers now." . . . They say the purpose of the research is to find the answers. "Well, wouldn't the money be better spent on projects of a less uncertain nature?" we ask. There is usually no response to that. Sometimes they say that what may come out of all this is defense of hard targets [missile silos]. But when we say: "If it's hard targets you want to defend, why do it in space, where it won't work and where the systems will be vulnerable? Why not do it on the ground, where it will work?" they say: "We won't get the money unless we do it in space." It's all circular. No one other than the president has made a clear statement, but no one among the Americans whom Europeans talk to thinks his concept is anything other than nonsense and fantasy.

That may be a little harsh. But certainly those who advised President Reagan before his initial speech do not appear to have thought

---

[3]If further evidence of this was needed, it came in an advertising campaign mounted by the pro–Star Wars lobby prior to the superpower summit in November 1985. One rather preposterous commercial featured a cartoon drawing of stick people, a dog, a house, and a sun. A little girl says in a cute voice: "I asked my daddy what this 'Star Wars' stuff is all about. . . . He said that right now we can't protect ourselves from nuclear weapons, and that's why the president wants to build a peace shield." The stick people and the sun frown as big red missiles come booming at them; but happily a domelike arc is drawn over the scene just in time and the missiles bounce off harmlessly. "It would stop missiles in outer space so they couldn't hit our house," continues the voice, "then nobody could win a war. . . ." The arch becomes a rainbow and the people and the sun smile. The house unfurls an American flag. "My daddy's smart."

through the implications of what they were proposing. In the circumstances, it was hardly surprising that even those disposed to be sympathetic to Star Wars sometimes ended up adding to the confusion. A case in point was an editorial in the usually level-headed *Economist* on August 3, 1985. The magazine carried on its cover a picture of a devastated Hiroshima in 1945, with the caption: "THE CASE FOR STAR WARS." It could equally well have labeled the picture "THE CASE FOR NUCLEAR DISARMAMENT," or shown a picture of London or Paris, fully restored and at peace for forty years, with the caption "THE CASE FOR DETERRENCE." The editorial began, strikingly, like this:

> The time is, let us say, 1925. The French army possesses a force of about 8,000 tanks, impervious to machine guns and ordinary artillery and unstoppable by other tanks, which can crunch its way through to Berlin within 24 hours. The German army has about 8,000 tanks of its own which can do the same to Paris. The conventional wisdom of 1925, nodding sagely, says that this will prevent another Great War because both sides know that if they march for the other's capital they will lose their own: it is the safety of deterrence. Enter an inventor, claiming that he thinks he knows how to make an anti-tank weapon which can stop at least a fair proportion of these hitherto unstoppable monsters. Is he told to forget it?

Assuming that no one could answer yes, the *Economist* proceeded to the point: "On next Tuesday's 40th anniversary of the dropping of the atomic bomb on Hiroshima, a world which has long believed that the only defense against nuclear mass slaughter is to threaten nuclear mass counter-slaughter should be contemplating the nuclear equivalent of that parable of the tanks." Certainly it should, yet not in the manner the *Economist* was suggesting. Soon after 1925 the French *did* believe they had come up with a weapon that could "stop at least a fair proportion of these hitherto unstoppable monsters." It was called the Maginot line. Only it ended up stopping precious little. Had France decided to stick with its force of 8,000 tanks it might well have wound up defeating the Germans, not losing to them. Besides, as the *Economist*'s cover graphically illustrated, there is a world of difference between tanks and nuclear weapons. Nuclear deterrence works precisely because nuclear weapons *can* inflict such ghastly destruction; if the French had had 8,000 nuclear weapons rather than tanks, Hitler would have had to be very mad indeed to have attacked them.

On one count, at least, there was agreement between Washington and the European allies. Whatever the doubts about Star Wars—what Caspar Weinberger called Reagan's "inspiring vision"—no one doubted the need for *research*. This belief, of course, was enshrined in the Reagan-Thatcher Camp David accords. It was easy to see why.

From the beginning, the Soviets had attacked Star Wars noisily, self-righteously, and at every available opportunity. But for all the moral outrage they expressed, they were scarcely innocents in the field. They themselves were busy exploring potential defensive weapons; indeed, as one U.S. official put it, America was in some respects a Johnny-come-lately in the business.

Let us glance back a moment. The Russians, like the Americans, began working on antimissile defenses in the late 1940s, and in the 1960s they constructed an actual system around Moscow, called Galosh. It was, to be sure, a crude affair, unlikely to stop much. But it was enough to spur Washington to launch an ABM program of its own—and also to ensure that Washington pressed ahead with the development of multiwarheaded missiles, MIRVs. Eventually, both sides decided to forswear proper defenses by signing the 1972 ABM treaty, which outlawed the testing or deployment of weapons in space. The Soviets, fearing America's vaunted edge in high technology, showed themselves anxious to avoid an additional arms race in antimissile systems, while Washington, for its part, had been at best halfhearted about ABM development. There was little support for ABMs in Congress, where they were seen as likely to cost vast sums and prove ultimately futile. A leak-proof system did not look remotely feasible, and although the ABM treaty *did* allow the construction of two ABM systems per side (later reduced to one), Washington chose not to make use of this concession. So while the Kremlin preserved their Galosh network around Moscow, the Americans were quick to mothball one they had planned to deploy at a missile field in Grand Forks, North

Dakota. Basically, the ABM treaty codified one of the central truths of the nuclear age, however perverse it might seem: that attempting to defend yourself would lead only to an intensified arms race and make the world more unstable for both sides. Security, as Winston Churchill had put it in the 1950s, would be "the twin brother of annihilation, and safety the sturdy child of terror."

Despite this, the Soviets have never quite accepted the notion of a defense-free world. They have espoused, instead, a policy of "damage limitation." Their civil defense effort has always been on a grander scale than America's; they have plowed more money into hardening missile silos and command centers—and into antiaircraft defenses. By some estimates, they have spent, during the 1970s and early 1980s, as much on defense as they have on offense.

In doing this the Russians have taken full advantage of their license under the ABM treaty to modernize their Galosh system around Moscow, deploying, in the early 1980s, two new kinds of antimissile missiles, the SH-04, designed to hit warheads in space, and the SH-08, designed to strike warheads that have reentered the earth's atmosphere and are on their way down to their targets in the reentry phase. In the early 1980s, too, the Russians have been developing a new high-performance surface-to-air missile, the SA-12 (code-named Gladiator by NATO), supposedly for use against aircraft, but capable of striking targets at a height of more than 100,000 feet. In 1983 and 1984 the SA-12 was tested on several occasions against a target vehicle sent into space by a tactical missile. Pentagon officials accepted the tests as legal under the terms of the ABM treaty but pointed out that the SA-12 could eventually be capable of intercepting incoming warheads, especially if armed with a nuclear warhead itself.

In addition to this, the Russians have constructed six large "phased-array" radars that could, the Pentagon believes, form the basis of a nationwide ABM system. One of these has been built just outside the village of Abalakovo, near Krasnoyarsk, in the heart of Siberia. A large building, about 100 yards long and 22 stories high, it touched off a flap in Washington when it was discovered, already half complete, by U.S. intelligence in 1983. The Krasnoyarsk area had not been subject to intensive satellite surveillance because no one had expected the Russians to build there. Under the conditions of the ABM treaty, phased-array radars are supposed to be built only on the perimeter of each superpower, not inland. On the perimeter, they can perform the vital role of providing warning of a nuclear attack. Inland, they can theoretically also be used to "service" an ABM system, by passing on precise information about incoming missiles to battle management radars, which would in turn be linked to antimissile rockets.

The arguments about Krasnoyarsk are complex. The Russians may have built their radar where they did not so much to service an ABM system, as because it was difficult to build it elsewhere; the northeastern border of the Soviet Union, beyond Krasnoyarsk, is impossibly marshy in summer and hard with permafrost in winter. There are no proper roads or railway lines. Clearly, the Kremlin wanted to plug a gap in the early warning coverage offered by its existing five radars, and Krasnoyarsk did this, enabling them to monitor the flight path American submarine-launched missiles would take if fired from the Pacific at the Soviet SS-18 and SS-19 missile fields to the south. But the fact is that Krasnoyarsk constitutes a violation of the ABM treaty. And by building it, the Russians have both strengthened the hands of those advocating Star Wars and, to an extent, complicated the task of those opposing it.

But only to an extent. Many defense and Soviet analysts find far-fetched the notion that the Soviet Union is preparing to "break out" of the ABM treaty and construct, with great speed, an effective defense against American missiles. Most of what the Kremlin has done is entirely consistent with the ABM treaty, and though Krasnoyarsk may be an exception, there are even doubts about this. The main dissent from the U.S. interpretation comes from Britain. The Russians claim that their Abalakovo radar is primarily designed for tracking objects in space, a function permitted by the treaty. The British government has argued that it will be impossible to tell whether the Russian claim is true or not until the radar is switched on and becomes fully operational. Because of its "special relationship" with America, Britain is in a strong position to judge (it has access to most of the intelligence data on the radar) and Downing Street's attitude has irritated, even amazed, Washington. "I am dumbfounded by the British attitude toward this," one U.S. official told me. "It seems to me they've been bending over backward to justify the Soviet position. It's uncharacteristic."

Perhaps. But what underlay the British case was a relatively benign assessment of the *military* importance of the new Soviet radar. Pentagon officials worried that it could have been built to play a key role in an ABM system, but this was widely disputed, and not just in London. A report by British intelligence analysts to the Thatcher cabinet's Joint Intelligence Committee in January 1985 (first revealed by the American magazine *National Journal*) concluded that Abalakovo was unlikely to be able to serve as an ABM radar. Interestingly, the British report drew on a secret CIA assessment, completed in 1984, which came to a similar view.

A number of experts, including some administration officials, have confirmed this assessment. They point out that the radar's face is not set at an optimal angle for ABM battle management, that there are no interceptor missiles or associated radars near the site (of the kind necessary in an ABM system), and that it will operate at the wrong frequency for a battle management radar. (They can tell from the way the transmitters are spaced.) Finally, Abalakovo has not been specially hardened, and it presents a large and extremely vulnerable target—one likely to be "taken out" quite easily at the beginning of a war. The best guess, say these experts, is that it is an early warning radar in the wrong place, built inland because of the difficulties of construction on the Siberian border. (In various unofficial forums, the Soviets have themselves attempted to indicate that this is precisely what it is.)

Thus, while Washington is clearly right that the radar constitutes a violation of the treaty, it scarcely appears to present a grave threat. The same, according to many analysts, is true of other aspects of the Soviet strategic defense program. Though the Russians are certainly modernizing their ABM system around Moscow, the new types of nuclear-tipped interceptor—SH-04s and SH-08s—would cause problems if they were ever used, since the first to explode would probably blind the tracking radars. The radars themselves, colorfully code-named by NATO Pawn Shop and Flat Twin, are also relatively old-fashioned. (Pawn Shop operates entirely mechanically; the slightly more advanced Flat Twin is half mechanical, half electronic.) The technology, in short, is on a par with what the Americans were exploring in the late 1960s, when they planned, but subsequently abandoned, construction of an antimissile system in North Dakota.

The fear among some in the administration is that the Russians are secretly building and stockpiling a large number of these components for their new system (code named ABM-X-3), so that they can use them, eventually, not just to defend Moscow but the rest of the country too. There is no evidence to support this. The building work on ABM-X-3 appears to be leisurely, and is not expected to be complete until 1987. And at the research and testing site at Shary Sagan in south central Asia as well as at other major Soviet facilities, there is apparently no sign of the kind of frenetic activity that might be consistent with a massive production effort.

Despite this, the Reagan administration's rhetoric about the Soviet defense program became increasingly alarmist. "When you look at what the Soviets are doing in both strategic offense and defense," the president said in October 1985, "you realize that our SDI research program is crucial to maintain the military balance and protect the liberty and freedom of the West."

In the same month, Caspar Weinberger went even further. The Russians, he charged in a speech in Philadelphia, had abandoned "the notion of deterrence through agreed mutual vulnerability" and were racing ahead with their own antimissile defense program.

Yet the Defense Intelligence Agency, the most hard-line of the American intelligence agencies—initially set up because the CIA was considered insufficiently alarmist about the Soviet threat—has estimated in declassified testimony that it would take the Russians "up to ten years" to "break out" of the ABM treaty—in which time, of course, America could do the same. And a study done for the Joint Chiefs of Staff in 1985, drawing on DIA material, assumed, apparently, that though in ten years America might be able to field a reasonably effective space-based antimissile shield, the Soviet Union would by then be capable only of a relatively crude ground-based defense.

Testimony by the Pentagon's research-and-engineering department backed this up. In surveying twenty areas of high technology, it identified the Americans as behind the Russians in none, equal to them in five, and ahead in fifteen—even though in some of these it suggested the gap was closing. Some officials dispute the report, pointing out that the Russians are ahead in some areas of laser and particle beam research. But even if that is true, and if the Russians have developed a capacity to blind American satellites with laser beams, few believe that they are anywhere near achieving sufficiently powerful lasers to shoot down missiles. Besides, in the most crucial area of all—computers—the Pentagon suggested that the American lead was actually increasing. (The Russians are still struggling to master third-generation computers, whereas the Americans have already mastered the fourth generation, able to transact 100 million instructions per second and, as we have seen, are working on a fifth generation.) General Abrahamson, SDI's director, states that "in the key technologies needed for a broader defense, such as data processing and computer software, we are far, far ahead."

The Pentagon's rhetoric about the Soviet antimissile effort reminded some defense experts of American alarm over the alleged "missile gap" between the Soviet Union and the United States in the early 1960s. (There *was* a gap—in America's favor.) These experts accept that the Russians take defense very seriously. (After all, they have tried to protect their national capital; America, though it could have opted to do the same, did not.) They accept, too, that the Russians have spent a lot of money on air defense, civil defense, and the like (though a survey of thousands of Russian émigrés in America conducted during the Reagan years found the evidence of a massive Soviet civil defense effort very flimsy). What many experts did not accept was that the Russians were about to break out of the ABM treaty, or that Moscow believed it could construct anything resembling an effective defensive system.

Weinberger's argument that the Russians have abandoned deterrence, therefore, appears to be stretching a point. Arguably, in fact, the Russians have taken certain steps since the late 1970s that *reduce* their incentive to build a full-blown defense. They have developed two types of land-based mobile missile, the SS-24 and the SS-25, and though the SS-25 constitutes a breach of SALT II, which permits the building of only *one* new missile per side, the decision to "go mobile" is one that, in principle, many analysts welcome. (It will make the Soviet Union's land-based force less vulnerable, thus reducing the temptation for the Kremlin to "use it or lose it.") And for all the controversy it has created, the Abalakovo radar is stabilizing in the sense that it completes the early warning coverage of what might, in a crisis, be a very nervous Kremlin.

Then there is the evidence of Soviet military doctrine. In the 1960s and early 1970s, as we have noted, a number of prominent military men in the Soviet Union made statements suggesting that a nuclear war might be winnable. Such statements are not heard nowadays. Since around 1977, Soviet political leaders—and some Russian generals too—have stressed that nuclear war would lead to catastrophe for both sides, and significantly there have been no statements to the contrary. The Soviets may not have a word for deterrence, and they may not call the balance of terror mutually assured destruction, but they nevertheless appear to accept the concept. Besides, if what the Pentagon fears is a Soviet break-out from the ABM treaty, then Reagan's Star Wars initiative, far from encouraging Soviet restraint, is likely to have the opposite effect.

In June 1985, for example, a prominent Soviet analyst with ties to Gorbachev told an assembled group of Washington's defense specialists and Kremlinologists that the key to stability was each side's capacity to deliver a crushing retaliatory blow against the other. Against this background, he said, SDI marked a qualitative change. But SDI wasn't going to work, he went on. It was a nonstarter, technically. Consequently, there must be *another* aim behind the initiative. The official proceeded to spell out the common Soviet view that, because of the contradictions, SDI *must* be designed for offensive purposes, in order to give America a first-strike capability over the USSR. We have worst-case planners, too, he said. We also have to be pessimistic. The implication—that Moscow would react to the American program, and react strongly—was clear enough.

Some in Washington, indeed, were concerned that Reagan's Star Wars plan might give the Soviets an excuse and an incentive to effect the very break-out from the ABM treaty that everyone feared. In a Senate Armed Services Committee hearing in March 1984, a year after Reagan's speech, Senator Sam Nunn of Georgia, the Democrats' lead-

ing defense expert, raised this question with Richard Perle. "I am
... concerned," said Nunn, "that the Soviets may feel they have been
given help, public opinion-wise, because the president made such a
pitch publicly about what we were going to do in the whole ABM area
and how that was such a wonderful thing for world peace. It seems to
me they have been given a carte blanche propaganda tool they can use
very much to go along with an ABM break-out [that is, a sudden
decision to flout the treaty and erect a defense]. I don't think the
president intended to do that. I am not suggesting that." But that,
clearly, was the danger. "All they have to do is quote back how these
ballistic missiles defenses are wonderful for peace and make the world
safe and abolish offensive weapons and all that business. . . ." Perle
elected to address the question off the record, but many in Washington
shared precisely the fear Nunn expressed.

What, then, were Reagan's critics recommending?
First, that quiet, low-key research, such as that which had been
proceeding before Star Wars arrived, was important and should continue. It provided a hedge against possible Soviet breakthroughs and
might one day, far into the next millennium, yield the kind of technology that *would* make population defense thinkable. The Star Wars
initiative, on the other hand, with the political heat it generated,
seemed calculated only to raise false hopes and to spur the Russians on
to greater efforts.
Second, the critics believed that the key to preventing an uncon-
strained and horrifically expensive space race lay in arms control. In
order to succeed, an arms control deal, like previous deals, would have
to be modest, and though the subject of precisely what could happen
in negotiations is beyond the scope of this book, the shape such a deal
might take is apparent as I write: it would involve both sides accepting
that research must go on, a cast-iron commitment to the ABM treaty
(with considerable tightening of its language and with the Reagan
administration agreeing, perhaps indefinitely, to renounce testing and
deployment of space-based systems), and cuts—perhaps quite substantial cuts—in the offensive forces of both sides. Conceivably, both sides
could also agree to modify the ABM treaty to allow more extensive

deployment of ground-based defenses for protecting missile silos. (If this was done as part of an arms control agreement, it might win the political support in America it would otherwise lack—though, as I have suggested, it might not be sensible.) But perhaps most crucial of all, a new treaty would outlaw or dramatically constrain testing of antisatellite weapons, or ASATs.

ASATs, of course, are already with us. The Russians have a fully tested system and the Americans, at the time of this writing, are beginning to test one. The prospect of large-scale ASAT deployment, however, still lies in the future. It is in neither side's interest for this to happen. If it *does* happen, the West will suffer the most. Indeed, from NATO's point of view, it is hard to imagine a more nonsensical weapon than one capable of destroying satellites.

Satellites play many critical roles. In a crisis, for example, reconnaissance satellites would provide vital early warning of a possible nuclear attack. If one side were able to blind the other by knocking out its reconnaissance satellites, the dangers would be intense; the side that has been blinded might suspect it was about to be attacked and, under the circumstances, decide to get its blow in first. Blinding your adversary in the nuclear age, as E. P. Velikhov, vice president of the Soviet Academy of Sciences, puts it, would be "tantamount to repeating the biblical story of Samson. The blinded adversary will let the skies fall on his head and on the enemy's head, too, of course."

Those in the Pentagon who dislike the idea of an ASAT ban rest their case on two arguments. First, they say, an ASAT ban would be impossible. The Russians have already deployed a system: it is small and could be easily hidden in holes in the ground. There would be no chance of the West being able to verify adequately that the ban was being observed.

But the Russian ASAT is a very crude device. It weighs two tons and has to be propelled into space by a huge, liquid-fueled, SS-9 booster rocket. It is so crude that it has little chance of success unless it is fired from the ground when the designated target is immediately overhead, which means that its firing crew may have to wait up to twenty-four hours for the rotation of the earth to bring it into the right position. Then, once this blunderbuss is launched, it cannot make a direct ascent but has to do at least one and probably two orbits of the earth before it is ready to blow up its target with a warhead that explodes in a hail of shrapnel. This process may take up to three hours, and after that time the odds are still high that it will miss; in twenty tests between the 1960s and mid-1985, almost half have been failures. The new American ASAT, by contrast, is much more sophisticated. Launched by an F-15 jet fighter at an altitude of about 18 miles, it can speed toward its target, boosted by a two-stage solid-fueled rocket, at 500 miles a minute, much faster than its Russian counterpart, and it can *theoretically* reach that target in only half an orbit.

The argument that a ban is impossible because of the existing Russian ASAT is nonsense. In the first place, if they were forbidden to carry out further testing, the Russians would soon lose any vestige of confidence they may currently have in their system. At the same time, some relatively modest changes in American satellites could make them unassailable unless the Russians developed something new: these changes would involve building better-protected satellites, making them more agile, so that they could take evasive action if threatened, and, in some cases, sending them into higher orbit—much of which is being done anyway. Given this, the Russians would derive no benefit at all from secretly storing their current ASAT weapons in holes in the ground.

The second argument that can be heard in defense of ASATs is more complicated. It goes like this. NATO is an alliance divided by water: in a war on the central front it would depend on being able to bring vital reinforcements and supplies across to Europe *by sea*. The Soviets, however, would be able to use their ocean reconnaissance satellites, called RORSATs, to track allied shipping, making it possible for submarines (and perhaps bombers too) to wreak havoc. To protect its convoys, therefore, the West has no option but to develop ASATs that could destroy the Soviet RORSATs in the event of war.

This argument is as untenable as the first one. For one thing, the U.S. Navy believes that it is already able to interfere heavily with RORSATs by jamming and other electronic means. Even if the navy is exaggerating its capacity—as some believe it does—the West is overall much more dependent on satellites than the East, whatever the danger posed by RORSATs. The Warsaw Pact, for example, can depend on land lines for communication; NATO cannot.[4] And for intelligence, reconnaissance, and surveillance, the West depends on satellites to a much greater extent than the Warsaw Pact.

There remains only one argument left to justify ASATs, an argument not much aired in public. The argument is that Star Wars will not be possible if ASATs are banned. Under the ABM treaty, it is permissible to proceed with ASAT testing, and this loophole, the Pentagon hopes, will enable it to test some of the technology that will eventually be vital for SDI. Many SDI weapons, indeed, will have to perform a very similar role to ASATs, only they will have to be able to shoot down missiles as well as satellites. So by agreeing to an ASAT ban the Pentagon would be agreeing to radical constraints on the Star Wars program. It does not wish to do that. Thus the Reagan administration's certification to Congress that it was negotiating in good faith to ban ASATs in arms control could be compared, as Republican Senator Charles Mathias put it, to the game played by Alice in *Through the Looking Glass* in which she tried to believe as many as six impossible things before breakfast.

The arms control deal I have suggested would scarcely represent a dramatic breakthrough. Smallish cuts in missile arsenals, a recommitment to the ABM treaty (a way would have to be found of solving the problem posed by Krasnoyarsk), and a ban on ASAT tests would scarcely amount to the "inspired vision" of SDI. But in a profoundly complicated and divided world, it is probably the best that can be hoped for. An ASAT deal, in particular, might avert a race in especially silly and destabilizing weapons. Arguably, too, the West should seek a ban on ATBMs—anti*tactical* ballistic missiles. These are systems potentially capable of shooting down medium- and short-range ballistic missiles—systems like the Soviet SA-12, which, though ostensibly an antiaircraft weapon, has been tested in an ATBM role. The West has

---

[4]The present generation of Soviet ASATs cannot threaten communications satellites, since they are in geosynchronous orbit, and hence beyond their range. But future generations undoubtedly will.

nothing comparable to the SA-12, and a ban on ATBMs would close a major loophole in the ABM treaty.

The irony of Star Wars, of course, is that by launching it, and by scaring the Soviets, Ronald Reagan may have put himself in a better position to achieve such a deal than any previous administration. "I don't think this genie should ever have been let out of the bottle," one very senior American official told a friend in early 1985, "but now that it has, I'm going to make them pay to stuff it back in again." And as John Newhouse, who worked for the Arms Control and Disarmament Agency during the Carter administration, observed, the Soviets might be prepared to pay: "Their internal problems are a litany of woes; their empire in Eastern Europe is trembling on its foundations; and they are caught up in an unending race with the United States—a faster horse —around the weapons-technology track."

At the time of this writing, however, the prospect of such a deal does not look likely. True, the opposition to SDI is likely to grow. There are signs that the Joint Chiefs of Staff, who rashly endorsed the project in 1983, are beginning to have second thoughts. As pressures on the defense budget grow they will face hard choices, and SDI is unlikely to seem a priority to their various services—though the chief of naval operations, Admiral Watkins, remains personally devoted to it. And, to be sure, defense projects *have* been canceled in the past: take the embryonic ABM system of the late 1960s, or America's once extensive air defense network, or the Divad gun. A wise investor does not pour "good money after bad," say the optimists, and sooner or later the American government, which is strongly influenced by economic forces, will have to drop Star Wars whether it does a deal or not. Better, then, to do a deal while the currency is still worth something.

Whatever happens, though, Ronald Reagan will never persuade the Russians to accept not just disarmament, but Star Wars too. As *Washington Post* columnist Robert Kaiser put it, asking them to "accept an entirely new and staggeringly expensive competition to build defensive weapons" together with "the elimination of a large fraction of their offensive weapons" is like telling them "there's about to be a famine, so please throw out all the canned food in your basement." It just won't happen. Arms control and Star Wars will not be able to coexist, and if Star Wars does not die, then arms control surely will.

Not only will the prospect of all future agreements evaporate, but so will existing ones—such as the ABM treaty—as both sides engage in an out-and-out race in defensive and offensive arms.

The trouble is, however, that despite the talk of arms control, there are a significant number of people in Washington who would welcome precisely that. Ronald Reagan may believe that both Star Wars and arms control are achievable, but they are not. They believe that arms control, as practiced to date, has been a one-way street, both pointless and dangerous, and they would gladly be rid of it. The Kremlin, they argue, has consistently fared better at the bargaining table than the White House. Unfettered by public opinion, unlike democratic governments, it has been able to play a tougher hand and to lull America into a false sense of security, while, unnoticed by the public, the military balance has tilted dangerously in favor of the East. Not only that: the Soviets have not even respected the agreements they have signed. They have brazenly cheated, as in the case of the Krasnoyarsk radar.

Those who doubt the value of existing agreements say that what they are after is "real" arms control, but the kind of agreements they envisage are now—and will always be—beyond the bounds of the possible. What these people believe, then, is that America will have to resign itself to an arms race, and that it had therefore better try to win it.

From this perspective, Star Wars makes sense. The United States would almost certainly *lose* a purely offensive arms race; the Soviets would be able to deploy more new missiles, and deploy them faster (as they have done, indeed, for years). Take MX: initial plans to deploy 200 under Carter had shrunk by 1985 to 50 in vulnerable silos. And some Pentagon officials wonder gloomily whether America will *ever* be able to win support for another land-based missile after MX.

But in an arms race involving both offensive *and* defensive weapons, say the hard-liners, America would have some advantages. First, the Russians would be forced to divert rivers of rubles from potentially lethal missiles into relatively harmless defensive systems (a bonus for America). Second, the Soviets would be competing with America in an area where America would indisputably be stronger—at the leading edge of technology. What's more, according to this school of thought, the Russians would never be able to keep building their offensive forces, *and* develop countermeasures to America's Star Wars program, *and* build their own Star Wars at the same time. They simply would not be able to afford it.

Following this logic, therefore, the hard-liners not only don't care whether arms control collapses; they want it to. They want to make the American Star Wars program unstoppable by the time Reagan leaves office in 1989, and to this end, they believe that if the Soviets start working flat out on space systems, and flagrantly break out of the ABM treaty, it will only help their cause. Congressmen will see what is happening and realize that America has no alternative but to follow suit, and they will cough up the funds accordingly. Otherwise, as one insider put it, they will be faced with a "technological Pearl Harbor" —a world in which the Soviet Union has a defensive shield and America does not.

What the hard-liners want, then, is an out-and-out offense-defense race. They believe that the United States may eventually emerge on top; the Soviet economy, already perilously strained, will be unable to stand the competition. The United States will have restored its "lost security," not through arms control, but through its own technological efforts. ("The days when we were the only bully on the block with a big stick have gone," as one SDI researcher put it. "Some of the advocates of SDI believe that if we can take Russia's stick away and go back to being the only bully on the block then we'll be all right again.") The Soviet Union, finally, will collapse, bankrupt, onto the "ash heap of history." That vision, it seems to me, is the real driving force behind Star Wars.

On July 31, 1984, the official newspaper of the Soviet Communist party, *Pravda,* ran a piece under the headline "DANGEROUS ILLUSIONS IN WASHINGTON." The article was not about Star Wars but about cruise missiles, which the newspaper attacked, as follows. The United States, it said, "once sought to outdistance the Soviet Union in ballistic missiles, and that did not work. . . . It tried with independently targetable multiple reentry vehicles, MIRVs, and again that did not work. It won't work this time either." For all the piece's bluster and self-righteousness, *Pravda* had a point. America invented MIRVs, but the Soviets soon caught up, and because they began with bigger missiles (and no public opinion problems), they were able to deploy more of them than the United States. Similarly, America devised cruise missiles as a system it would take the Soviets years and billions of rubles to match. But just two months after the *Pravda* article appeared, the first Soviet cruise missile deployments, on submarines and bombers, were announced. In the long run, as we have seen, this deployment will probably turn out to be against Western interests, too. The *Pravda* article did not mention Star Wars, but the implication was clear: if the United States went ahead with SDI, they would too. (Indeed, many believe that the Soviet Union will only become *capable* of building Star Wars if America pioneers the way first; just as Moscow made the crucial breakthrough in MIRV technology by acquiring vital components from the West, so they would probably have to acquire crucial pieces of Star Wars technology from America in order to construct defenses.)[5]

If the Americans and the Soviets do begin a flat-out arms race in defensive and offensive weapons, there is no guarantee that the Americans will "win" it, even if they had anything to gain by doing so. The only certainty is that the race itself would be extraordinarily dangerous. On this we can call in the testimony of Caspar Weinberger. "It takes very little imagination to realize what a vastly more dangerous world this would be if they [the Soviets] attain this ability to destroy our missiles, and we did not have a similar capability," he said on one occasion. And on another: "If the Soviets get strategic defense and we don't, it would be very much like the world in which the Soviets had a nuclear weapon and we did not."

If the Soviet Union gets Stars Wars and America does not, in other words, America will be at a desperate disadvantage. It will know that the Soviet Union can attack it with impunity, or relative impunity.

---

[5] When the Russians first attempted MIRVing in the 1960s, they ran into all kinds of snags because they lacked the precision tools necessary to manufacture key components of a MIRV guidance system (specifically, the requisite ball bearings). Their problems were solved at the beginning of the 1970s when they acquired 100 Centaline machines from the United States. Secretary of State Henry Kissinger approved the sale over the objections of the Pentagon.

But what happens if America gets Star Wars first? Would not the world suddenly become "vastly more dangerous" for the Russians? Would they not suddenly realize that America had the potential to strike *them* with relative impunity? There are some who say the Russians could not possibly believe that, on the grounds that Westerners are the "white hats" and not aggressive, but this is naive in the extreme. *Whichever* side lost a Star Wars race would feel desperately insecure, and almost certainly put its offensive forces on a hair trigger. And the fact that whichever side won would probably end up with a less than effective system does not change the argument. As Richard Garwin points out, even a dud strategic defense could threaten stability. "Think of a plastic gun used in a robbery. Thieves armed with nothing more have been shot and killed."

The truth about a Star Wars race is that the *winning* side—the side that got Star Wars first—would have acquired, in the eyes of the *losing* side, a first-strike capability much more real than any that could come from offensive missiles alone. For the sake of argument, let us assume that America wins the space race. As seen from the Kremlin, America would now be in a position to land a crushing nuclear blow, knocking out many Russian missiles, while at the same time being protected against the inevitably "ragged" retaliatory strike the Soviet Union would then be capable of sending back. Would the Russians allow this to happen? They would know that they might come off better if they struck first; that way, using *all their missiles,* they would have a good chance of overwhelming America's defense with sheer numbers. It might seem preferable to being destroyed and unable to mount a proper retaliatory strike. So Star Wars could, contrary to the wishes of its advocates, make both sides not less but much more jumpy than they are now.

The situation, as one prominent defense analyst puts it, can be expressed in medieval terms. Imagine two knights, each of whom possesses only a sword: that is the situation we are in now. Each can strike the other, but he knows that if he does he will be struck back. But suppose one of the knights obtains a shield. Then he knows that he can strike the other with impunity—and catch the return blow on his shield. This is what the world would be like if one side got Star Wars and the other didn't. The analogy can be carried further. If both sides got swords and shields then each would strive to find another weapon

—say, a mace—in order to be able to disarm *both* the other's sword *and* his shield. An SDI race, in other words, would be dangerous throughout; in an atmosphere of distrust, with no arms control, and each side fearful the other might achieve a workable defense first, there would be frequent temptations for small-scale attacks on satellites or even preemptive strikes. The race would be one that neither side could afford to lose. As a result, each side might simply decide to shoot down any weapon put into orbit above its territory. Only with extraordinary cooperation between the superpowers would Star Wars make sense, and the irony of the project is that those who advocate it most strongly are those least disposed to believe in the likelihood of such cooperation. Besides, such a perfect relationship as here envisaged would surely obviate the need for Star Wars.

And even if both sides reached the promised land of fully deployed defenses, neither's would be perfect, and both would be dependent on what one scientist described as "paranoid computers"—computers primed to react to the slightest sign of a possible attack, whether a genuine or an accidental threat (such as a stray satellite moving too close to a sensitive platform). These computers could interact in frightening ways, and it is not beyond the bounds of possibility, as we saw earlier, that they could actually cause a nuclear war.

Finally, it is worth returning to the matter of cost. No one has a clue as to what this might be. Estimates range the whole way up to $1 trillion—a pile of $100 bills 67 miles high, to use Ronald Reagan's image. It could, of course, be more, especially if improved air defenses to deal with cruise missiles are added in. Most defense projects, as we have seen, end up costing far more than anyone anticipates, and for something as vast and teeming with unknown engineering problems as Star Wars (it would be the biggest enterprise in the history of mankind) this would be more likely than ever.

In the early 1970s, when James Schlesinger served in the White House Budget Office, one of his responsibilities was to review the U.S. Army's plans for the construction of the Safeguard defensive system then being contemplated for protecting American missile fields. "The Safeguard system," he later said, "turned out to be the only weapon system development in my experience in which staggering overruns were already revealed *prior* to the inception of work."

What would be the consequences of spending billions on a vast, probably futile, and unnecessary attempt to bolster deterrence? There would be a shortage of funds for other things. Money spent on Star Wars is money *not* spent on something else, and either the defense budget would have to expand dramatically—an unlikely event given America's ballooning budget deficit—or the Pentagon would have to change its priorities. Let us glance back again to what happened when Safeguard was on the drawing board: "The fiscal 1971 budget, first submitted by the Pentagon, proposed a reduction of seven army divisions and a substantial Europeanization of European defense. Of course, the Army did have the honor of developing the Safeguard system. But it also seemed embarked on the path to eating itself out of house and home—at the cost of its conventional capabilities."

If Star Wars ever goes ahead, this problem will recur—on an infinitely grander scale. The sums poured into constructing the fantastic gadgetry of Star Wars would be money that, if properly applied, could make a huge difference to America's conventional forces—perhaps the difference, in a war, between whether or not nuclear weapons had to be used. No wonder, then, that Sir Geoffrey Howe worried in his speech to the Royal United Services Institute about the effect of Star Wars "on all the other elements of our defenses, on which Western security will continue in large part to depend." All the evidence suggests that pursuing the chimera of a space-based defense, unless the Russians make it impossible not to do so, would be a disastrous course. It would be disastrous not because it is based on an ignoble vision—it is not. Nor because scientists are incapable of devising gadgets to shoot down missiles; that, someday, may be possible. And not because "live Americans" are not better than "dead Russians," to use the false choice often put forth. But because, considered in terms of what it would have to achieve, it *would not work.* It is not a project worth betting the future of the Western world on. Its legacy would be utterly different from Reagan's vision of what it might be, and almost entirely bad. It would cripple arms control, and it would place a great, perhaps intolerable, strain on the Western alliance—an alliance that, as we will see in the next chapter, will have problems enough to overcome in the years ahead without the added burden of Star Wars.

13

The Future of NATO

Late in 1981, during the super-power talks about Euromissiles in Geneva, Yuli Kvitsinsky, the chief Soviet negotiator, told Paul Nitze, his American counterpart, the following story.

A bear was traveling by train when he noticed, hopping along the corridor outside his compartment, a rabbit. The rabbit seemed nervous, so the bear asked: "What's the matter, rabbit?" "I think the inspector is coming," said the rabbit, "and I don't have a ticket." "Never mind," said the bear. "Come in here next to me and I'll protect you." The rabbit hesitated, but decided he had better do as he was bid. He hopped onto the seat next to the bear. Moments later, they heard the inspector coming down the corridor. "What am I going to do?" said the rabbit anxiously. "Don't worry," said the bear. "I will hold you out of the carriage window by your ears, so the inspector won't be able to see you. Then, when he's gone, you can come back in again." The rabbit looked rather

dubious about this but felt he had no option but to agree. So the
bear picked him up by the ears [and at this point Kvitsinsky
clenched his right fist] and dangled him out of the window. When
the inspector came in, the bear showed him his ticket. But the
inspector was suspicious. "What have you got in that hand outside
the window?" he asked. "Oh . . . nothing," said the bear.

And Kvitsinsky suddenly unclenched his fist and held up an empty
hand.

The story was offered to Nitze with no explanation or moral, and
Nitze accepted it in the same spirit. It was conceivable, however, that
Kvitsinsky had a moral in mind: allies don't matter, he was saying; great
powers should abandon them when it seems necessary to do so. Certainly such a moral would have been appropriate, because the Soviets
at the time—preceding the cruise and Pershing deployments in Europe
—were attempting both to persuade the Americans to renege on their
commitment to deploy (to make the bear drop the rabbit), and to
persuade the Europeans that the Americans were not negotiating seriously.

Trying to drive a wedge between America and its allies, of course,
has been a long-term preoccupation of Soviet foreign policy, and the
impending deployment of cruise missiles provided an opportunity to
practice it. The problem, for the West, is that the alliance is becoming
more and more vulnerable to attempts to divide it. Differences between
Europe and America are greater now than they have ever been on a
whole variety of issues, and many analysts forecast that things will get
worse. The old conventional wisdom, that NATO is forever facing
crises and forever weathering them—German rearmament, Suez,
France leaving the military structure, the Vietnam War, MLF, INF
—is gradually being replaced by another: that NATO is bound eventually to collapse, and unless dramatic changes are made may do so by
the end of the century. An increasing number of people on both sides
of the Atlantic are questioning whether it should be preserved, or
whether the time has come to tear up the North Atlantic Treaty, send
the supreme allied commander back to Washington, and pension off
the secretary general.

*   *   *

On the face of it, it would not be altogether surprising if the alliance was due for a shakeup. If, in the beginning, NATO was an arrangement whereby the United States provided most of the effective defense of the West, while Europe, to everyone's advantage, got on with rebuilding its political and economic institutions, then clearly things have changed.

The idea of being hitched to Europe, in an alliance lasting forty years, would have been anathema to America's Founding Fathers. "Europe has a set of primary interests," George Washington declared as he left office, "which to us have none, or a very remote relation. . . . It must be unwise in us to implicate ourselves, by artificial ties, in the ordinary vicissitudes of her politics, or the ordinary combination and collision of her friendships and enmities."

The current of isolationism runs strongly through American history. In both World War I and II the United States hesitated before becoming involved, and after 1945 many influential figures resisted the notion of an Atlantic alliance on the grounds that America stood to gain little, that it didn't need Europe, and that, in the last resort, a Russian takeover of the continent would not matter much. Why not retreat behind the atomic bomb and two oceans and construct a Fortress America? Even President Truman, in the act of sending troops to Europe, made it clear that he found inconceivable the possibility of a *permanent* American military presence there. In the end, Europe would be strong enough to make the arrangement unnecessary. "Eventual European unity and European self-defense were corollaries of the North Atlantic Treaty," observed the historian Theodore Draper in a 1982 article in *Encounter*. "It is doubtful whether the U.S. Senate would have approved of the treaty if it had not been for these two presuppositions."

Yet the arrangement persisted, and it did so without Europe moving toward unity or self-defense, and despite some fundamental changes. In the first place, the Soviet Union, a "European" power when the alliance began, armed only with conventional weapons, steadily expanded its influence abroad and built up a nuclear arsenal to rival America's. The nuclear umbrella that America extended confidently over the Atlantic came to look less watertight to those it sheltered and more like a lightning rod to its bearer. Meanwhile, coinciding with the

USSR's rise to nuclear parity were profound developments in both America and Europe.

The changes are familiar enough: America's political center of gravity has moved gradually west and become less Eurocentric. The people who shaped America's postwar foreign policy were, for the most part, members of the "old East Coast establishment"—bankers, lawyers, and industrialists whose views had been shaped in New York and, above all, on Wall Street. Their understanding of Europe was based on frequent contact with its institutions and travel to its cities, and their belief that the economic health of America was intimately bound up with the health of Europe, and that America would be perilously exposed if the European continent went Communist, translated into the firm conviction that the forward defense of America began on the Elbe.

There are still many in the State Department and the Pentagon who hold this view. But the influence of the old East Coast establishment in American politics has declined. As the old smokestack industries of the North and East have faltered, so new industries, many of them based on high technology, have sprung up in the West and South. According to the nationwide census, 4 million people decamped from the so-called "frost belt" to the "sun belt" in the 1970s alone, and the shift has been reflected in Congress: New York State had 47 representatives in 1946, now it has 34; California had 25 representatives in 1946, now it has 45. Inevitably, as America's center has moved westward, Europe has come to seem less important, both culturally (with most of America's new immigrants coming from Mexico, Central America, and Asia) and economically (with the discovery of new and expanding markets in the vast Pacific basin). California, after all, is almost twice as far from Europe as New York is. "Economically, Europe is a good trading partner for the U.S.," wrote an international businessman who wants NATO dissolved.

> But Japan is a bigger trading partner than any country in Europe and soon will overwhelm Europe in this role. Southeast Asia has some of the fastest developing economies in the world and has more people than all of Western Europe. Then there is East Asia, so vast in its potential as to stagger the imagination. There is also

the Pacific rim of South America and beyond that South Asia and
Africa wait. . . . Indeed, when we measure the near-optimized
markets of Europe and its 250 million persons against the near-
unoptimized 1.5 billion to 2 billion people of the Pacific basin
alone, Europe seems a puny affair.

In the pages of the *Wall Street Journal* and other former bastions
of transatlanticism, such sentiments have become familiar. They are
not yet typical, but they may become so. The economic interdepend-
ence of Europe and America is no longer as strong as it was. The
Atlantic, as Sir Oliver Wright, the British ambassador to Washington,
pointed out in a 1982 speech, has "grown wider."

As America has changed, so too has Europe. It is no longer the
battered, impoverished continent it was in 1949, when NATO was
founded. Theoretically at least, it is capable, now, of defending itself;
it has about the same gross national product as the United States and
it generates more international trade. In some respects it has become
an "economic superpower" in its own right.

But as Europe has gotten back on its feet, so, as in America, has
a new generation come to the fore, a generation more skeptical of
military power, more unwilling or unable to understand its role in
keeping the peace, less concerned about the Soviet Union, and less
sympathetic toward America. It is a generation that remembers dimly,
if at all, the Stalin purges or the building of the Berlin Wall. As one
British analyst has noted: "America does not connote to them the
Marshall Plan and the Berlin airlift, or even John Kennedy, but rather
Vietnam and Watergate."

The starkest evidence of this anti-Americanism is in the European
Left, especially in the modern-day peace movement, which is much
stronger and better organized than its 1950s predecessor. To the antinuclear Left, the overwhelming desire is to be rid of America, and it
seems to be this, as much as a fear of nuclear weapons, that lies at the
heart of unilateralism. For as Theodore Draper put it in his admirable
essay: "The campaign to get nuclear weapons out of Europe is at the
same time a campaign to get the United States out of Europe."

This campaign reached new heights in the wake of the cruise

decision; the nuclear weapons being objected to, of course, were American ones, under the control of a president whom the protesters did not trust. Their fate was in his hands, and in their view the risks of such dependence now greatly outweighed its benefits. Sometimes, indeed, America seemed even *worse* than the Russians. "The United States seems to me the more dangerous and provocative," wrote E. P. Thompson in the *New Statesman* in 1981, "and its general military and diplomatic strategies, which press around the Soviet Union with menacing bases. . . . It is in Washington, rather than Moscow, that scenarios are dreamed up for 'theatre' wars. . . ."

But where such hyperbole is the hallmark of the antinuclear leaders, distrust of American policy has grown in European capitals, too. European governments have become more ready to criticize, and less passive. On the whole, they distrusted Carter as weak and indecisive, but found Reagan's confrontational attitude toward Russia equally if not more upsetting. Differences of perspective showed up in successive rows—over Poland, Grenada, the building of the Siberian gas pipeline, the handling of international terrorism—as well as in festering disagreements about U.S. policy toward Central America and the Middle East. Though there have always been rows, European leaders, responding to grass-roots pressure, have become less willing to accept U.S. leadership of the alliance than they once were. Where the left-wing West German politician Egon Bahr may talk, rather absurdly, about the United States treating Europe as a protectorate, Helmut Kohl, the West German leader, makes a similar point about the changed relationship, though more politely, when he characterizes the transatlantic relationship as "friendship and partnership, but not dependency." Or as Ambassador Wright said in his Massachusetts speech: "The change in the power relationship between Europe and America has meant that Europe considers its view of the Soviet Union as valid as America's view and as equally worthy of consideration and discussion."

At the heart of the changed relationship, of course, is money, and the vexed question of "burden sharing." Given its own relative rise in wealth, and America's decline, is Europe doing enough for its own defense? With the surge in American defense spending of the early 1980s has come a parallel surge of resentment against Europe for not paying its way. While the United States was increasing its defense budget by around 7 percent a year, the pledge by the allies to increase theirs by 3 percent a year was, as one U.S. official put it, "more honored in the breach than in the observance." "I thought we cut a deal," one congressman told me, "but you guys haven't stuck to it." The American buildup, as he and other politicians were quick to point out, entailed sacrifice: more guns equaled less butter, or at least less help for the poor, and it was not just the American Right that complained. Senator Sam Nunn, the clever Georgia Democrat who chaired the Senate Armed Services Committee during the Carter years, consistently gave it as his view that unless Europe got its act together the security commitment might have to be rethought. "The American poor and working class," he told a private breakfast on Capitol Hill in 1982, "are becoming increasingly fed up at having to pay for the defense of the European rich and middle class."

Administration officials voiced similar sentiments. "We've gutted our social programs. You have not," said one State Department man. William Brock, U.S. trade representative before he became labor secretary, echoed his sentiments: "Forty percent of American workers have had their pay frozen or have actually taken pay cuts. Europeans have made no such adjustments. They're just going their merry way."

In this atmosphere, the spectacle of regular European antinuclear marches did not help. The peace movement seemed, to some U.S. politicians and officials, to exemplify a deeper malaise in Europe. ("Protestant angst," Richard Perle called it.) The "rivers of appeasement," it was thought, ran deep. Not only were European governments conspicuously reluctant to pay their share for the common defense, they were seen as failing, at the same time, to mollify the "cry babies," as one White House man labeled them, who criticized and in an important way *undermined* the defense America was trying to supply. *Not only, it seemed, did Europe not want to be defended by America, but large segments of it did not want to be defended at all.* The sight, on American TV screens, of protesters milling about U.S. bases and shouting abuse at American soldiers hardly enhanced support for the alliance; apart from anything else, the behavior appeared unfriendly and rude. When a London Weekend Television film crew visited Parma, Ohio, in the heart of "middle America," they came back, not surprisingly, with shots of residents saying they were "hurt" by

Europe's attitude, fed up with its criticism, and convinced, in the words of one businessman, that "European countries [should] take control of their own destiny."

This kind of sentiment was reflected in Mansfield-type stirrings in Congress. In the early 1970s Senate Majority Leader Mike Mansfield of Montana introduced a series of amendments calling for large-scale troop withdrawals from the central front. The amendments always failed, though not always by a large margin, but there are plenty of people in the Congress of the 1980s who are prepared to pick up Mansfield's banner. In 1982, the Senate Republican whip, Ted Stevens of Alaska, called for a reexamination of America's "commitment to Europe"; he and Senator Larry Pressler had been dismayed by the "hostile attitudes" toward the U.S. military they discovered on a trip to West Germany. More tangibly, both House and Senate have cut back the funding for some fairly routine European items, such as a Pentagon request for $6 billion toward providing prepositioned equipment for two extra American divisions intended to reinforce the troops on the central front in time of war. And in 1984 the staunchly pro-NATO Sam Nunn introduced an amendment that, if passed, would have led to a phased withdrawal of 90,000 U.S. troops from Europe by the end of the 1980s unless Europe took certain steps to boost its own defense. Nunn's salvo was intended as a warning shot across Europe's bow—it was even questionable whether he wanted it to pass—but it illustrated how the irritation with Europe in the Senate was not limited to one party or the other but was becoming more and more widespread. "Uncle Sam," as one Midwest senator put it, "just can't do it all anymore."

The "case against Europe" was often exaggerated. Uncle Sam was not doing it all, or anything like it. As their ambassadors in Washington were frequently pointing out, European nations would supply 85 percent of the ground forces and 80 percent of the aircraft at the outset of a war on the central front, though the arrival of American reinforcements would radically change that ratio. But disagreements between West and West have grown steadily more difficult to resolve, and the prospect of NATO falling, or drifting, apart is no longer unthinkable.

The unhappiness on both sides of the Atlantic feeds on itself, symbiotically. The American deficit is like a cancer: its effects, hidden at first, are liable to become more visible, and as it takes its toll the American defense budget will come under more and more strain. As that happens, the cries to reduce the "European" share will intensify.

The precise size of that share is hard to measure, but a fair estimate is about 30 percent. In 1984 the Pentagon counted the "incremental operating costs" of stationing U.S. forces in Europe at about $2 billion, the total cost of European-deployed forces and early reinforcements at $90 billion, and the total cost of *all* forces that might be committed to a European war at about $177 billion. Some analysts use even higher figures. They point out that most equipment currently being designed and built for U.S. forces, such as the M-1 tank and the Bradley, is designed with Europe in mind, and that the whole *thrust* of American army and air force procurement is Europe oriented. One analyst, Earl Ravenal, writing in the magazine *Foreign Affairs*, estimated in 1985 that on current trends and allowing for inflation, "Europe will cost the United States $2.2 trillion" over the next ten years. To Ravenal and others this is too much. "Americans," he says, "are faced with an increasingly demarcated choice: the salvation of Europe, or their own solvency and safety."

I do not believe Americans are faced with any such choice. But let us consider, first, the consequences of NATO falling apart, or being formally dissolved. Would either Europe or America benefit from such a move?

Those in the United States who advocate the disbanding of the alliance believe that both America and Europe are now better placed to look after their respective security interests separately rather than together. They believe that, if forced to do so, Europeans would overcome their differences and unite to form a common defense pact solid enough to stand up to the Russians. Equally, they believe that America, free from the tiresome burden of defending Europe, would be freer to pursue its own national interests than it is now. There is no evidence that either of these propositions is based on anything other than wishful thinking.

Take Europe first. Faced with the military strength of the Soviet Union—a strength that the West as a whole finds it tough to match —Europe would have to exact a colossal sacrifice from its people to have any hope of mounting a credible defense on its own. The whole structure of postwar European defense has been built around its alliance with America; to start again, and fashion a new and more ambitious pact, would require a superhuman effort, one that would probably be beyond Europe's economic and political reach. Without being able to count on American troops, or American reinforcements, it would have to develop not just massive conventional forces of its own, but a credible nuclear component. (The idea that the United States could still plausibly threaten retaliation for a nuclear attack on Europe once the alliance had been dissolved, and American troops removed, is fantasy.)

The beginnings of a European nuclear deterrent exist, of course, in the shape of the independent forces of Britain and France. But these are small, and suited principally to protecting the two countries that possess them. Would West Germany ever believe they would be used on its behalf? West German politicians are nervous enough about the American guarantee. They would be much more uncertain about a Franco-British one.

For Europe, the likeliest outcome of a dissolved NATO would not be the development of a robust, unified defense but a gradual, confused slide into neutralism. Indeed, far from remaining a nuclear power in its own right, Britain might actually lead the way. After long flirting with unilateralism, Britain's opposition Labour party is now wedded to it. If it wins an election, it is committed to removing all nuclear weapons from British soil. The independent deterrent would go, without even the pretense of negotiations. That in itself would scarcely cripple the alliance, but *all* other nuclear weapons in Britain would have to be scrapped or removed as well, and all American bases closed down. In the current climate, of course, this would be precisely the kind of action that might trigger the end of NATO—a goal Labour says it does not want, though its policy suggests it does. Judging from policy documents, Labour appears to hope that having disarmed itself, Britain would be able to continue to find shelter under the American nuclear umbrella, a strategy characterized by one State Department official as "NATO without the risk."

If Labour did disarm Britain, however, it could cause the already simmering discontent in Washington to reach a boiling point, and the pressure to withdraw American troops, the main military pillar of the alliance, could prove unstoppable. That in turn would leave West Germany, the country in the front line, considerably more exposed, and many believe that West Germany would then gradually seek a greater accommodation with the East, and be followed in the process by the other smaller nations of Central Europe.

West Germany might choose an alternative course: it might develop its own nuclear arsenal. In doing so, however, it would take a perilous step, one that would horrify the European Left (which fiercely opposed German rearmament in the 1950s). Since World War II, there has been a taboo on the German possession of nuclear weapons, and the Russians, with memories still vivid of the suffering they endured at German hands during that war (20 million dead), have always made it plain they would regard such a move as intolerably provocative. Nevertheless, with West Germany polarized and demoralized, there would be bitter dispute between those who, in effect, wished to move toward nuclear arms and those who wished to move toward Moscow's arms. In the circumstances, the Kremlin might find irresistible the temptation to interfere. Berlin, in particular, would suddenly be intensely vulnerable.

A neutral Europe, of course, would not worry the peace movements. They would welcome the removal of American troops and nuclear weapons. They believe that in a Europe left to its own devices, tensions would subside and the chance of war, especially nuclear war, would be less. They might be right. But they rest their case on a total faith in Soviet good intentions. They believe that the Kremlin would not attempt to exert pressure on Europe, either peacefully (by, say, interfering in the political process of other countries) or by the use of force, and that even if it did Europe would find ways of resisting. The experiences of Afghanistan, Vietnam, and Algeria, the British left-wing politician Anthony Wedgwood Benn has observed, "may prove" that "a determined people is the best guarantee against permanent domination from outside." This is no doubt of great comfort to the Afghans, the Vietnamese, and the Algerians, and it may even reassure Mr. Benn.

But Europe would be plunging into neutralism at a time when Moscow faces terrible, perhaps intractable problems, at time when it might feel more and more tempted to use the one element that makes it a superpower: its military strength. A neutral Europe, therefore, would scarcely guarantee a more stable world. If NATO collapsed, the chances of a miscalculation by the Russians would be greater and of a war between the superpowers just as great. And Europe, even if not directly involved, would probably still be devastated by such a war (both sides regarding the continent as a prize they could ill afford to lose). The peace movements would prefer to be Red rather than dead. They might end up both.

But those in America who advocate the withdrawal of U.S. troops are just as wrong-headed. They believe that an America cut loose from Western Europe—"Prometheus unbound," as one commentator put it—would be freer to act unilaterally and follow its own national interests. In fact, there is no evidence that America would become any more decisive, ruthless, or comfortable with the use of military force than it is now. Besides, it is hardly in America's "national interest" to allow the Soviet Union to intimidate and perhaps take over the European continent: if that happened, America would be far more vulnerable than it is now.

An America without allies, of course, is precisely what the Russians would like to see. "We must divide the West," said Nikita Khrushchev in a 1961 speech, "not unite it by crude attacks on capitalism." Yuri Andropov, then general secretary of the Soviet Communist party, told an audience in Karelia (Soviet-occupied Finland): "The Soviet Union's European policy remains unchanged. . . . Our position is clear. Europe must become a continent of peace and good-neighborly cooperation. Here, in Karelia, we have to emphasize the significance of the Soviet Union's good-neighborly cooperation with Finland. Soviet-Finnish relations today . . . represent the very kind of détente which makes for a more lasting peace. . . ."

A weaker America and a Finlandized Europe—both, clearly, would suit the USSR in its bid to achieve what Russian theoreticians have referred to as the "Era of Global Democratic Peace." The Russians will continue to exploit differences within the West, and though many of their propaganda campaigns have been strikingly crude, and arguably counterproductive, they are likely to get more and more help.

It is not surprising, therefore, that European diplomats joke that

SDI really stands for "Soviet dream item"—for at heart Reagan's Star Wars plans are profoundly isolationist. Consider the words of the eminent star warrior Edward Teller in a March 1983 speech: "We need to be in a situation where no matter how other conflicts come out, we can at least be safe at home, without allies."

Or as Lawrence Freedman, professor of war studies at London's King's College, has put it, from another perspective:

> Should the Americans succeed in creating this protection for themselves, it's unlikely that it would be as successful with regard to its allies and thus [America] will become in a way isolated from its allies, protected by its own fortress, and no longer as interested or sensitive to their interests. Indeed if the Americans do succeed in eliminating offensive nuclear weapons, in removing nuclear weapons from the security equation, then that removes from the Europeans one of the basic stabilizing factors of the last four decades that has helped keep the peace in Europe.

It is to be hoped that a potentially dangerous row over Star Wars can be averted. Politicians on both sides of the Atlantic must hold on to the conviction that world stability cannot possibly be improved by the fragmentation of the West—that NATO, despite all its problems, is worth preserving. "There is only one thing worse than fighting with allies," said Winston Churchill, "and that is fighting without them." Or as an American diplomat put it to me: "Whichever way you look at it, the West would be worse off without NATO than it is with it."

14

Conclusion

It is easier to identify NATO's problems than it is to prescribe solutions. After all, it is in the nature of defense that you may not know whether you have got it right until it is too late. As Dame Rebecca West once suggested, military planning before a war seems an exact science, like astronomy; afterward, it seems more like astrology.

There are, however, two facts that need to be borne in mind in contemplating the future of Western defense. The first is that the pressure to "get it right" is greater now than it has been in the past: if there is another world war, it will almost certainly be fought much faster, and be settled more swiftly, than any previous conflict. It has been estimated that the first twelve hours of artillery fire in a war on the central front would use up more ammunition than the whole of the Battle of El Alamein. There will be no time to gear up industrial production, to redesign hardware, to make elaborate changes in tactics.

The second inescapable fact is that Western defense ministries are going to become increasingly hard up. If defense budgets continue to rise, they will not, in real terms, rise very much. America's buildup in the early 1980s has been financed by huge federal deficits, deficits that threaten to burden the country for at least a generation and which mean that from now on, defense will get a smaller slice of the cake.[1] Indeed, the Reagan defense buildup, ironically, has insured that there will not be another such buildup in the near future, and it may mean that there will be *less* money available for defense in the late 1980s than there would have been had the buildup been more modest in the first place. In Western Europe, where America's allies are facing growing domestic problems (declining industries, rising unemployment, etc.), there will be no extra money for defense either. Budgets may keep pace with inflation, but they are unlikely to do more than that. So whatever NATO does, it will not be able to tap into any vast new resources. No amount of blood-curdling rhetoric about the Soviet threat will change this. Besides, trying to do too much, as we saw in the last chapter, will end NATO. The alliance will simply fall apart under the strain.

Yet modern weapons are getting more expensive at a dizzying rate; every year we can buy fewer planes, fewer ships, and fewer tanks. The cost of hardware is rising much faster than defense budgets are likely to. Congressman Denny Smith estimates that each new generation of weaponry costs between two and five times as much as the previous one. So if we are not to have a constantly dwindling defense establishment, the money will have to go farther. We will have to gain more "output" for less "input."

In both America and Europe, therefore, there is urgent need for change in the way people think about defense. The hope has been that a numerically superior enemy can be defeated by harnessing the latest in high technology, that we will be able to fight a "sanitized" war in which our weapons will be able to stop the enemy, as often as not, before he has even crossed the horizon and had a chance to fire back. As David Evans, a Marine Corps lieutenant colonel, wrote in the *New*

---

[1]The Gramm-Rudman Bill, passed by Congress in late 1985, which seeks to achieve a balanced federal budget by 1992, seems certain to have a dramatic effect on defense.

York Times in October 1984, there are two assumptions behind this "video-game vision" of defense: "First, the enemy will accommodate us by charging blindly into the teeth of this technology; secondly, he will continue to do so in the face of unacceptable losses. In short, a predictable foe destroyed by arms that always work perfectly."

The Soviets, as we have seen, are unlikely to oblige us by charging blindly into the teeth of Western technology, and the weapons are unlikely to work perfectly. Instead, weapons designers, seeking to squeeze an extra 5 percent capability out of a given system by cramming in the latest gadgetry, often add an extra 30 percent or more to the cost. And many of the enormously expensive weapons they produce are chronically unreliable and ill conceived. Watching the process, one is reminded of the British peer who was given to exclaiming, "My God, why can't they let it alone?" Like the sorcerer's apprentice, the Pentagon knows how to start the magic, but not how to stop it.

It is in America, as we have seen, that this high-tech bias is most deeply rooted. In part, it is a cultural phenomenon, an outgrowth both of America's utopianism and of the pioneering spirit. The history of American society is a history of frontiers being tamed and new ones being sought to conquer. It started with wagon trains moving west, but increasingly the tools of discovery have become high-tech tools and the heroes have become the wizards of high tech—the astronauts in the space program, the doctors who can produce manmade hearts, even clever salesmen like Steven Jobs, the founder of Apple Computers. The danger is that technology, instead of being simply regarded as a useful tool to help us do things, is becoming the be-all and the end-all. The ultimate view of technology is that it can manufacture worldwide peace for ever and ever, amen. Thus, a White House aide was quoted as saying at a Star Wars "pep rally" held on the eve of the 1985 superpower summit that the program was powerfully assertive policy, like the Republican Party itself. "It asserts the fundamental morality of peace through strength, and the fundamental morality of peace through technology." It takes something like the space shuttle disaster of January 1986 to remind us that there are limits.

In the defense establishment, the high-tech bias is bolstered by enormously powerful institutional forces. It is in everyone's interest to press ahead to "the next generation." The effectiveness of individual service chiefs tends to be measured more and more by their ability to squeeze money out of Congress rather than by any potential ability to win wars. The temptation to exaggerate requirements, and to exaggerate the threat, is ever present. The first responsibility of defense contractors is to their shareholders, rather than to the national interest, and when they turn out weapons ill suited to any battlefield they "salve their conscience," in the words of the Pentagon's inspector general, Joseph Sherick, by saying "Well, we'll never have a war, and we won't use that, and if we do, we'll always fire ten of them anyway." Meanwhile, Congress meddles insistently in the military. Some twenty-four congressional committees and forty subcommittees oversee the Pentagon, which, according to the *Washington Post*, fields more than a half million telephone inquiries from Capitol Hill every year. But Congress's collective urge is to "micromanage" rather than to reform. In the end, for individual congressmen, short-term parochial interests almost invariably triumph over broader strategic ones.

I must confess that, in the light of this, and in the light of similar pressures in Europe, I see little prospect of dramatic changes in the way NATO organizes its defenses and procures its weapons. The forces that pervert or prevent rational planning are too strong to permit fundamental change. To that extent, this is a pessimistic book. I have no magic cure-all to propose, no bold new strategy to propound, certainly no new technological gimmick to offer. I write principally on the assumption that the most necessary requirement, if there are to be even small changes, is a well-informed and concerned public. I am conscious, however, that as weapons get more and more complicated, and the strategies used to justify them more and more abstruse, the difficulties for laymen in making sensible judgments about defense become ever greater.

With all that in mind, I will offer one or two basic, and perhaps obvious, thoughts about the future. There are few ideas of reform with which NATO has *not* toyed at some stage or other, and I can scarcely claim that the suggestions I make are original. In some cases, they simply involve doing more of the things that are being done already. In no cases are they grotesquely expensive or especially glamorous. Nothing, indeed, could be more literally down to earth than the first.

Creating More Obstacles on the Central Front

"What is the object of defense?" asks the great Prussian strategist Karl von Clausewitz at the beginning of book six of *On War*. And he answers: "Preservation. It is easier to hold ground than take it. It follows that defense is easier than attack, assuming both sides have equal means. . . ."

In Central Europe both sides do not have "equal means." But one of the West's advantages is that it *owns the land* that would be under attack. The Russians, as we saw in Chapter 6, would attempt to smash through NATO's defensive line at weak points, and as fast as possible. One way of making this harder for them to do is better preparation of the terrain close to the border. As historian John Keegan has put it, the best way of rendering the central front impenetrable is "to take a pick and shovel to it."

A system of barriers, or obstacles, does not need to be as elaborate as France's Maginot line—far from it. It does not even need to involve constructing extensive mine fields and barbed-wire fences (at least in peacetime). Much could be done to slow a potential armored thrust through the creation of "natural" obstacles—planting trees or hedgerows across principal corridors of attack, for example. Tanks cannot knock down trees; they would have to be cleared, a difficult and time-consuming process and, in war, a dangerous one. Other possibilities include constructing more manmade lakes close to the Inner German Border; building "steps" into canals to render them impassable to tanks; arranging for the flooding of low-lying areas by canals and rivers in time of war; and building more dikes alongside roads that run parallel to the border. Tanks have difficulty getting past even three-foot walls. Such walls are not unattractive—they run alongside countless country lanes all over Europe—and building more of them would put difficult obstacles in the way of invading forces bent on moving fast.

A certain amount of so-called "terrain enhancement," it is true, has already been carried out. And much of West Germany already presents formidable obstacles to a would-be invader. "The most important manmade peacetime obstacles to the movement of enemy forces exist already," says John Tillson, a Pentagon analyst. "These are the cities and towns in the defensive zone." But more natural obstacles would not go amiss, and NATO could—and should—create more artificial obstacles too: trenches, antitank positions, and the like. It could and should prepare more of the 12,000 bridges in the defensive zone for demolition in time of war. Tillson estimates the total cost of "prechambering" half of these bridges for explosives, and preparing an equal number of roads and other features for demolition, at about $900 million, and a "landscaping program" at about the same amount—the cost altogether of two armored divisions. (Obviously, these prechambered bridges and roads would not be packed with explosives until war began and would not be blown until the Russians were close by.)

Finally, NATO could take advantage of a liquid explosive called nitromethane. Nitromethane, like many inflammable chemicals, burns only gently if it is set alight in the open air. If, however, it is compressed and then blown up with a two-pound charge, it can do considerable damage. What its advocates propose is the laying of lengths of plastic pipe across critical "axes of advance" on the central front, close to the border. The pipe, 6 inches in diameter, would be buried 7 feet underground, deep enough to ensure that, once down, it would not interfere with farmers ploughing the soil or sowing crops. It might be laid in 300-yard sections. All that would be visible, at various roadsides, would be the end of the pipe protruding aboveground and covered with a cap and a pressure valve.

In a crisis, diesel tankers, probably owned by civilian companies, could be filled with nitromethane at military storage sites. The chemical would then be poured into the plastic pipes, and explosive charges would be set. If the crisis abated, the fluid would be pumped back out and restored to its original tanks. If not, it would be triggered, probably by reserve soldiers watching from observation posts near the pipes. The resulting explosions would create ditches about 10 yards wide and 20 feet deep, quite impassable by tanks.

Action like this would cause chaos with the fine timetable of a Warsaw Pact invasion and hours of delay. Engineering units would have to be called up to erect bridges over the ditches, or fill them in, and in the meantime they—and the tanks waiting to cross—would be vulnerable to NATO fire. It is hard to imagine a more effective way of disrupting an attack. "If NATO wants a proper conventional defense of the central front, it has to prepare the ground better," one Pentagon man, who has spent years studying Soviet tactics, told me. "The fact that we are not doing this tells me we're not serious." Israel, by contrast, which *is* serious, relied heavily on fortifications and barriers to defend itself against much larger Syrian forces in the 1973 Middle East war.

The West German government, always reluctant to take the kind of steps that might signify a permanent division between itself and East Germany, is not enthusiastic about barriers, though some West German generals are more sympathetic. But the separation of the two Germanys is a fact of life. And the argument sometimes made that barriers are offensive, and would give NATO a better position from which to launch an attack, is far-fetched. They are considerably less offensive than futuristic, deep-strike weapons that might be fired at Soviet backup forces, and they are no more offensive than maintaining large standing armies in Germany, as NATO does at present. Besides, they would require relatively little land—less than 0.01 percent of West German soil, in one plan—and they would be simple and cheap.

A persuasive case can be made that West Germans, in exchange for the continued American commitment to their defense, should be prepared to make the relatively modest sacrifice that a better system of barriers would entail.

There is another problem with barriers, of course, quite apart from the political one. They generate little enthusiasm among procurement executives for the obvious reason that planting hedges and laying plastic pipes scarcely constitute exciting projects at the cutting edge of technology. They have none of the allure of supersonic fighters or nuclear-powered aircraft carriers. In short, as one Pentagon official put it, "They're not sexy. . . . The military planners have turned the defense program over to the high-technology guys and the big corporations, and they're going to rue the day."

A Greater Readiness to Explore
Operational Alternatives to Gadgetry

The ill-fated Divad antiaircraft gun having finally met its demise, the
U.S. Army has now turned its attention to finding a successor. And it
is a fair bet that a whole new series of horror stories will soon come to
be written about a gold-plated "son of Divad." At the time of writing,
it is unclear precisely what kind of follow-on to Divad the army might
pursue. By the time this book comes out the defense industry will be
hard at work developing one.

Instead of seeking a sophisticated followup to Divad, however,
why doesn't the army contemplate an operational solution? One possibility, suggested to me by a former U.S. Army officer, would involve
arming small units of infantry with much shorter-range antiaircraft
weapons, and deploying them close to the front line—out in front of
the main body of tanks and infantry—so that they would be able to
shoot down helicopters *before* they posed a major threat to U.S.
forces.

In the same vein, NATO would do well to think more carefully
about how it might use what the military likes to call "civilian assets"
during a war. One example: as was illustrated during the Falklands
War, oceangoing tankers and cargo vessels can be adapted to provide
alternative launch platforms for vertical takeoff jets and helicopters.
This, during a war at sea, would enable NATO to disperse some of its
jets and helicopters more widely—for reconnaissance, close air defense,
etc.—and that would make a lot of sense. Aircraft carriers, after all, are
extraordinarily expensive and concentrated targets. NATO might even
work out an arrangement with shipowners and operators under which,
in exchange for a contribution to costs, new vessels are equipped, or
older ones adapted, to carry appropriate launch platforms and other
facilities that could be used in a war.

This is just one instance where more thought about tactics, and
less about technology, would benefit America and the alliance in general. There are all kinds of others, as I suggested earlier in the book:
moving the emphasis, in air power, away from "deep strike" towards
"close air support" and, at sea, from aircraft carriers toward smaller

vessels, land-based aircraft, and submarines, are two of the more obvious alternatives put forward.

Better Use of Manpower

With NATO likely to find it increasingly difficult to maintain fully
manned, well-trained armed forces in the late 1980s and the 1990s, the
importance of reserves has come to loom steadily larger. Already, the
West Germans are capable of mobilizing a million men in under a
month, and other continental European countries can also call on large
forces of trained reserves. Many defense experts see properly equipped
and trained reserves as the key to a stronger NATO defense and have
developed elaborate plans for their use.

There are others more qualified than I to assess these plans, but
there is clearly a strong argument for allowing reserves to train with
equipment every bit as good as that used by regulars, a lesson that the
United States seems to have learned more thoroughly than the Europeans.

The question of how and where reserves should be deployed is
more controversial. Some argue that the most effective role they could
play would be close to the front line, where they could provide greater
"defense in depth" by freeing more heavily armored regular divisions.
This, however, would require an extraordinarily well trained and highly
motivated reserve force, and while West German reserves might measure up, those of other NATO nations probably would not. Wherever
deployed, though, reserve forces would provide valuable extra manpower in any war on the central front.

For though NATO obviously needs tanks—to regain ground that
has been lost and, if necessary, to make counterattacks—infantry
armed with TOW missiles or their European equivalent can go a long
way toward offsetting the disparity in tank numbers between the Warsaw Pact and NATO that so exercises military planners.

To digress for a moment, the tube-launched, optically tracked,
wire-guided missile is a relatively effective weapon. Critics argue that
operating the TOW entails considerable risk for the soldiers involved.
This may be true, but it is hard to find any effective weapon that can

be operated without danger, and those who argue that NATO should cease trying to build weapons that seek to remove all risk, as I do, can scarcely have it both ways by arguing at the same time that weapons like TOW are silly because they involve risk.[2] Besides, the TOW is not as risky as has sometimes been suggested. The idea that, to fire it, soldiers will have to stand up, exposed, on the battlefield for ten seconds or so is stretching a point. TOW missiles travel 1,000 meters in three or four seconds, and soldiers firing at tanks are not likely to be more than 1,000 meters away. Moreover, they are likely to be standing in some sort of cover—among trees, for example—rather than in the middle of open terrain. Finally, the cost-effectiveness of the TOW missile—priced at about $7,000, it can destroy a Soviet tank worth $500,000—is a strong argument in its favor.

More emphasis on reserves, and on the potential of dismounted infantry, would facilitate the kind of tactical changes needed to give NATO greater defense in depth. Some of these tactical changes are already being made. The U.S. Army, as we have seen, has developed a new doctrine, one that places more emphasis on maneuver and less on fighting wars of attrition. And the four NATO armies responsible for the northern sector of the central front, to take another example, have been organized into a more efficient and more "integrated" fighting unit.

The moving spirit behind these changes was a British general, Sir Nigel Bagnall, who commanded NATO's Northern Army Group in the early 1980s. What Bagnall did, essentially, was to form a new "backup" force for his four armies. This new force, made up of the so-called "operational reserves" (as distinct from the *national* reserves—i.e., part-time soldiers—which we have just examined), is three times the size of the old one (which was composed of separate units from the four army corps of the Northern Army Group: the Dutch, the West Germans, the British, and the Belgians). And the new force, heavily equipped with tanks, would enable the Northern Army Group to pro-

---

[2] The "fire and discard" Viper, described in Chapter 2, is a different matter: it simply was not a very effective weapon.

vide more defense in depth, to mount counterattacks on Soviet forces, and even, if it seemed necessary, to thrust into East Germany itself.

Bagnall's changes have had to be carefully wrought. The West German government is understandably sensitive about any retreat from forward defense. But German generals, in particular the German chief of staff, General Hans-Henning von Sandrart, have quietly helped implement the new concept of operations, and each of the defense ministries has given its approval. Furthermore, writing in *Sixteen Nations*, a magazine that covers NATO, General von Sandrart warned against an "over-literal interpretation" of forward defense; like others in the German military, he appeared to recognize the growing need for a more fluid deployment of forces on the central front.

It is from changes like these—from the better use of existing manpower and resources, rather than from any acquisition of shiny new hardware—that NATO will benefit most.

In this context, recent developments in France clearly benefit NATO. After 1965, when it left the military structure of the alliance, France sought to have the best of both worlds. Through Gaullism, it avoided the political problems of belonging to NATO—and having American nuclear weapons on its soil—while at the same time being defended in spite of itself. For as Theodore Draper has observed, France "is in the peculiar position of needing the alliance in order to benefit from staying out of it." It knows that despite possessing its own nuclear weapons, it would be perilously vulnerable if NATO ever collapsed or became too weak. (Would the French *really* go nuclear to stop a Soviet conventional attack? It seems unlikely.) Thus François Mitterrand, having savaged the alliance in his autobiography as an empty shell based on "the fiction of American intervention in Europe in time of war," has taken a very different tone since becoming president of France. And France, under Mitterrand, has become steadily more worried about the military weakness of the alliance and, above all, of its neighbor, West Germany.

The consequence has been that French military policy has in the early 1980s has evolved in a more European direction. The French have reorganized and strengthened their conventional forces. They have created a new 47,000-man *force d'action rapide*, designed to operate beyond France's borders, and have exercised this with the West Germans. If war came, the best guess, now, is that French forces would move into West Germany to assist the common defense, and for NATO, this is obviously welcome.[3]

Injecting More Sense into Procurement

The spate of stories about gold-plated ashtrays, coffeemakers, and lavatory seats may be an illustration of the law developed by C. Northcote Parkinson—that the importance of an item is inversely proportionate to the attention given to it. In one sense, however, the attention given to such trivial examples of Pentagon profligacy has served a purpose. It has helped trigger a growing restiveness about the inadequacies of the U.S. procurement system—a restiveness that now embraces politicians of many different political hues.

Gone are the days, indeed, when critics of U.S. procurement could be dismissed as "liberals" whose real aim was to cut the Pentagon budget. In the vanguard of those now calling for sweeping reforms are Senator Barry Goldwater, the staunchly anti-Soviet chairman of the Senate Armed Services Committee, and other leading conservatives. This is a natural enough development. Conservatives, after all, have traditionally abhorred waste. (One might add that conservatives have also, traditionally, had a very strong sense of the limits of the possible and been inclined to distrust grandiose visions such as that offered by the star warriors.) Public attacks on the Pentagon's procurement system are increasingly coming from the Pentagon itself. Take David Evans, the Marine Corps lieutenant colonel who once worked in Caspar Weinberger's office:

---

[3] It makes sense for France as well. Just as the French attempted before World War II to construct a purely national defense (ignoring allies) and ended up being badly beaten, so the Gaullist approach would avail them little in a modern crisis. Alistair Horne commented in *To Lose a Battle:* "There are moments when one feels that—like the Bourbons, only worse—France has learned nothing and forgotten everything."

Speaking for myself, I think that exaggerated force requirement, inappropriate technology and high costs are symptomatic of a runaway system. A 45 percent real increase in defense spending over the past four years has been necessary just to keep the force from shrinking. The former Army Chief of Staff, Gen. Edward C. Meyer, was on target when he said: "Either we are going to spend ourselves into extinction, or we have to come up with alternative strategies and new ways to allocate resources."

So what should be done? The loosely knit coalition of "military reformers" in Congress, in government, and in assorted think tanks have many and varying ideas. While everyone agrees there is a problem, and that it is getting worse, no one can quite agree on what needs to be done. There is a long list of prescriptions, some of them sensible, some not so sensible, and some of them quite unworkable.

Still, there are certain measures that could do nothing but good. One is firing a large number of the 54,000 bureaucrats who do the Pentagon's shopping. (A good place to start might be with those who break the law. Most critics of the Pentagon accept that the laws governing procurement practices are adequate; it is just that they are inadequately enforced.)

A second measure that makes sense would entail subjecting the Pentagon's modern creations to vastly more realistic testing than the farcical "success-oriented" variety they tend to go through now. The situation at the moment, as one senator has put it, is "like having a student grade his own final exams." Under pressure from Congress, the Pentagon *has* created an Office of Operational Test and Evaluation, intended to be independent of the people responsible for weapons development. But at the time of this writing the office is very small, with a staff of 17 and a budget of under $12 million, and scarcely up to the task of monitoring the 140 new weapons currently in the pipeline. Similarly, a new Joint Live Fire Test Program has been instituted to test the survivability of planes and combat vehicles by firing live ammunition at them. But when the army, after "intense negotiations," agreed to let its Bradley Fighting Vehicle be tested under this program in December 1985—with results that predictably suggested, according to one of the officials involved, that the atmosphere inside the vehicle became "simply intolerable" after each hit due to ammunition fires or the triggering of the automatic fire extinguisher—the Army immediately disputed the verdict, contending that the Bradley had met its requirements and only minor modifications were necessary to make it more resistant to attack.

The army's reaction illustrates the problem. The services dislike intensely the notion of independent testing because it threatens to jeopardize programs in which they may have invested years of effort and millions, if not billions, of dollars. (The navy flatly refuses ever to let its ships be subjected to the Joint Live Fire Test Program.) Without compulsory full-scale independent testing, however, the endless procession to the battlefield of fragile and overcomplicated hardware will continue.

A third reform, often proposed, involves blocking off the "revolving door" between the Pentagon and industry in order to disrupt what is currently a highly incestuous partnership. I recognize that this is a difficult issue. Clearly, the Pentagon can benefit from hiring some industrialists—they are familiar with the tricks contractors can play, for one thing—and clearly, the defense industry can benefit from hiring people who understand the Pentagon's needs. Finding a way of slowing down this two-way traffic is, nevertheless, desirable, and possible, though, as with other changes, it will require considerable more vigilance from the top, and a greater readiness to enforce the law.

A more obvious reform would involve strengthening, and making more independent, the Joint Chiefs of Staff, in particular the chairman. At the moment each of the chiefs, except the chairman, is totally beholden to his service. The chairman himself has no real powers, and military procurement is thus dominated by the individual services, each of which dreams up strategies to justify the weapons it wants, rather than the other way around, and pushes tenaciously for its "share" of the budget with scarcely a nod in the direction of overall planning. Each service concocts grossly overambitious lists of what it wants, and in the end, through a process of haggling and compromise, the chiefs reach agreement on what each can have. The idea that *real* choices are made—giving up, say, a wing of F-15s for an army division—is a joke. There is a glaring need for a more centralized system, and for a more powerful and more independent JCS organization—one less beholden to the individual services. A revamped JCS might be made up, not of the heads of each service, as now, but of other, specially selected senior military officers, and it might be headed by a chairman with considerably strengthened powers.

The defense industry, meanwhile, would clearly benefit from a dose of what Senator Grassley calls "creeping capitalism." In the present climate there is too little of the free enterprise on which America prides itself. Many big defense contractors, as monopoly suppliers to the Pentagon of particular pieces of equipment, are virtually handed a license to waste money. They face no competition, and all too frequently have no incentive to cut costs or improve quality. Unless that changes, the U.S. defense industry will continue to produce weapons that are grotesquely overpriced, overelaborate, and, all too often, ineffective.

The argument that Europe should build a stronger defense industry of its own, and become less dependent on American weapons, is a compelling one. In part through increased cooperation on defense projects, Europe has already moved in this direction. In the 1970s, for example, the United States sold Europe about nine times as much equipment as it bought in return. Now that ratio has dropped sharply. In 1984, for example, the fourteen European nations in NATO agreed to buy $3.81 billion in defense goods from the United States while at the same time arranging sales to the United States totaling $1.19 billion —a U.S. advantage in the transatlantic arms trade of three to one, well below the 1970s average. Such a trend may not altogether please America, which, although it has long borne the brunt of financing NATO, has also enjoyed the profits from its large surplus in the arms trade with Europe. But as the *Wall Street Journal* has pointed out, "Extravagance and fraud in the U.S. defense industry haven't placed American arms contractors in the best position to complain about administration support for a more competitive European arms industry." On the whole, the United States can only welcome increased signs of cooperation and independence in Europe.

Such cooperation could be dramatically increased, as I have argued, if national defense establishments were more willing to compromise. In the late 1960s, Britain had a golden opportunity to collaborate with the Dutch in the building of a new frigate. The collaboration, strongly backed by the British defense minister, Denis Healey, would have suited both countries admirably. Each was saddled with frigates whose hulls were wearing out; both shared a long naval tradition; there even appeared to be a natural division of labor—Britain could concentrate on ship design and propulsion, while Holland took care of the electronics. The Dutch had one stipulation. The new frigate must be short enough to fit into their docks at Den Helder, The Royal Navy, however, designed a warship that failed to meet this requirement, and the collaboration fell apart. As a result, Britain wound up building the Type 22, a heavily gold-plated vessel with an aluminum superstructure and elaborate missile systems of dubious effectiveness. The cost: about $299 million. The Dutch, meanwhile, built a smaller, simpler frigate for approximately half that, which has since enjoyed considerable success on the export market.

Two other British examples illustrate the best and worst of European procurement.

Consider first Britain's determination to preserve its own torpedo industry. (It is the only European country that refuses to buy torpedoes from the United States.) In the late 1970s, faced with a choice between buying the American-made Mark 44 lightweight torpedo (to be modified under a "near term improvement program," known as NEARTIP) for around $575 million, or developing its own (known as the Stingray), the U.K. government opted for the Stingray. The result: a program whose cost spiraled upward to about $2.3 billion. Admittedly, the British Stingray is ultrasophisticated, a true guided weapon that can be fired from a submarine or dropped from an aircraft and then home in, automatically, on its target. But it has cost Britain four times as much as buying American would have done. Indeed, the money that would have been saved had the British bought American might have allowed the Royal Navy to purchase three or four new frigates.

A more encouraging project—indeed, an object lesson for NATO procurement bureaucracies—was Britain's Hawk. The Hawk is a training aircraft, though some countries have bought it with a more ambitious role in mind. Designed in the mid-1970s, it is a light and simple airplane, easy to fly. When it went into production, the RAF offered

British Aerospace handsome bonuses if the company could beat the maintenance standards it set. Offered the incentive, British Aerospace did precisely that, and through a clever, economical design created parts that would last longer and be easier to change than on most aircraft. The result was that Hawk has enjoyed enormously successful export sales. It is one of NATO's minor success stories, an illustration of what can be achieved through businesslike procurement.

It is not beyond NATO's wit or means to develop a more robust conventional defense, and to do so without hefty increases in spending. Such a defense would not have to be impregnable, it would simply have to appear solid enough to deny the Soviets a quick victory, the only kind of victory they would contemplate trying to achieve. Any extension of the length of time NATO could hold out before coming under pressure to go nuclear would work to the West's advantage. It would allow more time for reinforcements to arrive, more time for negotiations, more time for cooler heads to prevail. It would postpone the moment when the West might be tempted to take a fateful decision and enter a room, in the words of one British general, "which no one's ever been in before." And though modern conventional weapons—those that work —can wreak terrible havoc (a modern shell can split into a million fragments, a thousand times as many as its World War I equivalent), conventional weapons would not, if used, risk destroying the globe. Nuclear weapons would.

Existing NATO strategy, which envisages the first use of nuclear weapons, is not very plausible. It seems to many a bluff that, though useful for deterring war, would not be very helpful if war actually occurred. Richard Betts, a senior defense analyst at the Brookings Institution in Washington, has called it a "great white lie"—white because it is told for the best of intentions, but a lie nonetheless. There is, of course, the danger that in a war in Europe the Russians themselves might decide to go nuclear first, thus forcing NATO to respond. But just as we in the West can imagine the consequences of nuclear escalation, so it follows that the Soviet leaders can, too. The point is that the onus of going first would have been switched to them. They, not NATO, would have to make the agonizing decision to start a nuclear war.

*   *   *

There remains the problem of what the West should do about its existing nuclear arsenal. The short answer is not much. Nuclear deterrence, I have argued, is considerably more robust than it is often assumed to be—either by the peace movements or by American conservatives. It would matter little if several years went by without the West deploying any new nuclear weapons. We would not be one whit less secure. Having said that, there is clearly a case for *some* modernization, both for political and strategic reasons: all weapons, whether tanks or nuclear delivery systems, wear out sooner or later and, in the end, need to be replaced. The trouble with the nuclear freeze is that it would freeze everything, good or bad, necessary or unnecessary.

The guiding principle for NATO should be "sufficiency"—by which I mean maintaining as a deterrent to an attack on Western Europe a relatively small arsenal of battlefield nuclear weapons, and maintaining just enough strategic weapons to be sure of being able to mount a devastating retaliatory strike on the Soviet Union, even after enduring a first strike. What NATO does not need is a vast redundancy of such weapons: this is both pointless and a waste of money. Equally pointless, and potentially dangerous, is the deployment of new "destabilizing" weapons that might threaten the nuclear stalemate and lead one side or the other to entertain the notion that it might get away with a preemptive strike.

Experts disagree as to what "sufficiency" means, but one thing it does not mean is matching the Soviets system for system. The Soviet buildup, of course, is excessive. "They feel they don't just need a belt and braces, but a piece of string as well," as one British official put it to me. Viewed from Moscow, the Soviet Union is a land ringed by enemies, forced to consider not just the U.S. arsenal but the independent deterrents of Britain and France, as well as a growing threat from the Chinese. Soviet paranoia is probably increased by NATO's implicit threat of nuclear first use, which the Kremlin is determined to demonstrate would be a foolhardy act. It is bolstered, too, by a "production line mentality"—a tendency to crank out systems that appear to be effective in great numbers.

But the fact that Moscow overproduces nuclear weapons does not mean that the West needs to follow suit. The SS-20 is a good example.

At the time of writing there were 441 of these missiles in place, two-thirds of them trained on Western Europe. Doubtless the Soviets fear that some SS-20s might not work, and that others might be destroyed by conventional weapons before they could be used. But so huge a deployment still makes little sense. There is no reason the alliance should allow itself to be intimidated. If the Soviets choose to invest millions of rubles in weapons that can make the rubble bounce, that is their privilege. It should not force the West to waste millions of dollars in response.

To an extent, the idea of sufficiency is already catching on. When, after initial Western deployments of cruise and Pershing missiles, the Soviets began deploying an array of new short-range weapons "in retaliation" (SS-21s, SS-22s, and SS-23s), NATO conspicuously declined to react. And when, also in retaliation, the Russians announced that they were going to deploy more nuclear-armed submarines close to the American coastline, President Reagan sensibly said that he would not be losing any sleep over this. Both Soviet gestures were pointless and likely to yield no military advantage. NATO has committed itself to pulling out a total of 2,400 nuclear weapons from the central front. And the United States, since the early 1960s, has eliminated 8,000 warheads from its strategic arsenal and cut the "payload," or destructive capability, of that arsenal roughly in half.

Nonetheless, America's current strategic program remains unnecessarily ambitious. Does the United States *really* need—in addition to its Star Wars program—not just new Trident submarines, but the MX, the B-1, Midgetman, Stealth, several new types of cruise missile, and the array of new warheads that are being developed? Surely not. Budgetary pressures will certainly ensure that many of these programs are scaled back, but the cuts will probably be as irrational as the buildup. One way of making the process more rational might be for the White House to create a standing commission on nuclear forces similar to the Scowcroft Commission, which was formed in 1982 to advise the president on strategic matters after the MX missile got into trouble in Congress. The Scowcroft Commission was temporary; a permanent bipartisan commission along the same lines, however, might make nuclear weapons procurement less subject to the vagaries of presidential politics and interservice rivalry, and help defuse unfounded scares like the missile gap and the window of vulnerability. In general, the whole nuclear issue could benefit from nothing more than what William Kaufman, the veteran defense expert, calls "a dose of benign neglect."

The kind of nuclear program that might emerge from a more rational assessment of the threat, and of NATO requirements, would be considerably less ambitious than the existing one. It would not include MX, but it might include the B-1. The B-1 is a versatile weapon, able to perform a conventional as well as a nuclear role, and though complicated and expensive, it has the distinction of coming off the production line at almost exactly the anticipated cost and (amazingly) slightly ahead of schedule. There is an argument for pursuing Stealth technology, though not for installing it in yet another bomber. If Stealth works, it will surely be adequate to apply it simply to air-launched cruise missiles, making them (and thus the B-1) better able to penetrate Soviet air defenses. Given the worries about the vulnerability of land-based missiles, the Midgetman program may be worth preserving, too.

But the most important piece of nuclear modernization, by far, is the Trident program. Some strategists argue, and I accept, that America would have done better to stick to its original, less accurate C-4 version of the missile system, rather than pressing on to develop the more sophisticated D-5. Apart from anything else, this would have caused fewer headaches in Britain, which needs to modernize its existing Polaris deterrent, and which, in the interests of commonality, has followed the United States down the D-5 track, even though C-4 would have been perfectly adequate for its needs. It is true, too, that the Trident submarines being built reflect the U.S. Navy disease of "giantism"; a larger force of smaller submarines would have been better than the small force of huge ones presently taking shape. But the sea has become, and is likely to remain, the best place for nuclear weapons— especially for the West, which is far ahead of the Soviet Union in submarine technology. And to that extent it makes sense for America to concentrate most on the sea-based leg of its nuclear triad.

No doubt someday we will have to confront the spectacle of "submarine vulnerability," just as we have confronted "ICBM vulnerability." There is no doubt that, when we do, its dangers will be exaggerated. Even now, both sides are working to make the sea "transparent"—though it is in neither's interests to be successful—the Americans mainly through the development of listening devices, the Russians by concentrating more on "nonacoustic" methods of detection. Already, alarmist reports have circulated in the Pentagon about Soviet developments in the field of synthetic aperture radar. Moscow hopes that this, based on nuclear-powered satellites, may eventually enable it to identify American submarines from their "internal waves" (i.e., their wakes). But American ballistic submarines are very quiet, can travel very deep, and when moving slowly send to the surface only the faintest internal waves. It is likely to be at least another generation or two before the Russians make the kind of breakthrough necessary to track them.

In the effort to preserve nuclear stability, arms control is clearly important. But its contribution is likely to be modest. The notion that the superpowers' arsenals will ever be negotiated down to very low levels, and perhaps eventually to nothing, is fantasy (with or without Star Wars). Nothing in history, either before or since World War II, suggests that this is even a remote possibility. Holding out the hope that it might happen is dangerous: it raises expectations that can never be satisfied and it places an intolerable burden on the whole arms control process.

Thus, neither SALT I, nor its unratified successor, SALT II, has done much to slow down the arms race. They have not enabled defense establishments to become smaller; they have not noticeably reduced the risks of war; they have done nothing to limit the likelihood of appalling casualties if war occurred—in short, they have done little to further the kind of goals that were laid out by arms control experts such as Thomas Schelling and Bernard Brodie in the 1950s.

This is not surprising. The United States and the Soviet Union see the world very differently, and a host of factors—geographical, political, and military—make equitable agreements hard to achieve. What looks fair to the West usually looks unfair to the East, and vice versa. How do you take into account America's technological edge, for example, or the USSR's imposing air defense network, or the fact that the Soviet Union is ringed with enemies, or that the United States is

separated from its allies by an ocean? Arms control negotiators invariably strive to obtain a political and military advantage for their own
sides, and it sometimes seems, in the words of former National Security
Council staffer Helmut Sonnenfeldt, that "what is negotiable is not
significant and what is significant is not negotiable." Even some of the
more far-ranging agreements that *have* been reached—banning nuclear weapons on the seabed, or at the North Pole, or on the moon,
for example—outlaw things that neither side much wants to do anyway.

　　Nevertheless, arms control has lent a measure of "predictability"
to the arms race. The very process of talking, over the last twenty years,
has made dangerous misunderstandings between the two sides—about
particular programs, about strategic intent—less likely than they might
otherwise have been. Moreover, arms control answers a political need
in the West. There may be a grain of truth in the jibe that it is
"conducted for the amusement of the allies," but people in America,
as well as in Western Europe, would be less inclined to keep supporting
high defense budgets if it was jettisoned. And though the Soviets
undoubtedly have some questions to answer regarding violations of
existing agreements, the charges are often overdone. Overall, the Soviet
compliance record has been good. Their more questionable behavior
may stem, in part, from the general deterioration of East-West relations during the late 1970s and the early 1980s; treated as a pariah by
Washington, as the "evil empire," their incentive to "play by the rules"
radically diminished.

　　Thus, as one expert put it, "we may not be able to design a whole
new city, but we can at least try and mend the potholes in the road."
It is worth, for instance, continuing the attempt to agree on "confi-
dence-building measures"—improvements in the Moscow-Washing-
ton hot line, exchanges of information over military maneuvers, and
other steps intended to prevent crises blowing up through misunderstandings, or getting out of hand if they do occur. In nuclear negotiations, the main focus of Western efforts should be less on balancing
numbers than on channeling and restraining developments in technology. Balancing numbers is very hard, as we have noted, and it tends
to encourage both sides to hang on to old, unnecessary weapons as

bargaining chips (America's Titan missiles; the Russian SS-4s and SS-5s), and even to deploy new ones for the same purpose (America's MX). Even if the vision being discussed in Geneva as I write—a 50 percent reduction in the strategic arsenals of the superpowers—became reality, it would have more symbolic than military value. Both sides would still be able to make the rubble bounce several times over. Indeed, if both sides had very small arsenals, the dangers might be greater than they are now: if you have a large arsenal, the difficulties the other side has in imagining a way of destroying it in one fell swoop are correspondingly large.

So what can arms controllers do about the march of new technology? Clearly they cannot halt it, even if this were a desirable end. As the Washington defense analyst Barry Blechman has written:

> Technological change can no more be stopped—or "frozen"— than knowledge of how to design and manufacture nuclear weapons can be banished from the minds of men and women. . . . It is unrealistic and counter-productive to assume that national leaders will agree to cease applying the products of new technologies for the enhancement of the security (or the power) of their nations. If anything, we should assume that the evolution of weapons technologies will accelerate in the future, in keeping with the general trend in the rate of technological change.

But proposals for a blanket ban on new technology—such as that implicit in the nuclear freeze movement—are probably not desirable anyway. Some future developments may benefit the West, just as some past ones have: photo-reconnaissance satellites, which have given us a much clearer picture of the size and character of Soviet forces; "permissive action links" and other nuclear safety mechanisms, which have greatly reduced the risks of nuclear war starting by accident.

Many developments in technology, however, are potentially destabilizing, more likely to cause both sides headaches than to enhance anyone's security. It is too late to ban MIRVing, one such development, or cruise missiles, another. But it is not too late, at the time of writing, to ban or drastically restrict the testing of antisatellite weapons.

ASATs must be strong contenders for the prize of "most destabilizing weapons ever devised," and will cause terrible problems for both sides, perhaps especially for the West, if they are developed into effective satellite killers and are allowed to proliferate. The arguments for a ban on the testing of both existing and new systems are overwhelming. A ban on the testing and deployment of ATBMs would also make considerable sense.

So, I believe, would a complete ban on the testing of nuclear weapons. In 1963, after Kennedy and Khrushchev "stared into the abyss" during the Cuban missile crisis, the superpowers agreed on a Limited Test Ban Treaty that forbade the testing of all nuclear devices in the atmosphere. Two subsequent agreements, in 1974 and 1976, sought to limit underground tests to no more than 150 kilotons (though these have never been ratified by the U.S. Senate).

Various arguments have been made *against* a test ban. One is that testing has allowed both superpowers to develop smaller, less destructive warheads. A second is that such a ban could never be verified. A third, advanced by the Pentagon, is that the West needs to keep testing in order to ensure that its weapons work properly. A fourth is that the United States is behind the Soviet Union in the nuclear arms race and must test so that it can develop the new weapons it needs to catch up.

I find these arguments unpersuasive. Why do both sides need to go on developing smaller, more accurate warheads? It is precisely such developments that have encouraged the fantasies about fighting and prevailing in limited nuclear wars. Verification is certainly a problem, but developments in seismology have made it possible to monitor and identify even small nuclear explosions, and America would be fully justified in arguing not only for an adequate number of seismological stations on the soil of both superpowers but also for "on-site inspections" to ensure against cheating. (American officials say that they need a better understanding of the geology of the Soviet test site at Plesetsk for effective monitoring of tests.) But the Russians have already indicated that they might go along with this. Why not challenge them and see?

A test ban would make it far harder for both sides to develop new and destabilizing weapons. It would also make it harder for them to feel confident about existing ones, which, in turn, would reduce concerns about a first strike. To seriously contemplate striking first, you must be confident that all, or most, of your weapons will work perfectly. Deterrence does not require anything so demanding. You simply have to know that *enough* of your weapons will work to make possible a devastating *retaliatory* strike. Since the superpowers now possess about 25,000 nuclear weapons each, they would remain utterly confident of this, even after a comprehensive test ban. The Reagan administration suggests that a major reason why billions of dollars need to be spent on Star Wars is to "complicate" Soviet plans to attack and thereby make a first strike seem implausible. But a comprehensive test ban would achieve the same result at vastly lower cost and bring all kinds of benefits in its wake. It could, in effect, close the window of vulnerability—in the eyes of those who believe it exists—a window Washington has fretted about ever since President Reagan entered the White House but has done nothing whatsoever to close. A test ban, finally, could play an important role in reducing one of the greatest dangers of our age: that of nuclear proliferation. Third World countries, watching the superpowers continue to expand their arsenals and test new weapons at the same time as they preach the virtues of nonproliferation, are understandably less than impressed. A comprehensive test ban, however, signed by both America and the Soviet Union, and joined by France and Britain, would be perfectly possible to enforce. (Under such circumstances, for example, were Libya's Colonel Khadafy to obtain a nuclear weapons facility, the United States would be fully justified in attacking and destroying it. The Soviets would have no choice but to accept such an outcome.)

As we have seen, however, there are a great many careers tied up in the nuclear weapons business, and the institutional pressures against a test ban are strong. Nevertheless, the case for ratifying the two existing treaties, and then for negotiations aimed eventually at ending testing altogether, is a powerful one. In the long run, it would undoubtedly save money, since it would slow down the process by which both sides keep making additions to their arsenals. A ban on nuclear testing, indeed, could be followed by a ban, or a drastic restriction, on the number of *missile* tests that could be carried out by each side.

In addition to striving for a ban on ASATs and nuclear testing, the West should also, as I argued in Chapters 11 and 12, adopt a much more cautious attitude toward Star Wars.[4] The likelihood is that if the current enthusiasm for space-based defense is allowed to proceed unchecked, the world will end up a considerably more dangerous place. It is clearly in the interests of both sides to amend the ABM treaty—taking into account recent developments in technology—and at least for the foreseeable future, to agree to stick to its provisions. It makes sense to do this even if it is impossible at the same time to obtain deep cuts in the nuclear arsenals of both sides. Otherwise we may end up in the world envisaged by George Kennan: ". . . [fleeing] like haunted creatures from one defensive device to another, each more costly and humiliating than the one before, cowering underground one day, breaking up our cities the next, attempting to surround ourselves with elaborate shields on the third, concerned only to prolong the length of our lives while sacrificing all the values for which it might be worth while to live at all."

Even that, unfortunately, scarcely captures what the world might be like if both sides were to enter into an untrammeled Star Wars race. In Chapter 11 I described Star Wars as the quintessence of the new Maginot line, the ultimate technological fix. But France's Maginot line was static, and conspicuously defensive. It was bad for France, because it absorbed too much money and lulled the French into a false sense of security, but it constituted no casus belli. Arguably, in fact, it was in Germany's interest that it should be built. A Maginot line in space, however, would be in *no* one's interest; it would be a defense that would decrease *everyone's* security; not only would it cause desperate instabilities as it was being constructed (and probably once it was complete), but it would also, almost certainly, have an offensive capability.

The reason for this is blindingly obvious. Whether satellites in low orbit armed with kinetic energy interceptors or "directed energy" de-

---

[4]It is worth noting, incidentally, that one reason for the Pentagon's reluctance to pursue a nuclear test ban is the belief that nuclear technology may play an important part in a space-based defense. The X-ray laser being contemplated for boost-phase defense will require an intense and protracted series of underground tests, and these tests have already begun.

vices, weapons in space powerful enough to destroy missiles soon after liftoff would probably also be powerful enough to destroy, at the very least, "soft" targets on the ground. According to Robert English, a Pentagon policy analyst between 1982 and 1985, two separate studies —one by a private research firm, the other by a science laboratory— "have concluded that space-based lasers could incinerate flammable targets and set numerous fires on the enemy's home soil." Such laser devices, whether based on satellites or bounced off mirrors from ground stations, might be able to destroy everything from early-warning radars to communications centers. They might, in fact, find this easier to do than striking rocket boosters rising quickly out of Soviet silos. (There would be none of the tracking or discrimination problems.) And though, initially, space-based weaponry would probably be unable to destroy intercontinental ballistic missiles in their silos, or other "hard" targets, that possibility, too, might eventually open up. And at that point, as Robert English wrote in the *New Republic* in February 1986, the situation would become hazardous in the extreme.

> The "surgical" precision of such weapons would make the tempta-
> tion of a first strike much harder to resist. Even more disconcert-
> ing is the extraordinary speed with which space-based weapons
> could attack. To date, none of the numerous advances in strategic
> weaponry over the past 20 years have been able to make a first
> strike credible. No matter how overwhelming one's advantages in
> megatonnage or accuracy, no attacker could ever escape devasta-
> tion as long as the enemy had enough time to launch his missiles
> in retaliation. However, space-based weapons might reduce a half
> hour of warning to a mere two or three minutes. Of course, the
> side that felt threatened by such a system might well be compelled
> to shift from a "launch-under-attack" or "launch-on-warning"
> posture to one of "launch-under-crisis" for fear of losing the bulk
> of its retaliatory force before it even knew it was being attacked.
> A more hair-trigger world is hard to imagine.

Neither the peace movement nor the radical Right are likely to be much impressed by the arguments I have made in this book. Their fantasies are curiously similar. The peace movement believes in the complete abolition of nuclear weapons. But nuclear weapons will never be abolished. A nuclear-free world could never be verified; the knowledge of how to make the weapons is freely available and will remain so. And even if the superpowers pulled off the miracle of scrapping their arsenals, it would make a conventional or chemical war seem more possible, and mean that the world had become vulnerable to any dictator sufficiently power-hungry or wicked or unscrupulous to decide to build nuclear weapons and threaten their use. We cannot "abolish war," or "reinvent politics," or do any of the other utopian things the disarmers would have us do.

But it is not only the peace movement that dreams romantic dreams. The star warriors want to abolish nuclear weapons too— through the wonder of modern technology. Whereas CND and the Greens express the wish to get back to a lost world in which nuclear weapons no longer exist, the radical Right entertains notions that have just as little relevance to the planet we live on. In debates on defense, common sense is often in short supply.

The truth is that the West is going to have to learn to live with less security than it might want. This is difficult, especially for America, sheltered as it is by two oceans that, for most of its history, rendered it effectively invulnerable. But in the nuclear age there is no such thing as absolute security, and by striving to attain it we risk ending up worse off than we are at present. In the words of Frederick the Great: "He who strives for absolute security often ends up with no security at all."

Those who advocate a no-holds-barred arms race with the Russians court just such a fate. They say that arms control is a snare and a delusion, that the West's best course is to keep upping the ante, developing more and more sophisticated strategic weapons until the Russians, exhausted and bankrupt, finally give up. We are richer and smarter than they are, the argument goes: we can win. But the Russians will not give up. And if they do find themselves facing bankruptcy, what then? Will they give up quietly, abandon their empire, surrender? Or will they in desperation decide that they have no choice but to go to war? In any case, an unbridled arms race would probably bankrupt the West as surely as it would cripple the East. Even if it did not, it would leave our economies so damaged as to raise the question of whether the effort was worth it. If you destroy your economy, after all, you have destroyed the very fabric of the society you are seeking to defend.

Even the argument that intensive military research yields all kinds of benefits for the civilian economy has less credibility now than it once did. There have undoubtedly been important spinoffs from developments pioneered by the defense industry—computers, jet engines, even graphite tennis rackets—but many argue that military technology has now become so exotic there will be far fewer such spinoffs in the future. Indeed, some argue that the emphasis on the military applications of science is weakening America's ability to compete with Japan in other areas of technology. Jerome Wiesner, a former president of MIT who served as science adviser to Presidents Eisenhower and Kennedy, believes that there is a danger, if current trends continue, of America becoming a "totally military culture."

Achieving real security for the West is more than a matter of simply inventing more and more sophisticated weapons. The real challenge for the rest of this century and beyond will be managing the East-West conflict in such a way as to minimize the chances of disaster. The idea shared by the peace movements and the radical Right—that it all comes down to weapons—is silly. As Michael Howard pointed out in the *Times* of London in January 1984:

> We must look deeper for the things that really matter. . . . Can the Soviet Union continue to control its East European empire? Will that control remain, indefinitely, and be politically acceptable to the West? Can the Germans, East and West, incrementally develop a relationship which will not call in question the entire postwar settlement of the Continent? Will the nations of western Europe be reduced to ungovernability by the social discontent arising from their economic problems and thus once more constitute an attractive target for Soviet penetration? And most important of all, will the United States continue to regard western Europe as a region so vital to its own security that it will persist, in spite of all the frustrations and humiliations involved, in maintaining so complex an alliance?
>
> Factors such as these will determine whether the balance is stable or not; not SS20s, Pershing 2s or numbers of Soviet tanks.

> If the underlying political structure remains stable it will not be
> disturbed by weapons imbalance, or be at the mercy of crises,
> accidents and misperceptions. If it is not, then peace cannot be
> preserved either by anxiously matching weapon for weapon or by
> dramatic gestures of one-sided disarmament.

These are wise words. The Russians are, in the end, as much a political as a military problem. We must lean on diplomacy as heavily as we lean on technology. When former Soviet foreign minister Andrei Gromyko met President Reagan in September 1984, he talked about the "push of technology," and according to one account "repeatedly wondered aloud whether the great powers would be able to control arms or whether arms would take control of them." One might well argue that during his thirty-year tenure in the Soviet foreign ministry, Gromyko contributed little to the business of controlling arms. But like President Eisenhower in his warning about the powers of the military-industrial complex, he was expressing a very real danger. We must be careful lest the technocrats take us over completely, lest technology becomes an influence that dwarfs all others in the shaping of foreign policy. We have already progressed some way down the road, and Star Wars threatens to take us considerably farther.

My prescription for western defense—a gradual, incremental improvement in conventional forces, less reliance on nuclear weapons, and a greater emphasis on diplomacy—may not be a very exciting one. But it is, I believe, more realistic and less dangerous than the goals of the star warriors or the utopian dreams of the unilateral disarmers. It is also less risky. The danger to be faced is that an attempt to rely too heavily on technology could lead to more than just mutual bankruptcy. It could lead, in Winston Churchill's graphic phrase, to a return of the Stone Age "on the gleaming wings of science."

Source Notes

I have not cited personal interviews. All books referred to, and others I have drawn on, appear in the bibliography. The following abbreviations have been used: *NYT*, for *New York Times; WP, Washington Post; WSJ, Wall Street Journal; LA Times, Los Angeles Times; DT, Daily Telegraph* (London); *ST, Sunday Times* (London); *FT, Financial Times;* IISS, International Institute for Strategic Studies in London.

Introduction

vii   "He was not": M. Guizot, *The History of France,* p. 551.

viii   "planted against": Christopher Duffy, *Siege Warfare,* p. 9.

viii   first use of breech-loading rifle and artillery: Michael Howard cites both these examples in "The Forgotten Dimensions of Strategy," in Philip Towle, ed., *Estimating Foreign Military Power,* p. 264. But he adds: "This [technological] superiority was far from decisive: the Franco-Prussian War in particular was won, like the American Civil War, by superior logistical capability based upon a firm popular commitment."

x   "Trying to offset": Steven Canby, "The Alliance and Europe: Part IV, Military Doctrine and Technology," Adelphi Paper 109, IISS.

xii   "They could not agree": Kaufman, *The McNamara Strategy*, p. 104.

xiii footnote: Robert Reich, "High Tech, a Subsidiary of Pentagon Inc.," *NYT*, 5/29/85.

xiv   "nearly enough": Fred Hiatt and Rick Atkinson, "Is the Trillion-Dollar Buildup Exacting a Hidden Cost?" *WP*, 12/1/85.

Chapter One

3   taking threat seriously: see, for example, Robert Neild, *How to Make Up Your Mind about the Bomb*, p. 9 and seq.

4   "Relaxation of tensions": remarks by Leonid Brezhnev at Twenty-fifth Congress of the Communist Party of the Soviet Union, Foreign Broadcast Information Service, FBIS-SOV-76-38, 2/28/76.

5   "your first thought": CBS Television, "The Defense of the United States," 6/14/81.

7   "When the Russians": quoted in John Barry, "A Week in Politics Special," Channel 4 Television (U.K.), 3/30/84.

11   "has never attempted": United States Military Posture for Fiscal Year 1976, statement by chairman of the Joint Chiefs of Staff, General George Brown, USAF, p. 70.

11   "In this increasingly": Dr. Malcolm Currie, Program of Research, Development, Test and Evaluation, FY 1976, statement submitted to the U.S. Senate Armed Services Committee, 3/7/75, pp. 1–2. Both Currie's and Brown's remarks are also quoted in "New Weapons Technologies," by Richard Burt, Adelphi Paper 126, IISS.

12   "rests on": quoted in Etzold.

12   "Technology . . . is": text of speech appears in *Current Policy*, no. 220, published by the State Department under the title "Essentials of Security: Arms and More," 9/18/80.

13   *Titanic* story: William Kaufman tells this in *The Defense Budget* (Washington, D.C.: Brookings Institution, 1983), p. 99.

13   "Be reassured": Alistair Horne, *To Lose a Battle*, p. 104.

15   "Rapidly, the Maginot": ibid., p. 63.

Chapter Two

16   "silly transaction": Bill Keller, "3 Navy Officers Relieved of Duty in Ashtray Case," *NYT*, 5/31/85.

17   "Whenever in the old days": Wavell, *Generals and Generalship*, p. 3.

18   "hardly reassuring": George Wilson, "Army Gun Said to Be Vulnerable to Cold," *WP*, 3/6/85.

18   "Unless the army": ibid.

19   "Pretty soon": Gregg Easterbrook, "Divad," *Atlantic Monthly*, 10/82, p. 31.

21   Divad test in early 1982: ibid., p. 37.

23   "In a flir-to-flir duel": ibid., p. 31.

24   "jammed so frequently": "Sergeant York Musters Out," *Newsweek*, 9/9/85.

24   "Knocking out a tank": Bill Keller, "Demise of the Sgt. York Gun: Model Weapon Turns to Dud," *NYT*, 11/28/85.

24   "Soviet pilots": ibid.

24   "The program": ABC Television, "20/20," 12/13/84.

25   "I would say": ibid.

25   "like testing": Gregg Easterbrook, "Why the Divad Wouldn't Die," *Washington Monthly*, 11/84.

28   "To demonstrate": ABC Television, "20/20," 2/13/84.

30   "died of embarrassment": *NYT*, 11/28/85.

31   "enemy outnumbers you by two to one" argument: F. W. Lanchester, *Aircraft in Warfare: The Dawn of the Fourth Army*.

32   "What we're dealing": John J. Fialka, "Embattled Weapon," *WSJ*, 2/17/82.

33   "If it gets": ibid.

33   "powder keg": Gary Hart, "Our Soldiers' Lives Depend on Reform of Way We Buy Arms," *Newsday*, 2/85.

34   The Bradley is . . . cramped: "The Winds of Reform," *Time*, 3/7/83.

34   "Unfortunately, while": Edward N. Luttwak, *The Pentagon and the Art of War*, p. 226.

36   defense of M-1: ibid., p. 223.

36   "The overwhelming evidence": George W. S. Kuhn, "Ending Defense Stagnation," in Richard N. Holwill, ed., *A Mandate for Leadership Report: Agenda '83*, p. 99.

37   "The competition": Richard Barnard, "U.S. Comes Through Gut-wrenching Tank Games in Third Place," *Defense Week*, 6/29/81.

38   Rasor study: Dina Rasor, "Fighting with Failures," *Reason*, 4/82.

38   problem with Mark II system: study by Franklin C. Spinney, quoted in Kuhn, "Ending Defense Stagnation," p. 89.

39   "In the early 1970s": Ibid., p. 92.

39   "The Army's": ibid., p. 92.

41   "there isn't any": George Dvorchak, "Getting It on in the All-Aspect Arena," *Tactical Analysis Bulletin*, 7/25/79.

43   Murray on AMRAAM: "AMRAAM: 'An Expensive Bird' of Limited Use?" *National Journal*, 7/24/82.

44   "When you're up": CBS Television, "The Defense of the United States," 6/17/81.

44   "In massed fighting": Dvorchak, "Getting It On in the All-Aspect Arena," *Tactical Analysis Bulletin*, 7/25/79.

46   "in the year": Rone Tempest et al., "Servants and Masters," *LA Times*, 7/10/83.

46   F-16: best account of its development in James Fallows, *National Defense*.

47   "the greatest": quoted in Mary Kaldor, *The Baroque Arsenal*, p. 189.

47   price of German Tornado: Roger Boyes, "The Tornado Rattles Bonn's Defence Planners," *FT*, 8/21/80.

48   "critical . . . targets": letter from Air Chief Marshal Sir Denis Smallwood, *DT*, 4/22/77.

48   problem with helicopters: Gregg Easterbrook, "All Aboard Air Oblivion," *Atlantic Monthly*, 9/81.

50   "The 60 percent": Morton Mintz, "Fiasco in Weaponsland," *WP*, 7/25/82.

50   "If the question": ibid.

50   "don't like the gun": ibid.

51   attacked telephone poles: CBS Television, "The Defense of the United States,"
     6/17/81.

52   "Clearly it didn't": Morton Mintz, "Air Force's Maverick Missile: Troubled but
     Inevitable," *WP*, 2/23/82.

52   "It's like": ibid.

53   "What you get": Mintz, "Maverick: Pressing for Production," *WP*, 2/25/82.

54   "I'd have": Frank Greve, "Dream Weapon a Nightmare," *Philadelphia In-
     quirer*, 5/2/82.

54   "swamp of . . . waste": William Greider, "The Education of David Stockman,"
     Atlantic Monthly, 12/81.

54   "You want something": "Where to Cut Defense," *Newsweek*, 12/20/82.

55   tendency . . . to explode: Walter Pincus, "Army Kills Controversial Anti-Tank
     Arm," *WP*, 9/30/83.

55   "its accuracy": George C. Wilson, "Pentagon Makes 1.6 Billion Bet on Shell,"
     WP, 4/11/83.

56   "Thus . . . it will": ibid.

57   "including two steerable": Bill Sweetman, "Unmanned Air Vehicles Make a
     Comeback," *International Defence Review*, vol. 18, no. 11, p. 85.

57   "The air frame": ibid.

58   Hellfire: Walter Pincus, "Cheaper Addition to Laser System Growing in Ex-
     pense," *WP*, 9/7/83.

60   "Indeed . . . those": Anthony Farrar-Hockley, "The Scope and Direction of New
     Conventional Weapons Technology (2)" in Adelphi Paper 144, IISS.

Chapter Three

61   "We can spend": "Arming for the '80s," *Time*, 7/27/81.

62   army "hollow": Richard Halloran, "Pentagon Taking Renewed Pride in Its
     Personnel," *NYT*, 5/16/85.

62   "America's . . . computer edge": Thomas H. Etzold, *Defense or Delusion?*, p.
     102.

64   "dune buggy": Dennis Farney, "High-Tech Soldiers: Army Division Tests Un-
     conventional Gear to Increase Mobility," *WSJ*, 6/26/85.

64   ". . . its tactics": ibid.

65   "one of the few": CBS Television, "The Defense of the United States, Part 3:
     Call to Arms," 6/16/81.

65   "You are left": ibid.

67   exclusion of JDA: "Defense Organization: The Need for Change," Staff Report
     to the Committee on Armed Services, U.S. Senate. (Washington: U.S. Govern-
     ment Printing Office, 1985), p. 368.

67   "The JDA's": Michael Duffy, "Grenada: Rampant Confusion" (*Military Logis-
     tics Forum*, July/August 85), p. 23. Also see committee report cited immediately
     above, p. 368.

67   "continues to purchase": Armed Services Committee report, p. 365.

67   ". . . the Army elements": ibid., p. 365.

67   "We blew them": Edward N. Luttwak, *The Pentagon and the Art of War*, p.
     19.

Chapter Four

71   "I've been trying": Michael Kramer, "$1.5 Trillion for Defense? How to Under-
     stand Reagan's Big Buildup," *New York*, 6/22/81.

72   "without doubt": Jon Connell, "Man behind the U.S. Navy Buildup," *ST*,
     9/11/83.

72   "would lead": ibid.

73   "I take an oath": *ST*, 9/11/83.

74   "The mighty whale": Luttwak, *The Pentagon and the Art of War*, p. 221.

74   "very much in harmony": Bill Keller, "The Navy's Brash Leader," *NYT Maga-
     zine*, 12/15/85, p. 38.

74   "I have yet": *ST*, 9/11/83.

74   "Even if Lehman": interview with the author, but also see Robert W. Komer,
     Maritime Strategy or Coalition Defense?

75   "the likelihood fallacy": Komer, *Maritime Strategy*, p. 69.

75   "What is really": ibid., p. 59.

76   carriers "never" sunk: Etzold, *Defense or Delusion?* p. 101.

76   "The modern Aegis": editorial, *NYT*, 4/2/84.

76   "the centerpiece": see, for example, Fred Kaplan, "Navy Defense System Criti-
       cized," *Boston Globe*, 2/7/84.

77   "were not as low-flying": Charles H. Mohr, "Republican Charges Ship Missile
       System Fails," *NYT*, 2/7/84.

77   "operational requirements": *NYT*, 4/2/84.

77   "a serious mismatch": ibid.

78   "The consequent imbalance": Kuhn, "Ending Defense Stagnation," in Holwill,
       A Mandate, p. 73.

78   crew had "dwindled": Keller, "The Navy's Brash Leader," *NYT Magazine*,
       12/15/85.

79   "Give the navy": Komer, *Maritime Strategy*, p. 73.

80   "In rejecting": Kuhn, "Ending Defense Stagnation," pp. 96–97.

81   "because conventional": ibid., p. 97.

Chapter Five

82   "Nothing so inefficient": Rone Tempest et al., "Servants or Masters?" *LA
       Times*, 7/10/83.

83   General Dynamics saga: best account in extensive series of articles in *St. Louis
       Post-Dispatch* (e.g., 3/17/85 and 5/22/85).

83   Extent of abuses: "Fraud Probes Target 45 Defense Contractors, Panel Told":
       Washington Times, 4/25/85.

84   "a log floating": Rick Atkinson and Fred Hiatt, "Defense Inc.," *WP* 5/20/85.

85   "If all": David Martin, news report, CBS Television, 2/5/85.

85   whistle: detailed report in Atkinson and Hiatt, "Defense Inc.," *WP*, 5/20/85.

86   Council on Economic Priorities study: see Gordon Adams, *The Iron Triangle*.

86   cost of HARM: Atkinson and Hiatt, "Defense Inc.," *WP*, 5/19/85.

86   "the surgical removal": ibid.

86   "They've got": ibid.

88   "If we told": J. Ronald Fox, *Arming America,* p. 138.

88   "Everyone's missed": Atkinson and Hiatt, "Defense Inc.," *WP,* 5/19/85.

89   "The lesson": editorial, "Dogfight of the Decade," *NYT,* 4/23/85.

89   "to get something": Atkinson and Hiatt, "Defense Inc.," *WP,* 5/19/85.

90   tax study: see Robert S. McIntyre, "Disarm the Deficit: End Corporate Tax Dodges," *WP,* 3/24/85.

90   "It's like": Atkinson and Hiatt, "Defense Inc.," *WP,* 5/31/85.

90   "Anything that succeeds": Atkinson and Hiatt, "Defense Inc.," *WP,* 5/20/85.

91   navy study: Atkinson and Hiatt, "Defense Inc.," *WP,* 4/1/85.

92   poll: Peter Grier, "Support Fades for Bigger Arms Budgets," *Christian Science Monitor,* 5/15/85.

93   PAC money doubles: Rone Tempest et al., "Servants or Masters?" *LA Times,* 7/10/81.

93   "a public works": ibid.

94   "Joe, they've built": Steven V. Roberts, "Political Aims of Lawmakers Bring Military Budget Rises," *NYT,* 5/17/85.

95   Record argument: see, for example, Jeffrey Record, "Ground the F-18 Program," *NYT,* 11/2/81.

95   contractors double "government . . . offices": Rone Tempest et al., "Servants or Masters?" *LA Times,* 7/10/81.

95   "We know": CBS Television, "Defense of the United States," 6/17/81.

96   "I speak": Fox, *Arming America,* pp. 128–29.

96   "target list": excerpts from Congressional Contact Tally Computer Log obtained by the Project on Military Procurement, Washington. Released 6/14/82.

97   Ptarmigan: see Jon Connell and Sarah Hogg, "Defence: Last of the Overspenders?" *ST,* 1/31/82.

98   NATO study: Klepsch Report, *Two-Way Street, USA-Europe Arms Procurement.*

99   "Without Nimrod": James Adams and John Witherow, "The Scandal of Nimrod as Cost Soars Past 1.5 Billion Pounds," *ST,* 7/28/85.

100 shortages: See James Adams, "Can Carrington Revive Nato?" *ST,* 6/24/84.

101 "If the C³I": ibid.

101 request to "go nuclear": ibid.

102 team of U.S. engineers: Captain J. W. Kehoe and K. S. Brower, privately circulated paper, "U.S. and Soviet Weapon System Design Practices," 10/81.

102 "rough casting": ibid., p. 34.

103 boxer losing shorts: Viktor Suvorov, *The Liberators*, pp. 62–75.

103 "The total number": Kehoe and Brower, "U.S. and Soviet Weapon System Design Practices," p. 34.

104 "Comrades, make it simple": quoted in Kehoe and Brower, "U.S. and Soviet Weapon System Design Practices," p. 1.

104 "There's a sort": CBS Television, "The Defense of the United States," 6/17/81.

105 "The worry": ibid.

105 "The Soviet": interview with Andrew Cockburn. For full exposition see *The Threat.*

105 "We believe": David C. Isby, *Weapons and Tactics of the Soviet Army,* p. 104.

106 "By ignoring": report by Franklin C. Spinney, privately circulated paper, "Defense Facts of Life," 12/5/80, p. 128.

107 "Technology proved indecisive": Jeffrey Record, *WP,* 7/29/84.

107 Skipper: Atkinson and Hiatt, "Defense Inc.," *WP,* 5/21/85.

107 "They used": ibid.

Chapter Six

109 Soviet plan of attack: John Barry, "A Week in Politics Special," Channel 4 (U.K.) Television, 3/30/84.

111 "brought us": Phil Stanford, "The Automated Battlefield," *NYT Magazine,* 2/23/75.

112 Interview with Tegnelia, quoted in Michael R. Gordon, "Highly Touted Assault Breaker Weapon Caught Up in Internal Pentagon Debate," *National Journal,* 10/22/83, pp. 2152ff.

112   account of Assault Breaker tests: Michael R. Gordon, " 'E. T.' Weapons to Beef Up Nato Forces Raise Technical and Political Doubts," *National Journal,* 2/19/83, p. 364.

115   "If you attach": ibid., p. 367.

115   paper on Assault Breaker: Steven L. Canby, "The Conventional Defense of Europe: The Operational Limits of Emerging Technology," Working Paper 55 delivered to the Wilson Center, 5/29/84.

116   "operational maneuver group": C. N. Donnelly, "The Soviet Operational Maneuver Group, a New Challenge for Nato," *International Defence Review,* 15, no. 9 (1982).

117   "are not going": Barry, "Week in Politics," 3/30/84.

117   "one shot one kill": Richard Burt, "New Weapons Technologies: Debate and Directions," Adelphi Paper 126, IISS, p. 15.

Chapter Seven

121   "moment of . . . truth": Fred Kaplan, *The Wizards of Armageddon,* p. 298.

121   Khrushchev speech: ibid., p. 292.

122   "with high confidence": ibid., p. 299.

123   "the low tens": ibid., p. 301.

123   "If ever": ibid., p. 301.

124   "In long conversations": Robert S. McNamara, "The Military Role of Nuclear Weapons: Perceptions and Misperceptions," *Foreign Affairs* 62, no. 1 (Autumn 1983).

126   "[The] resourcefulness": John Foster Dulles, "Challenge and Response in United States Policy," *Foreign Affairs,* 10/57.

126   "If seventy divisions": Robert Endicott Osgood, *NATO: The Entangling Alliance,* p. 109.

127   Carte Blanche: ibid., p. 126.

128   "In Europe": ibid., p. 125.

128   "more rather than less": ibid., p. 107.

133   "the balancing act": J. Michael Legge, *Theater Nuclear Weapons and the NATO Strategy of Flexible Response.*

135 "it would be": Field Marshal Lord Carver, "Nuclear Weapons in Europe," Council for Arms Control, Second Annual Lecture, 10/9/83.

135 "war fighting": see, for example, Colin S. Gray and Keith Payne, "Victory Is Possible," *Foreign Policy,* Summer 1980.

137 "The area between . . . ": In the ensuing discussion I have drawn on an unpublished draft paper by Paul Bracken.

137 "Were Nato": ibid.

139 problem of stopping war: see Desmond Ball, "Can Nuclear War Be Controlled?" Adelphi Paper 169, IISS, 1981. Also Bracken, *The Command and Control of Nuclear Forces.*

141 "islands of force": Bracken, *Command and Control,* p. 232.

141 "If there is": ibid., p. 231.

Chapter Eight

143 "two scorpions": J. Robert Oppenheimer, "Atomic Weapons and American Policy," *Foreign Affairs,* 7/53.

144 "American forces": Richard Burt, "US Stresses Limited Nuclear War in Sharp Shift on Military Strategy," *International Herald Tribune,* 8/7/80.

144 "prevail and be able": Richard Halloran, "Pentagon Draws Up First Strategy for Fighting a Long Nuclear War," *NYT,* 5/30/82.

145 "Combat operations": Joseph D. Douglass, Jr., and Amoretta M. Hoeber, *Soviet Strategy for Nuclear War,* pp. 22–23.

145 "There is profound": Douglass and Hoeber, *Soviet Strategy for Nuclear War,* p. 7.

145 "It is . . . madness": quoted in "Soviet Military Power: Questions and Answers," *Defense Monitor,* vol. 1, no. 1, p. 82.

146 "a strategic nuclear": quoted in Theodore Draper, "How Not to Think about Nuclear War," *New York Review of Books,* 7/15/82.

146 "Some of": Wieseltier, *Nuclear War, Nuclear Peace,* p. 36.

147 "gave us": George C. Wilson, "The Missile Gap the MX Can't Close," *WP,* 12/14/80.

148 "It's our . . . feeling": Fred Kaplan, "Would U.S. Missiles Hit or Miss?" *Nuclear Times,* 4/83.

150 "We had": editorial, "Ornery Missiles," *NYT*, 12/8/84.

150 "I'm always": ibid.

150 "purple plague": Kaplan, "Would U.S. Missiles Hit or Miss?" *Nuclear Times*, 4/83.

151 "Guaranteeing to launch": *NYT*, 12/8/84.

153 "It has never": R. Jeffrey Smith, "An Upheaval in U.S. Strategic Thought," *Science*, 4/2/82.

153 "it does not": ibid.

153 "A far more": ibid.

154 "The Soviets": ibid.

158 "the trees chase": "The MX System: Boon or Boondoggle?" *Newsweek*, 5/26/80.

161 "If only": quoted in Elizabeth Drew, "A Political Journal," *New Yorker*, 5/9/83.

163 ". . . to the degree": *Science*, 5/2/82.

163 "to a certain extent": ibid.

164 "What in the name": quoted in ibid.

Chapter Nine

168 "no better than even": John Barry, "The Nuclear Double Talk Tearing NATO Apart," first of three articles, *Times* (London) 8/17/81.

171 the "specter": Barnet, *The Alliance*, p. 373.

174 "perhaps the most": "A headache for arms control," *FT*, 2/15/77.

178 Schmidt's IISS speech: to IISS, 10/28/77.

179 pressure of flexible response: see Gregory Treverton, "Nuclear Weapons in Europe," Adelphi Paper 168, IISS (Summer 1981).

Chapter Ten

184 "the symbol": Richard Barnet, *The Alliance*, p. 376.

185 "His administration": Zbigniew Brzezinski, *Power and Principle*, p. 304.

193   "place us": E.P. Thompson, *Protest and Survive*, p. 43.

194   "the resistance": U.S. Arms Control and Disarmament Agency, "Soviet Propaganda Campaign against Nato," 10/83, p. 16.

194   "Washington's design": ibid.

197   GAO report on Cruise: see Fred Kaplan, "Much Ado about Wonder Weapons," *Boston Globe*, 11/22/81.

197   "a signal": Michael Howard, letter to the *Times* (London), 11/3/81.

198   "The belief": ibid.

In Chapters 9 and 10 I have drawn heavily on the following works:

John Barry series in the *Times* (London), 5/31–6/2/83.

John Barry, "Revealed: The Truth about Labour and Cruise," *ST*, 2/6/83.

John Barry, "The Elephant and the Monorail," Channel 4 Television (U.K.), "Week in Politics Special," 12/11/83.

David C. Elliot, "Decision at Brussels: The Politics of Nuclear Forces," Discussion Paper 97 for California Seminar on International Security and Foreign Policy, 8/81.

Lynn E. Davis, "U.S. INF Policy," paper prepared for meeting of Danish Commission Security and Disarmament Affairs on "Nuclear Modernization in Europe," in Ebeltoft, Denmark, 4/27–28/83.

Second Interim Report on Nuclear Weapons in Europe, prepared by the North Atlantic Assembly's Special Committee on Nuclear Weapons in Europe for the Committee on Foreign Relations, U.S. Senate, 1/83.

James A. Thomson, "The LRTNF Decision: Evolution of U.S. Theater Nuclear Policy, 1975–79," 4/84.

Chapter Eleven

202   President Reagan's speech (excerpted): *Survival*, vol. 25, no. 3 (May-June 1983).

203   submarine-based missiles not nuclear: "Election Extra," *Newsweek* 11/12/84.

204   "With firelit intensity": James R. Mills, "A 1971 Conversation with Ronald Reagan," *San Diego*, 12/85.

205   "technological end run": Lieutenant General Daniel O. Graham, *High Frontier: A New National Strategy*, p. 3.

205   "The kind of superiority": Frank Greve, "Out of the Blue: How 'Star Wars' Was Proposed," *Philadelphia Inquirer*, 11/17/85.

206   "primary motivations" speech: Dr. G. A. Keyworth II, to the Fifty Club of Cleveland, 5/6/85.

207   McFarlane's role: see, for example, Lawrence I. Barrett, "How Reagan Became a Believer," *Time*, 3/11/85.

208   "He and Reagan got on": *Philadelphia Inquirer*, 11/17/85.

209   "McFarlane interjected": *Time*, 3/11/85.

209   president "dazzled": report by Marvin Kalb, "The Real 'Star Wars'—Defense in Space," NBC Television, 9/8/84.

210   "Edward . . . like it": ibid.

210   "Don't worry, gentlemen": Elizabeth Drew, "A Political Journal," *New Yorker*, 5/9/83, p. 49.

211   Pentagon demonstration: see, for example, Jon Connell and Peter Wilsher, "Collision Course," *ST*, 6/17/84.

214   "firefly in a darkened room": Union of Concerned Scientists, *The Fallacy of Star Wars*, p. 56.

215   "They have to go": Edgar Ulsamer, "The Battle for SDI," *Air Force*, 2/85, p. 49.

215   DeLauer testimony: U.S. Congress, House subcommittees on Research and Development and Investigations, hearing on H.R. 3073, People Protection Act, 98th Congress, first session, 11/10/83.

217   missiles without buses: see, for example, Union of Concerned Scientists, *The Fallacy of Star Wars*.

217   number of satellites required: see Zbigniew Brzezinski, Robert Jastrow, Max M. Kampelman, "Defense in Space Is Not 'Star Wars,' " *New York Times Magazine*, 1/27/85. See also R. V. Jones, "New Light on Star Wars," Policy Study 71 (London: Centre for Policy Studies, 1985).

218   destruction of Sidewinders: see R. V. Jones, "New Light on Star Wars," p. 11.

219   footnote: see, for example, *Newsweek*, 6/17/85, p. 37; and Jones, "New Light on Star Wars," p. 18.

220   "perhaps one-tenth of a second": *Air Force*, 2/85, p. 52.

220   Jones on laser accuracy: "New Light on Star Wars," p. 12.

221   "They must be deployed": Edward Teller, letter published in *Commentary*, vol. 79, no. 3 (March 1985).

222   Dauphin program: Malcolm W. Browne, "Stopping Missiles with Energy Beams," *Discover*, 6/83, pp. 30–31.

222   "You . . . have to get": ibid., p. 31.

225   "the long pole": "Star Warriors," *Newsweek*, 6/17/85.

227   "future historians": Jonathan Jacky, "The 'Star Wars' Defense Won't Compute," *Atlantic Monthly*, 6/80, p. 20.

227   "Instead of fielding": ibid., p. 20.

228   quotes from panel of scientists and Keyworth: ibid., pp. 21–22.

228   "many of the . . . features": ibid., p. 22.

228   "Keyworth's . . . suggestions": ibid., p. 22.

229   Bracken study: Bracken, *The Command and Control of Nuclear Forces*.

230   "It's like a . . . bunch": "Star Warriors," *Newsweek*, 6/17/85.

231   "If you start": interview with Erik Amfitheatrof in "Upsetting a Delicate Balance," *Time*, 3/11/85.

232   estimate of "extra" missiles: Stephen M. Meyer of MIT, quoted in Charles Mohr, "What Moscow Might Do in Replying to Star Wars," *NYT*, 3/6/85.

232   "Any defensive system": testimony to U.S. Congress already cited.

232   "a submachine gun": "Star Warriors," *Newsweek*, 6/17/85.

233   "It is suggested": James Schlesinger speech to National Security Issues Symposium, 10/25/84.

234   "send a series": Malcolm Browne, "Stopping Missiles with Energy Beams," p. 32. For possible countermeasures also see, for example, Richard L. Garwin and Kurt Gottfried, "Even Halfway Is Wrong," *NYT*, 2/12/85.

235   "Some of the biggest": William J. Broad, " 'Star Wars' Research Forges Ahead," *NYT*, 2/5/85.

237   "the difference": "Star Warriors," *Newsweek*, 6/17/85.

237   "Many . . . scientists": "The Real Star Wars," NBC Television, 9/8/84.

237   "The laws": Union of Concerned Scientists, *The Fallacy of Star Wars*, p. 50.

238   "American . . . enthusiasm": R. V. Jones, "New Light on Star Wars," p. 24.

238   "We need to remember": ibid., p. 25.

241   "Are the Soviets": Schlesinger speech, National Security Issues Symposium, 10/25/84.

242   "light-reflecting aerosols": Bill Keller, "Air Force Seeking More Wily Missile," *NYT*, 2/11/85. Also see Keller, "Defense Department Seeks More Money for Secret Weapons, Analyst Says," *NYT*, 2/12/85.

242   "You can always beat": ibid.

Chapter Twelve

245   polls: *Washington Post–ABC News* poll, *WP*, 8/14/85.

245   "Is it any wonder": "Star Warriors," *Newsweek*, 6/17/85.

246   "computing in support": Charles Mohr, "Scientist Quits Antimissile Panel, Saying Task Is Impossible," *NYT*, 7/12/85.

247   "state of mind": John Newhouse, "The Diplomatic Round," *New Yorker*, 7/22/85.

248   "The keystone": speech by Sir Geoffrey Howe, reported in *Times* (London), 3/16/85.

250   "the justification": Schlesinger speech, National Security Issues Symposium, 10/25/84.

250   "However large": Newhouse, "The Diplomatic Round," *New Yorker*, 7/22/85.

251   "probably the only person": ibid.

253   footnote: testimony by Frank Miller, hearings before the Subcommittee on International Security and Scientific Affairs of the Committee on Foreign Affairs, House of Representatives, 11/10/83, 4/10/84, 5/2/84, and 7/26/84.

253   "of strategic defense": quoted in Leslie H. Gelb, " 'Star Wars' Advances: The Plan vs. the Reality," *NYT*, 12/15/85.

254   "early demonstrations": William J. Broad, "Science Showmanship: A Deep 'Star Wars' Rift," *NYT*, 12/16/85.

255   Leak on X-ray laser: R. Jeffrey Smith, "Experts Cast Doubt on X-ray Laser," *Science*, 11/8/85.

256   "In terms of": Howe speech, *Times* (London), 3/16/85.

256   *Times* editorial: "Howe's UDI from SDI," *Times* (London), 3/18/85.

257 boosting deterrence: see, for example, Fred S. Hoffman, "The SDI in U.S. Nuclear Strategy," Senate testimony reprinted in *International Security*, vol. 10, no. 1 (Summer 1985).

260 run it to the end: see David Ignatius, "In Star Wars Debate, Tactical Issues Nearly Get Lost in the Shuffle," *WSJ*, 10/15/85.

261 "protecting missile silos": quoted in ibid.

261 "held out to American citizens": Schlesinger speech, National Security Issues Symposium, 10/25/84.

262 footnote: Lloyd Grove, "The 'Star Wars' Soft Sell," *WP*, 11/4/85.

262 "The answer is": Newhouse, "The Diplomatic Round," *New Yorker*, 7/22/85.

263 "The time is": "The Case for Star Wars," *Economist*, 8/3/85.

266 British report: Michael R. Gordon, "CIA Is Sceptical That New Soviet Radar Is Part of an ABM Defence System," *National Journal*, 9/3/85.

268 "When you look at": Gerald M. Boyd, "Reagan Sees Soviet 'Deception' on Arms," *NYT*, 10/13/85.

268 Weinberger speech: Caspar Weinberger to the Philadelphia World Affairs Council, 10/3/85.

268 Pentagon testimony: FY 1986 Department of Defense Program for Research, Development and Acquisition, 3/7/85.

269 "in the key technologies": R. Jeffrey Smith, "Star Wars Chief Takes Aim at Critics," *Science*, 8/10/84.

271 "I am . . . concerned": part 7 of FY 1985 Defense Department authorization hearings by the Senate Armed Services Committee, 3/15/84.

274 six impossible things: Hedrick Smith, "U.S. Strategy of Toughness: A Counter to the Russians," *NYT*, 8/23/85.

275 "I don't think": "Star Wars: Will Space Battle Stations Work?" *ST*, 2/24/85.

275 "Their internal problems": John Newhouse, "The Diplomatic Round," *New Yorker*, 12/31/85.

275 "accept an entirely new": Robert Kaiser, "A Disarming Lack of Candor," *WP*, 3/10/85.

278 "It takes very little": ibid.

280 "The Safeguard system": Schlesinger speech, National Securities Issues Symposium, 10/25/84.

281   "The fiscal 1971 budget": ibid.

281   "on all the other": Howe speech, *Times* (London), 3/16/85.

Chapter Thirteen

282   "A bear": story appears in John Barry, "Geneva behind Closed Doors," *Times* (London) 5/31/83. See also John Wallach, "Walk in the Woods," *The Washingtonian*, 1/84.

284   "Europe has": quoted in "NATO's Death Is Now Thinkable," *International Herald Tribune*, 11/14–15/81.

284   "Eventual European unity": Theodore Draper, "The Dilemma of the West: A Transatlantic Parting of the Ways?" *Encounter*, 3/82.

285   "Economically Europe": Ronald E. Nairn, "Should the U.S. Pull Out of Nato?" *WSJ*, 12/15/81.

286   "grown wider": Sir Oliver Wright, British ambassador to the U.S., "The Atlantic Grows Wider," speech to the Fletcher School of Law and Diplomacy, Tufts University, Medford, Mass., 4/21/83.

286   "America does not connote": Stephen F. Szabo, "The Successor Generation in Europe," *Public Opinion*, vol. 6, no. 1 (February–March 1983).

286   "The campaign": Draper, "The Dilemma of the West," *Encounter*, 3/82.

287   "The United States": quoted in Alun Chalfont, "The Great Unilateralist Illusion," *Encounter*, 4/83.

287   "friendship and partnership": Draper, "The Dilemma of the West," *Encounter*, 3/82.

287   "The change": Wright speech, "The Atlantic Grows Wider," 4/21/83.

288   London Weekend Television film: "The NATO Alliance: Still Europe's Best Hope?" "Weekend World," London Weekend Television, 4/8/84.

289   dismay of Stevens and Pressler: see, for example, "Scowls across the Atlantic," *Economist*, 1/7/84.

289   European share: see, for example, Timothy Garton Ash, "Goddam Nato and Goddam Tories," *Spectator*, 8/10/85.

290   "Europe will cost": Earl C. Ravenal, "Europe without America: The Erosion of NATO," *Foreign Affairs*, Summer 1985.

292   "may prove": Draper, "The Dilemma of the West," *Encounter*, 3/82.

293 "We must divide": quoted in Phillip A. Petersen and John G. Hines, "Military Power in Soviet Strategy against Nato," *RUSI Journal,* 12/83.

293 "The Soviet Union's": ibid.

293 "Era of . . . Peace": ibid.

294 "Soviet dream item": Michael Howard, "Is Arms Control Really Necessary?" Council for Arms Control, Fourth Annual Lecture, 10/8/85.

294 "We need to be": "The Old Lion Still Roars," *Time,* 4/4/83.

294 "Should the Americans": "Weekend World: The Arms Talks: What Chance of Success?" London Weekend Television, 3/10/85.

Chapter Fourteen

295 planning like astronomy: Philip Towle, ed., *Estimating Foreign Military Power,* p. 30.

297 "video-game vision": David Evans, "A Runaway Pentagon," *NYT,* 10/3/84.

298 "salve their conscience": Rick Atkinson and Fred Hiatt, "To Prepare for War, We Need a Revolution," *WP,* 12/15/85.

298 twenty-four congressional committees: ibid.

299 "What is . . . defense?": Karl von Clausewitz, *On War,* p. 357.

299 "take a pick": quoted in Glenn Pascall, *The Trillion Dollar Budget.*

300 "The most important": John C. F. Tillson IV, "The Forward Defence of Europe," *Military Review,* 5/81.

300 "prechambering": estimate in ibid.

304 change in Northern Army Group: see, for example, David Fairhall, "Nato Clears the Way for a Non-nuclear Defence," *Manchester Guardian Weekly,* 6/23/85.

305 "over-literal interpretation": Lieutenant General Hans-Henning von Sandrart, "Forward Defence—Mobility and the Use of Barriers," *Nato's Sixteen Nations,* 1/85.

305 France needs Nato: Draper, "The Dilemma of the West," *Encounter,* 3/82.

305 "the fiction": quoted in ibid.

307 "Speaking for myself": David Evans, "A Runaway Pentagon," *NYT,* 10/3/84.

307   "like having": Michael R. Gordon, "Billion-Dollar 'Failures' May Slip Through Pentagon Weapons Testing Net," *National Journal,* 7/24/82.

307   "intense negotiations": Michael R. Gordon, "Army Disputed on Tests of Weapon," *NYT,* 1/26/86.

308   "simply intolerable": "The Folly of Untested Weapons" (editorial), *NYT,* 2/7/86.

309   "Extravagance and fraud": Gary Putka, "Arms-Trade Balance with Nato Nations Turns against the U.S.," *WSJ,* 11/8/85.

311   "great white lie": Richard K. Betts, "Compound Deterrence versus No First Use: What's Wrong Is What's Right," *Orbis,* vol. 28, no. 4 (Winter 1985).

317   "Technological change": Dr. Barry M. Blechman, "New Technology, Stability and the Arms Control Deadlock," in F. W. Mellenthin et al., *NATO under Attack.*

320   "like haunted creatures": George Kennan, *Russia, the Atom and the West.*

321   "have concluded": Robert English. "Why Star Wars Is Offensive," *The New Republic,* 2/24/86.

321   "The surgical": ibid.

323   "We must look deeper": Michael Howard, "Peace: The vital factors," *Times* (London), 1/13/84.

324   "push of technology": Newhouse, "The Diplomatic Round," *New Yorker,* 12/31/84.

Bibliography

Adams, Gordon. *The Iron Triangle: The Politics of Defense Contracting.* New York: Council on Economic Priorities, 1981.

Barnet, Richard J. *The Alliance: America-Europe-Japan, Makers of the Postwar World.* New York: Simon & Schuster, 1983.

———. *Real Security: Restoring American Power in a Dangerous Decade.* New York: Simon & Schuster, 1981.

Betts, Richard K. *Cruise Missiles: Technology, Strategy, Politics.* Washington, D.C.: Brookings Institution, 1981.

———. *Surprise Attack.* Washington, D.C.: Brookings Institution, 1982.

Bracken, Paul. *The Command and Control of Nuclear Forces.* New Haven and London: Yale University Press, 1983.

Brodie, Bernard. *The Absolute Weapon.* New York: Harcourt, Brace, 1946.

Brzezinski, Zbigniew K. *Power and Principle: Memoirs of the National Security Adviser, 1977–1981.* New York: Farrar, Straus & Giroux, 1983.

Calder, Nigel. *Nuclear Nightmares: An Investigation into Possible Wars.* London: British Broadcasting Corp., 1979.

Clausewitz, Karl von. *On War.* Edited and translated by Michael Howard and Peter Paret. Princeton, N.J.: Princeton University Press, 1976.

Cockburn, Andrew. *The Threat: Inside the Soviet Military Machine.* New York: Random House, 1983.

Coker, Christopher. *U.S. Military Power in the 1980s.* London: Macmillan, 1983.

Deitchman, Seymour J. *New Technology and Military Power: General Purpose Military Forces for the 1980s and Beyond.* Boulder, Colo.: Westview Press, 1979.

Douglass, Joseph D., Jr., and Hoeber, Amoretta M. *Soviet Strategy for Nuclear War.* Stanford, Calif.: Stanford University Press, 1979.

Duffy, Christopher. *Siege Warfare: The Fortress in the Early Modern World, 1494–1660.* London: Routledge & Kegan Paul, 1979.

ESECS (Report of the Europe Security Study). *Strengthening Conventional Deterrence in Europe.* London: Macmillan, 1983.

Etzold, Thomas H. *Defense or Delusion? America's Military in the 1980s.* New York: Harper & Row, 1982.

Fallows, James. *National Defense.* New York: Random House, 1981.

Fox, J. Ronald. *Arming America.* Cambridge, Mass.: Harvard University Press, 1974.

Freedman, Lawrence. *The Evolution of Nuclear Strategy.* London: Macmillan, 1981.

————, ed. *The Troubled Alliance: Atlantic Relations in the 1980s.* London: Heinemann, 1983.

Gansler, Jacques S. *The Defense Industry.* Cambridge, Mass.: MIT Press, 1980.

Graham, Daniel O. *High Frontier: A New National Strategy.* Washington, D.C.: Heritage Foundation, 1982.

Guizot, M. *The History of France from the Earliest Times to the Year 1789.* London: Sampson Low, Marstan, Low & Searle, 1873.

Holst, Johan J., and Nerlich, Uwe, eds. *Beyond Nuclear Deterrence: New Aims, New Arms.* New York: Crane, Russak, 1977.

Holwill, Richard N., ed. *A Mandate for Leadership Report: Agenda '83.* Washington D.C.: Heritage Foundation, 1983.

Horne, Alistair. *To Lose a Battle: France 1940.* London: Macmillan, 1969.

Isby, David C. *Weapons and Tactics of the Soviet Army.* London: Jane's Publishing, 1981.

Kaldor, Mary. *The Baroque Arsenal.* New York: Hill and Wang, 1981.

Kaplan, Fred. *The Wizards of Armageddon.* New York: Simon & Schuster, 1983.

Karas, Thomas. *The New High Ground: Strategies and Weapons of Space-Age War.* New York: Simon & Schuster, 1983.

Kaufman, William. *The McNamara Strategy.* New York: Harper & Row, 1964.

Kennan, George F. *Russia, the Atom and the West.* New York: Harper & Brothers, 1958.

Klepsch Report. *Two-Way Street: USA-Europe Arms Procurement.* London: Brassey's, 1979.

Komer, Robert W. *Maritime Strategy or Coalition Defense?* Cambridge, Mass.: Abt Books, 1984.

Lanchester, F. W. *Aircraft in Warfare: The Dawn of the Fourth Army.* London: Constable, 1916.

Legge, J. Michael. *Theater Nuclear Weapons and the NATO Strategy of Flexible Response.* Santa Monica, Calif.: Rand Corp., 1983.

Lunn, Simon. *Burden-sharing in NATO.* London: Routledge & Kegan Paul, 1983.

Luttwak, Edward N. *The Pentagon and the Art of War.* New York: Simon & Schuster, 1984.

Mearsheimer, John J. *Conventional Deterrence.* Ithaca: Cornell University Press, 1983.

Mellenthin, F. W., and Stalli, R. H., with Subik, E., ed., *NATO under Attack,* Durham: Duke University Press, 1984.

Neild, Robert. *How to Make Up Your Mind about the Bomb.* London: André Deutsch, 1981.

Osgood, Robert Endicott. *NATO: The Entangling Alliance.* Chicago: University of Chicago Press, 1962.

Pascall, Glenn. *The Trillion Dollar Budget: How to Stop the Bankrupting of America.* Seattle: University of Washington Press, 1985.

Pearton, Morris. *The Knowledgeable State: Diplomacy, War and Technology since 1830.* London: Burnett Books, 1982.

Pringle, Peter, and Arkin, William. *SIOP, Nuclear War from the Inside.* London: Sphere Books, 1983.

Rasor, Dina, ed. *More Bucks, Less Bang: How the Pentagon Buys Ineffective Weapons.* Washington D.C.: Fund for Constitutional Government, 1983.

Scheer, Robert. *With Enough Shovels: Reagan, Bush and Nuclear War.* New York: Random House, 1982.

Schell, Jonathan. *The Fate of the Earth.* New York: Alfred A. Knopf, 1982.

Schwartz, David N. *NATO's Nuclear Dilemmas.* Washington D.C.: Brookings Institution, 1983.

Smith, Dan. *The Defence of the Realm in the 1980s.* London: Croom Helm, 1980.

Smith, Gerard. *Doubletalk: The Story of SALT I.* New York: Doubleday, 1980.

Stein, Jonathan B. *From H-Bomb to Star Wars: The Politics of Strategic Decision Making.* Lexington, Mass.: Lexington Books, 1984.

Suvorov, Viktor. *The Liberators.* London: Hamish Hamilton, 1981.

Talbott, Strobe. *Deadly Gambits.* New York: Alfred A. Knopf, 1984.————.*Endgame: The Inside Story of SALT II.* New York: Harper & Row, 1979.

Taylor, William J., Jr. *The Future of Conflict.* Washington, D.C.: Center for Strategic and International Studies, 1983.

Thompson, E. P., and Smith, Dan, eds. *Protest and Survive.* Harmondsworth, England: Penguin Books, 1980.

Towle, Philip, ed. *Estimating Foreign Military Power.* London: Croom Helm, 1982.

Union of Concerned Scientists. *The Fallacy of Star Wars.* New York: Random House, Vintage, 1984.

U.S. Department of Defense. *Soviet Military Power 1985.* Washington, D.C.: U.S. Government Printing Office, 1985.

Wavell, Archibald. *Generals and Generalship.* New York: Macmillan, 1943.

White, Andrew. *Symbols of War: Pershing II and Cruise Missiles in Europe.* London: Merlin Press/European Nuclear Disarmament, 1983.

Wieseltier, Leon. *Nuclear War, Nuclear Peace.* New York: Holt, Rinehart & Winston, 1983.